This is *not* the way

The practical anti-manual for facilitating strategy, innovation and creativity

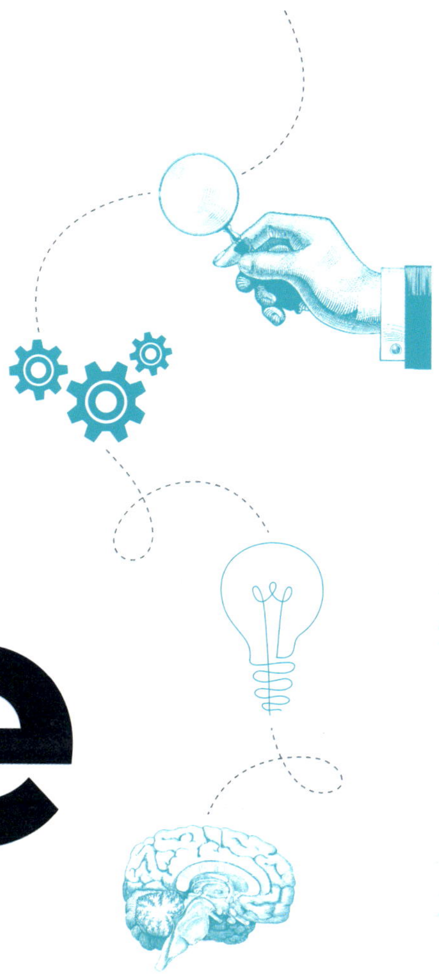

Andy Reid

FOUNDER OF

GENIUS BOX

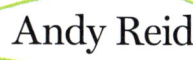

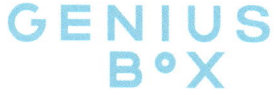

Author's note

This is me

My name is Andy Reid. I'm the founder of GENIUS BOX; a company on a mission to inspire a different approach to problem solving. It was an idea borne from a conversation around a kitchen table in 2009. I wrote this book because what I do isn't easy. Creative projects design and facilitation takes skill; and I'm frustrated that people like me and the work we do is still misunderstood.

I started my working life as a teacher, helping young people from all walks of life tackle challenges each day. I learnt that every problem has an answer if you listen carefully. I also learnt that when adults get stuck, they behave like children.

After teaching, I was drawn by the glittering allure of marketing and advertising – believing I could generate meaningful ideas like they do in the movies. But in reality, I endured unproductive back-to-back meetings, mind-numbing PowerPoints and witnessed smart people kill starter ideas.

I also worked in consulting for a while, where clients ignored the crucial business issues and instead preoccupied themselves with the size of their logo or insisted a branded lanyard would re-energise their culture.

I've headed up innovation in a bank. The CEO invited me to provoke the business. I left upon receiving feedback from the board that I had 'exceeded the organisation's appetite for provocation.'

I'm nostalgic. I make cocktails for my wife on a Friday while listening to 80s' music. I'm left-handed. I'm terrible at mental arithmetic. My teenage kids make me hoot with laughter. I have a model railway in my shed and a 1984 Lotus in bits on my driveway. Creative tinkering is in my nature.

This book is a window into how I think, solve problems and have ideas. I'd like to help you do the same.

Andy

Foreword by Chris Clark

What is the value of a truly breakthrough idea in your business today?

Will it be the thing that saves you from the personal inferno of failure? Or will it make you a corporate superstar and have your name in lights forever emblazoned on the company head office? Or will it more likely help you build a team-based response to a thorny issue you face, or an opportunity so far not realised?

Winning ways of working that embrace creativity and ideas are much misunderstood. In some companies, they are perceived as 'strokes of luck' that someone happened to fall over on their way to the canteen. In other organisations, they are the stuff of alchemy and dark arts that those guys in (insert dept here, marketing, product development, digital, etc.) cook up around a cauldron bubbling with eye of newt and wing of bat.

My heartfelt point of view is that ideas and innovation are a whole company discipline and responsibility. Not that every minute of every day sees every employee lying on a beanbag with a magic marker in hand waiting for inspiration to strike, but that it is important to understand how to bring together all the great minds in your company. These are the people who understand your products, your customers, your competitors, your history and, moreover, bring them together with sound process to generate strategically based breakthroughs.

To this end we must learn and embrace the noble art of facilitation. The bringing together of the right folk, from the right departments, in the right place, with the right amount of time and suitable stimulus and permission to explore the art of the possible with structure and clear outcomes.

If this sounds like just what you need, then grab this book with both hands and get learning. I have been lucky enough to share in the work of Andy Reid and his teams over the past 15 years. It works, it's fun and it will change what you do and how you think for the better.

Breakthroughs and change are not born out of luck. You get to make your own luck, so load those dice with sound facilitation practices. Like all difficult things it takes effort and courage. I've always been a fan of John Paul Getty's success formula, 'Get up early, work hard, strike oil', or, in this case, strike inspiration.

Chris Clark

Chris Clark is Chairman of Aviva UKD and a non-executive director of Aviva Insurance Ltd. He's also a former Global Head of Marketing for *HSBC* and Group Director of *Saatchi & Saatchi*.

Foreword by Jamal Benmiloud

Dear Potential Reader,

If you're looking for a guide to becoming a mediocre facilitator who leads teams down the path of bland and uninspired ideas, then *This is Not the Way* is definitely not the book for you.

This book is not for those who are content with average outcomes, nor is it for those who want to continue to facilitate projects, workshops or teams in a way that doesn't help to build their business. In fact, if you're satisfied with being a facilitator who produces lacklustre strategies and unremarkable products, then we suggest you stop reading right now and go back to your usual way of doing things.

But, if you're looking to take your facilitation skills to the next level, to become a master of leading teams to innovative ideas and building a successful business, then this book is for you.

This is Not the Way is a guide to help you avoid the common mistakes and pitfalls that hinder the facilitation process. Through Andy's tips, tricks and real-life examples (honed after working on thousands of projects), you'll learn how to empower your team to create outstanding strategies, products and services that truly set your business apart from the competition. You'll also learn how to create an environment that fosters collaboration, builds trust, and empowers your team to create outstanding ideas whilst having a huge amount of fun along the way!

If you're ready to become a great facilitator to help your team develop the right strategy, innovate the right products and services, or generally have amazing ideas, then dive into *This is Not the Way*. Just remember, this book is not for the faint of heart. It's for those who are willing to take risks, push boundaries, and truly lead their teams to greatness. But, be warned: once you've read it, there's no going back to mediocrity.

Jamal Benmiloud

> Jamal Benmiloud is a non-executive director and Board Advisor at *Huel*; Global Marketing Advisor for *Anheuser-Busch InBev*; Former VP of Marketing at *Monster* and Head of Marketing for *Red Bull*.

Contents

About this book 8

Introduction:
Premium creative facilitation 10

1

You (specifically your fabulous and creative brain) 26

Quality thinking, more often 29
Neurons and stuff 32
The creative brain's parts 34
Interview: Danny Denhard 36
Brain vs mind 38
Luke and Yoda 48
Heuristics and habits 54
Brain hemispheres 56
Your ARAS 58
States of mind 60
Interview: Nina Riecks 62
Upside-down pyramids 64
Connecting brain to process 68
Topping up the warehouse for you and others 74
Interview: Chris Baréz-Brown 76
20 lifestyle challenges 78
It's all about the brain 82

2

The Genius Way 84

The GENIUS BOX model 88
Interview: Dave Lewis 96
Using the model 98
The process – a story in four parts 100
Mavericks make the method 102
Client, sponsor, problem owner – who's who? 106
Interview: Hannah Feely 108

3

The Process 110

1_SCOPING 112
Intro bit 114
The Tools and Insights Discovery 116
Tool 001 Whyhaus 120
Tool 002 Tissue session 124
Interview: Jeff Tan 128

Tool 003 Mixing desks & honeypots	130
Tool 004 Rumsfeld's Matrix and Columbo's Question	138
Tool 005 Angels & Demons	142
Interview: Kirsten Gillard	146
Tool 006 Pirates vs Navy	148
Tool 007 Mozart tool	152

2_INSIGHT — 156

Intro bit	158
10 tools to insight utopia	166
Connection games	168
Interview: Henrietta De Souza	178
Metaphor games	180
Insight framework	198
Interview: Esra Demir	216

3_IDEAS — 218

Intro bit	220
Thoughts vs ideas	222
Interview: Sue Woodley	230
Best behaviour for ideas	232
The 'Big Six'	242

Interview: Sarah Christensen	250
More on idea capture	252
Ideas coaching	254
Idea DNA	255
Idea trees	256

4_SELECTION — 260

Intro bit	262
Auditing	264
Audit Tool 001 Piles of purpose	265
Audit Tool 002 Kill your darlings	268
Audit Tool 003 Grey's Anatomy	269
Audit Tool 004 Jazz session	270
Audit Tool 005 Smile	271
Interview: Joeri Schilders	274
Scoring	276
Scoring Tool 001 Save in a fire	278
Scoring Tool 002 Comparative assessment	279
Scoring Tool 003 Sheriff badge	282
Scoring Tool 004 Grade boundaries	283
Tools for getting unstuck	285
Embedding	290

Finding The Way — 298

Developing your way	300
The cube revisited	301
Process and Strategy	302
Interview: Sanjay Patel	308
Environment and Behaviour	310
Competency and Team Culture	316
Creative session planning	318
Interview: Adam Howe	326
The shift	328
The Way	332

Acknowledgements	336

About this book

If a manual is a book with detailed instruction on what to do, this book is an anti-manual; one that is designed to bend rules, break spells and bust myths.

There are hundreds of ways to brief in instruction to a group, so this anti-manual is written to inspire you to brief in a hundred more.

However, there is a structure to the way I've organised the topics and content. That structure is based on a story which starts and ends with you and your impact on your project team and business.

This book is also peppered with top tips and interviews with brilliant facilitators from around the world – they have shared their perspectives and stories for you to learn from too.

1

Part 1 is all about you, the individual. It's about having greater awareness of how your brain makes connections, thinks things through and arrives at answers. Creative masters are deliberate in the habits they practise to keep their minds fresh and active. It's no surprise that people who are perceived by others as being creative are constantly engaged in 'creative things'. However, I believe we all have the capacity to make new and creative connections – creative thinking isn't a dark art that only special wizards can master. Part One of the book will help you understand more about how and why you think the way you do and offers some advice on getting the very best out of the most powerful creative tool you as a facilitator have: your brain.

2

Part 2 of the book introduces a model that you and your team can use to build stronger facilitation capability. The model will help you build awareness of everything else that has an impact on the tasks you'll be set over time as a facilitator. It enables you to consider, and therefore manage, the context around the innovation challenges you'll face. This is our GENIUS BOX model, not *the* model. But I hope it inspires you to develop your own personal model that suits you and your team's approach to facilitating projects in the future.

Our model helps you to lead aspects of facilitation that are inside your control: the process, your behaviour and your own competency – and to manage other aspects that have a wider impact on a project, which are the physical environment in which you're working, the culture in the project team and the delivery strategy you deploy.

3

Part 3 is all about the core of our model: the Process. It covers the four main aspects of the creative facilitation process and suggests tools and activities for each one that you can use to guide your project team. Together, these tools will enable you and your team to create collaboratively and creatively. They are designed to forge new connections and greater energetic relationships within your project content, all inspired by what we have learned about the brain and how this can amplify the mental state needed to make new connections.

There are four stages to our creative process: Scoping, Insight, Ideas, and Selection – each of which has its own chapter – and a number of tools are shared within each one. Here you can pick and choose the content you want to use as needed. There are no right ways to facilitate innovation projects. Whilst we at GENIUS BOX have our approach, there are other approaches, too. You will have tools and activities in mind that you've used in the past and will use again in the future. We have adopted (stolen!) tools from project facilitators we thought delivered 'cool things' with great results. Over time our particular spin has become our IP and style – use all we share here as stimuli for your own creative toolbox. And if you spot something you've seen before, then be reassured the tool clearly works.

My advice here is embrace our process and tools loosely. If you remain utterly wedded to using the same tool in a specific way every time, your ability to work with agility and creativity is hindered. You'll become stale. So will your projects. THIS IS NOT THE WAY!

Dip in and out of our process, steal what you like and in the words of a talent show host 'make it your own'.

4

Part 4 revisits our GENIUS BOX model and invites you to consider your role in building the brand of facilitation and your own creative style of facilitating.

This part of the book is less about tools and tactics, but broader provocations, principles and inspiration for you.

A good project facilitator will be confident in explaining to a group what to do and why. But a brilliant facilitator, a creative, imaginative and inspiring facilitator, will create the conditions for other people to solve business problems and build teams' capabilities at the same time.

In Part Four, I invite you to find and lead your way…

Now let's begin.

Introduction

PREMIUM CREATIVE FACILITATION

 There is a skill in facilitating strategy, innovation and creativity – or, better expressed, there is a skill in being able to facilitate strategically, innovatively and creatively.

We need facilitators who not only possess the ability to manage people in a room confidently, but who also have expert knowledge and some experience in the art and practice of creativity and innovation.

Combining these strengths makes for a model that powers brilliant facilitation and, as a result, secures successful commercial output.

I believe that businesses should invest in facilitation capability. For too long, projects have been run by bad facilitators charging low fees for poor instructional design.

Bad facilitation is easy, brilliant facilitation takes skill. I'm on a mission to improve the quality of business strategy, and to inspire people involved in innovation projects by championing the role of premium facilitation. Better quality facilitation leads to better output; better output makes for brilliant projects, and brilliant projects benefit your people and your business. *Everyone wins.*

And here's why: the fundaments of business haven't changed, things have just become more complex. A bit like a car engine – spark plugs, pistons, a drive shaft and wheels still take us from one place to another, but the operation of ancillary systems outside of the engine, designed for efficiency and comfort, are a mystery to us all. And with the switch to electric vehicles, even fewer of us will genuinely know how our cars really work. 👉

Social and tech revolutions have entirely transformed the way business is conducted; changing trends re-write established approaches to the management of organisational operation. Therefore, investment in all aspects of business development has risen. This is good, of course. And with luck we will all soon be leading carbon-neutral lives of leisure and self-fulfilment in a world of better conditions for all humanity (ahem).

But the way people are actually taught how to be strategic, innovative and creative hasn't kept pace. Subsequently, I believe a few things most other people don't:

1. There is an imbalance between the strategic investment in new technology and the amount invested in human capital, training and people development.
Organisations think nothing of spending £250K on an 8-week tech consulting project, but they buckle at the thought of spending the same amount on a core group of people who could deliver impact time and again. People development is the first thing to get cut when economic times are hard. Training budgets disappear, apprenticeships are culled and recruitment is frozen. I believe this is wrong.

2. When human capability development is finally signed off, it's crap.
Firstly, the content has little to do with the business need. Myers Briggs or mindfulness topics are the vogue for one learning programme whilst 'personal branding' and 'presentation skills' (sigh) are delivered at another. How do these really answer the needs of the organisation? Secondly, this questionably relevant content is usually delivered in an appalling fashion. It is still essentially chalk and talk. The delivery may have evolved onto PowerPoint or Prezi, but it's still dated and it's still dull. Thirdly, audiences with no understanding of why they've been selected arrive with no prep on how to be effective learners.

3. Superficial training and poor project facilitation lead to a fragmented workforce.
People put themselves in false boxes – an 'analytical *this* or *that*' or an 'I can't work creatively because…' – providing labels and excuses for them to *not* get involved in projects at work. People are often operating from mental maps based on pseudo-science that can potentially hinder their beliefs and careers.

4. Finally, while I believe we are *all* creative, I don't believe we are *all* capable of facilitating the creative process for project teams.
The art, science and skill of being a facilitator isn't regarded as highly as it should be. Senior leaders are less supportive of work that takes employees away from their current responsibilities; they are often reluctant to sign off any training or creative project facilitation. And who can blame them, especially if their personal experience of it was ineffective, meaningless or miserable.

In addition to poor attitude and poor financial investment when it comes to facilitation of new ideas, a major issue is simply that it is just hard to make change happen. Change is no longer as simple as one person suggesting a new idea and it being readily accepted by others. It is complex, political and slow. People accept that they need to change, but no one actually likes being changed. New ideas, no matter how well positioned, still threaten our happy status quo – and our minds (as we'll see in Part 1) are quick to dismiss ideas. And, paradoxically, organisations will actually say that they *are* constantly changing, and that transformation and evolution are necessary for survival in a highly competitive market. The mantra still exists: innovate or die – and yet anything new, at an individual level, is treated as a subconscious enemy within our world of work.

So, it's even more essential that strategy, innovation and creativity should be facilitated. It won't 'just happen' by putting

In 2009, Dustin Curtis logged onto the American Airlines website to book a flight. He discovered that the website was difficult to navigate and created a needlessly cumbersome customer experience. Coincidentally, Curtis worked in 'user interface' and felt compelled to write an open letter to American Airlines criticising the website, but also offering up an alternative design for the front page. An American Airlines employee wrote an open reply to Curtis, here's part of it:

"The problem with the design of aa.com... lies less in our competency (or lack thereof, as you pointed out in your post) and more with the culture and processes employed here at American Airlines. Let me explain. The group running aa.com consists of at least 200 people spread out among many different groups... We have a lot of people touching the site, and a lot more with their own vested interests in how the site presents its content and functionality... It only takes a few hours to put together a really good-looking one, as you demonstrated in your post. But doing the design isn't the hard part, and I think that's what a lot of outsiders don't really get..."

The website to this day still remains as is with only marginal gains in navigation and ease of use. It's unclear whether Curtis was thanked or even acknowledged for his efforts, but this example neatly illustrates the frustrations that anyone in business (regardless of the size of enterprise) will empathise with:

It is hard to make change happen.

enough meetings in the diary and a logo about 'one team' in email signatures. There are processes, tools and techniques that can be lifted and utilised to engineer positive outcomes for individuals, teams and business units. But those tools and the way they are used, and the briefing of a group on what to do and how to do it, need to be shepherded by creative facilitators who know what they are doing and why. We need facilitators who are able to bring their personal magic to any given business situation.

My re-expression of this whole sorry situation is a monopoly board – the pieces would be a Filofax, a laptop, an iPad and a Twitter handle (to represent the workplace generations). And while sexy technology, big data and social collaboration projects are all getting signed off on Mayfair and Park Lane budgets, down the road in HR the projects that actually invest in people are being forced into lunchtime sessions over sandwiches, 60-minute workouts or a 'Hey! Watch this link on TED' sent over email. It's all Old Kent Road – low rent and low impact.

All this leads to a growing gap between people's natural ability to solve problems and their capability to do so in the increasingly complex work landscape we navigate. And businesses continue to pay low rent for poor quality project facilitation and ineffective training to address it. It's a sad situation.

Enough is enough.

THIS IS <u>NOT</u> THE WAY.

Championing ingenuity

Another problem lies in that fact that we're not actually being taught how to solve problems, we're just expected to do it. And while schools and colleges reward us with qualifications, our confidence in our achievements can quickly fade when we join a profession hoping to be mentored by others. Some of us may be lucky and join a team where there's an abundance of positive thinking and co-creation. The not-so-lucky ones sit in a silent office, tapping figures into an Excel sheet, gazing up at the clock, occasionally sighing at the plastic pot plant. This is not an environment for innovation. Grey Formica offices lead to grey Formica ideas.

Worse still was the experience of those who joined the working world during the COVID-19 pandemic; a laptop teetering on one end of the kitchen table and a fragile internet connection. Then, amongst the laundry, dirty pots and family members or flatmates, new innovative connections had to be made… how?

In 2000, Thomas Homer-Dixon wrote of an 'ingenuity gap', a widening space between the growing complexity of modern life and our increasing inability to solve its problems. I believe his predictions are as true today as they were twenty years ago.

The pioneers of our business world had fewer competitors – and sustainability, workforce diversity and GDPR weren't topics on the agenda. Globalisation and its impact on the environment probably wasn't considered. Perhaps even the demands of stakeholders were less political. Widgets were welded and panels were punched. And all this was done without high-speed internet, portable calculators, lasers, phones, instant photocopying and wifi… there were just top-down instructions, slide rules and little regard for health and safety – perhaps happier times, if you could survive them.

A century on and the working world is far more complex. Change isn't as easy as pulling a lever (metaphorically or literally). For businesses to be more innovative and creative, and to move with more agility and pace, people need to engage in the broader purpose of change rather than just executing management will. Creative briefs now are less about new products, plans and widgets, and are more associated with vision, mission, purpose, engagement, culture and ways of working. The ingenuity gap is getting bigger – the world is getting more complex each day and we're spending less time skilling people up on how to solve problems and have ideas.

The mantra 'fail fast and learn sooner' is an oft-cited cliché, but there are few people in business who have been recognised for their failings and then asked to lead the next innovation project. The truth is that business is designed to trap us – it's not deliberate, it's just far easier to manage a people machine that has 'rules and procedures' instead of 'mindsets and attitudes'. And whilst kooky start-ups are keen to promote their flexible working and pop-up operations, most businesses are built on designs that are easy to scale, easy to manage and lead in a top-down fashion.

At GENIUS BOX, we believe that facilitating successful internal projects provides evidence that your business is being creative. Investing in facilitation translates the rhetoric of 'fail fast to learn sooner' into tangible proof points. People can point at project output and say 'we're innovating around here'. And importantly, those who facilitate the creative process develop their capability in a way that builds confidence, engagement and personal joy.

OPPOSITE:
If we're to spend one-third of our waking lives at work it ought to be a positive experience.

The skill of facilitation

For too long the responsibility of project facilitation or the development of creative capability has fallen between the stools of HR, L&D and COMMS, with each department trying hard to grow capability without success. Instead, facilitation has become an assumed skill of outside agencies commissioned to deliver work for large organisations. But agencies who specialise in advertising, AGILE or digital transformation aren't necessarily filled with brilliant facilitators.

Designing and delivering working sessions that shepherd people through process and secure output is a skill on top of and in addition to being familiar with creativity and innovation. And I would advise bosses to regularly review the calibre of their preferred providers on their roster. How well do they answer your capability brief? How relevant is 'what they deliver' to your original question? Are real life alternatives making their content look dated? Are your people still sitting facing a PowerPoint?

There needs to be a shift from skills-based training to long-term capability building; doing so is a profit strategy. It's your money, but if you keep paying your current agencies to deliver poor content in the hope that you'll become more innovative, you won't – and they'll just keep delivering more poor content. If the pandemic of 2020 gave us anything, it was a high volume of advice about how to run meetings remotely. Most of this advice was obvious or dull – have we not been running meetings for decades, centuries even? Are we not one incredibly powerful global workforce? It appears as though there's a tiny percentage of us building electric cars, search engine algorithms, cryptocurrencies and alternatives to single-use plastic, while the rest of the working world (if LinkedIn is to be believed) is struggling with the basics of running a meeting on Zoom.

For any change and transformation to happen it needs to be facilitated. And you need a specific set of tools and skills to facilitate that change. But where does the help to acquire these tools come from?

Facilitation of innovation, strategy and creativity requires a set of skills and behaviours that extend far beyond the ability to just run a meeting to time. At GENIUS BOX we believe that the weakest link in the change and transformation journey is often the person or people who ultimately have to facilitate the creative sessions that translate the direction of work into tactical action. It's when person A has to explain to person B what is going on and why, and then asks who has any further ideas on what to do next. Therefore, it's essential to build that facilitation skill.

Unfortunately, these skills aren't taught in schools or in graduate recruitment programmes. You're unlikely to find a 'creative facilitation module' as part of ongoing PDP. In large organisations L&D won't have an internal 'innovation facilitation curriculum' either, and business literature isn't that useful.

It is always the same organisations who are cited as bastions of innovation and creativity – Google, Apple, Netflix, Tesla, etc. And even though they do provide exciting stories of success, in reality only a small percentage of the global workforce work for them (and it's an even smaller percentage who actually make stuff happen). Yet this tiny cluster dictate what has become the accepted model of innovation and creativity – and this is not tactical help on what you can do in an insight generation session on a Tuesday morning at 10:00am. No. We're constantly being led to believe that the only way is the current way: trial and error, watching others stumbling through projects, participating in agency activities and jumping in… **There must be better way.**

The GENIUS BOX approach

There isn't a single way… but some ways are better than others. And at GENIUS BOX we're on a mission to *inspire*. I lead a team who are passionate about innovation, people, culture and creativity. Each team member has run over 100 innovation projects and between us we've done so across 40 countries for over 250 businesses. We've trained over 15,000 people in innovation skills and behaviours and we've smashed the puzzle on how to do that online too. We're all different, but are aligned and united in the belief that in the right conditions anyone can make creative connections and have impact in business. It's our role as facilitators to make that happen.

Premium facilitation and the role of the creative facilitator are key, they establish the conditions in which people are inspired to think differently so that **projects get done and change happens**. It's about working hard, not about hard work. When people are inspired it's easy for them to make creative connections, ask pertinent questions, uncover insights and have ideas. It's our role as a team to design and deliver that environment (the box) so people can make those new and novel (the genius) connections. Brilliant facilitation is about delivering inspiration – that's what we do.

Hence this manual, born from the collective experience of our projects and training sessions. It's designed as a source of inspiration and stimulus to help you lead smarter when it comes to facilitating strategy, innovation and creativity. The GENIUS BOX approach to the design and delivery of our innovation projects is visual and practical, so expect that in the book from now on.

Expect to see images, photos, analogies and examples, all of which will help build your facilitation toolbox. You can dip in and out of the book, and just focus on the part of the process you want to fix – much like using a handy repair manual. But I encourage you to take time to absorb the lot; it's all stimulus for you. And then, as you wish, steal what resonates and make it your own. There is no 'right way' to facilitate, but there certainly are areas where high standards, clear briefings and super-tight instructions will secure better project output.

Above all, develop a point of view. Don't be neutral. Share your opinion about facilitation and use your perspective to stimulate debate, discussion and eventually decision making. Your voice needs to be in the room – it helps people

get from A to B – otherwise you're all sitting in silence. Being neutral isn't being positive, and the creative process needs positive intention to get it moving. I would argue that if you're actively avoiding getting involved and sharing opinions then your actual impact is negative. Think about it: people are happy to share opinions in social situations where they're not being paid (over drinks on a night out) and perhaps their perspective isn't even welcome (commenting on your friend's political opinion) so why remain neutral when your business clients have commissioned you to facilitate?

Signalled up front, personal opinion is a powerful tool that unlocks 'the stuck' and spikes up creative sessions. Opinion is at the heart of most conversations; there is no need to censor your mind. Facilitation is NOT coaching, so asking 'what do *you* think you should do?' time and again won't move things on. Given all the things a facilitator has to do in prepping projects and training sessions, opinions can be offered freely and take no time to plan.

Opinions, thoughts and perspectives are an extension of who you are and what you stand for, and that has value for any creative process. Being consistent with that over time builds a credible brand for your skill as a facilitator. Your audience will fill in the gaps – they're bright people, they'll work it out. If you stay neutral, with nothing to say, then you're simply warming a seat.

The world is a needlessly complex place.

You're amazing at what you do.

Your business needs you.

Innovate or die.

Now, read on, make a difference.

And have some fun.

What does good look like?

Let's start with Jenny. A mid-level marketer, Jenny works for one of the world's largest banks. She has her own team, and reports to the area general manager of the bank with a dotted line to the Regional Head of Marketing. You may empathise with Jenny. She's busy, active and has many responsibilities, as she operates in a matrix organisation where decision making can be slow and getting things done takes patience and political effort.

One morning, Jenny is called into the GM's office and issued a business challenge: **Sell more loans**. Banks make money by depositing credit into people's accounts and charging interest. Increasing the value of the bank to its shareholders means having more bottom line growth. This comes from managing the deposits and investments, and having people borrow against them. This is good for the economy as businesses can lean on the bank's support as they deliver their plans to grow.

'Helping everyone achieve more' was a core part of the bank's global strategy – in the retail side of the bank, where Jenny and her boss sat, that meant 'sell more loans'. More loans equates to more interest payments. And more interest payments is good for business.

But Jenny's shoulders sank.

At that time, in her part of the world (the Philippines), received wisdom was that saving for a rainy day is good. Investing for the future is good. And having loans – being 'in debt' – is really bad news. In fact, it's a sign of a poorly managed character to have spent beyond your means. Being in debt was seen as a great shame, especially being indebted to an international bank. To sell more loans to consumers who at a cultural level reject debt of any kind felt impossible. But Jenny had a secret weapon.

Jenny and her team had solid knowledge and understanding of the creative process. Jenny also knew how to facilitate her team along this process using a series of tools and activities. She knew that if given space, she and her team could arrive at new and differentiating outcomes. This would be good for the bank, because they would succeed in getting a project over the line, and good for Jenny, as leading this project successfully would be a personal victory for her career. She began.

Firstly, she pushed back on the brief.

In discussion with her GM, the original 'sell more loans' was the commercial driver of the bank, the brief that best described what the business wanted. Intuitively, Jenny and her GM agreed that advertising banking rates didn't feel appropriate as a campaign when marketing's remit was to build brand. Nor did that brief match with other marketing activities at a regional level. Jenny finally confirmed with both her GM and Regional Head that her brief was to **build awareness that the bank provided loans**. Awareness correlated to customer behaviour and Jenny's bank was confident that if consumers knew about them when they considered borrowing money, it was likely that this consideration would translate into behaviour where people chose them for their loans.

Jenny then ring-fenced her team. She suspended business as usual for a few days, split her team into pairs, and assigned them 'insight adventures'. The pairs were to complete a mixture of desk research and observations out in the field. Desk research was mining the usual reports and performance papers of the bank and its competitors, whilst field research was to suspend the ordinary commissions of research agencies and instead save money by going out and about themselves.

Team members were encouraged to head out into the bars, cafes, restaurants and shopping malls where people spent time together. They were asked to speak with families about what they were up to and how they were spending time together – importantly, to find out what they were spending money on. Jenny's team didn't need to identify themselves as bank employees, and they didn't need to speak specifically about money, they just needed to 'hang out' with people and strike up conversation. Something that would be easy and natural to do as her team were enthusiastic, keen and eager to help.

The findings from the team were that, contrary to perception, people in the Philippines didn't 'save for a rainy day'. Nor did they 'invest in the future' by hoarding capital. In the Philippines, family is at the centre of community and society. Many generations live, work and play under the same roof. And leisure time was something the whole family often enjoyed together. A key insight that emerged was that 'investing for the future' manifested in the behaviour of 'spending time and money on each other'. The big theme emerging across Jenny's insight work was:

Spending time on doing things we love is a sign we're investing in our future, because the next generation is our future.

Significantly, finances or loans were never mentioned in conversations. The story of family was something that emerged time and time again across all the field research.

This insight inspired a simple but effective marketing campaign. Jenny worked with her ad agency to capture shared family moments. For example, father and son enjoying a rollercoaster ride, mother and daughter laughing together under balloons, grandparents and grandchildren enjoying a shared smoothie – simple vignettes of moments that mattered and ones that told, at a glance, the story of generational love.

The ad copy was loosely 'Don't put off until tomorrow what you can do today', followed by 'enjoy further moments that matter with the help of our family-friendly loans' all smattered with the bank's iconic global branding.

The campaign was launched and originally planned for a 3 to 6-month window. When measured against competitors, research showed that consumers considering a loan held Jenny's bank top of their mind and that this intention correlated to a sharp uptick in actual loan approvals made by the bank during that period. The campaign was extended for a further 6 months.

On a visit to the bank's HQ in Hong Kong, I saw a copy of Jenny's ad framed on the wall. It's still there to this day.

Facilitation framework model

Jenny's project is a story I tell time and again as it demonstrates three factors essential for great innovation:

Jenny, the individual: her personal mastery and confidence in the creative process, her relationship with creative energy and her own talents and attitude. At the centre of this project was her commanding stewardship, energy and facilitation. If it wasn't for Jenny's facilitation, the project wouldn't have worked.

Jenny's team: the team used tools and activities and followed a process to get from A to B. The next time they ran a project together they adapted their approach from the feedback of the previous project and mixed things up a little to keep everyone fresh. They didn't simply repeat exactly the same approach, using exactly the same tools, in exactly the same fashion. This is not the way! Jenny's team were creative in what they did and how they did it.

The task: in this instance, the task – to devise a campaign to market the selling of more loans – helped shape which elements of the 'process' *(see Part Three)* were used, and which tools and tactics Jenny and team chose to deploy.

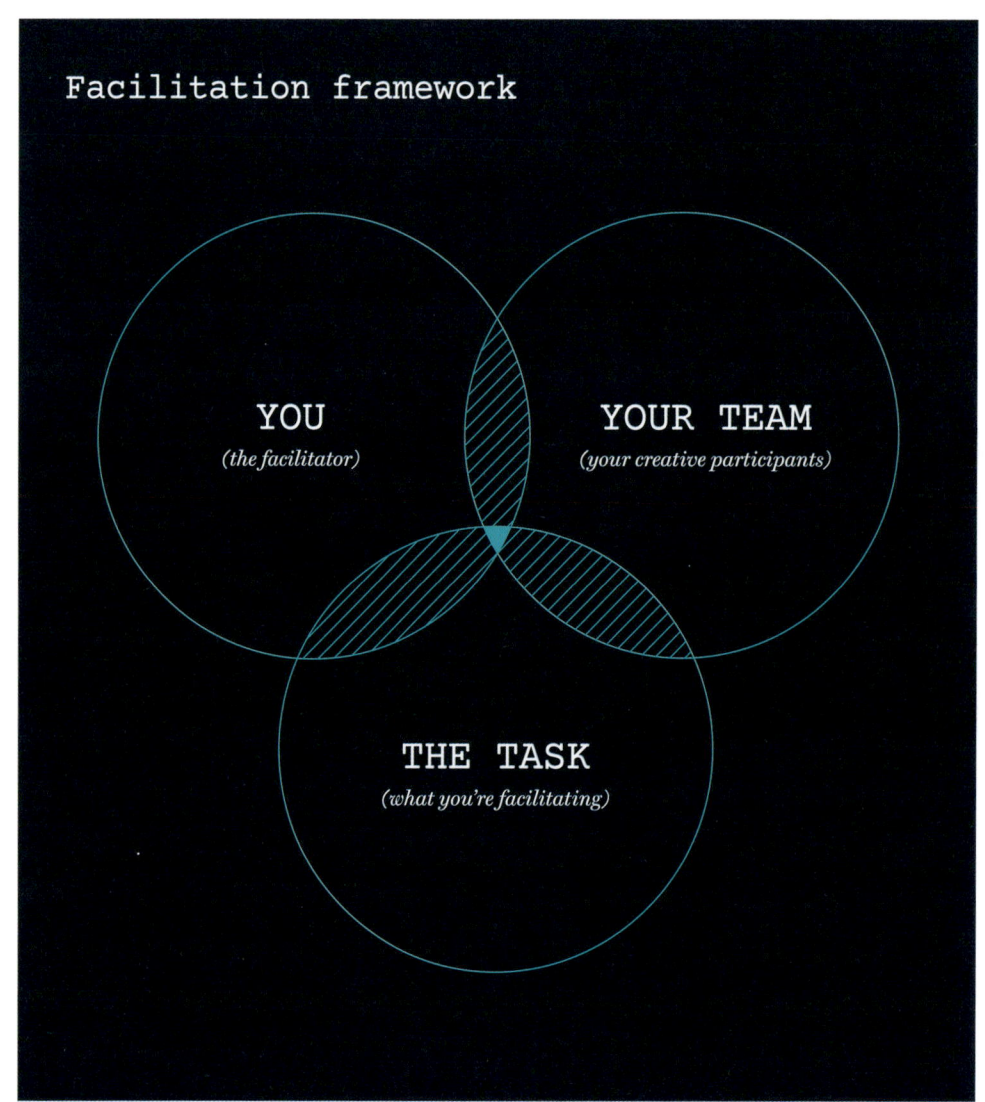

A facilitator's task can be big and small. So in any given business situation, knowledge and understanding around the context in which that task is set is critical to performance.

Jenny's story is powerful as it neatly illustrates the three factors of our facilitation framework. It is this foundation that helps us design a session, whether it's one lasting a few hours or one that might be part of a large programme lasting several weeks. And it is this framework that needs to be scaled when creative capability is embedded at an enterprise level.

I believe that mastery of the framework begins with the individual. When individuals command control of their own creative abilities, they will be able to confidently facilitate other people through a creative process. And when a team has collective awareness of their combined powers, they'll be able to adjust their approach to meet the tasks set by the business, and be all the more capable of scaling their efforts across an organisation.

In summary, it's people who drive the process, not the other way around. Let's now take a closer look at you and your incredible brain so you can start to learn how to facilitate as confidently and creatively as Jenny.

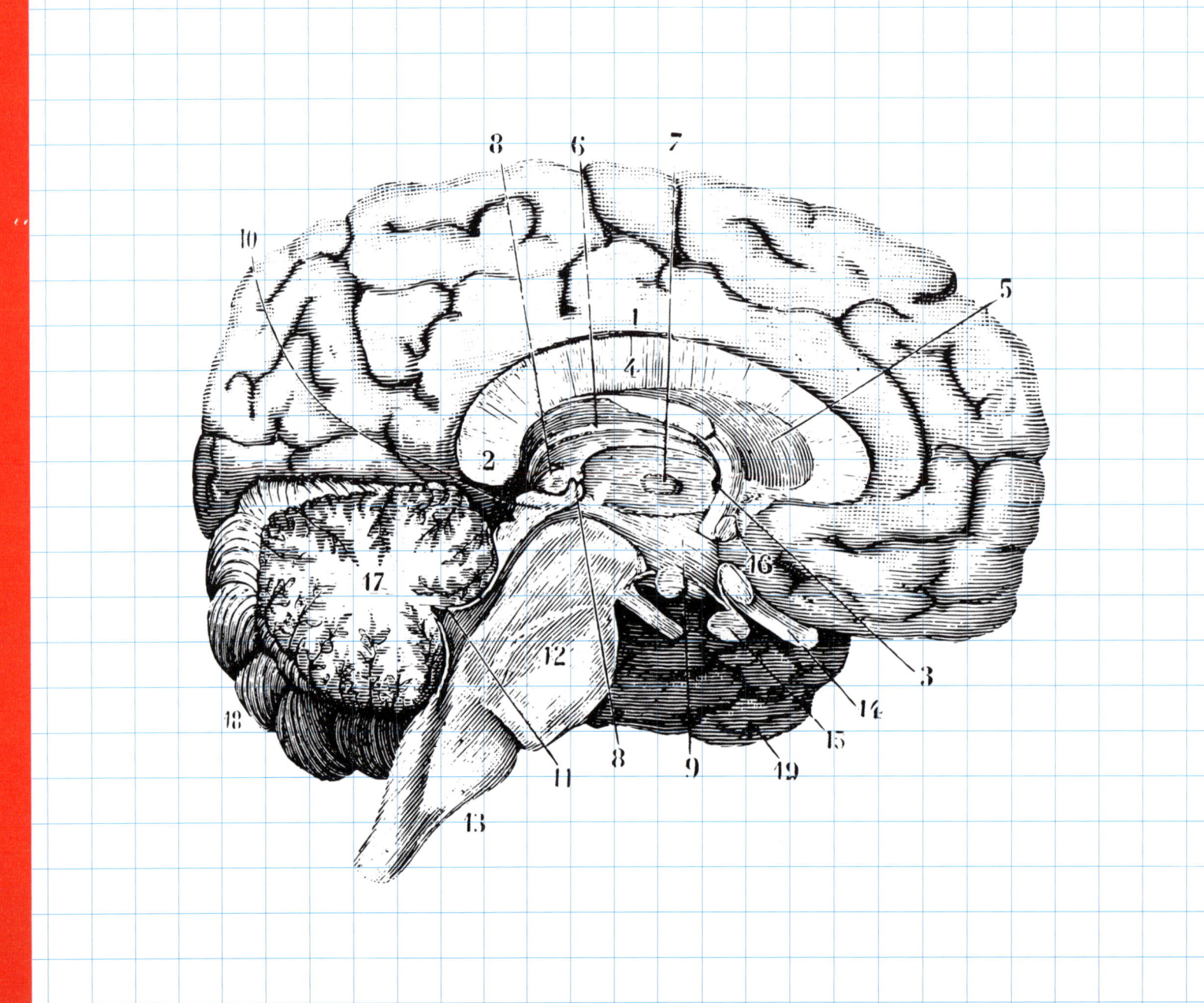

Part 1

YOU

(specifically your fabulous and creative brain)

Before you facilitate the creative process, you need to be your own creative master and know how best to make new connections. You can then help others make connections, sniff out ideas and facilitate strategy. Having a little knowledge about your brain, therefore, is a good thing.

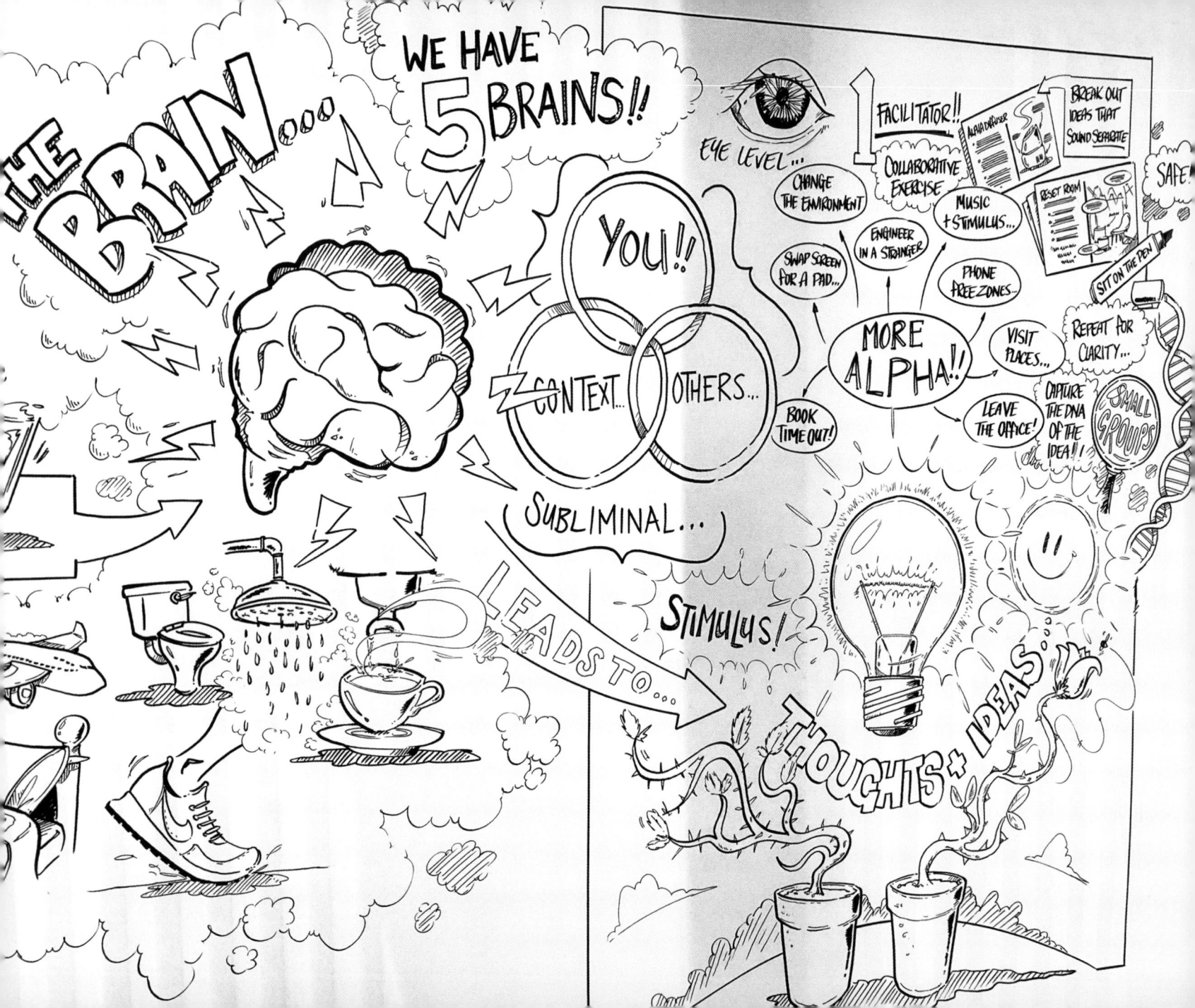

Quality thinking, more often

If you're tasked with facilitating strategy, innovation and creativity in a business it's because that business needs ideas. Facilitating people, in a way that makes ideas happen, requires you to be a different type of thinker and doer to the average Joe.

Before you design interventions for others, it's important to invest in creative structures for yourself. That way you stay fresh and sensitive to any opportunity around you. People will follow how you behave and what you do, far more than the instructions you brief and the emails you write.

Part One of this book is all about you and your creative connection-making brain. We start this journey by asking you a question.

Where do you have your best ideas?

(Clue: it's unlikely to be at the office, in poorly organised brainstorms.)

Consider these questions, too:

- **Where are you when have your best quality thinking?**
- **Where are you when you find it easier to make connections?**
- **Where are you when your thoughts flow at their easiest?**

There are many variations on the same theme as you'll interpret the questions in different ways, but please be specific about your answer. Spot the exact place and time, if possible. For example, it could be 'late at night whilst having a long bath', or 'on a long car journey as a passenger and gazing out the window' or 'vacuuming the house, ideas just pop in my head!' Make a note now…

We've asked this question *a lot* – and probably heard answers from 10K+ people from around the world – and 99% of the time people are describing activities not usually associated with working in an office or working on a task linked to a professional assignment. Typically, answers are:

- When exercising (running, walking the dog, on a rowing machine, at the gym, etc.)

- Washing up, making the beds

- Late at night (putting out the bins maybe…)

- Listening to music and laughing with friends, 'Just after I bumped into someone in town and we had a quick chat.' 👉

- Having a think about something and then later in the day realising the answer 'arrived' out of nowhere

- At the beach, in the mountains, watching a sunset

- Having a shower

- While on the toilet

Very rarely has anyone answered 'I get my best ideas when I'm sitting at my desk in a busy office, staring at an Excel chart, starved of time and energy with an approaching deadline'. Although it happens from time to time, it's not a scalable or welcome solution in business.

It would be tempting to advise that all you need to do to have better quality thinking, and therefore more creative ideas, is relax a little, avoid sitting at a desk and run a hot bath. But this is *not* the way. That technique only works for some people, some of the time.

There will have been times in your career when you had amazing creative breakthroughs at work, so saying that creative thinking is exclusively found away from our desks is also bad advice. However, there must be a certain quality of thinking within our brains when we're 'at the gym' or 'walking the dog' that is also present during those times in the office when we've had our creative breakthroughs. If we spend time understanding a little more about *how* we think, we can deliberately engineer our environment and working routines to recreate those conditions time and again. We can also ensure they're present when we design and deliver our facilitation projects so we help other people to get their heads in the best space to generate quality creative thinking, too.

The most creative minds are very deliberate when it comes to 'thinking hard' and indulging not only in a problem but also in their approach to answering it. So, understanding the brain and how we think is an important foundation of being innovative.

And let's not shy away from the science. A little knowledge of what's going on inside our heads will help us understand how we think. When we understand what's going on, we can take steps to amplify the conditions around us (and others) to do more of that 'good thinking'.

Some of what you'll read here about the inner workings of the brain is true in any context, but mostly we've re-expressed and described in the context of business. We do this because fine nuances (and possible truths) can get lost – we've found that using some of the material out there about the brain is useful to a point, but quickly becomes specialist and academic. This book should be a north star to help you have better ideas and also to help you help other people have better ideas. Use the material as a stimulus for your own journey into the brain. If you spot a better way to describe the brain then use it. There is no 'one right way' to make creative connections, and no one way to accurately explain the magic of the human brain.

We all have a deeply personal relationship with our own thinking that far exceeds the insights from 'experts'.

In every project we do, we strive to unlock something new about the way we think that the team didn't know before. That said, here's everything you need to know about the brain and how it makes creative connections...

RIGHT:
Asking people when and where they have their best ideas yields interesting results.

Neurons and stuff

Let's start with the foundations. The basics of the brain. Meet our fabulous friend, the neuron.

Neurons are specialised cells that transmit nerve impulses. Like all nerve cells, they have a body containing a nucleus and two other main components: an axon and dendrites.

Dendrites are fibres that project out from the neuron body and receive signals from other neurons. If we used a computer term to describe their function (dangerous!) then they are all about input. A single neuron can have any number of dendrites, from one to several thousand.

The axon is the longest fibre projecting away from the cell. It's all about output; it directs electrical information away from the neuron. Although a neuron only has one axon (generally), the axon has many branches so it can connect to as many as a thousand other neurons. Despite meeting a few people in your time who appear not to have any life in their head, the human brain has over 80 billion neurons. That's more than the known number of stars in our galaxy. When

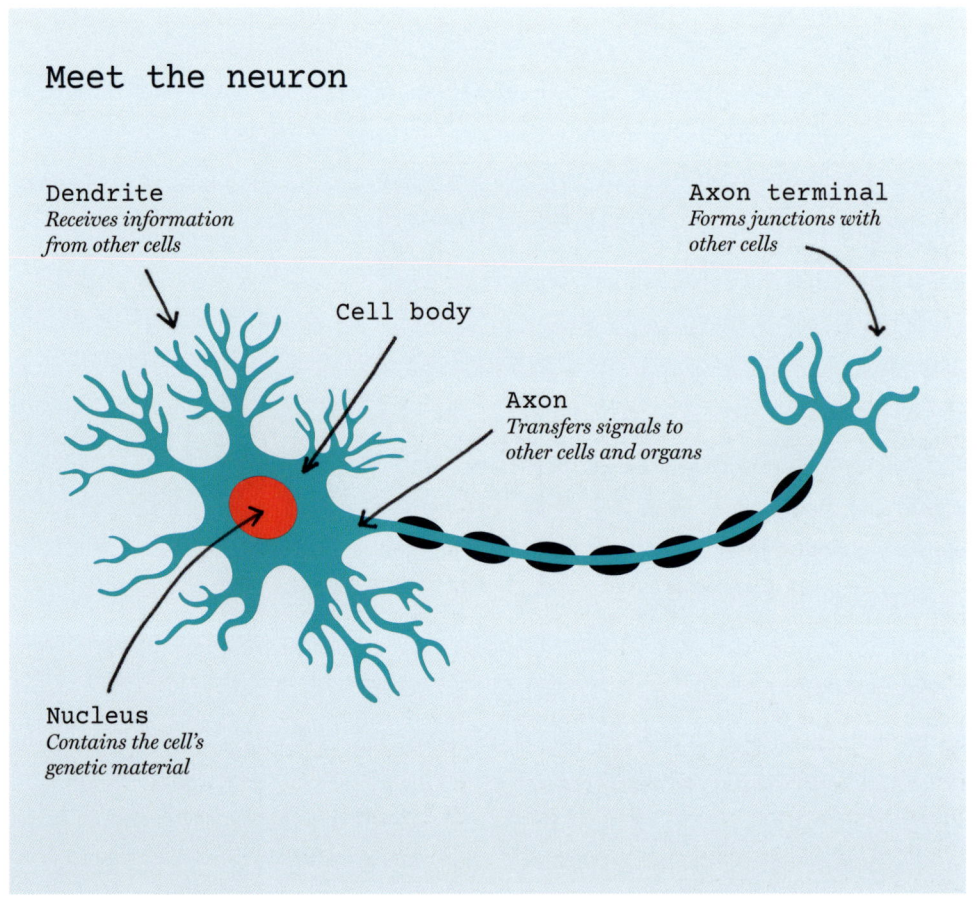

Meet the neuron

Dendrite *Receives information from other cells*

Cell body

Axon terminal *Forms junctions with other cells*

Axon *Transfers signals to other cells and organs*

Nucleus *Contains the cell's genetic material*

you truly consider the interactions of all of those dendrites and axons, you see that the neural network in the brain has billions of connections. Billions.

The dendrites of some neurons receive information from other neurons although they are not physically connected; there is a tiny gap between the two, known as the synapse.

The main function of a neuron is to carry 'messages' from one part of the body to another. To do this, our nervous system uses a combination of two processes – electrical and chemical. An electrical impulse travels through the neuron, then the impulse is transferred between neurons (across the synapse) as chemicals. Our brain is made up of these electrochemical signals, all firing billions of times a second. There are between 86 billion and 17 trillion 'action potentials' (the term for cells firing off) per second in the average human brain. And synaptic firing rates would be closer to 100 trillion+ per second. That's magical.

Are these creative thoughts?
Are these creative ideas?

No.

Once a neuron has 'fired' it returns to its resting state. There's no change to the electronic state of the neuron after it's fired; there is no 'memory' in the electronic state of the neuron. However, each time a neuron does fire, the chemical state of the relevant synapse is altered. This means that each time two neurons fire in sequence they will become more sensitive; they will be more likely to fire next time there is electrical stimulation at the synapse. The increase in sensitivity is the only trace of there having been some experience.

Our memory and imagination are not stored as electrical settings of the neurons. Instead, they are stored chemically as the greater likelihood of a particular set of neurons reacting to a new sensory input.

For any thinking that can be labelled as a 'thought' or an 'idea' in the brain, we need to see billions of neurons firing.

Unlike a cartoon of an idea appearing in a specific space in our brains between just two brain cells, our thoughts are present when billions of synaptic firings happen at the same time; the whole being far more than the sun of the parts.

Consider how a picture in an old newspaper was made from lots of tiny black dots – when seen from afar we see the whole image. And for an analogy more akin to electrical signals in the brain, consider lightning firing on and off within a big storm cloud... That's what is going on inside your head.

The creative brain's parts

If you're reading this with a PhD in neuropsychology it's probably best you skip ahead as you may feel compelled to get your red pen out. Remember, our approach is to make it easier for you as a facilitator to understand what's going on, so you can help others make connections.

Let's start with the top of your brain and work down.

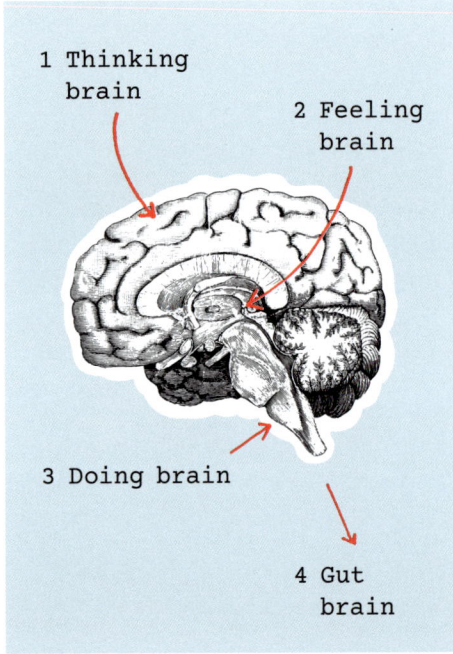

1 Thinking brain
2 Feeling brain
3 Doing brain
4 Gut brain

Brain: Part One is our **thinking brain**. Yes, yes, even though there are billions of neural connections throughout the entire brain, it's mainly the top cortex that's doing the heavy lifting. It's a few hundred thousand years old – in evolutionary terms, very young. This is what sets us apart from other mammals on the planet. We have our cortex to thank for working out sudoku puzzles, reading maps, understanding IKEA instructions and, of course, building language so we can tell our friends and family how much we love them. Our cortex is only a few millimetres thick, but it can handle the rules of grammar and infer meaning simultaneously, so you can process information on this page even if the wrods are selpt incorrecntyl.

Sixteen billion nerves connect the thinking brain to the next part of your brain: Part Two – what we call the **feeling brain**. Scientists call this the limbic system. A few million years old, it is the seat of motivation, emotion, learning and memory. Most of your behaviour is driven by the limbic system and its number one goal is survival. It craves consistency, as it takes energy to start doing things differently. Food, shelter, being loved and staying alive are top of the list.

The limbic system weighs up the effort to do something new versus the risk. You can play a game to test limbic processing by throwing different sized breadcrumbs at birds and seeing which birds are brave enough to hop towards you for the sizeable reward of chunky crusty bread. Remember, birds don't speak, solve crosswords or read maps – it's all basic programming such as eat, sleep, fly, chirp...

If you are feeling pain or emotion it's because your limbic system is sensing a challenge to its safety. We get easily spooked in a dark alleyway late at night because all those pre-programmed survival instincts we inherited from our ancestors are locked away in our limbic system's DNA. It's the 21st century, no facilitators should be in dark alleyways late at night. Unless they want to be.

Your limbic system connects to what we'll call the **doing brain**: the brainstem – Brain: Part Three. This is the oldest part of what we'd call 'our brain'. Essentially, it's a more developed part of our nervous system. This nervous system grew with us, becoming far more complex as we developed from aquatic life forms to living on land. Our earliest mammal ancestors date back a few hundred million years, when the signals in the brainstem would primarily be running simple support systems such as respiration and circulation of oxygen. We began to look human-esque around 2 million years ago and our Neanderthal forefathers were using basic tools around

800,000 years ago. Since then, while life has got increasingly complex for our fresh and developing thinking brain, our primal brainstem has continued the basic function of managing our survival and automatic functions in the body, such as heart rate, breathing, blood pressure, balance and digestion.

Brain: Part Four is your **gut brain**. Yes, in your actual gut. Your gut contains 500 million neurons that connect to your brain through the vagus nerve. So your gut communicates directly with your brainstem and limbic centres. This is a clear connection between body and mind, it's a bi-directional messaging system. If you are stressed – properly stressed, like in a pandemic, divorce, debt or death – then your brain sends messages to the gut that make it leaky and not ready to digest food. Equally, if you put dodgy food in the gut and don't chew properly, your gut sends unhappy messages to your brainstem and limbic centres making you feel rough. Do this often enough and bad things happen to your health. Yet so many people eat at their desk, typing emails with one hand whilst trying to eat a sandwich in the other...

Bad for your belly. Bad for your business.

Finally, we need to mention the **microbiota**. This is the entire population of bacteria living in and on the human body. Our gastrointestinal tract has the largest number of bacteria living in it. Many researchers talk about the 'microbiota-gut-brain axis'. So this collection of microbes, bacteria, fungi, viruses and their genes living inside and on our bodies is definitely worth considering as an extension of our gut brain. Although microbes are so small that they require a microscope to be visible, they contribute in big ways to our overall health and wellbeing.

This superhighway of information connecting mind to body and body to mind means that your body is not just a vessel to carry your thinking box to work, and that your brain is an electrochemical machine. However, unlike a machine that follows fixed operations, the brain is constantly creating and losing neural connections. When we think, electrical signals turn into chemical signals and back again into electrical signals as thoughts fire across our synapses. Your body is your creative thinking box, and the health of the body drives how well we think, how resilient we are, and how long we can deliver on our brilliant creative capacity. If you want to think well then it's important to eat well, drink well, move well and rest well. The best-cared for machines last the longest.

The facilitators who inspire us at GENIUS BOX are incredibly disciplined about their overall wellbeing. Gone are the times of living on coffees by day and martinis at night. You can do it occasionally, but as a long-term strategy for personal creativity the lifestyles of our rock music heroes aren't the ones to follow. As we'll see later, a hot bath and an early night on an insight project will work wonders for you, more so than a bellyful of wine and a cheese platter.

SUMMARY

- Your brain is an electrochemical wonder.

- Brain activity (thinking that leads to ideas) exists as the firing of billions of synapses between neurons. The more they fire, the more likely it is they'll fire again.

- Creativity, in this context, is making as many of those neurons fire in new and different places as possible – different connections will lead to different ideas.

- But if you pollute your brain with bad diet and lack of sleep; or ask it to operate on refined sugar, or too much caffeine and alcohol too often you'll wear down the creative magic...

Interview

Danny Denhard
CMO & EXEC COACH

Danny Denhard has over 21 years of experience in marketing, growth, product development and leadership. He has led some of the best-known brands and helped challenger brands actually compete. Danny is now a CMO/CGO and Exec Coach helping CMOs, VPs and Directors progress their careers and the performance of their teams and companies through workshop-based coaching.

How do you go about designing and facilitating a series of sessions to help a group of people agree and align behind a strategy of their own?
A strategy is a plan of which everyone has the same understanding. I believe it's particularly important that this plan is clear in telling everyone what they are not going to do just as much as what they should focus on – that's the best way I've found to align everyone. Tactically, I think a strategy can be kicked off by a presentation with some supporting slides (six slides, or a two-pager) that everyone keeps referring back to. This is what you save in a fire. Everyone needs to understand the same foundational elements: the purpose, the who, the why, the 'by when'. But the actual 'how' should be decided by the teams, departments and experts. If this isn't being decided then it's creating friction before you start. Strategy should be imperative and inclusive; no individual department should have its own strategy. And finally, when to review strategy: up to twice per year. When to change strategy: once a year, every year. I believe that's a good rhythm.

You've seen many processes, approaches, tools and language to describe and explain strategy; what has stuck with you?
Every leader has their own understanding of frameworks and what has worked in the past. Typically most organisations struggle to move away from the one they have and don't invest the time to find better frameworks or ways of working. The best framework I've found is the 'think big, act small, by when' framework – this helps everyone understand what they are working on. Then add the 'why' and then the builds – this helps people to understand the important levers and essential elements within the business: pricing, product, marketing, operations and how all that fits together. You'll see already that facilitating strategy is tough as there are both big and small topics of conversation.

When it comes to revisiting a strategy, is it better to get everyone in the room or just a few senior people who know the business inside out?
Strong strategy comes from everyone. It's not just a handful of confident people who you need to listen to. There isn't a 'one size fits all' approach either. I prefer a mix of generalists and specialists. Without this mix your emerging strategy becomes skewed and misaligned. Too many people over-index on inviting specialists to build a plan. Remember that generalists are the ones who often work to translate the elements of the strategy to others and can also be the glue between specialists. Anything more than ten people becomes too noisy for most to contribute, though, and I've noticed also that status is really highlighted in large groups.

There's bound to be disagreement between stakeholders on aspects of

> *"Strong strategy comes from everyone."*
>
> – DANNY DENHARD

an emerging strategy. What tips have you to manage differences of opinion?

Most people who facilitate strategy in businesses take the same steps. They approach the most senior people and listen to the HiPPO*. This might play as a successful tactical approach for an external consultancy, but often doesn't help build the best strategy. Ultimately departments and other leaders can't get fully behind a strategy that's built that way. To remove your own points of view and manage those of others, you have to take on board all of the insights, and all of the nuances in your discussions, take note of them, and keep them safe. Then invite other leaders to come to the plate and put across their points of view and their expert insight and feedback.

> *Business shorthand for: 'Highest Paid Person's Opinion'. HiPPO syndrome is frequently cited in failures at ExCo and board level, where it, along with 'group think', is often named as the root cause of bad decision-making and poor leadership. In some instances, HiPPO syndrome leads to businesses failing, stock prices falling and even impacts on the health, safety and wellbeing of employees.*

How do you manage any beliefs you might develop about your proposals being stronger than your client's point of view?

My job is to help drive positive change. When facilitating, my job is to probe, ask difficult questions and collaborate with the client. I work with the client and have to help them truly understand the strategy and how they progress it for short-term, mid-term and long-term success. Like most, I come up against resistance. On some occasions I have everyone agreeing, as it seems easier than doing the work to get it right. For many, building a strategy means a long slog or a fight with the boss. But I remind people that long before we had masses of data to help us, we'd go with an idea and then made it work with smart decisions.

What is a final nugget of genius you'd like to share?

Strategy is like baking a cake, you all start with the same sort of recipe. The difference between the best cake and the worst cake is time, tweaking the recipe and the confidence of the baker(s).

Brain vs mind

Look at the circle, dots and lines below – anything? No, didn't think so.

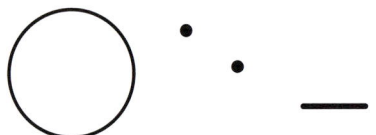

Now look at the following image...

Ooh! A face!

When our brain's optical processing department 'sees' those same shapes rearranged in a group we interpret them as a face. Somehow, the activity in our brain starts with optic neurons registering the lines. It then recruits other neurons and binds them together in a firing sequence until enough are recruited into a 'neural cloud' to represent the idea of a face in our mind. It will do that with the next three images too, and then recruit other neural clouds associated with faces and different emotions.

The neurons that make up these clouds are recruited because their synapses are sensitive to signals from the neurons at the start of the process. We've seen faces before, and we've seen simple diagrams before and learnt to interpret them as faces. The neural activity observing the images leads to the thought: ah, a smiley face!*

*Incidentally, if we turn an *object* upside down, we can perceive and identify it immediately. But turn a *face* upside down and something odd happens. We don't recognise the person as easily; we have to work harder and find it more difficult. This is because faces have their own dedicated processing areas in the brain...

We design baby carriers to face inwards, so babies see the smiling, loving faces of parents and carers. This helps their brains 'store' faces and then 'things that look a bit like faces' in an efficient manner. Perhaps if had we grown up in forward-facing prams we might not be as good at the emoji game... The point is that everything we do has the potential to help us when it comes to creativity, as it's all getting remembered, stored and catalogued in the warehouse that is our amazing brain. Our brain has the capacity to work with random information and turn it into thoughts that our mind can understand.

Psychologists, philosophers, and latte-drinking advertisers have agonised for decades about the difference between the brain and the mind. And whilst that full conversation has merit, it doesn't serve us well in the context of this book. So, best leave that for another time (or another book!)

It's helpful to consider that neural clouds have more collective power than the sum of the neurons from which they are made – a cloud of neurons will do more 'thinking'. Of course, technically, none of this is true as we're just talking about electrochemical signals, and it's hard to define where and what a thought is at neural level. This may be because up until now I've been talking about 'the brain' and it's probably better to now shift and talk about 'the mind.'

Whilst the brain has the capacity to sense activity from the optic nerve and then fire and recruit more neurons to process black shapes, as seen in the pictures above, it is the mind that responds to the neural clouds and observes the spaces between the shapes. The mind fills in information, makes connections, builds more meaning and spots things that aren't there…

In psychology, a 'gestalt' is a term that means the whole of anything is greater than the sum of its parts. To the brain, small black shapes are triggers for a sequence of neural networks firing, but it is the power of the gestalt across these neural clouds that gives the mind its fabulous processing ability. Again, had we not played with toy blocks (triangles, spheres and Loch Ness monsters) perhaps our minds would struggle to fill in the gaps.*

> Here's something to think on, too. The nature of perception involves so much more than simply combining those small black shapes together… we fill the space with what our brain thinks best fits; it's our perception making educated guesses. We like to think that what we see accurately matches what exists in the real world, but that isn't always the case – we know this from visual illusions. And sayings such as 'the map is not the territory' remind us that there's a marked difference between what we believe to be true and what is actually real. A powerful reminder that the way we see the world is constructed by us. 👉

Creativity, then, is something we all have the capacity for, given the right start. And it's never too late to start relearning how to think. Look at the text below and read what it says:

Aoccdrnig to a rscheearch at Cmabrigde Uinervtisy, it deosn't mttaer in waht oredr the ltteers in a wrod are, the olny iprmoetnt tihng is taht the frist and lsat ltteer be in the rghit pclae. The rset can be a toatl mses and you can sitll raed it wouthit porbelm. Tihs is bcuseae the huamn mnid deos not raed ervey lteter by istlef, but the wrod as a wlohe.

The jumbled up text is a lovely way of showing that our minds are working out how to process the world without our conscious help. They interpret 'meaning' in the world from the signals the brain is processing. Corrupt the signal (with food, sleep, diet, etc.) and our mind's ability to process accurate meaning from its surroundings becomes compromised.

The impact of people and the environment also compromises the mind's ability to think creatively. It's unsurprising, then, that we don't arrive at our best ideas sitting at a desk, 'thinking hard' or stuffing an energy bar into our face during a brainstorm after a day of sales updates.

The basics of the brain and mind described here offer a plausible explanation of how we think, so that when we're charged with the responsibility of coming up with new ideas, we know how to adjust our thinking, and the thinking of others, to arrive at new and different ideas. If we keep thinking the same way about the same problem we'll arrive at the same answer. In order to arrive at new ideas, we need to know how our mind thinks and what habits we've got into that keep reinforcing that way of thinking. 👉

RIGHT:
With more potential connections than stars in the galaxy, your brain is the greatest source of new ideas.

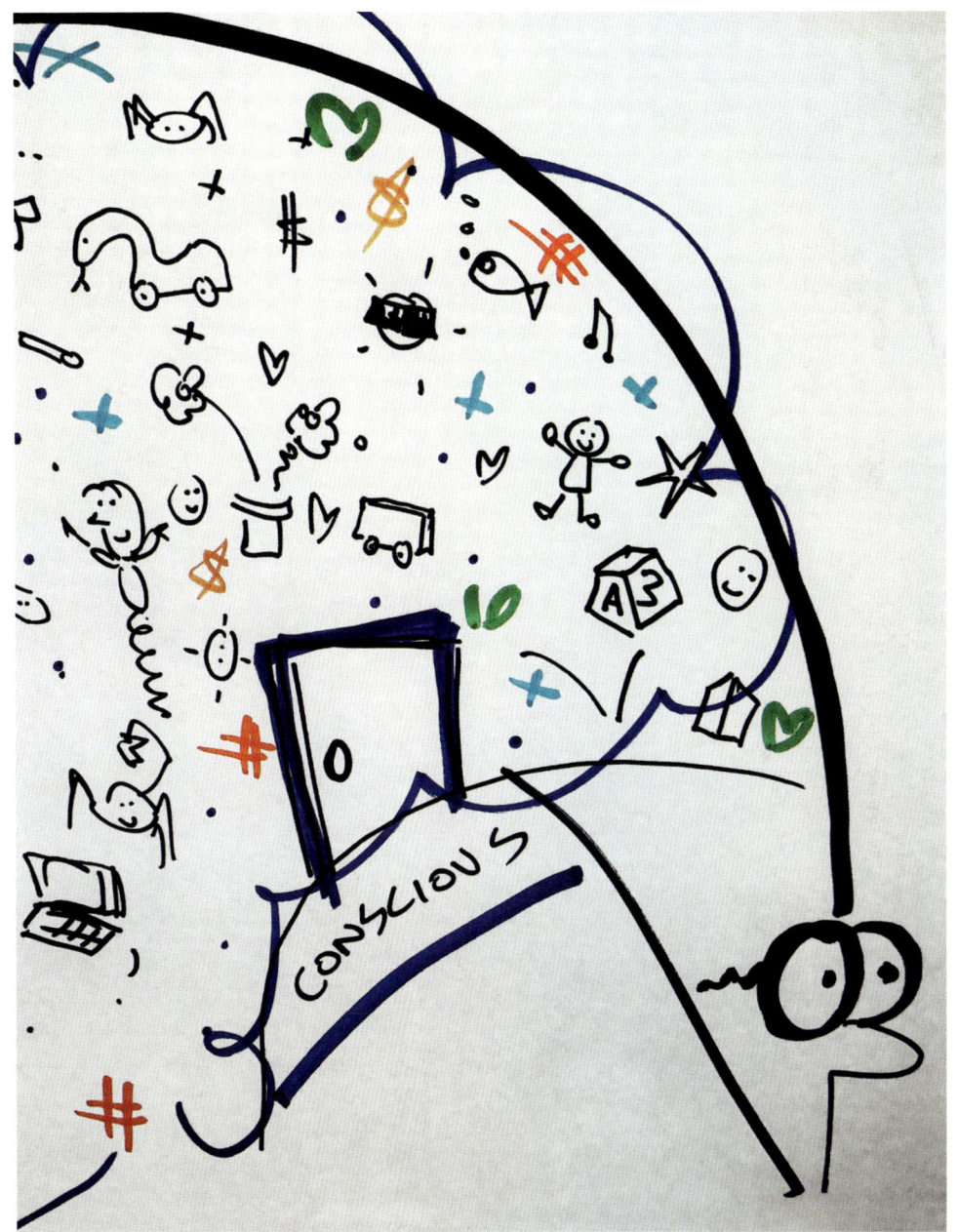

When considering the workings of the brain in the context of innovation and creativity, we need to move away from academic science and use analogies and metaphors. Such tricks of language allow us to describe our behaviours in different ways. Sentences that start with, 'It's a bit like' are gold dust to the creative facilitator; metaphors and similes unlock people's thinking and help us understand each other more easily. (Metaphors in previous sentence = 'gold dust' and 'unlock'.)

Our brain is a bit like a warehouse. You store things in it.

There's a small reception at the front where things are initially inspected and identified, and then fork-lifts, robots and scanners sort, label, package and, ultimately, put things on shelves. The way your mind deals with any kind of information is pretty much the same.

Imagine your brain as a super-efficient (and brilliantly organised) warehouse with an almost infinite number of shelves. Remember this is a metaphor. Your brain/mind doesn't *actually* operate this way, but this metaphor really does help. In the Disney Pixar film *Inside Out* (2015) we see memories stored as balls on shelves. These shelves seem to stretch into infinity, and of course there are also the lost memories deep in the darkness, too. A lovely analogy. Similarly, on the

Netflix series *Locke & Key* some of the characters use the 'Head Key' to unlock their minds – the character Kinsey, for example, visits memories of her dad stored in catalogued coloured boxes. The metaphor of a warehouse, with the ability to 'store' and 'access' material, is therefore a good one to use. It's one we can all easily understand.

Within the warehouse of your mind are all the memories, experiences, data points, sensations and knowledge of your life – all the ingredients needed to solve problems, have ideas and, of course, memories to refer to. Only the scale is much greater than any Amazon warehouse's wildest dreams. You can increase the volume of your mind-warehouse and the ability to cross-reference items by adding more experiences into your life. Breaking habits is a great way to 'do more things' and as a result expose yourself to more stimuli.

The longer you live, the more you can add to the warehouse. And the more varied the experiences you have, the more interesting, exciting and creative your ideas and insights will be, because all that 'stuff' can be used to generate new things. If creativity is about making new connections then the more 'stuff' we have to make connections from the better. However, adding more 'stuff' in a deliberate and ongoing fashion takes effort and energy. 👉

It's crude to use computer analogies to describe the brain, but if our cortex is like the RAM, it can only go so fast and handle so much information before it becomes overloaded and 'crashes'. When we work our bodies too hard in the gym, we pull a muscle. When we work our heads too hard, we get a headache. Thinking hard takes energy, so our brains are naturally wired to be energy-efficient and avoid unnecessary stress. We default to our old ways of processing the world. Very quickly (using pre-programmed chemical codes that decide whether 'new' is useful or a threat) our brains decide what to do with new information. Our mind-warehouse is hardwired to organise 'like with like'.

At my old agency we used to play a guessing game by asking people to write down the answers to these sorts of questions about each other:

- What sort of car do you think they drive?
- What's their favourite type of music?
- Do they like seafood?
- What makes them laugh?
- What do they do on holiday?

(...and other wilder questions depending on the workshop vibe!)

And of course, not knowing these intimacies at first, participants would have to guess. They'd make assumptions based on what they had inferred from each other in the time we'd had together. As a warm-up to insight work it introduced the point that we all carry a story about ourselves and we make conclusions about others in comparison to that story. We might not know what type of car Jane drives, but she says she lives in a big house near a small village in the countryside – so, maybe she drives an old green Land Rover and owns a shaggy dog. People from our past who look and sound a bit like Jane also liked walking holidays, read the *Telegraph* and laughed too loud at public gatherings – maybe Jane is like that too.*

This activity is a way of bringing to life some of the theories on social perception. We tend to form a first impression of someone in less than 100 milliseconds (that's less than one tenth of a second). This is largely based on their facial appearance (imagine the impact of Covid masks...) We also engage in something called 'thin-slicing', which is the ability of our subconscious to find patterns in situations and behaviour based on some very narrow slices of experience. We form impressions of someone's character based on extremely brief snippets of behaviour and use these to make assumptions. This leads on to attribution theory – do we attribute someone's behaviour to themselves (their personality traits) or to their situation (other people, stuff that's happened that day)?

In fact, people make fundamental attribution errors all the time where they overestimate the extent to which someone's behaviour is due to internal factors and underestimate the role of situational factors (e.g. the checkout assistant was grumpy with Gabriel and so Gabriel assumes that she is just a grumpy person... actually, she had a fight with her boyfriend that morning, her car wouldn't start and her cat's unwell). What's even more fascinating is that our minds can often maintain this narrative for people we've made judgements about and carry them forward into the future. We can take an instant dislike to Aunt Jenny back in the day for something minor and hold on to that narrative because of attribution error. Even if she turns up early one Christmas Eve, cooks us dinner and gives us all handmade and thoughtful gifts, we'd still dislike her as 'that's just the type of manipulative thing she'd do'.

Making creative connections takes energy; the brain wants to work as efficiently as possible.

So, the brain makes these 'looks like/sounds like/I've been here before' connections at lightning speed instead. A super-fast classification 'goes in this box' type of brain is good for efficiency. Once we've learnt how to drive, the operation of most vehicles with a steering wheel and pedals remains the same. Learning to type on a QWERTY keyboard becomes a transferable skill to a touchscreen. Our brain spots things that 'sort of look a bit like X and therefore Y isn't that different' all the time. A good deal of problem solving rests on knowledge and experience we've gathered previously.

But our assumptions can sometimes be wrong. We can easily make a mistake about people and situations – and assumptions can disconnect us from what really matters to people. Whilst it's a survival strength of our brains to follow like-with-like behaviour, we must deliberately inject new information to disturb assumption-making patterns – something we'll revisit in the Insight chapter (see 156).

Additionally, to keep efficient we crave routine. And we get into subconscious habits that keep us locked in those routines. We don't have to think hard and waste precious energy when we're in routines – we can live our life on cruise control. Consider:

• Do you always sleep on the same side of the bed?

• Do you have your tea or coffee 'just so'?

• Do you always read your news from the same website?

• Do you have the same sorts of songs on your playlist?

• And, despite a huge range of options, do you opt for the same pizza?

Comedians thrive on these types of observations, and we laugh because

SUMMARY

- Your mind is like a warehouse.

- It stores all your experiences in your head in coloured boxes with neat labels. (it doesn't *actually* do that, it's a metaphor).

- Its like-with-like filing system is super-fast, super-efficient and super-helpful for living our busy lives, as we don't have to think about things too hard.

- *But*, this keeps us in a rut and the trap of routine.

- New information is hard to file easily and, as a result, new ideas may get dismissed in creative sessions.

- Take care when making assumptions (but don't feel bad about yourself that you do – *everyone* does it).

they're true. It's the same in our working world – it's filled with routines and subtle behaviours that keep us exposed to the same sort of inputs throughout the day, but ironically keep us from the very thing that will enrich our creative potential: something new. To recap:

- The same kind of inputs get sorted like-with-like in the warehouse of the mind.

- Our brains develop to store like-with-like experiences on top of each other.

- This embeds learning and skills for survival.

When a baby lies on its back looking at its hands for months on end, it is processing the signals and senses required to connect intention to muscle memory. We don't consciously ask our fingers to grip the handle of a mug, instead 'we take a sip of tea'. I'm not consciously aware, as I type this sentence, of my fingers in space above the keyboard, but I'm instead doing my best to tell you the story of how I believe creativity works in the brain.

The takeaway from this section is that the brain is brilliant at acquiring and storing information and, to keep it efficient, like is stored with like. But creative thinking is all about mixing things up. So, the creative process, and how it's facilitated, needs to engineer deliberate rule-breaking and process-disrupting moments for 'new' to take hold in someone's mind.

ABOVE LEFT:
Filling your brain with the same experiences leads to the same ideas. More new experiences provide more resources for new ideas.

Luke and Yoda

(the conscious and subconscious* mind)

I've described the brain as a warehouse where information, experiences and sensations are stored in an orderly fashion. Your mind sorts those inputs without any direct instruction from 'you' and keeps that information locked up safe until it's needed. Consider how you won't be consciously thinking right now about which words in this paragraph are nouns or adjectives. But that knowledge, along with all the rules of grammar, needs to exist somewhere in your mind for you to comprehend the structure and meaning of what I'm writing here and throughout the rest of this delicious book.

The mind 'thinks' on its own without us being aware of what it's up to. This means

Freud used the terms 'subconscious' and 'unconscious' interchangeably, but when psychologists use these terms they tend to do so for different specific reasons. In this book, both terms are used interchangeably, and used in the context of creative thinking, making connections and interacting with others.

Most times, as a facilitator, you'll be aware of what you're doing and why. On other occasions, whether in groups or on your own, you won't be aware of some of your thinking, behaviour or actions – this is what I mean by unconscious and subconscious, it's the stuff that's going on in the background.

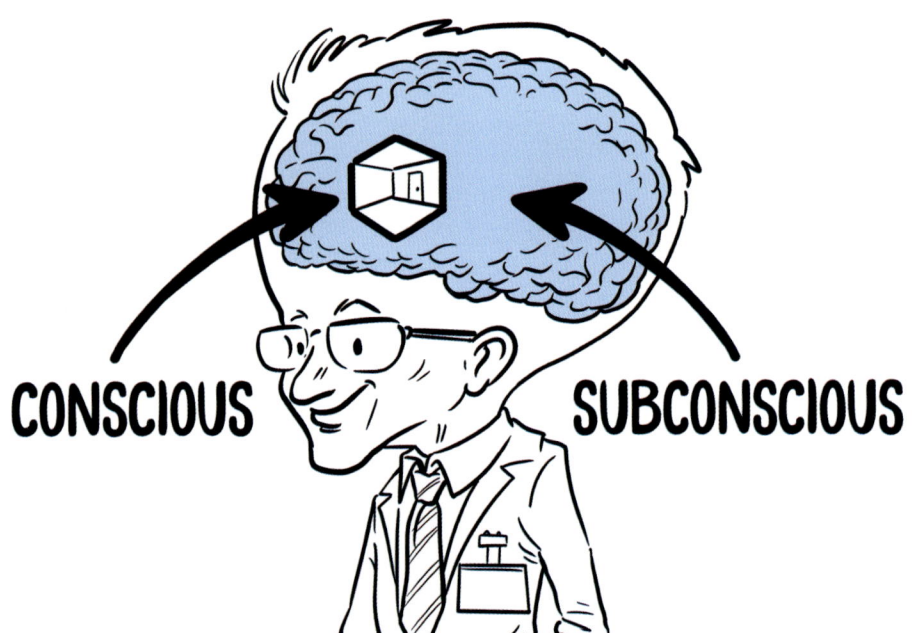

LEFT:
We're aware of what we're thinking about consciously. There's far more thinking and processing at a subconscious level.

that the tasks we're involved in, and how we're interacting with those tasks, will affect the quality of that thought processing. The brain is processing information billions of times per second, but for the purposes of facilitating creativity (and to the annoyance of the psychology professors who fact-checked my writing), It's helpful to consider the mind as operating on two levels. One level is navigating moment-to-moment (we can call this 'conscious') whilst at another level activity is happening deeper and at a much faster pace without us knowing (we'll call this 'subconscious').

The creative power of the conscious/subconscious comes from a partnership and is not an either/or state.

Things like breathing, circulation and digestion we'll put at an even deeper level, as there's not a great deal our mind can do about it. Largely, the functions we need to stay alive are driven automatically by the brainstem (see p34). Let's accept it's like our own version of MS-DOS: a body operating system, and leave it alone!

The concepts are usually grouped as follows:

- Subconscious system = intuitive/automatic/super-fast processing

- Conscious system = intentional/limited/slower processing (we're aware of what we're thinking – it's that voice in our head)

Most psychologists are in agreement that our minds operate on a two-system basis. To help land learning, at GENIUS BOX we find it helpful to re-express these systems as characters from movies and TV. If our dual mode mind had characteristics, they'd be Luke and Yoda from *Star Wars*. 👉

In the past GENIUS BOX has offered up other famous partnerships from popular culture as a metaphor for the dual mode thinking of our mind. Kirk and Spock from *Star Trek* worked well, the 1980s cop duo Dempsey and Makepeace less so!

Interestingly, we've spotted that enduring TV programmes from the past had characters that we all enjoyed watching and were invested in. The four characters from *The A-Team* (Face, Hannibal, Mr T and Murdoch) have similar drivers and behaviours to the four characters from *Sex in the City* (Charlotte, Miranda, Samantha and Carrie). Perhaps it was deliberate that the scriptwriters designed these characters from specific psychological models and behavioural theory. Perhaps it's accidental. But in our millions, we'd tune into each episode to see what adventures our favourite character got up to that week.

We'll return to the power of metaphors and re-expressions in the Insight and Ideas chapters. A picture paints a thousand words – and so too can a character, with whom we identify, help us to picture the way we think and behave.

Yoda is super intuitive. He spots the connections between unrelated things. He considers all alternative perspectives way before Luke.

He has the knowledge and the capacity to connect to all energy in the galaxy. Yoda is our 'hunches', our insights, and our random ideas that appear when we are in the shower, out for a walk or on the rowing machine at the gym. Yoda is your mind's subconscious system.

On the other hand we have Luke – he's slower* and he tires quickly. Learning to control his light saber, at first, takes effort. Lifting downed TIE-fighters out of the lake using his mind takes effort. His thoughts are controlled and explicit. He almost says his thoughts out loud as they happen. His thinking system has limited capacity and is cognitively demanding (it's hard work saving the galaxy when you grew up on a farm). It's also easily overloaded by information good and bad ('Luke, I am your father'). Luke is like your mind's conscious system.

> In the early days of the *Star Wars* saga, Luke is certainly slower than the super powerful 'look-at-me-connected-to-all-the-universe-being-able-to-shape-shift-and-stuff' Jedi version he becomes in the later movies. Spoiler alert.

Re-expressing the mind's subconscious and conscious processing as Yoda and Luke sounds a little like the 'System 1 and System 2 thinking' made popular by the Nobel Prize-winning author Daniel Kahneman in his book *Thinking, Fast and Slow*. System 1 is Yoda and is fast and automatic (using previous patterns to save energy). Our System 1 mind can:

- Complete the phrase "Romeo and… "
- Know instantly the answer to 2 + 2
- Ride a bicycle
- Know what our true love gave us on the 5th day of Christmas

System 2 is Luke and is slower and effortful (taking more energy from the brain). System 2 can:

- Spend time reading Romeo and Juliet to answer questions about a specific passage
- Execute mental arithmetic and calculate 57 x 3*
- Read the map when out on a bike ride
- Say out loud backwards the months of the year starting with December 👉

You likely said to yourself 'so that's (50 x 3) + (7 x 3), so that's 150 + 21' – and it took a few moments as you had to consciously handle all that information all at once.

PART 1 — YOU

THIS IS NOT THE WAY

Finally, System 1 (Yoda) thinking is much better at determining comparisons between things. It is very good at arriving at the *average* of things, and not the *sum* of things.

Here's an example:

In the image here, quickly determine what the average length of the lines is.

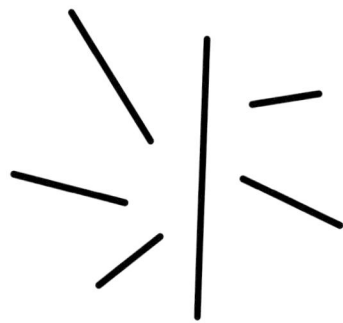

You've immediately got a sense of how long that is. And if you drew that line off to the side you could show it to someone else. This thinking took less than a second – right?

Now, how would you determine the sum of the lengths of all of the lines? This activity requires System 2 thinking – and probably some maths!

A word of caution: the danger in re-expressing our processing powers as Yoda and Luke is that we form the belief that we are either in one or the other systems of thinking. This is not so. Yoda and Luke work in partnership and in parallel. The deeper, cooler subconscious power of the Yoda system is in the background and filters out all the unnecessary information Luke doesn't need. For example, until I made you aware of it, you weren't thinking consciously about the colour of the top you are wearing right now, or what you had for dinner last night. Ha! You are now, eh? Clever.

Our deep, Yoda-like subconscious processing is happening all the time, unbeknown to us. When we're deep in the moment, focused on one thing 'over here', our subconscious processing is pondering something else 'over there'. If you've ever opened an eye-level cupboard door in a kitchen and have something fall out, or accidentally knocked a cup from your desk, your instant reaction is to catch it. There's no conscious thought – you simply do it; it's a primitive reaction no doubt steeped in survival instincts. This is our reflexive system in operation – our subconscious superpowers.

The processing power of our Yoda subconscious is infinitely greater than the conscious processing power of our Luke brain. Luke only has access to a small part of our warehouse storage. Yoda can scan all the shelves at all times. In psychological terms, the basic operation of System 1 thinking isn't impaired when the observer is cognitively busy. In other words, Yoda will always be able to operate effectively, but System 2 (Luke) will start to tire, make errors and draw more energy from the brain when overloaded with information and distraction.

I mention this now as that's useful to know when it comes to:

• Running brainstorms in busy offices (don't!)

• Selecting ideas (we should trust our Yoda/System 1 thinking)

It is Luke who attends the business meeting, but it is Yoda who ponders what everyone discussed while on the commute home, as you gaze out the window and when washing up that evening. It is our Yoda brain that makes connections at a deeper level while we sleep and then, when we wake having 'slept on it', we have a better perspective about a challenge we're facing. It's Luke who sets the alarm, but Yoda who wakes us seconds before it goes off, as though he's been counting time perfectly while we slept. It's Luke who spots that tehse wrods are the worng way aunord but Yoda who makes ssnee of it all. Genius.

"Everybody is a genius. But if you judge a fish by its ability to climb a tree, it will live its whole life believing that it is stupid."

— **ALBERT EINSTEIN**

Heuristics and habits

Fact: the cards above have a number on one side, and a colour on the other.

Question: Which cards need to be flipped over to prove that all even numbers have red backs?

Got it? Make a note of your answer.

The correct answer is to flip over two cards: the number 4 (to make sure it has a red back) and the blue card (to make sure that it *doesn't* have an even number on the other side). Most people suggest flipping over the 4 and the red card – this is wrong, as it doesn't matter if the red card has an odd number on the other side as the posit would still be true. If you chose '4' and 'red' I have some self-esteem-saving news:

- Around 90% of people say '4' and 'red'
- You're still creative
- I'm just using this test as a way of illustrating how your mind processed the puzzle and decided on the answer

This is the Wason Selection Task (or 'Four-card Problem'). A logic puzzle devised by Peter Cathcart Wason in 1966, it's one of the most famous tasks in the study of deductive reasoning. Here, it illustrates how the brain hears instructions and immediately and automatically initiates default modes of thinking. Often acting on only partial information, the brain suggests the answer. Your brain has seen lots of card tricks before, and races ahead with an impulse answer, only concerned with 'red' and 'even'. With good intention it is trying to solve the riddle as efficiently as possible. It's only when we get shown the answer, or have the chance to indulge in more time to think it through, that we hear how Yoda may have mooted to Luke, 'consider the blue card you must.'

As mentioned before, the brain likes patterns and sequences; they are helpful

RIGHT:
If not addressed, heuristics and habit can trample new creative thoughts.

SUMMARY

- It's efficient for our brains to run default heuristic programmes to navigate the complexity of daily life. In most cases, this is useful. But for problem solving and especially for making new connections (the creative act!), we need access to *all* of our subconscious processing power and to not have our default heuristics take over.

- What happens in business meetings more often than not is that we're given a challenge without being allowed time to think about it fully and so our heuristics kick in.

- We don't indulge the problem or scope it out enough to provide all of our mind with the stimuli it needs to knock it out of default heuristics mode.

- Worse still is when we're placed in a hot and stuffy meeting room and asked to 'brainstorm' the answer in one afternoon. This is *not* the way to creative thought.

when storing information in a like-with-like way (and like-with-'sort of like') in the early stages of brain development. Our repeat habits reinforce the learning. It's much more efficient to continue using patterns and sequences to retrieve information, too. We continue to store like-with-like and we can create 'gestalts': ideas that are more than the sum of their parts. The default pre-programmes that kick in are called 'heuristics', and our brains use these heuristics to save precious energy.

When we think – particularly if we classify our thinking as problem solving – our intuition, heuristics and bias hit first, in most instances acting on only parts of information, guessing the rest and filling in the blanks. If our awareness is there, of course, then conscious and deliberative thinking takes over, but this takes energy.

There's a relationship between the heuristics, or defaults, within our mind that we use in our thinking process, and the gestalts, or ideas, we create to understand the world. They reinforce each other. Consider how many quirky puzzles you've tackled in the past. I share one here to demonstrate how your heuristics kick in and say, 'Hey, I've got this, I've seen something like this before, here's the answer – go for the red card.'

Brain hemispheres

Much has been written about the two sides of the brain and their functions. But how much of it is true?

A quick internet search will reveal surprising lists about what each side of the brain does, but beware as science can be nasty. In his 1981 Nobel lecture, the neuroscientist Roger Sperry (a founder of split-brain research) summarised the prevailing view of the right hemisphere: 'not only mute and graphic but also dyslexic, word-deaf and lacking generally in higher cognitive function'. In short, the right side of the brain was thought to be pretty useless – we know this can't be true. It would be foolish to assume that if we took half our brain out we'd still be able to function perfectly. But what is going on in specific parts of our mind? Is there literally a bit of our head that 'makes things up' and generates 'the creative idea'?

We know the right side of the brain sort of looks after the left of side of the body. And one of the most common misconceptions about left-handers is that they are more creative than right-handers. I'm left-handed and so will of course indulge this point of view! But these debates over lateralisation in the brain and where creative thought sits are never resolved easily. We do know that in the association of new and unrelated concepts (creative thought) there are greater activations in the right hemisphere – so there's definitely something going on there.

A little knowledge about what goes on inside our heads sets the context for developing our innate intuitive and creative powers. When facilitating people who can sometimes believe that they have little creativity, I think this information is a powerful coaching tool.

In recent times, psychologists have noticed that many patients with right hemisphere damage had serious cognitive problems even though the left hemisphere had been spared. Some of these patients couldn't understand jokes or sarcasm or metaphors. Other patients found it hard to use a map or make sense of paintings. At first it seems these issues of a lack of humour and an inability to read a map have nothing in common. But when looking at that statement from a different perspective, you'll see the right hemisphere of your brain trying to find connections between unrelated things.

In the realm of creativity, I believe the right side of the brain helps spot existing patterns in information or helps you uncover and create new patterns made from disparate information. Just as our mind creates bigger pictures to make sense of the world, and relies on patterns to save energy and navigate problems, our brain can also be taught to make new pictures of seemingly unrelated things, and can create new connections from a variety of different stimuli.

Facilitating creative behaviour is making the effort to create 'new' repeatedly, and forming a conscious and deliberate habit to do so. This is initially hard as we're already in a pattern of subconscious habits and behaviours. If you define creativity as being a gifted artist (be you right- or left-handed) then that's one manifestation, certainly. For others, it is being smart with numbers. Creativity for some is being super musical or fast-brained, it's socially magical and only for the extroverted. This isn't helpful in the context of a business project. To make the point – sometimes you'll be facilitating someone who says they're not creative. Ask them if they have they ever done any of the following:

- Cooked without a recipe

- Taken a photo at an angle with their phone and adjusted the filter afterwards before posting on an Instagram feed

- Searched the internet for an image to represent a particular message on a PowerPoint slide

- Spotted a gift for someone because it was 'just so'

These are creative acts. This is the mind making new connections. It is the right side of the brain igniting with possibility. It was also the case when colleagues conceived an answer to a business issue at work. So yes, if we define our creative ability through just one lens (artistic or musical) we can easily fool ourselves into believing we're not creative. But when we realise we can form a habit of doing new things often enough that it coaches our right hemisphere to spot new connections, then we're all equally powerful participants in the creative process.

When we have our best thinking or moments of insight, and when generating new ideas, it is our right hemisphere working in partnership with all that's found in the left. This is a harmony of System 1 and System 2 thinking (Yoda and Luke) and it's also more likely to happen when we're open to stimuli and possibility – just like we are when gazing out the window on a train journey rather than in a hot and stuffy office.

SUMMARY

- Your right hemisphere does a great deal of work to make sense of unrelated things.

- It's important to make deliberate efforts to experience a range of stimuli in our lives, and especially in ideas sessions, in order to stimulate the brain.

- Insights and ideas come from mixing up a range of stimuli (left-brain activity) and making connections between them (right-brain activity).

- The key as facilitators of the creative process is to set the best conditions for that to happen often. Importantly, our role as insight and ideas facilitators is to manage the energy and stimuli throughout all aspects of the project you are involved in, so people can make connections on demand.

LEFT:
Access to both hemispheres of the brain is required for our best creative thinking.

Your ARAS

Conscious thought – such as sitting at your desk and 'thinking hard' or having a forced brainstorm that feels uncomfortable – can only get you so far.

To make new and creative connections of true brilliance, we must grant ourselves access to the whole of our mind. We want to wander all the shelves of our mind warehouse so the right hemisphere can help us make connections. Access to all areas of our mind warehouse is governed by our selective attention and, specifically, the part of the brain that's dedicated to levels of conscious awareness. This part of the brain is called the Ascending Reticular Activating System, or ARAS. It's deep at the base of our brainstem and is responsible for levels of attention and alertness.

While we're busy navigating our day in self-talk, our ARAS is making decisions for us about what's important. And it's raising those messages to our conscious attention or it's filtering out what isn't needed. This is an automatic system and probably has echoes from our pre-historic ancestors who needed to be alert for noises at the mouth of the cave. Our ARAS would pose the conscious question necessary for survival: 'Is that scratching sound something that I could eat or should kill, or is it something getting ready to eat or kill me?'

Thankfully, such immediate threats are scarce in modern business, but our DNA carries those codes. And in the 21st century your ARAS will (usually!) wake you in time for your train stop, even if your head is pressed against the window in commuter slumber. It will hear your voice being mentioned in a crowded room, a phenomenon known as the cocktail party effect. Your ARAS will spot a sequence of numbers that might have a one-digit difference to your own telephone number.

In short, it lets you know what's important and what else that information is connected to. Therefore, in terms of a creative tool it's brilliant at spotting patterns, making connections and filling in gaps. Again, the more information you fill your mind with as a result of ongoing, deliberate fresh experiences, the more potential connections your ARAS can make when it switches on your attention and focus.

As with so many things, it's most helpful to remember what the ARAS is and how it works with the help of a metaphor. To describe the ARAS as something like a door, which is either closed or open, is a little misleading as, in truth, there is always a thoroughfare of information across the brain, billions of times a second. It is perhaps easier to think of this area – the connection between subconscious and conscious – as a digital filter effect on an image. Some filters dull down light and create shadows, other filters boost up sharpness or brightness. In all instances, we're simply changing the light settings allowing more or less light through. It's the same with the communication between our subconscious and conscious thought.

For a creative epiphany, your ARAS works best when you're in a particular state of attention. We don't want

pre-programmed heuristics to take over, but instead need to be both stimulated and focused on a task (thinking about a problem or crafting an idea), whilst also rested and relaxed, and open to new possibilities.

If I ask you where you have your best thinking (be that new ideas or moments of insight), 99.9% of the time you are not going to be at work. You might be at the office or having a conversation with a colleague, but the conditions of that exact moment are quite particular. You might be having a one-to-one conversation in a comfy seating area, walking across the office campus outside or having a moment of 'fun' with your team during an off-work topic. And, as listed earlier in the chapter, more often than not people say they have their best thinking when running, walking, washing the car, washing up, hoovering the house, in the bath, on the toilet, doing DIY. This isn't a coincidence, it's directly related to your state of mind. 👉

States of mind

In the late 1920s, psychiatrist Hans Berger discovered and pioneered the science of electroencephalography (EEG).

His rudimentary machines plotted the electrical signals within our brain. As I've described, our thoughts, emotions and behaviours all arise from the electrical activity of brain cells. When neurons fire, a bioelectrical current ripples through the axon. When many cells fire at the same time, electrodes on our skull can detect a shift in tiny voltages – this process forms the basis of EEG. A typical EEG chart reveals rhythmic crests and troughs, reflecting rising and falling voltages in groups of neurons. These dynamics are sometimes called 'brain waves' and are typically measured in hertz.

The first publications on the topic identified two major categories of brain wave: alpha waves (7–12Hz) and beta waves (12–30Hz). In the decades that followed, researchers defined additional rhythms, including delta (0.5–4Hz), theta (4–8Hz), and gamma (32–100Hz) waves. We typically spend a great deal of our day in a 'beta state' – faster brainwaves associated with a state of outwardly focused concentration. We're in 'doing mode' – typing emails, sending texts, switching screens on Zoom calls and working through life's to do list. There's little communication with our ARAS; the doorway to our subconscious is shut.

Unsurprisingly, when asked to 'come up with some ideas' by an insistent colleague, our minds struggle to do so. We painfully scan the room waiting for someone to offer a suggestion. Beta state is not good for creativity.

However, in moments where we're partially focused and absorbed in something needing little of our conscious attention (maybe washing up or walking the dog) our bodies relax and so do our minds. We fall into an 'alpha state'. Our minds are idling along, free from energy-demanding concentration, we're able to daydream a little and ponder other matters in our lives. Our ARAS is in harmony with our thoughts; the doorway to our subconscious opens

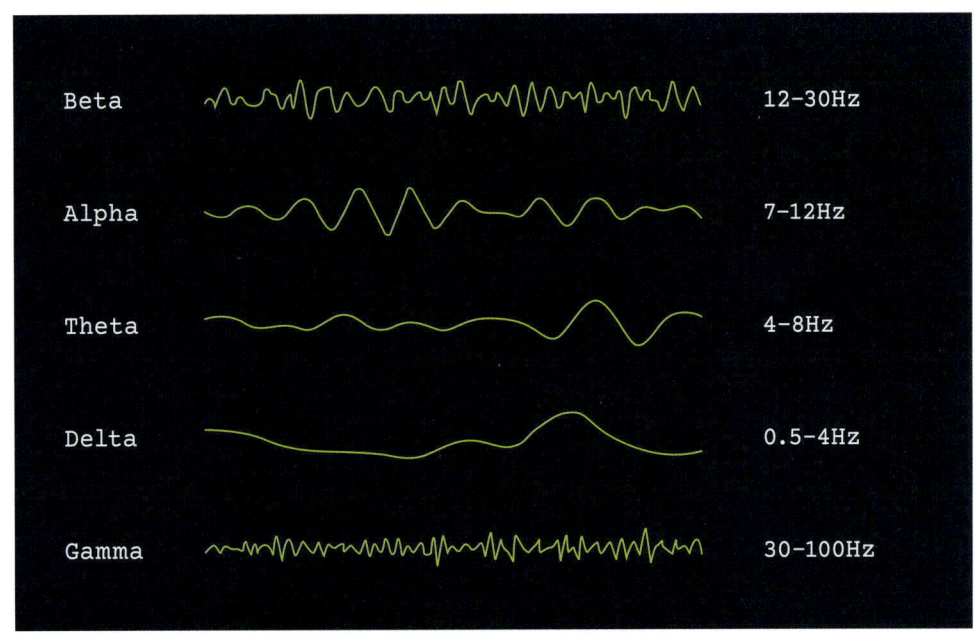

further, and 'eureka!' our right hemisphere makes connections hitherto hindered when taken by surprise. We craft insights. We tune in to other people's emotions. We're more empathetic and open to stimulus – we have ideas.

Another creative brain state is a 'theta state' – a realm between sleep and being awake; a junction, if you like, between dream and reality. The doorway between conscious, rational and linear thought is wide open and we have full access to our subconscious. Brahms, Klee, Dali, Tolstoy, Twain, Puccini and Wagner are all said to have used hypnotic routines to help them drift into a theta state for creative inspiration. We all have creative idols from the modern era, too, and you may know of some people who are disciplined in crafting time to expand their minds. But, while a theta state is brilliant for personal creativity, it's tough to facilitate.

Inviting the board to indulge in floatation tank hypnotherapy isn't likely to win you any innovation favours.

And from personal experience, I found bobbing around in salty water a bit irritating at first and just as I drifted off to sleep the buzzer sounded and the tank drained – along with the beginnings of my creative epiphanies.

ABOVE:
'Sleep on it' is good advice; our minds still make connections long after we've drifted off.

Interview

Nina Riecks

IDEAS COACH, FMCG

Nina Riecks is Russian-born. She now lives and works in Salzburg, Austria. She's been facilitating creative sessions as part of annual business planning across Europe for over ten years. As part of her training and development, Nina has coached hundreds of FMCG marketers across the Middle East and Asia, and buddied up on the design and delivery of sessions that led to many brand build events and experiences.

You work in an organisation famous for its big ideas. When facilitating a session what's that pressure like?

It's not a pressure I feel. Instead, I feel a sense of expectation from myself. It is not in our nature to give people pressure as that's not what this business is about. It never happens that someone steps into a meeting room and says, 'We need a business idea and you've only got 3 hours.' We have plans and a process that help to grow our ideas over time. No one is scared to share ideas around here, we all know how to deal with them. I've realised that I live in a culture where we say 'why not share the idea' and that's what is very liberating.

You see ideas that are both fully formed and also in their infancy. What have you noticed about the advice you give to people when you coach them in both instances?

You can't just leave things as they are. You need to do something in both instances and with each type of idea. My approach is to check people's passion behind an idea. I have far more understanding about an idea when people tell me a story about what it is and how they see it happening. I can feel their passion. It's often the case that they don't really capture the idea, but instead describe the benefits of the idea. And, of course, we can't 'do' the benefits. I've learned that I know an idea is ready when I get a sense that people want to start working on it immediately.

What do you do to personally manage your energy and keep yourself inspired about creativity?

Whether to keep me going when things are good or if I feel stuck and need a boost, I use my personal philosophy: 'Tomorrow will always be better than today'. It's a growth mindset. I see two ways of thinking and living. You can be fixed and accept that there are things that are just too hard and too difficult. Or you can adopt a growth mindset where everything is up for being explored and learnt from. I choose the growth mindset. I understand from my strengths profile that I am 'a learner'. My curiosity will naturally bring me joy. When I take on new skills and choose to learn new things I get joy from doing so. And creative thinking always forces me to seek out new experiences and learn new things. So, the joy from learning is what keeps me going.

Are there any transferable techniques you've used across different projects?

Aha! Of course! In any project you will always find me and my project team on 'alpha walks'. They don't know it's an alpha walk – I don't need to share with them any science. I just do it. We can spend 20 minutes around the campus discussing an aspect of a project, or the start of a new idea. Sometimes, I think it is just enough to listen to someone talk something through out loud. I've realised a walk helps me connect to that person on a different level and we both end up with a new perspective on the topic we've discussed. We're lucky here in that our office is in such a wonderful setting – but anywhere will deliver the same feeling.

If you could give advice to anyone beginning their facilitation career in a big organisation, what would it be?
I've two parts to my answer. The first is 'you are what you believe'. You've got to keep trying new things out, experimenting and giving things a go. It is simply not good to say 'this is the one way to do things'. All business is different and so all the projects you run will be, too. Be confident, even when you feel things aren't going well. 'Fake it until you make it' is a saying that captures that philosophy. And the second part of my answer is 'find a buddy'. You create a two-way support unit that has no fear, no judgement and a shared passion to do the right thing. It is hard to facilitate. It's really hard, scary and exposing to do so on your own. It's far easier when you have a buddy, as you can tackle what you perceive to be impossible together.

What is a final nugget of genius you'd like to share?
There's a great quotation that I love: 'If you have an apple and I have an apple and we exchange these apples, then you and I will still each have one apple. But if you have an idea and I have an idea and we exchange these ideas, then each of us will have two ideas.' That's such brilliant way of looking at the power of sharing ideas with people, spending time with people when being creative and doing good – that keeps me going.

> *"You can tackle what you perceive to be impossible together."*
> – NINA RIECKS

Upside-down pyramids

Q: What word links these three: AGE, MILE and SAND ?

Now you have the answer, did you feel *where* that happened in your brain? Unlikely, but you recognised the moment happen. A sense of energy, perhaps, flooding around your head and heart. A satisfactory 'got it' glow.

I think it's worth recognising what's going on during those breakthrough moments as you think problems through. If I hooked you up to an MRI machine, we'd see your right hemisphere hugely active when you make connections. Those aha! moments are happening in and around your anterior superior temporal gyrus (or anterior STG) to be exact. When you made the connection between those three words (the answer is STONE, by the way) in your head, your anterior STG fired off! And thirty milliseconds after that it fired off gamma waves, too. Literally, new connections being made. How healthy it is to wrestle with a problem (rather than type the question into Google)?!

Here's another experiment devised by those clever psychologist types:

Picture a giant, inverted steel pyramid. It's balanced perfectly on its point. Any movement of the pyramid will cause it to topple over. Underneath the pyramid is a $100 bill. How do you remove the bill without disturbing the pyramid?

Almost everyone begins by visualising the pyramid. System 1 thinking (Yoda) does his thing and the right hemisphere starts making pictures. Your next thought probably involves some sort of apparatus that would lift the pyramid (alas, such a device breaks the rules.) And next come other suggestions* involving troops of monkeys, giants, magicians and branches of the armed forces – all suggestions involve somehow lifting and suspending the pyramid off the ground long enough so someone (or perhaps a trained mouse on stilts) can reach in and grab the $100 bill.

For most people no workable answer comes to mind which is why suggestions dry up. You, too, might get stuck. And thinking harder won't help. In the experiment, the subjects (you've gotta

* Interestingly, as a teacher I set this sort of puzzle for my year 7 pupils (11 years of age) as an energiser to break up long lessons or pass time in tutor periods. There was no shortage of suggestions from the groups, and after a few moments more elaborate answers would come forth – all insanely impractical and farfetched, but joyous, playful and imaginative.

Unlike the experiment referenced here, I sought no 'correct' answer, but instead wanted my pupils to grow ideas with each other and without judgement. Being creative as an adult relies on our confidence to think imaginatively and free from self-doubt.

While the experiment is great for highlighting the (perhaps true) functioning of our brain, there is still an implied message of one 'right' answer against a high volume of 'wrong' answers. The popular debate that creativity is being knocked out of our children by our education system, is certainly something worth pondering.

love how scientists call people 'subjects') were then given hints. Cards with the word 'fire' in a sentence were flashed subliminally before them or subjects were told to think about the meaning of the word 'remove'. Interestingly, such nudges of stimuli worked far more effectively when presented to the left eye – connected to the right hemisphere of the brain.

If you're still wondering, the solution is to set the $100 bill on fire – the puzzle states 'remove', remember. The chances are your heuristics kicked in and made the assumption that 'remove' meant 'to pull away and keep', because in language that's often what we mean and want by such an instruction. While your left hemisphere was trying to lift the pyramid into the air (the 'obvious' way to 'remove' the money), your right hemisphere thought about alternative approaches to the problem. This is a fascinating experiment and carries strong messages:

1. Creativity can be driven by **deliberation** (the conscious 'thinking hard' bit) and **intuition** (the subconscious system). They both need to be present so new connections can happen.

2. The subconscious system, when stimulated by flash cards and hints, made connections that weren't possible before. We need to make a conscious effort when we're stuck in order to stimulate the brain and mind. Therefore, deliberate and apparently random sources of new information are an absolute must when running projects or creative sessions as part of a creative process. In short, 'new stuff' = 'new' connections = 'new' ideas.

3. Creative genius is driven by novelty and insightfulness, but also by purposefulness. The novelty/insightfulness tends to be driven by intuitive/subconscious processes that allow our attention and focus to spread, but the purposefulness is driven by realistic/conscious thinking. Solving pyramid problems, word games and tricks with matches, tacks and candles are great for studying 'the brain' and how we think – but ideas in laboratories are different than those needed in the working business world.

For any innovation training to be effective it has to be connected to reality and the needs of the adult learner. This is why all our work at GENIUS BOX is linked to live challenges and immediate commercial needs. You'll see more of that in our model later in the book. Developing the creative capability of your project team will work best, therefore, when they are tasked to think differently whilst working on a live brief. Anything else risks simply becoming an isolated academic exercise and an expensive day out of the office.

SUMMARY

- Access to our subconscious is governed by the ARAS.

- Moments of clarity and insight are more likely to arise when the whole of the brain is engaged and both the left and right brain are working together. One half sees the information whilst the other makes connections.

- Specific parts of the brain (e.g. the anterior STG) will respond to stimuli.

- Stimuli (new things) interrupt the habitual patterns and heuristics familiar to System 1 and System 2 thinking.

- Deliberate framing of an issue, a slight focus on a simple task and a degree of idle mental wandering places us in an alpha state.

- When in alpha state, the above conditions are all the more likely to align. The door to our subconscious will open…

…and we will have creative ideas.

It starts with you…

As facilitators of the creative process, we need to become better at solving problems, and this starts by changing our personal behaviour. I believe working through a problem requires effort; it's no longer sound advice to tell you to run a hot bath, breathe deeply or go for a walk as a lone tactic to generate your creative epiphany. Instead, you need to accompany how you behave with some mental tools, to help you with what to think during the problem-solving process.

- Thinking about a work problem on the drive home.

- Needing to come up with a new brand name whilst making notes by the pool on holiday.

- Going to the gym shortly after taking that conference call.

- Walking on wet grass in the morning before switching on your iPhone.

These are all perfect examples of a well-trained mind. But this is only half of the magic.

The remaining half consists of the tools and techniques that keep your mind focused (in alpha state) and help to engineer positive creative outcomes.

The process and tools I describe in the rest of this book work, as they encourage practical and physical interaction with your innovation topic. As you journey through the pages, be aware how these tools maintain conscious purposefulness and serious playfulness – great behaviours for a facilitator of strategy, innovation and creativity to adopt.

Whilst you're running sessions for other people to solve the business problem, keep a note of any connections your own brain is making during discussions. I think great facilitators make conscious decisions to share (or not) the thinking they've been doing as additional stimulus for a project team.

All this advice might sound obvious but ask yourself: when have you genuinely stepped away from a business problem and given yourself the space to think? Sitting at our desks and 'thinking' is not the right way to solve a problem.

However, it's not enough to hope that switching off our phones and relaxing will garner results either. To be mentally fit and fertile we must work hard when we think. Making use of the simple, accessible and creative tools described in this book makes working hard feel less like hard work.

PART 1 — YOU

THIS IS NOT THE WAY

68

Connecting brain to process

Remember Jenny, the mid-level marketer, from our opening story?

Jenny is someone who, like you, having read about the brain, was aware of how she made creative connections. Before she planned the design and delivery of her project, Jenny took time out to connect to the brief and make note of her own thoughts, feelings and reactions.

Great facilitators – like you from now on – will do this.

Jenny knew that her own interpretation of the brief, along with her perceived insights and starter ideas were her brain's System 2 thinking kicking in and immediately flooding her conscious mind. While such thoughts are all potentially useful, they can also be distracting to the facilitator who has to manage (and brief in) the long sequence of events that everyone else will experience.

Be aware that you will naturally develop a point of view about whichever project you are helping to facilitate. And at each stage of the process you will be inspired by the activities and your own thinking. You'll develop your own insights and ideas, and your own strategy on how to deploy them in the business or for the client who commissions you. But this is not the way! You are meant to be *facilitating* the project, not *solving* the project. There's a difference.*

My tip regarding project facilitation is: do not fight your natural inclination to problem solve but keep notes of your own ideas in parallel to the inputs and outputs of the project 'proper' as you facilitate it. You can decide to what extent your own endeavours are embraced at each stage of the project process. And you can let go of any personal conflict you may feel in having insights and ideas along the way.

Let's look at two things Jenny took time over to secure her success. Firstly, she applied her knowledge of the brain to the design and delivery of her facilitated sessions. Immediately, they stood out from ordinary workflow, becoming something interesting for others to be involved with. Secondly, Jenny adopted the personal discipline of injecting tiny differences to her daily routine. This constantly topped up her mind with fresh experiences and stimulus, helping build more resources in the warehouse of her mind. As a result, Jenny could make more connections linking different topics together and build stories, insights and, importantly, ideas in response to the world around her. Jenny became a creative master. 👉

> *You can, of course, agree up front that your own perspectives can be offered into the project either as a stimulus for other people or as an actual contribution to the content – too much of the latter, however, can stifle everyone else's thinking.*

Applying knowledge of the brain to facilitation

Jenny's success also came from mastery of her own thinking due to new knowledge about the way her brain works. Revisiting her project design will reveal direct connections from this knowledge to the quality and nature of her instruction and facilitation.

Jenny took time to create environments for her team to think in alpha state. Specifically, instead of having people sitting at their desks thinking hard, she changed the physical environment at the office, creating an 'incident room' for insight discussions to take place. Her brain and her team's brains would have responded to this change in environment. She encouraged colleagues to work away from the office and to observe people in cafés, restaurants and shopping malls. Everyone's brains would have been all the more attuned to the context in which observations were made.

Next, Jenny instructed her team to capture information freehand and on coloured paper. Their brains would have responded very differently to information in this format than if facts and figures were neatly presented on white paper or in PowerPoint form.

Jenny started each insight session with light-hearted energizers and word games. Her brain and her team's brains would have made better connections between the data collected as a result. The games would have 'warmed up' their brains in the same way an athlete stretches before physical exercise. We'll explore more of these games in the Insight chapter of Part 3 (see p156).

She also stuck materials up on the wall – pictures, charts, photos, instructions and reminders of what the team had agreed in previous sessions. This information would have been absorbed into the collective unconscious of the project team. As a result, the faster and deeper processing power of everyone's thinking would have been aligning.

Jenny made personal invites to the creative sessions, played favourite music tracks on the team playlist and sent weekly reminders with short personalised stories mentioning everyone in the team by name for their positive contribution to the project. Her brain and her team's brains would have felt loved and this built a strong team culture of 'we're innovating around here'.

Knowledge and understanding of the brain allowed Jenny to consider not only the tasks needed at each stage of the process, but also the manner in which she briefed the team, the time taken to run activities and the method of capture and communication at each stage.

In short, she established an 'alpha environment' for her own brain and the brains of everyone in her team, and maximized the collective, creative, connection-making power of the group.

Good habits

Jenny also established the personal habit of deliberately and consistently exploring new challenges. As a result, she became a *creative* facilitator – someone who delivers far more impact than if they were simply issuing instructions. Creative facilitators will constantly discover and develop new tools to achieve the outcomes they want and find new methods for explaining the tools they use. Being a creative facilitator ensures that the innovation projects you facilitate yield creative output, novel ideas and answers that your business clients desire.

When I describe creativity in the context of business facilitation my definitions are:

Creative = new connections being made.

Creativity = the ongoing and deliberate injection of fresh experiences, which results in maximizing the potential power of System 1 (unconscious) and System 2 (conscious) thinking combined.

I've chosen these words carefully. Allow me to explain:

- **Ongoing:** not a 'one off' act. Timetabled, scheduled, routinely followed and structured.

- **Deliberate:** designed, engineered and considered. Not just 'lucky happenstance'.

- **Injection:** consciously seeking the value to you. Leaning into 'it'. Being active. Showing up. Not just being passive.

- **Fresh:** new, novel, different from the norm, perhaps occasionally uncomfortable.

- **Experiences:** things to see, hear, read, do. Visceral. Physical changes.

Being a creative value-adding facilitator means that you'll be one who does things differently, leading to positive change in your business. I believe you need to engineer the ongoing, deliberate injection of fresh experiences into your own life so that you get used to 'change' and don't see 'new' and 'different' as a difficulty.

Whilst people sign up to the idea of innovation and creativity, it ultimately means change, and no one actually likes being changed.

As mentioned earlier in Part One, we are creatures of habit. It's efficient for our brains to seek the same routines, both big and small, in our lives. This eases cognitive load and also maintains and reflects our personal narrative of who we are and what matters to us. The story of our lives is reflected in our behaviour. We are the product of our surroundings – the people we spend time with the most and the activities we always make time to do. We're social animals. Our sense of safety comes from our connection to the herd – and, of course, that herd is a sophisticated and highly developed social network of friends, family, colleagues, and a wider web of digital connections.

A consequence of having an ambition for a business to be innovative is more 'new' and more 'different'. And new and different, in the herd, creates uncertainty. We know from social science that in moments of uncertainty, we look to each other and to those with whom we identify for what behaviours to adopt. This inevitable and unavoidable phenomenon is known in psychology as 'Social Proof'. Misleadingly, the term has been used in business this way:

" ...and when a certain percentage of people in your organisation adopt 'the change' and behave differently, then everyone else will follow... "

No. They don't.

We change our behaviour based on our own self-interest.

We calibrate the change against the reactions and interactions of those around us. And we adjust our story of why we've changed so we appear to have acted favourably compared to those we follow and who we believe follow us. That's why in business, change, transformation, innovation and creativity are hard. Our ability to deal with 'new' and 'different' is stifled because we're all stuck in habits that ease personal cognitive load. And very quickly we can believe that any change, big or small, is 'unwelcome' and 'difficult'.

In order to lead other people in a creative process, we have to 'go there first'. We need to be comfortable experimenting with new tools and techniques and not be wedded to pre-conceived notions about what output looks like. Hence, change (new, different, innovative, creative) needs to be facilitated. That's what Jenny did. And that's what I believe you will need to do, too.

If you just pick up the manual and brief people in the tools without consciously changing your own personal relationship with creativity, then this process won't work. And like many attempts to embed and then scale innovation in a business, your approach won't work either.

Being innovative isn't like downloading a Microsoft update overnight and everything being all shiny, new and fault-free as a result. And it isn't just about following the steps perfectly in a linear and clinical fashion. Being innovative is about creating value though deploying 'the new', and that new comes from creative connections. **The keystone in creative facilitation is you.** You need to demonstrate how enriching, positive, and rewarding it is to make new and creative connections as part of the way you live your life.

LEFT:
Whilst we might intellectually understand and sign-up to the benefits of change, actually making changes to our routine is a challenge for many.

Topping up the warehouse for you and others

In order for you to be the best creative facilitator you can be, you'll need to work your brain as hard as your body. You need to be able to get into alpha state quickly and also inspire your project participants to do the same.

If the greatest source of information is the 'warehouse' of your mind, then it makes sense to constantly top it up with fresh experiences and new knowledge from which to draw (and that means more 'stuff' that could be used for making creative connections in the future). Constantly making fresh habits for yourself forces you to switch out of default behaviours, and makes it easier to step into alpha state. The patterns of System 1 and System 2 thinking are shaken up, energized and challenged. You become far more alert and sensitive to what's around you if the setting is unfamiliar.

In closing Part One of this book, I want to link this new knowledge about how the brain makes connections to the way a process, such as the one outlined in Part Three, will help forge new connections around a business project.

I see the process as an 'external mind', that mirrors the internal workings of your creative mind. The external process can be like scaffolding for the team, on which personal and individual experiences are hung.

If we stick predictable input into our process, and power that process by people who are stuck in routines, then we can only expect the same sort of predictable outcomes. If we change up our personal routines, we'll have fitter, better, more creative minds. And if we power a flexible process with those people, our innovation projects should be better for it.

There's a whole world of personal habit-breaking behaviour out there, and I invite you to explore it. Chris Baréz-Brown at *Upping Your Elvis* is my personal champion of experiments and hacks that get us out of routines, and also make us more impactful and fresh as creative people. I recommend following his advice if you want to stretch your personal creative self. Also, check out my interview with Chris on pages 76–77.

To start your habit-breaking journey, on the following pages I've included 20 challenges from a list that I created for a bank. As the bank began a cultural change of learning how to be more innovative and creative, we needed to start by addressing personal habits. Over time, stories emerged of how people had changed their routines and spotted things they hadn't seen before. It's this type of awareness that improves insight development and idea generation.

Interview
Chris Baréz-Brown
AUTHOR & ENTREPRENEUR

Chris Baréz-Brown is a British author and entrepreneur. He is the Founder of Upping Your Elvis, *a business on a mission to help people get their energy right so that work becomes easier, more fun and more meaningful. Chris is also the founder of* Talk It Out, *a wellbeing tech start-up with a mission to put a dent into global suffering by offering mental and emotional wellbeing support to anyone in the world, for free. When not helping people reset their energy he'll be singing about it with his guitar.*

You've a particularly deep knowledge and understanding about experimenting with energy – tell me more.
When speaking to hundreds of people across the world who I believe live and breathe high-performing project delivery in innovation and creativity, there's one palpable factor that dictated the success of those projects. It's the energy those people bring. In a tacit way, those people are experts at managing that energy. They bring the best version of themselves to the work they do. And yes, there's process to follow and there are tools that are needed, but after a while it's clear that creativity flows when you're relaxed, your behaviours are tuned in and you're open to possibility. Process falls away and you can be far more intuitive. Instead of leading a process, you're leading the energy.

That state can be fragile, though; we've worked together and leaders have had a huge impact on the energy in the room…
Yes. Many a time the leaders impact on the energy of a team negatively. I am often asked to help leaders learn how to inspire the conditions for their people to be brilliant rather than be a huge fun brake. It's all about getting them into the right energetic state. You can't learn this stuff intellectually – you have to feel it. But once they do, they are changed forever. Leaders tend to be deeply associated to their personal story. And they can be quite wedded to a picture of how they believe they need to be perceived. I've got better at creating meaningful experiences for them that shift their identity, so the behaviour change is sustained. That affects the hit rates substantially with leaders, but creating such a shift is an art more than a science.

What can we do to create new perspectives and behaviours to change our energy?
We've spent the last few years with the world's best energy experts. They have challenged us to try all sorts of wonderful things to see if they enhance our energy. The ones that work have now become baked into our lives. The discipline of finding new and different ways of living is key to staying fresh and creative.

Our findings are that most of the time we cement habits and routines into our lives. And that's good for efficiency and safety. But in reality, it means we spend huge chunks of life on autopilot. Life can become pretty rigid and grey. But thankfully, we have neuroplasticity. Our brains can constantly make new connections. We also have what I'll call life plasticity, too. We can make new connections in our lives that power new connections in our minds. We can energise our whole system by forcing ourselves to pay attention to what's happening around us and engaging with it far more consciously.

Is this why you advocate lots of little experiments?
We need to push ourselves. The more we stretch ourselves and step out of our comfort zones, the more energetic we'll become. And if the whole body is involved, then the ability for us to make new connections – that rewiring – will be embodied when we take a deep breath.

Think about what I'm asking you to do in an objective fashion. What really is the worst that can happen – nothing bad, right? We catastrophise life. We fill our minds with harrowing stories about how bad things can be. But those stories, by definition, can't be reality as it's our imagination – it's pure fantasy. We turn ourselves into people we're not by needlessly listening to negative stories and the mistakes we believe we might make. In the big bad world our actions are actually pretty insignificant. If we let go of the negative stories, we'll be far more open to a life worth living.

What is a final nugget of genius you'd like to share?
I've learnt that life has been far easier and more interesting when I'm not static and imagining the future or trying to rewrite the past. I am far more in the now. As a result, I'm better with my family, friends, clients and the work I do. In fact, when you wake up in the morning, you're *you* at your most natural state. The rest of the day there are few moments when you're not thinking about your to do list, you're not flooded with an imagined future or recalling a memory from the day before. You're just you. And that's enough. In fact, it's just perfect.

"...creativity flows when you're relaxed..."

– CHRIS BARÉZ-BROWN

20 lifestyle challenges

1. Wear your watch on the opposite wrist this week
For years you've looked down at your wrist several times a day – it's a subconscious and automatic action. By realising you've moved your watch to another wrist, you're training your brain to be more conscious and present.

2. Go 24 hours without a negative thought
Some of us are professional idea assassins – how often have you heard your inner voice say, 'that won't work, we tried it before'. Play this silent game, and every time you spot yourself saying 'no', reset the 24 hours. This teaches your brain to deal without absolutes and prepares it for the ambiguity of the creative process. You're not committing to anything – you're engineering the positive experience of letting go.

3. Get off the tube two stops early and walk the rest
Our commute is filled with habits: our favourite seat, the usual route, even the same spot in the car park... Get off, get out or park further away and walk the rest. Or walk a different route. Look up and around you and notice what catches your attention. It might just be your missing piece of stimulus.

4. Ditch 70% of the stuff on your desk
Have a clean. Go on. Touch everything in and around your desk area and ask honestly: 'what is this here for and do I need it?' It will get your mind consciously asking questions about the materials it needs to make creative connections. Time to make physical space to think.

5. Change the hours
The standard 9–5 is a working paradigm from the early industrial revolution. But our modern world just keeps going. Experiment with a different start and finish time over the next two weeks. Try 08:00–16:00, 10:00–18:00 and (controversially) 13:00–21:00! You'll discover how much time is productive and how much time you're physically present but mentally elsewhere.

6 No note-taking
In the next big meeting you attend, don't take any notes. Listen. There's a good deal of science that suggests if we're writing all the time we're not truly listening to what's being said or *how* it's being said. Tune in to the quality of the information. Use your intuition to choose the next question you ask. Wait in silence after each answer and allow the insight to emerge.

7 Ask for someone else's playlist
Having our 'go to' music works wonders, but it can also reinforce a false belief that you can 'only' get things 'just so' when certain songs do their thing. Tuning up (literally) to other people's playlists freshens the mind and stimulates the senses. And you'll be much more interesting at a dinner party too.

8 Begin with a story
Start your team meetings with a story from the business that celebrates success. It could be a learning, an insight, a change in thinking – anything promoting human endeavour and fresh thinking. Over time, the habit of storytelling becomes the norm and the spirit and values of what matter to your team emerge unconsciously.

9 Apply for another job and have the interview
When was the last time you objectively captured your strengths and talents, and communicated them to someone else in an organised forum solely about you? Exactly. Imagine the benefits of getting valuable feedback. It would be a fantastic way of calibrating how you perceive yourself and how you actually appear in the eyes of others.

10 Get up an hour early each day for a week
It's up to you how you use your hours, but the main reason is to change the assumption that 'there is never enough time'. Psychology shows us we find the time to do the things that are important to us. When we own how we use our time, rather than believe we're at the mercy of it, our lives take on more meaning and purpose.

11 Ask for feedback
The most often cited, high-performing teams in business are those built on feedback. Every team member takes personal ownership of their development and seeks out feedback daily. It gives you more information about you and gives you specific data. It's a simple question: 'how am I doing?'

12 Ask 'what's my big thing today'
This is more than, 'oh, I must process my expenses'. No, focus on the big-ticket item. The one chunky task you know a lot about, that needs to happen, and won't get done without you taking ownership for it. Take a moment at the start of the day to consider what you'll do to make progress in that 'big thing'. Do so consciously and calmly. Then set a reminder in your diary at the end of the day for a moment of reflection. Ask 'how well did I tackle my big thing?' Over time, your personal productivity will grow and you'll spend less time priding yourself on 'being busy'. 👉

13 Go email-free for an afternoon
This may take a bit of organising with your team. Unplug, turn off Wi-Fi, switch off the phones and drop out of range. You're then free to motor into a piece of work uninterrupted for a few hours. Notice how the quality of your work changes and how liberating it feels to be unplugged.

14 Be the Swiss railway
By having arrival and departure times such as 10:23 and 14:37, and frequently changing the timetables, the Swiss railway effectively got people taking more responsibility for their timekeeping. Set your meetings at different start and end times and keep to under an hour. This will get people watching the clock for the right reason.

15 Three is the magic number
Have three ideas, not one. You can do this by asking more questions, spending more time suspending judgement and experimenting with 'what if' scenarios and outside stimuli. Over time, you'll grow creative capability. You'll forge new connections, create more penetrating insights and the quality of your ideas will improve.

16 Ditch the coffee for a week
What! But I love coffee! But coffee is also a vehicle for stimulants (caffeine) and nasties (sugars) of which too much is bad for us. Have a mini detox and enjoy the moment of discovery when you say 'no thanks'. It's a moment of consciousness where ordinarily you'd habitually say 'yes' without thinking.

17 Pass the pen
Take it in turns to run the weekly meeting. Mix up the style, stories and delivery. Sharing the responsibility for meeting organisation sends the important signal that 'every member of this team is responsible for the way we work'. Over time, different approaches from each team will be shared and adopted.

18 Try a different desk every day for a week
Moving from one desk to another shifts your perspective. You'll sit with different colleagues who can stimulate your thinking in new ways and vice versa. Being portable also keeps you portable; you'll find it hard to carry around bags of material, and ditching the hard copies nudges your brain to be free from clutter.

19 When it's done. Go home!
Presentism creates presentism. When you've done what needs to be done, go.

20 Drink the champagne
Many people keep champagne on a shelf at home for 'the special occasion'. But what is special enough? Our brains process negativity more intensely than positivity; it's time, therefore, to celebrate the little things that all add up. And sharing fizz with someone means you have to tell them how wonderful you are. Go on, get popping!

It's all about the brain

Let's recap all we've learned in Part 1 about you and your fabulous and creative brain.

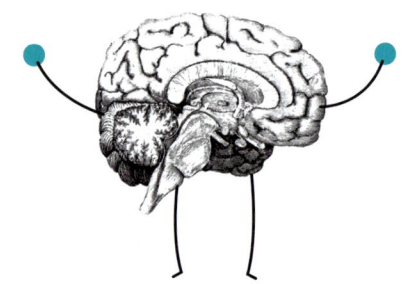

Our brain is brilliant at acquiring and storing information.

That takes energy. And to keep energy efficient, 'like' is stored with 'like'. But at the heart of any creative act is a new connection whereby 'like' is connected to something new: 'like goes with not-like'. It's as if our minds are actually hardwired to hinder creative thought!

Our minds keep efficient by defaulting to System 1 thinking; this is our 'Yoda' mind with its heuristics – fast pre-programmed assumptions based on previous experience. This is like connected with like, all happening at super-fast speeds deep within our unconscious mind. Super-efficient. However, creative thought requires greater effort – System 2 thinking: our 'Luke' mind with its conscious, hard-working awareness of thought.

Connecting new with old, and like with not-like, and making new connections across the warehouse of experiences and knowledge in our mind can be extremely energy draining.

We've also learnt that old methods of brainstorming don't work. Access to our unconscious mind is closed if the systems surrounding our consciousness aren't stimulated.

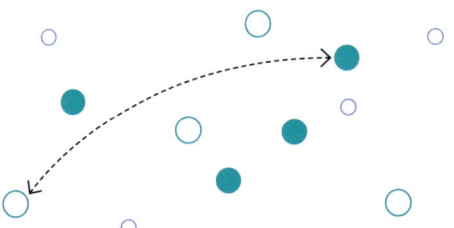

Sitting at our desk 'thinking hard' won't work.

Specifically, our Ascending Reticular Activating System (ARAS) is like a doorway 'closing off' the capacity to make new and interesting connections.

However, when we are in alpha state, we make those connections more easily – and it's energy efficient.

Individually, we're in default mode most of the time. We're unaware of these behaviours. Our routines keep us safe and efficient. Collectively, in business, routines and habits define culture; 'new' isn't necessarily welcome.

Breaking routines deliberately shakes up the way we process information. Both System 1 and 2 thinking are challenged. We're more alert, sensitive and attuned to what's happening around us and the thoughts we have. New routines are good for our warehouse mind – as it's more 'stuff' for the future.

For facilitators and project participants, it's necessary to get into new routines – and to make habits of breaking those routines time and again.

The creative process and the way it's facilitated needs to engineer deliberate rule-breaking and process-disrupting moments for 'new' to take hold in someone's mind. Brilliant facilitators, therefore, are interesting to work with because they are interested in topping up their mind warehouse as often as they can with new information, and in breaking the routines they know they have already established by default.

They are interested in the world and seek out new experiences all the time, to top up their personal storage kit of stimuli for the future – be that travel, food, music or sport. There is always something fresh and exciting to be distracted by.

Breaking routines is also important for creativity – it forces the mind to sort new information and create new categories of experiences and emotions. Remember, the more 'different' and 'new' things we can open ourselves up to, the greater the variety of answers and stimuli our neural pathways will connect to.

Breaking routines forces our minds to be more conscious and 'awake' than usual. As a result, you're more sensitive and alert to making use of stimuli. You're more likely to make fresh connections and find it easier to join up disparate topics to form novel insights and ideas.

So now we've discovered how your brain works, we're more aware of what's needed to secure more personal creative connections in your future. We also know to apply this knowledge to the design and delivery of your facilitated workshops so others can benefit from your creative magic. And you can re-enforce all of this by establishing the personal habit of deliberately doing (lots of little) things in new ways as often as you can.

Now, it's time to look at our GENIUS BOX model and how we use it to engineer an exploration of all the factors impacting successful creative facilitation. We need a model to help turn personal creativity into something that works for a project team. Without one, we're simply relying on good intention, chance and the hope that other people will understand what's going on. This is not the way. Let's look at what is.

Part 2

THE GENIUS WAY

Thinking out of the box requires that we have a box to start with. Let's look at what's in it, how it works and why.

"Alright stop, collaborate and listen."

— VANILLA ICE

The realm of personal creativity is very private, and the world of team creativity is very public. We need a model to help us navigate the difference between the two.

You now know a great deal more about the workings of your brain. You're aware of how you make connections more easily in one moment than in another, and how changing a few habits will create more chances for those creative sparks to fly. However, the workings of your mind are uniquely experienced by you and you alone. I have no concept of what it's like for you to think and feel your way to a new idea. Similarly, you've no idea (pardon the language) of what it's like for me to think and feel my way through a puzzle, solve a problem and arrive at an answer. As mentioned earlier, we're hopelessly poor assessors of other people's experiences. Whilst the chapter on the brain gives us knowledge on how to make more creative insights in the future, such knowledge isn't enough on its own to translate creativity into a team activity.

This book is all about facilitating other people so they have creative epiphanies, penetrating insights and new ideas for business. We, therefore, need something that can be used by you, the individual, as a facilitator of others. We need something that makes use of creative individual experiences and translates them into a collective, team experience. We need something that takes creative thinking from the private world of our own head to the public world of team thought.

In short, we need a model.

Our model was developed by working with some of the most creative minds in business. They all agreed that several factors need to be present for successful project facilitation. At GENIUS BOX, we've refined these down to six.

The GENIUS BOX model

Inspired by the idiom of 'thinking outside the box', our model consists of six interconnected factors that all need attention to secure facilitation success.

For project teams and project output to arrive at something new, fresh and different, a core set of principles and conditions all need to be met. This is where our GENIUS BOX model comes in.

This model translates the private world of personal creativity and connection making to the public realm of team creative discovery and idea generation.

Our model is a six-sided box. Each side is a key factor of successful facilitation design and delivery. Considering each side of the box in turn helps you, as a facilitator, guide your clients through the process of scoping briefs, gaining insights, developing ideas and selecting output to implement, whatever the project. Additionally, the model helps you consider other factors that influence the success of a project team as it operates within the inherited norms of an established business.

WHY WE NEED A MODEL

We need to get from this… to this!

Private	Public
Felt, thought and experienced personally	Seen, heard and experienced publicly
Individual	Team
Facilitator	Participants
'My brain' connections	'Our mind' connections
Few	Many

BOX OF GENIUS

Each of the sides of the box influences everything else and they all work together to inspire great facilitation.

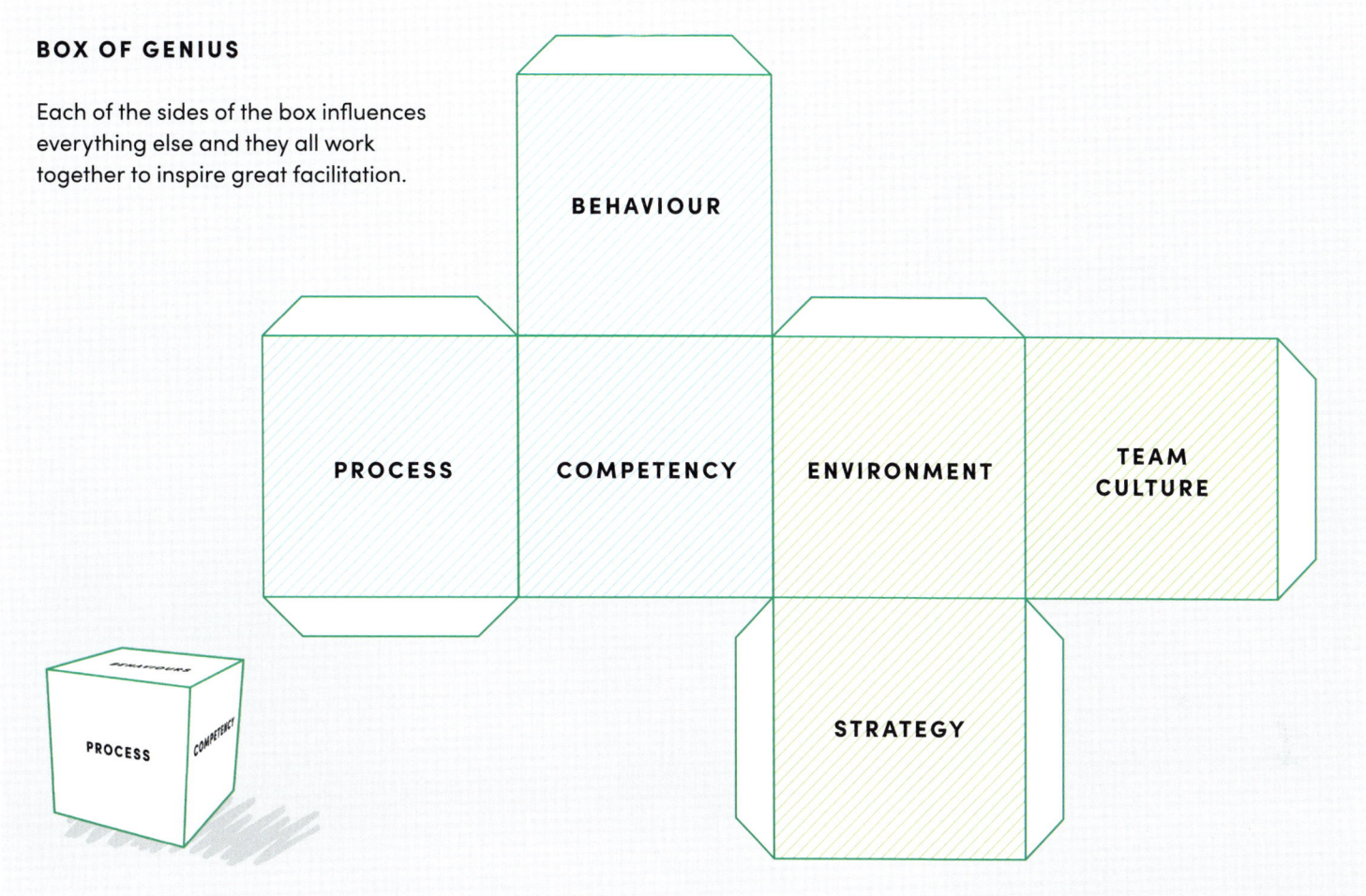

- Roughly speaking, half of the model is dedicated to aspects that are within our personal control – our own competency in being able to facilitate process and behaviour. I label these aspects loosely as individual inputs.

- The other half of the model concerns aspects of it that are impacted by our individual input, or influence the way we approach those individual inputs. They are our environment, the team culture and the strategy we adopt when we work.

Let's take a look at each aspect of the model in turn. 👉

1 Process

You are going to be facilitating groups of people through a process. Your style, charm, storytelling and behaviour will ensure you do so in a masterful fashion.

But good intention is not enough. You need a defined and designed process that contains a selection of carefully chosen tools to help you get the team you are faciliating to their destination. A badly designed process, filled with poorly executed tools, will stifle creativity and let you down. A well-designed process should give you the energy and stimuli to arrive at fresh perspectives and ideas. The four main stages of our GENIUS BOX process are Scoping, Insight, Ideas and Selection, which I explain further on pages 100–101 and in depth in Part Three, alongside the tools you'll need to put these stages into practice.

However, I also speak about the process as something of a 'misleading' sequence of events, as problem solving isn't something linear, but far more an ongoing behaviour. So, remember that not all puzzles are neatly presented with a brief at the start. I encourage you to think about how to cover all parts of the process, but (much like completing a puzzle or painting a picture by numbers) in an order that isn't necessarily fixed. There is no one 'right way' to do things, although there is certainly a wrong way to go about facilitating the tools and activities. When designing the sessions and interventions, good creative facilitators will combine their experience and skills to identify which parts of the process make sense to apply to different innovation challenges. Remember that one size fits no one.

2 Behaviour

If the process part of the model is 'doing', then behaviour is 'being'. Doing is what you instruct people to go and do. It is about task and action. Being, on the other hand, is the quality of your attitude (and everyone elses) when they perform those tasks you have given them as part of the process. A great process will only get you so far. We cannot keep thinking in the same fashion throughout the creative process and expect to arrive at new and different outcomes; we need, therefore, to change our behaviours at each stage of the process to reflect the unique situations we might find ourselves in at any given time.

For example, to **scope** a project statement well at the beginning of the process, we need to behave in a more considered fashion than we might if we were in an **ideas** session. To generate **insights**, we need to behave insightfully. And to move towards the **selection** of ideas and plan their successful implementation we need to be both playful and considered as we switch from idea-building mode to idea selection mode.

Behaviour is often spoken about in business – look no further than the documents in your own business that talk about corporate values. However, in the context of facilitating others through a creative process – and to be innovative yourself – you will need to change your behaviour from session to session, and from task to task, in order for the process to work. For each tool we suggest you use (see Part Three), I've mentioned the kinds of behaviours that ought to be present for the best results. I believe that you'll be able to infer which behaviour works best and adopt those behaviours as part of your briefing, your storytelling and in your delivery style each time you facilitate a session. 👉

OPPOSITE:
Using the model to map out thoughts regarding the design and facilitation of a future project.

③ Competency

The combination of process and behaviour is the input required for successful innovation – you need both to generate creative connections. But engineering positive creative connections needs facilitating. Knowing when to deploy these tools (the process) and how to deliver them (the behaviour) is what I call creative competency.

Brilliant facilitators are very good at managing their own energy and their impact on others, so they monitor what's going on for them and what's happening in the room around them. They'll have the awareness at any moment to ask and answer the question 'what's needed here?' They are sensitive to the immediate needs of the team, and to the impact the team has on both themselves and the quality of the task.

We all have our blind spots, however, and without being aware of our shortcomings we can sometimes plough on through a process, doing our best to add what we think is value, only to make it hard work for ourselves and the participants.

Similarly, we can overdo our behaviour, forget where we are in the process and find ourselves lost in an activity, and it then yields no useful output. That's why I advocate to always facilitate in a pair as

The Sweet Spot

YOU *(the facilitator)*

YOUR TEAM *(your creative participants)*

THE TASK *(what you're facilitating)*

Competency – you can manage your energy and getting the job done, but leave project participants confused if your instructions weren't clear. Keep the sweet spot in mind.

you're less likely to lose context and can support your facilitation buddy.

I believe that creative competency is a high-level professional capability. And people who find creativity and innovation motivating and rewarding should aspire to invest in their capability building. They'll run amazing projects and have rewarding careers as a result. Additionally, as I mentioned in the introduction, project facilitators all have a responsibility to raise their game and, as a result, the reputation of facilitation in general. This is why competency has a place on our model.

Those are the first three sides of the GENIUS BOX model. Process and Behaviour go hand in hand, and mastery of both is an aspect of Competency. Let's now look at the next three sides.

④ Environment

Now, let's take a look at the three key aspects that can have a profound effect on our process, behaviours and competency. First, the the physical environment in which creative work happens has an impact on our behaviour. Similarly, our behaviours will have an impact on the working environment in which processes are being followed – and therefore the quality of output. Change one, you end up changing the other.

If, at any time, you sense there is something 'up' with a session, most of the time it's because the behaviours aren't aligned with the task and tool in hand. And a contributing influence on our behaviour is the environment.

Environment and behaviour are the yin and yang of our model – inextricably linked. Together they combine to impact our psychological safety, energy and everyone's connection to the process and each other at any time.

The quality of this behavioural environment is something all of us can immediately pick up on when entering any room – our brains will very quickly assess the quality of the energy in seconds. So, active consideration needs to be taken concerning both the spaces we're working in and the behaviours we adopt to get the best out of the work we do. A grey room will lead to grey ideas. And (metaphorically) a grey personality will suck any colour from a conversation!

⑤ Team culture

Learnings from the world of psychology have helped us at GENIUS BOX to consider what it takes to build strong project team culture. Culture is an idea that rests on the assumption that we all have a joint and uniform experience of what it's like to be in a particular place – in business that's an experience of what it's like to work for a particular company. But findings reveal that employees' experiences will actually vary more *within* a particular company than between different companies.

A great team culture will lead to more ideas and, over time, that team will develop their own approaches to problem-solving and innovation. This is the ultimate goal of creative facilitation – to teach the teams you work with what good strategy and innovation looks like, and for them to have confidence they can replicate that approach in the future.

When we focus in on critical aspects of our experience at work, it's easier to see how cultural experiences vary more from team to team than company to company. Therefore, the idea of a 'company-wide culture' being something that's unique, unchanging and, importantly, a common experience for everyone is wrong.

What really matters is the culture in your project team.

Put simply, culture is literally how people think, feel and behave with each other when they're working together. And an obvious test of your project culture is how your participants are behaving when you're not in the room with them. There ought to be a tangible vibe in your project that's significant enough to be felt by everyone on your team.

A great project culture amplifies a 'can do' spirit; it's something binding and enduring. Importantly, I believe your project culture is portable. Everyone still ought to be feeling that 'can do' spirit not only when they're in the same room together, but also on the offsite or on a Zoom call. A strong culture will embrace and overcome the challenges a poor environment sometimes presents. And a strong culture will also maintain the behaviours and high standards necessary for everyone to say 'we're innovating around here'.

6 Strategy

Finally, innovation and creativity need to be planned. You cannot just turn up to your sessions time and again, sipping coffee and hoping that the answer appears by itself. Every project will be different – a point so obvious it's a cliché, but often one that's overlooked.

For many years, I worked with the same client as they headed into their business-planning season. Over time, this client reported back that the creative sessions had lost their spark, the tools failed to deliver new insights and the whole period felt tiresome as it dragged out over spring into summer. What had transpired was that exactly the same templates had been adopted year after year. The design and delivery of their planning was very much a cut-and-paste approach that had erased all the flexibility and freedoms people in the business needed to create new ideas. The team were missing time at the start of their planning season to review the learnings from the previous projects and work out how that feedback could help shape the design and delivery of the forthcoming planning season.

The etymology of 'strategy' is Greek, from a word loosely meaning 'the art of the general'. This 'generalship' is essential at the start of a project. When we're commissioned to facilitate any project, the team and I stick the GENIUS BOX model on the wall and use it as a prompt to help our high-level thinking, design and approach with the client. We use the model as a canvas to collect initial thoughts, questions, starter ideas and points of view about the project and the context in which it's presented. Sticking the model on the wall and using it as a canvas is good to do.

Creative problem solving and project planning can easily remain in the realms of people's heads, and being able to 'see' thinking makes it far easier to spot where connections are being made and where details are being missed. The 'business challenge' when written up and stuck next to the model acts as a reminder to you and the team about what you're working on. Having everyone's thinking physically in front of you, preferably at eye level, allows everyone to step back and 'see' the conversation emerging. It's far easier than trying to plan an answer inside your head whilst working out what's going on in other team members' heads too. When we're aligned that we've discussed all parts of the model, our project teams are good to go.

ABOVE:
As the facilitator, you're responsible for unpacking the model during the project design and delivery.

G — strategy
E — competency
N — environment
I — behaviours
U — culture
S — process

↑ This is our model in word form. Use it as a stimulus for the design of your own. You may take some or none of our elements; but you need *something*.

Facilitators who don't have a model, are just warming a seat.

THIS IS <u>NOT</u> THE WAY.

Interview

Dave Lewis

CREATIVE FACILITATOR AND CO-CREATION PIONEER

Dave Lewis has led start-ups and Global 500 corporations in developing new ideas and bringing exciting new propositions to market. He has over 20 years experience in facilitating creative processes across marketing, branding, NPD (new product development) and venture building. Dave is based in NYC.

You've experienced facilitating in many different contexts – what makes for successful creative facilitation?
For me, there are three key ingredients. Firstly, alignment. When I'm speaking to a client, I want to have this discussion: 'What outputs are you expecting and are we aligned around our shared vision of success?' I'm then able to know where we need to get to. The second element is the mixture of environment and behaviour that guides how we're going to act and interact on the journey – which has a huge impact on the quality of everyone's experience. And finally, all creative facilitation needs planning. To paraphrase Leonard Snart (DC Legends) 'Make the plan, execute the plan, expect the plan to go off the rails, create a new plan.' To those who say 'why have a plan anyway if you're going to change it?' It is because people are watching you and you respond to content arising in the moment. A new piece of information – an insight, an idea or just a simple comment – can be a build to your plan. That's different and new, and has more energy.

You've seen many processes, approaches, tools to deliver project success – is it all the same with different language or do differences genuinely exist?
At the core, the foundations and principles of collaboration, behaviour, psychological safety, positive mindsets and being open to improvisation are consistent in the best projects. There's no one, correct, 'just so' way of doing things. In honesty, all my sessions involve a new process, the invention of a new tool or a different approach to briefing something in. I'm always tweaking, but you'd recognise the foundations.

What do you do at the very first few sessions with a new team to get them engaged in a new project?
I want everyone to be clear on why we are there, what we're going to do and how we'll achieve it together. This can be an open discussion or homework I ask people to complete ahead of time. Either way, it's vital we cover that context up front. Too often, I see others rush into the content and asking people to get into 'go solve' mode without setting up the context.

On delivering the project vs skilling people up as you go – how do you navigate the two worlds?
I'm always carrying my personal compass, signposting where, why and how. And I use that as a reference from time to time so when we stop a project and have a conversation with people about activity, I can be clear on what we're doing right now and on what's next. If we're building output then I use *where* and *how* as a way to help make decisions on the path we'll take next. If there's a need for the group to grow its capability, I step away from the content and delivery a little and consider *why* we're doing what we're doing and how we might change activity in that moment to embed a new skill. Some projects are solely about delivery, but a degree of learning is inevitable in all we do.

You facilitate a very wide range of projects – from developing a new yogurt to an incubator project for a new digital platform – what are the main similarities and differences?
I still follow the same foundations – those behavioural principles that secure collaboration, psychological safety, a positive mindset and being open to improvisation. So, there's no compromise there at all. What's obviously different is the time I have to do that. Some projects could be days and in other instances projects last only a few hours. I therefore have to be incredibly forward and be almost 'telling' people what we'll do and how we'll do it. And then of course, if I've a six-month incubator, our core team has far more time to identify the behaviours it wants to emulate and I've time to stop the team and discuss how well we're living by those behaviours and principles. Activity neatly fills the time we allow for it though, so I've got to wrap my arms around time and take responsibility for it.

What is a final nugget of genius you'd like to share?
There's two things. Firstly, we all know the Gandhi quote about being the change you want to see. Great facilitators model the behaviour they want to see each day on a project. Everyone is watching you. If you fiddle with your phone, so will they. Be fully in the room, turning yourself towards people to fully engage in their conversations. Be present. You're the standard. Show up. And, secondly, I love creative facilitation as it's positive and puts me in a great place. Creative facilitation is not beanbags and sticky notes. It's delivering on purpose and is the result of working hard against clear foundations. But that ought to be a positive and enjoyable experience. If I'm going to put my name on a project, I'm doing that with a smile on my face.

"I've got to wrap my arms around time and take responsibility for it."

– DAVE LEWIS

Using the model

Now we've got a model, we're in a great place.

Our GENIUS BOX model enables us to organise our thinking about the design of a creative project we are going to facilitate, and to share that thinking if we're one of a pair of facilitators. The six aspects of the 'box' are a mixture of elements that influence the successful delivery of that project. And by looking at each element in turn, we can arrive at a great place; having explored a breadth of considerations about the project and its background. Importantly, using the model, we'll be excited as we've aligned behind a design and delivery plan we've created.

1 We can use the model to help land our own personal reactions to a business challenge, as it's inevitable and unavoidable that we'll have a point of view and our own ideas. However, as facilitators, we're not there to solve the business challenge, but to design the process for others to do just that. The model provides us with an opportunity to note and keep safe our own creative thoughts as stimulus for others to use should we need it.

2 The model also helps us, as facilitators, to consider the needs of project participants before, during and after creative sessions. As a (gentle) rule of thumb, I encourage my team to use the model at the end of each day during projects as a focus for our downloads, observations and changes to design. We work through the six elements in sequence asking ourselves what's going on for our project team participants; a simple discipline to keep us on plan, but flexible where needed.

3 Finally, the model helps us to design and deliver our projects. Specifically, it will prompt us to think about the series of interventions that, over time, will shepherd a group of participants (our project team) from A to B and arrive at an answer. We use the model to help choose which of all the tools, activities and exercises we have at our disposal. This keeps us from simply repeating and reapplying the same approach time and again to project delivery.

However, we still need to power this model with magic or it's just a collection of concepts and there's no unifying 'whole' that's greater than the sum of those parts. GENIUS is my one-word stamp of approval when I know that a project has that unifying whole. I will use 'where's the GENIUS?' as a quality assurance question when reviewing the design and delivery of a project with the team. And I can re-express that question as 'what's needed here?' in the moment when running a session.

***Process** is the doing (the what), **behaviour** is the being (the how), and masterfully managing the two is a core part of your facilitation **competency**.*

At the same time, remember all this will be influenced by the **environment**, your project team **culture** and the overall **strategy** you decide to adopt. The model is our way of taking our learnings from the brain (where so much is happening at a subconscious level) and lifting our attention to what's going on for you and others in a room to a more conscious state; making things far easier to manage, lead and facilitate.

A great deal of this book is given over to the process in our model. Understandably, a great facilitator will have many tools, activities and exercises all designed to help people make new and creative connections. And a successful project output is when all those connections have led to insights or ideas being created, and the business is happy with the decisions on what to do next.

Therefore, I want to share further insight on the link between process and behaviour. I'm going to offer an analogy to help you develop your competency. When you're facilitating creativity and innovation, you need to be operating at a GENIUS standard. You need to have a solid understanding of the creative process (in the context of business) and further awareness of how you're making a journey through that process ahead of the participants in your project team.

First let's look at the process. 👉

ABOVE:
Yours truly at the start of a project explaining who we are and what we do.

The Process – a story in four parts

Most, if not all, big consulting firms, agencies, co-creation partners, innovation teams and design studios, have a process they follow.

Similarly, the big idea accelerators and incubators who develop new products and services over time, have a process. Boutique consulting firms that take many short-term commissions a year have a process. I work in partnership with both internal and external creative propositions, and we all use a process.

A process, in the context of facilitating an innovation project, is something on which we can stick tools and language to help people navigate. We can shepherd a project team through a process. We can signal progress to sponsors by pointing to 'where the project is in the process'. Processes help us 'see thinking'. We can visually signpost the steps through which an idea will be born. We work a process from left to right, the mind makes sense of it and we can agonise over what colour the process boxes should look like when we type them up on a PowerPoint.

As an example, for a recent project my co-facilitator (Simon) and I discussed the 'process' we'd use to get our client from A to B (and then to C and to D) on a few scamps of paper. We then took a creative walk (to the local bakery) to talk things through further. We agreed where stages of the process should begin and end, and how they should be titled. And then, over an hour, we wrote it all up, stuck it on the wall and took the client through it – the process, not the wall!

Our model uses the environment, remember, so we didn't spend time typing up content, and instead more freely invited builds and amends by writing up our process on our pads. Our client, like your clients, sees the journey of a new project take shape through the context of a process. We associate process with predictability and safety; if there's a process the subconscious subtext is: 'it's

been done before, come with us on this creative adventure, here are the steps' – all this is very inviting and reassuring. So process is a good thing.

I believe there are four discrete parts to the creative process, and I see the same four phases in the process whether it's used to craft a new business strategy or a proposition for a new fizzy pop…

1. The scoping stage: some call it 'discovery' or 'define' or 'explore' (the list goes on). This stage is about finding the ambition of the brief, the scope of the problem, the boundaries and perceptions of what's known and unknown. In short, we're 'finding out what problem needs to be solved and why'. Additionally, a good process will also scope out the ability of your client's business to support the project, and how well any project output will be implemented. There is no sense investing in a project unless it can be realised by the client. Scoping is key. And when you don't scope – you get surprises.

2. The insight stage: where we explore all the topics and opportunities associated with the problem, so we're inspired to have new and refreshing ideas on how to solve the issue. There are many ways to arrive at an 'insight' and lots of ways to get you and your team acting more 'insightfully'. Facilitating this stage requires a particular set of skills. There are, in fact, many agencies out there who specialise (so they tell us) in insight alone. But in truth, we're all capable of arriving at new insights when properly facilitated.

3. Ideas: traditionally, this is where most pioneers cut their teeth in creativity. We've all been invited to 'innovation brainstorms' and been asked to come up with 'the brand-new idea' for the business. Sadly, brainstorms squeezed into the normal working day rarely yield brilliant output. Yet thousands such sessions happen globally every day. Output is often a mixture of thoughts and half-baked ideas captured in an unforgiving and inconsistent fashion. There's an art to the ebb and flow of an ideas session, and the energy needed to facilitate and manage participants in this part of the process is different than the scoping or insight phase.

4. The selection phase: ensuring the results of all the creative investment are secured. You need to *do* something with your ideas; choose them and structure them into the business, or you've arrived at the end of the process with little outcome. Embedding learnings and structuring for success is an important and creative part of the process. Being innovative here is just as key as it is at the insight and ideas stage.

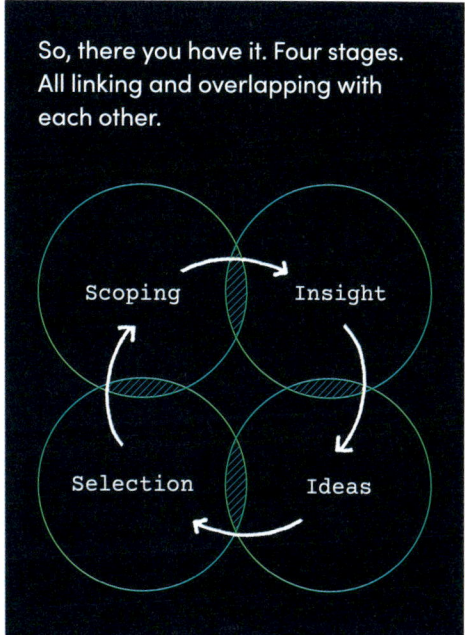

I call the process a misleading sequence of events, because in reality a project won't always visit each stage in turn, in sequence or with equal time spent at one stage before the other. The problem with writing out a process and projecting it onto a wall is that we give the subliminal message that the project team, over time, will start 'here on the left' and arrive 'there on the right'. Neatly titled boxes imply a steady rhythm to the work as if working through innovation is like ascending a staircase. The message is often 'follow this creative process and at the end we'll arrive at the answer.'

THIS IS NOT THE WAY.

As you now know from the model, **behaviours** are key to making that process work. For creative magic to happen we need an overall behavioural attitude to the way we facilitate that process. We need a quality of thinking that powers the process and its tools in different ways for each project, because each one is different and much overlapping of the stages will occur.

We need a quality of behaviour that forces 'new' each time. We need a quality of attitude and thinking that's present at the strategy meetings when you're planning the project and is equally present in the creative sessions and whilst briefing in any of the activities several weeks into a project.

We don't just need a process – we need a pilot!

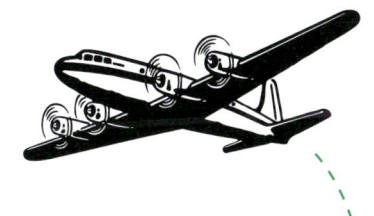

Mavericks make the method

"Don't think, just do."

— MAVERICK, TOP GUN

There's a great story from the pioneering days of the Apollo missions in the 1960s. Vast resources at the time were dedicated to solving a litany of frustrating scientific challenges in getting man to the moon. At the same time, the most rigorous of processes were employed to find the perfect people to pilot those trips. In addition to all the physical tests that the would-be astronauts undertook, they also endured tough psychological profiling and assessment.

Most Apollo astronauts were fighter pilots, had seen action in combat and had become test pilots for many of the US Navy's experimental aircraft. They really were the best of the best... of the best! But scientific testing wasn't helping the space programme differentiate one pilot from another.

After a while, it became clear that men made of the 'right stuff' saw the world differently and that the scientific methods alone weren't enough to identify them. On one occasion, a researcher passed a blank sheet of paper to John Glenn (who became the first American to orbit the Earth) and asked him to describe what he saw – Glenn sighed recalcitrantly, spun the paper around 180 degrees and slowly pushed it back across the desk to the researcher stating, 'You've shown it to me upside down.'

The very best didn't become the best by blindly following process. In fact, many of them didn't follow process at all and actively pushed against discipline, rules and procedures. It wasn't uncommon to find most test pilots driving too fast, drinking too much after hours or enjoying beers and BBQs long into the wee small hours before test flights.

Perhaps it was this maverick attitude that inspired Tom Cruise's character (Maverick) in the *Top Gun* films, who keeps buzzing the control tower and upstaging the other pilots. Maverick's skills and talents are legendary, whilst at the same time they upset the status quo. The Navy cannot 'train' pilots to fly like Maverick – least of all scale his credo of 'Don't think, just do.'

It's good to have a process and a method to organise work, but following processes in an exacting fashion when it comes to problem solving is a limiting strategy:

> *The definition of insanity is doing the same thing over and over again and expecting a different result.*

Attributed to Einstein (among others), this sentiment is almost cliché, but at the heart of it is something we intuitively know to be true. Some processes and methods within business are incredibly fixed (and rightly so) – a bit like the firing sequence of an engine, those pistons follow the same order as they rotate. But following the same order time and again won't yield 'new'. An engine needs lubricating oil to prevent it from overheating and seizing up. Without oil things don't move.

Maverick behaviours* are your method's lubricating oil.

Similarly, Will Smith's Agent J in *Men in Black* screeches a table across a polished floor in the recruiting phase of his enrolment into the undercover world of alien hosting. The scene neatly points out that the written test for all candidates was a nonsense distraction and the actual test was seeing how he and the other candidates dealt with the uncomfortable testing space and having the ability to think differently.

Simply having a process and following it won't get you to genius. Following the same process time after time will secure results and perhaps a modicum of predictability, but it can't deliver creative output; you won't arrive at new and fresh ideas because process alone won't allow for that. And if you think about it, if all organisations had the same process and followed it exactly, then the world would all look pretty much the same, and there'd be very little to get excited by.

To complement process, you need inputs and stimuli that aren't of the process. You

By 'maverick' we mean quirky, alternative, lateral, provocative and inspirational, not rebellious, disrespectful or negligent. Whilst powerful, those behaviours aren't necessarily that welcome in a business context!

need an injection of maverick thinking. You need to engineer deliberate breaks in the process to go 'off piste' and think (wait for it) 'out of the box'. But during the facilitation of a creative session, you can't afford the luxury of taking breaks all the time. To help, it's worth keeping in your head (like there isn't enough up there already!) a useful concept that will help you manage your facilitation competency. Let's take a look at the monorail and the radar.

The four parts of the process, I believe, are best facilitated in a parallel fashion, not a linear one. To show the importance of the facilitator in a project and how that differs to individuals personally generating ideas, a useful analogy is that of the **monorail** and the **radar**.

A monorail has a fixed track. People can see it stretching above them, carrying cars filled with passengers. The monorail track stretches out from one horizon to the other; looking up, people intuitively understand how it works. They get that jumping on at one stop will take them to the next. It's predictable; linear. Everyone knows what's happening, and when.

It's the same when it comes to the creative process. Regardless of the innovation methodology you're following – whether that be a week-long sprint or a capability programme lasting many months – just like a monorail, it's linear. You can liken the stages to stations and stops on the monorail. People will get to each stage over a period of time. Some stops are larger and more important than others. There may be several stops and stages that make up a process. You get the idea; a project team moves as one from one stage to the next, sequentially, on the project journey.

But it's different for the project facilitator. They have a creative radar. They sit at the helm with full line of sight of the whole process; the radar is spinning, constantly picking up all sorts of signals, not only from the process but also from the project team members.

Everyone on a project team, like you, has the capacity to make new and fresh connections. They can happen at any time.

A good project will be designed to stimulate people deliberately in different ways, and at different times, too. So, a project team of 12 people, for example, could at any moment on the monorail journey all be thinking about different parts of the process. They're either incubating some deeper thinking or spontaneously reacting to something in the project right there and then. It's the same for the facilitator; they too are a creative person and will also be making creative connections.

The radar (a metaphor, not literally) is a great friend to the facilitator as it allows them to calibrate where the project team is in the process (on track

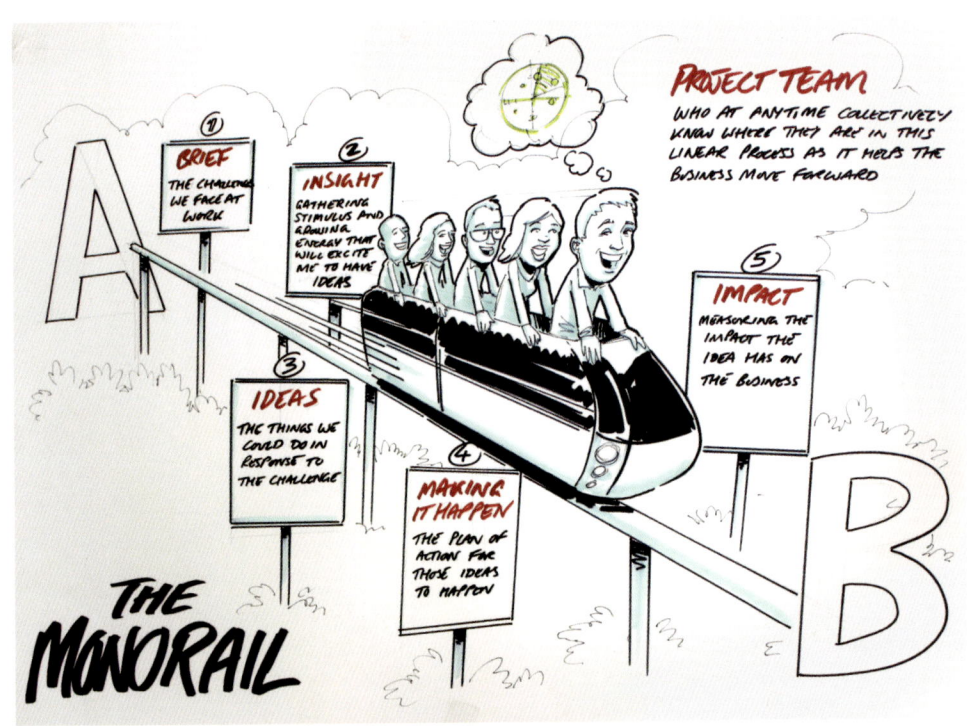

or behind schedule) compared to what everyone is thinking, saying and doing. Having a 360-degree view of the project process and being able to tune in to project team members allows the facilitator, at any given point, to work out the design and delivery of the next stage of the process and who to buddy up with whom. For example, we cannot help having ideas as soon as the project brief is presented. We've all been in briefing meetings or conference calls where a problem is being discussed and someone makes an immediate suggestion of 'let's do this!' It's energising and rewarding to have fast-brained people, but intuitively you and the team know more is needed than to implement the first suggestion.

The radar and monorail work hand in hand. To keep both front of mind when designing your facilitation next step, look at your hands and clasp them together. Your left hand is the monorail and the needs of the project team, what they expect, what you'll deliver for them. Your right hand is your radar and conscious awareness of your creative thoughts and reactions. Take a moment to consider both before making your next move.

SUMMARY

By connecting the magic of your creative brain to our GENIUS BOX model, you'll be able to design and deliver excellent creative projects.

The model's six sides are Process, Behaviour and Competency (our individual inputs) and Environment, Culture and Strategy (the aspects of facilitation impacted by our inputs).

But the model alone isn't enough – the 'genius' is the quality of competency that runs throughout the project design and delivery. Following the process in a linear fashion can be misleading – it's important to mix things up. Injecting maverick behaviours will help you make those planned and 'in the moment' changes when necessary.

The concept of the monorail (for the project team) and the radar (for you, the facilitator) is useful as it will help you ask and answer, 'what's needed here?' at any moment – when you confidently act on that, you're a GENIUS facilitator.

In Part Three, we'll break down our Process into its four constituent parts, and give you the practical tools and activities to help you get the best out of each one.

Client, sponsor, problem owner – who's who?

A golden rule (one that we've broken in the past and then remembered why the rule exists) is never to facilitate your own project.

As facilitators it's our job to manage our own energy and the energy of the team, and to manage the creative process. When we do that well, we'll arrive at an answer we can all be pleased with. Our role is to look after the context.

It's not for us to make decisions on what idea to go for, what pricing a product should be, what pillars go in the strategy, what proposition to lead with first, and so on. These are content matters, and decisions about content need to be made by someone in the business we're commissioned by. On our projects we call the business our **client**.

Seb, an old boss of mine, said 'if content is King, then context is the Emperor of the continent next door'. This is a rather *Game of Thrones* analogy for business project management, but the sentiment holds up well: be clear on the roles and buddy up when possible. When we run our projects, I personally like to facilitate *with* my client as they 'own' the content while I can 'own' the people in the room. That way, between us, we know we've got things covered.

If you're facilitating within a business, that agency–client dynamic isn't as clearly defined. So, it's imperative you call out where you and your project team's responsibilities begin and end. To help, here are some suggestions for language.

Whatever project you're commissioned to facilitate, there should be someone to whom updates and outputs are sent regularly. You don't 'send stuff' to the 'client'. Instead, you send updates to the 'problem owner'. The **problem owner** is someone who needs to have 'an answer' at the end of the creative process.

Sometimes the problem owner sets the brief, actively participates in every stage of the process, is present in the room to answer questions, co-creates insight with other team members, suggests ideas and even helps grab coffee and clear up. How brilliant is that! Sometimes the problem owner is on the other side of the world, and you've only an email to go on. That is also brilliant, as you've freedom to move.

Every project also has what we call the **sponsor** (the person who paid for the project). And every project will have a **decision maker.** Decision makers are what we call people who 'make decisions' (just to be clear!) when it comes to choices and options on what to do next regarding content.

There may be three separate people for each of these roles on a project, or it could be one person wearing multiple hats. A common scenario we find is there are two problem owners who criss-cross each other in a large business matrix.

As we'll see in the scoping tools, it's vital to have the conversation about **who** makes decisions about **what** topics when they appear. If it comes down to multiple people, with whom does the buck stop?

Interview

Hannah Feely

INNOVATION FACILITATOR, UK CIVIL SERVICE

Hannah Feely works in the UK civil service. She designs and delivers large development programmes and projects in software development. Hannah is Scrum Master, a Certified Agile Coach and Lean Practitioner. Her passions are for big group facilitation, and making outcomes better and people in business happier.

You've been facilitating projects in quite a technical and regulated environment, what's that like?

Working in my world can be challenging. There's lots of governance and red tape, and it can feel slow and immovable. People can very easily spend time talking and not doing. And it's easy to understand why negativity creeps in when process is hard to change. But the team and I respond to this by being ten times more upbeat than others. The key is to set those expectations around outputs and process right from the start. It's all about telling people what we're aiming to achieve, how we're going to do that and, importantly, why. If there's an elephant in the room around why things won't work, then I have to call it out. If people are part of that discussion right from the start, they are more likely to take ownership of the outputs, endorse the outputs and influence what happens to those outputs after our project sessions. In my world, success is about buy-in; getting people onboard at the start is key.

In a heavily regulated environment, new ideas threaten the status quo — what do you do to warm people to new thinking and new ideas?

I start by stating expectations, and putting language in the room that describes how potential naysayers might be feeling and what they might be thinking. I do that early and it helps everyone nod and take notice. I've given permission for people to say what they think at the start and voice their concerns before we then get to working on a problem. I will ensure we explain the purpose of our sessions, the outputs we imagine, who is in the room and why they've been chosen; that these people are important. I then get into the elephants that might be in the room and then it's explaining the process.

Creativity is essential if we're going to arrive at 'new' — how do you inject the creativity in your facilitated project sessions?

At first, I thought I wasn't a creative person. But over time I've realised that's simply not true. I can make connections all the time. And everyday I need to do so — and so do other people around me. I remind them of this by using case studies and examples. Simple and quick

"I like learning from styles that are different to mine."

— HANNAH FEELY

stories that I can tell to illustrate a point are an essential tool. My big learning is that taking insights from other businesses and sectors and making connections back towards our world always gives me ideas. It's far easier for my participants to build on a 'something' rather than try to have ideas from nothing. I've noticed we only need to share a few examples of someone else, or somewhere else, solving something similar to our challenge and that boosts a bigger conversation.

I've seen you buddy up with people and also run sessions on your own, what are your insights from working in those different formats?
I've noticed that when I buddy up, there's definitely more energy in the room and things are far more dynamic. I like learning from styles that are different to mine. And I believe people in the room benefit from that. For some large projects, I'll often be the Master Facilitator, though, and have a team of facilitators working different groups. I'm then moving from group to group picking up on how everyone is doing. That's a very different way of working as I'm a bit on my own and a bit in a team. My big spot is that when I do facilitate on my own, I can make decisions faster as I don't have to engineer a break or extend an activity to explain a change in delivery to my buddy or team members. This is handy when it comes to complex issues, but then it would be handy to have a buddy to bounce thoughts off.

Following a process will only get you so far – what are your thoughts on breaking rules, mixing things up, and engineering a bit of maverick thinking?
Oh! – you've got to have a set of tools. And having lots of tools will help you get out of a spot. But I've spotted I can avoid feeling that I'm in reactive mode by doing a 'pre-mortem' – this is where my co-facilitator and I work through the design of our sessions and imagine the outputs at each stage. We can rehearse what we'd do if output were half, or more, or nothing at each stage and then discuss and decide what we'd do in each instance. That way, when we arrive at those moments, we've mitigated against extremes. We've 'been' to them already, and we can brief into the group what feels like a logical next step.

What is a final nugget of genius you'd like to share?
Some advice to anyone beginning their facilitation journey, and that would be to always explain why activities are important. Whether that's at the start or end of an exercise, if people know why things are important, then they'll treat those actions with importance. Good for the project and good for the group. Always remember to mention the importance.

Part 3

Welcome to the GENIUS BOX process; a four-stage method designed to help you facilitate a project team's journey from problem to solution. Scoping, identifying insights, generating ideas and, finally, selecting and implementing output. At every stage there are different tools to use, each of which injects creativity, leaving a project team aligned and excited about the new ideas they've unlocked.

THE PROCESS

The Process

1_SCOPING

A great project will have a great project brief. Our definition of a great brief is a challenge that everyone understands thoroughly and is motivated to solve. Scoping that brief well is what will get it to greatness. Regardless of its complexity or scale, honest conversations are at the heart of scoping, and they add value along the way. Some projects can simply be time spent scoping to agree a sharper project brief! Whatever the context, always start by scoping.

The intro bit

I'd like to share with you seven tools, each with a catchy name, to help you facilitate scoping sessions for your projects. The tools are designed to:

- Establish the ambition and elicit further useful information about the potential project brief.

- Understand more about the problem owner and their motivations.

- Galvanise and align energy for you and your project team.

- Crystalise all your scoping efforts and prepare you and the project team for the insights and ideas phases of a project.

And they are:

Tool 1: **WHYHAUS** (pages 120–123)
Tool 2: **TISSUE SESSION** (pages 124–127)
Tool 3: **MIXING DESKS & HONEYPOTS** (pages 130–135)
Tool 4: **RUMSFELD'S MATRIX & COLUMBO'S QUESTION** (pages 138–141)
Tool 5: **ANGELS & DEMONS** (pages 142–145)
Tool 6: **PIRATES VS NAVY** (pages 149–150)
Tool 7: **MOZART** (pages 152–155)

These tools all need to be facilitated in different ways. Over time, you'll notice that some of them secure two or three of the desired outputs at the same time – how neat. Some are best explained by you, the facilitator. First, using the tool on the problem owner, and then de-briefing what happened to the team. Some tools are best explained first with an imaginary and unrelated topic and then everyone invited to have a go using the tool on the live challenge. Sometimes you can hide the tool in a conversation, sometimes it's best to be overt and say 'I'm going to use a tool to help us'.

The project context will help you decide what to do and how. A scoping session to align a marketing team around a yoghurt brand won't have the same context as a scoping session exploring the sales strategy for a global fintech. There isn't a 'right way' to go about scoping, so be sure to invest some time prepping (see pages 316–317). A discussion with your co-facilitator about what tools to use will always add value.

Eventually, you'll land particular instructions, phrases and advice that work for you and your style – and you'll tailor your explanations depending on the projects you're running. As you read through the tools in this chapter, we'll share some top tips on where and how we've used them, a bit of history about where they came from, and some stories on where they've been used, to help explain our advice and instruction.

All the tools are practical. They invite you and the project team to consider the project topic individually, in pairs or as a group. Some tools require the problem owner in the room with you, some are for just you and the project team to use. Some of them push output from one creative session into the input for another session. You can use all the tools remotely, but there will be a nuance to what you say and how you explain the sequence of events. Also, sometimes the time needed to complete the task when remotely facilitated is different to the time needed when everyone is in a room together.

It's also worth understanding what went into the design of our tools before you use them. For any tool to work the facilitator needs to connect to it and believe in its value. Simply going through the motions of completing templates, placing sticky notes on canvasses and ticking boxes doesn't add the magic. The tools alone won't unlock epiphanies around your potential projects either. They don't work like a calculator where clear problems are input for clever algorithms to provide you with an output. No, the tools need you, the facilitator, to respond to the content and conversation in the room as discussions unfold. A creative facilitator will use a tool to provide structure to a discussion and then allow people to explore the topics' tangents.

Innovation projects need conversations to explore 'the new' in order to arrive at something innovative; knowing 'the answer' on day one and organising a project team to implement that answer is wasteful. Scoping, therefore, is a critical but also creative stage of the process and you, as the facilitator, need to enjoy briefing in the tools as much as participants on your project team enjoy using them.

If agreement and alignment about a project's ambition will be the OUTPUT, then the choice of scoping tools, and how you brief them in and split your team up when using them, is the INPUT. The more creative your input facilitation, the more innovative your project output will be.

RIGHT:
Scoping is about understanding the question further and not leaping to idea generation straight away.

The Tools and Insights Discovery

There is a loose (and I mean really loose) connection between our tools and the preferences people demonstrate in Insights Discovery profiling – a globally known diagnostic tool that helps people understand themselves and the impact they have on others. Across our scoping tools we're confident that all types of thinkers/learners/doers can engage with the tools, the facilitator, the team and, importantly, the project topic. Insights Discovery starts with a simple and memorable model (below), which identifies four groups of behavioural preferences. We are all a mix of all four sections and can dial up any of them. However, we tend to have a preference for one or two sections. Remember, our brains save energy by developing patterns of behaviour. We are all motivated to succeed. We're naturally empowered, creative and driven to 'do things' and 'move forward'. The fact that you're reading this book means you've got a personal connection to innovation and creativity. You find it engaging and motivating – however, we're motivated to do things for different reasons and deep in our subconscious we're driven by these behavioural preferences. Insights Discovery explains our character traits as:

- **Fiery Red:** 'Do it now' – focused on action and results

- **Sunshine Yellow:** 'Do it harmoniously' – focused on being sociable, engaging and enthusiastic

- **Earth Green:** 'Do it together' – focused on listening, co-creation and collaboration

- **Cool Blue:** 'Do it right' – focused on precision and accuracy

At GENIUS BOX, when building our scoping tools over time, we've considered the different types of personality in the room; those of the problem owner, the facilitators and the project participants. We can't assume that everyone in a creative session is driven to 'do it harmoniously' so we must engineer our sessions to not only secure a great output, but also involve everyone so they are all fully engaged in this part of the process. The GENIUS BOX scoping tools aligned (loosely!) to our subconscious motivations are listed on the table opposite.

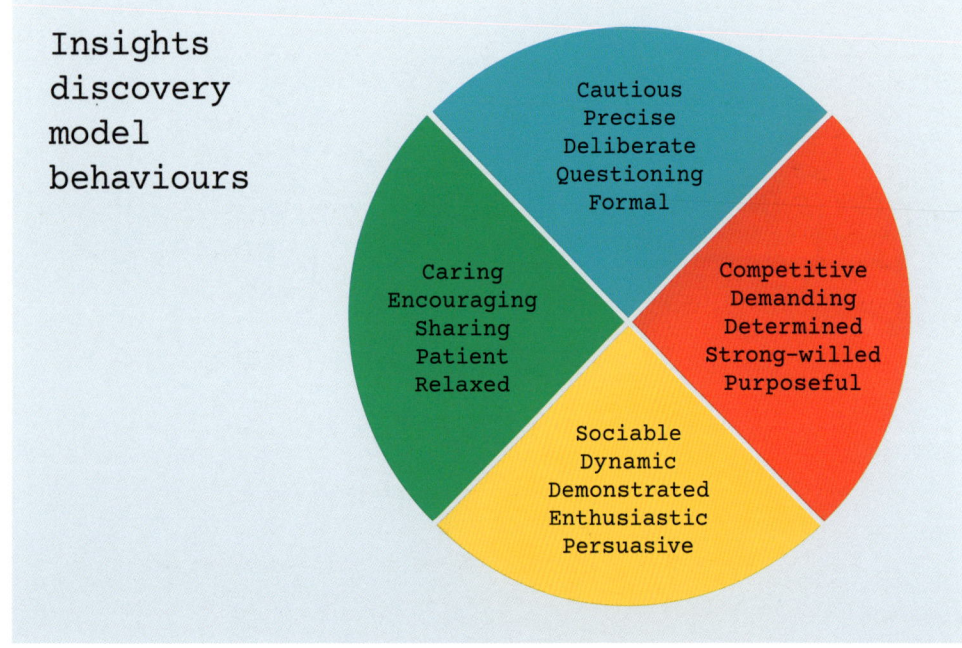

Scoping tool	*Insights Discovery* colours	What it looks like	What it aims to achieve
WHYHAUS	● Earth Green ● Cool Blue	Considered discussions. People who like to ask questions and think things through.	Uncover further context behind the business challenge by asking carefully chosen questions.
TISSUE SESSION	● Earth Green ● Fiery Red	Spontaneous reactions, animated, co-creation, dynamic discussion. People who like 'arriving at connections' in the moment.	Discover the problem owner's emotional connection to the project and therefore the threshold of what is in and out of scope by using ideas to stimulate conversations.
MIXING DESKS & HONEYPOTS	● Fiery Red ● Sunshine Yellow	A mixture of both 'open things up' and 'closing things down' discussion. Team explorations and lively debate. Allow for plenty of space and access to output from previous tools.	For the project team participants, the sponsor and the facilitator to agree the right ambition level for the project and to arrive at a single project brief.
RUMSFELD'S MATRIX & COLUMBO'S QUESTION	● Sunshine Yellow ● Cool Blue	Thoughtful, reflective, time for individuals.	For project team participants to individually and collectively exhaust final questions, comments and perspectives about the project brief.
ANGELS & DEMONS	● Earth Green ● Cool Blue	A team discussion, considered and empathetic.	To help map the people in the business who will influence the progress and success of the project.
PIRATES VS NAVY	● Earth Green ● Fiery Red	Team debate at speed, with passion vs team discussion and considered thinking.	Using a bit of fun and theatre to help the project participants gather energy and connection around the project brief.
MOZART	● Cool blue ● Sunshine Yellow	Making plans, making decisions, having a sequence of events that will get from A to B and therefore to the answer.	For the project facilitator and sponsor to agree the plan on how to answer the brief, now it's been thoroughly scoped.

EXAMPLE STORY

For several years we worked closely with the European Marketing Heads at a major drinks brand. Some of our tools for scoping, ideas generation and ideas selection were onboarded into their annual project-planning process.

They were very aware of the power that the right energy brings to any given situation. The process, therefore, wasn't led by tools, instructions and templates, but instead we signalled the different phases through the mindsets and energies that needed to be present at each stage.

Scoping became what we called the 'owl' stage. Owls are wise. They watch. They listen. They consider their environment carefully. Owls also spit out the unnecessary bones and undigestible parts of the prey they eat. Therefore, a successful owl stage required everyone to watch, listen and consider everything that was being discussed – and spit out unnecessary waste material! Across the brand's businesses in northern Europe (all languages and cultures) the energy of the owl was universally adopted. People 'got it' and arrived at the sessions with the right mindset and attitude, ready to ask 'wise owl-like' questions.

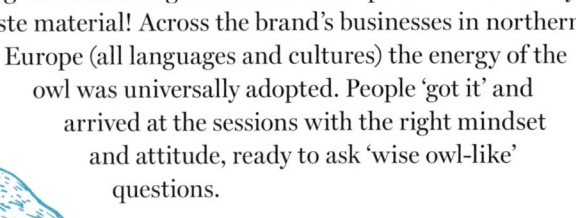

Remember that our preferred approach to problem solving can't be neatly dropped into one of four boxes. We're far more complex than that (thank goodness)! At any given moment all our proclivities are present, but some will be amplified in our interactions as we work with other people on business challenges. So, one tool isn't going to be enough to accurately explore a challenge; a range of tools are needed for people to gather context around an emerging business brief. Mix up a range of scoping tools so every participant in the project team understands, thinks and feels differently about the brief at the end of the scoping stage than they did at the start.

When you set up a scoping session, the explanations you give, and the anecdotes and stories you share, keep things fresh and new. Force yourself to introduce at least one new story or activity into your scoping sessions for each project. Be the new energy you want to see. Demonstrate the 'how to be' as well as the 'what to do' at each stage.

All of our tools link to each other, so there's no hard and fast rule on the specific order in which to use them. However, we advise starting with the WHYHAUS tool, as it's one that provides everybody with the opportunity to ask questions (and share immediate perspectives) straight away.

It's human nature to react to a stimulus immediately and try to make sense of anything 'new' by forming patterns and making assumptions. In the context of business those primitive survival instincts manifest as questions, ideas or intellectual rebuttals. People have a good deal of sceptical energy at the start of a project, so the WHYHAUS is a great way of defusing potentially hindering mindsets around the project brief. It's also the 'safest' tool to use, as what you're getting people to do isn't that much different from ordinary workflow – asking questions and taking notes of answers.

You're simply adding an extra layer of quality to it so the project scope gets established earlier.

Albert Einstein is quoted (apparently) as having said:

"If I had an hour to solve a problem, I'd spend 55 minutes thinking about the problem and 5 minutes thinking about solutions."

The point he makes is important: preparation has great value for problem solving. Scoping the problem so that it's properly and thoroughly understood is time well spent. Now let's explore each tool in turn. 👉

LEFT:
Our very own Einstein in a GENIUS BOX session. Hairbrush not included.

Tool 001

Whyhaus

Aim: to uncover further context behind the business challenge by asking carefully considered questions.

In the early 1920s, a pioneering group of German designers and artists founded the famous Bauhaus school of design. Their iconic HQ in Dessau is a temple to creative rule breaking. The Bauhaus attempted to unify the principles of mass production with an individual artistic vision and strove to combine function and form in new ways. From utopian visions of society shaped through architecture, to the design of humble chessboard pieces, nothing was off limits; everything could be re-imagined. The Bauhaus is an inspiration for us and was truly the first to ask, 'what if?'

In the creative process, it's essential to work on the right brief so you have a strong platform from which to move forward. Embracing the creative disciplines of the Bauhaus, we present our WHYHAUS tool. We're building a 'haus' (home) for our project narrative by asking 'why' in different forms. The tool is basically a great canvas on which to capture your first conversations with the problem owner at the start of an innovation project. If you're familiar with completing a SWOT analysis (strengths, weaknesses, opportunities and threats), then this tool is for you. We at GENIUS BOX love theatre, and this tool is a safe one to introduce project participants to creative and visual approaches to thinking, connection-making and exploration. It sets the scene for the future and immediately captures the conversation at project kick-off.

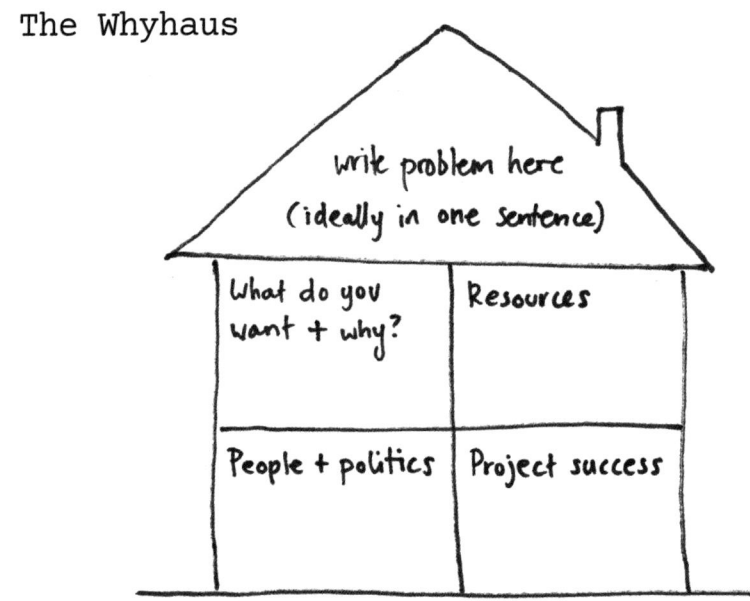

The Whyhaus

WHAT TO DO & HOW IT WORKS
Draw the 'haus' on the opposite page nice and big on a white board.

Have blank A3-size copies for individuals in the session, for their notes, and also A2-size for group work if needed*.

> **TOP TIP** If you are going to issue photocopies for people, then **draw them by hand and copy onto coloured paper**. Anything crafted by a software package will always look synthetic, almost pharmaceutical. Subconsciously, we associate neat boxes and typed fonts with nasty forms, such as insurance claims. We've experimented with all sorts of approaches in the past, but hand-drawn and copied onto coloured paper seems to work for us the best. It's easier to use the instruction 'place the completed pink sheets in that pile and the yellow ones in that pile' and see participants do so at a distance, than navigate an ocean of white A4 paper.

Start by asking 'what do you want and why?' It's likely you're reasonably informed of this starter brief ahead of the session, but asking overtly in the room makes the brief 'as public record' and your participants will be glad you're asking deliberately 'naive' questions. Allow the problem owner to put the brief in context; this is sometimes better requested in advance. It establishes the 'story so far' and sets the scene for the project.

Then it's over to you and the project participants to ask questions of the problem owner on the four topics in turn. As a starter, I've suggested four questions for each box for you below – but encourage the participants to ask *more* questions, if they aren't already.

① What do you want and why?

- Why is this project important for the business to answer now?
- How does this project affect the performance of other projects in your business?
- What happens if this issue remains unanswered?
- What's been achieved so far in answering the challenge – are there any learnings?

② Resources

- What resources (people, time, budget) are available to answer this brief?
- Have you an idea of a timescale for this project to be answered?
- Are there other demands on the business that might affect access to these resources?
- Have you got an idea of how this project brief will be given priority should tough decisions need to be made?

These then lead to a series of questions about people and the project's potential success. In any project, involving two or more people, there will be an element of politics. We all have different perspectives about the world. And people's perspectives about the right way to approach the project you're scoping will sometimes overlap and sometimes differ greatly.

Most of the time, projects die in business as no one is prepared to champion change. Projects mean more work for people; this can be both a chance for a problem owner to shine and also the school report that uncovers home truths about how some people and departments 'could do better'. Talking to people upfront and getting the answers straight away, therefore, is good to do before the 'people thing' becomes a 'thing'. 👉

3. People and politics

- You're our problem owner – who else is a sponsor of this project, and why?
- Who ultimately makes decisions – if there are two of you, who has final say?
- Who is 'Voldemort' and could stop this project before it starts?
- What's the word on the street about this project amongst the team and why?

4. Project success

- Revisiting your answer to 'what do you want, and why', be specific – success is... ?
- What is success for the other sponsors we've mentioned?
- What's in this for you? A promotion? A pay rise? Or just another 'to do' off the list?
- Why have you brought in all these resources and/or an outside agency to help? What's the feedback so far about what the end outcome might look like?

TOP TIPS

There are, of course, many overlaps between the questions, as you'll see in the examples – so the point is not to agonise on **where** to put the questions you and your project team wish to ask, but instead **that you ask the problem owner the questions and make a note of the answers**. The output of your WHYHAUS session will inform the content of other scoping sessions you run, and certainly help you complete the MOZART tool (see p152).

Over time, as a facilitator, you'll get a feel for the next type of question to ask given the answer to the previous question. This is something that becomes intuitive to you and your personal style. In the early stages, I'd advise always working in pairs so one of you can concentrate on the energy in the room and the focus of the problem owner, while the other can ensure all questions are covered and answers are recorded.

I like to have the WHYHAUS drawn up, large on the wall, and allow lots of space for answers to be scribbled down and seen. Take care when using sticky notes; they're really useful as they're accessible, flexible and people can rewrite questions and comments at speed and re-post their thinking – but one or two ALWAYS drop off. It only takes an important comment to float sadly to the floor and someone to notice it for the session to lose impact. Ensuring everyone's comments are captured to the WHYHAUS is a significant moment: it says 'I hear you, your voice is recorded, this answer is captured.'

There will always be more questions than will fit in the time dedicated to this tool. I think it's important for people to have a 'good time' rather than scope 'for a long time', so encourage teams to choose the three questions they're most excited by as a way of filtering out what needs to be asked. Sometimes it's better/easier for the problem owner to hear three questions in one go and form a coherent answer than one question at a time. People will always say more than is needed. The words 'problem', 'brief' and 'project' will be used interchangeably when using this tool – tell everyone this at the start of the session and they'll remain focused.

At the end of the session I often ask any unanswered questions be thrown into the 'car wash'. As you know, a car park is where vehicles are left to sit and gather dust. When people 'park' something in a meeting that's subtext for 'let's just forget we mentioned that, shall we?' A car wash, however, is a valet experience and vehicles leave spotlessly clean and tidy. Hand the questions to the problem owner to read over during the remaining time in the workshop, and have answers written up on the wall in and around the WHYHAUS. You can return to these at the start and end of each day or when people come back from the breaks – it's a great way to keep your project team focused on what's needed.

RIGHT:
You can facilitate the WHYHAUS using the floor when scoping with a large group.

Tool 002
Tissue session

Aim: to discover the problem owner's emotional connection to the project and therefore the threshold of what is in and out of scope by using ideas to stimulate conversations.

The origins of this tool link back to the pioneering days of advertising in the 50s and 60s. Back then, it would have been customary for the planners and brand owner to jot down suggestions on what to do in response to a new creative brief on their cigarette papers and notepads. They'd have thrown these starter thoughts and ideas into a hat (perhaps literally) and, one at a time, discussed their various merits.

Similarly, in those pre-computer days, concept drawings were sketched on tracing paper (known as tissue) and these 'tissue sessions' became part of the creative process. I use the tool here as a way of exploring the ambition of a project and the appetite for risk of the problem owner at the same time.

The WHYHAUS is a great tool for the head – you're asking questions and considering responses. The TISSUE SESSION is a great tool for the heart – you're noting down the reactions and emotions of your problem owner to ideas and provocations that you and the team put forth against the emerging brief.

You'll remember how our mind seeks patterns and craves familiarity. It wants to store information in a like-with-like way. New stimuli need to fit our story of the world. Any ideas or provocations that are perceived to threaten that narrative create emotional reactions and run the risk of being dismissed.

By using ideas (the wilder, the better) we can quickly uncover the threshold of what is an 'acceptable' story for your emerging project, and therefore the type of outcome your problem owner perceives as success. We can use ideas to establish the boundaries of a brief. Ideas cut to the chase. They present alternative futures to which our hearts and minds react. TISSUE SESSIONS uncover the deeper drivers of those reactions and allow you and the project team to capture further details on the motivations behind a project, for both.

WHAT TO DO & HOW IT WORKS

First, have everyone digest the output from the WHYHAUS tool. A one-page summary and wrap up meeting facilitated by you should help people connect to the project at this stage. Ask the team to think of two or three starter ideas that could be part of the answer to the brief. Importantly, these aren't positioned as the 'actual answer' but are used as equipment in the creative process to get you, the project team and the problem owner from the starting point to the first stages of progress. As one facilitator on our team likes to say, 'a bit like rock climbing equipment, those pieces of kit aren't the summit or the route, but you need them from time to time to conquer both.'

The ideas need to be easy to understand, and captured individually on separate sheets of paper and, at the session, you'll need space to create a bit of theatre around you. This tool is a brilliant opportunity for everyone to move around more, get animated, and literally 'think on their feet'. Being physical boosts the alpha waves in the mind and will help people remember more output from the session.

Have your problem owner stand on a rug or a square marked on the floor in tape. They are now the 'owner' of this island and only permit ideas that answer their brief upon it. Everything else is 'out of scope' and placed outside the island. Creative metaphors we've used in the past have been flying carpets, aircraft carriers, archery targets – you get the idea. Your problem owner is in charge of positioning suggested ideas close to them or far away. Either on the island or not.

Next, you, the facilitator, read out an idea. Be clear and precise. Ask your problem owner if they'd consider that idea as something that would somehow answer the brief and be acceptable to them as a possible project outcome. If it's a 'yes', ask them to place that idea at their feet on the island. If it's 'not in scope' ask them to place it outside the boundary. After you've done this a couple of times, invite other members of the project team to offer up their idea to the problem owner. You can step back and land discussions on a flip chart as you go. Importantly, you and the project team need to record the reason why this idea lands where it does. It's those principles and beliefs around what success looks like that matter to you at this stage, as you're still establishing the remit of your project brief.

During the conversations you might find team members debating the merits of the idea with the problem owner. Don't let this happen. Now isn't the time for lots of discussion. Instead, these ideas and provocations are quick ways to get immediate and unfiltered responses from your project owner.

Around 16–20 ideas is enough to scope the boundary of where the project begins and ends. Any further ideas are likely to be variations of others and glean little further knowledge or context. The session can run for an hour or so and, at the end, you ought to have a solid set of standards and principles to protect regarding the project and its next steps. You'll understand some of the emotional drivers from your problem owner, too, particularly what excites them and what makes them nervous.

TOP TIPS
The TISSUE SESSION is not an idea generation tool. You're not running a creative brainstorm. Remember to remind everyone (including yourself, as facilitator) that you are using ideas to stimulate debate and deepen further insight around what's perceived as 'in' and 'out' of scope for the project. This is something the problem owner often forgets as they get caught up in the session. One way to enforce the point is to lead with a handful of ideas that came from other projects similar to the one you're scoping. 'We could do 2-for-1 offers as we did for the other brand launch' is something that helps kick off the conversation.

If your project team arrives to the session with dozens of starter ideas, ask each person to choose the one idea they have the most energy for or would most like to see the problem owner react to. Avoid the obvious ideas that the problem owner is bound to agree with, and instead offer up the ideas that you believe challenge the status quo. It is here you'll find more insight. 👉

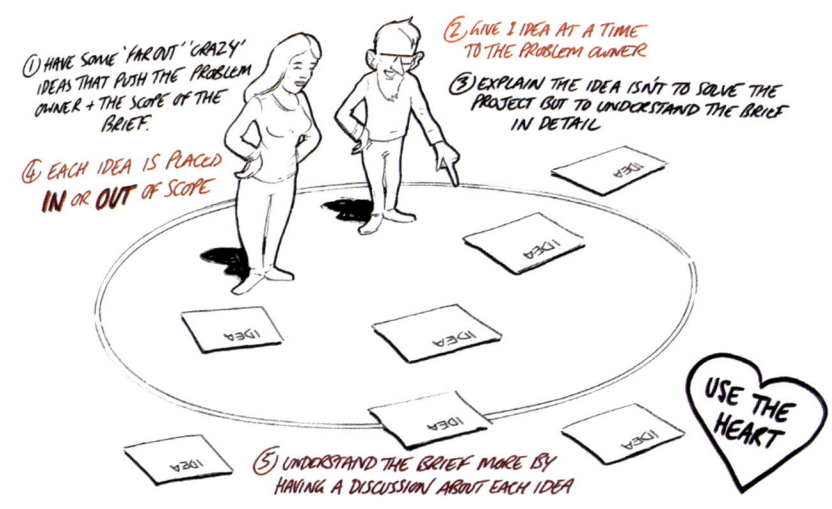

EXAMPLE STORY

On running a session with HSBC, we suggested that customers who are overdrawn be locked in stocks and have the branch staff throw rotten veg at them. This wasn't the first idea, but part of a light-hearted discussion during the session. The then UK Head of Branch Network said 'Yes! – in scope'. Now, it's not that she wanted to literally punish people, but on asking why she liked that idea she told the story of how she was in a queue buying perfume in a US branch of Victoria's Secret.

The customer in front of her was taken aside by the store staff and congratulated for making her purchase, and was awarded the accolade of 'Angel' and given a discount there and then for her loyalty. The occasion was marked with confetti and an impromptu glass of fizz. After the commotion had settled, our HSBC boss had stepped forward as the next customer and paid for her purchase without any fuss from the staff. She said exasperatedly, 'But I want to be an Angel, too!' She explained that in that moment she felt envious of the attention the customer in front of her had received. She told us how excited she was when she stepped up to the cashier desk, only to feel crestfallen that no such confetti and fizz was coming her way. It was an insight about her own emotions in an otherwise transactional experience that provided her with an understanding about staff and customers in a bank branch.

A queue normalises everyone. She had noted, 'There's no way staff can tell in advance of an interaction what customers' needs are. We require a way of helping staff to differentiate their approach to helping customers, depending on whether they need a £1,000 loan, a £1,000 overdraft or to cash in a £1,000 cheque. To the bank, it's a transaction that has commercial risk, but to the customer those values have far more meaning, utility and importance. All that is lost when you stand in a queue.' Being deliberately irreverent and suggesting 'stocks and mockings' prompted this story from the UK Head and unlocked a deeper level of insight than originally thought of by the project team. The project was no longer about 'reducing queue times' (a perceived need) but instead 'the customers' overall experience in branch' (a value-adding output).

It's easy to get caught up in the theatre of this session. With the problem owner moving around and placing papers on the floor, and yourself or a co-facilitator hastily jotting outputs on a flip chart, take care to spot any contradictions. Scoping a brief with Emirates Airlines about First Class Lounge access, we spotted the problem owner placing 'premium' types of ideas in scope in addition to 'access for all' type of ideas. This was contradictory. Similarly for beverages, 'naturally sourced local ingredients' and 'at global scale' can't co-exist without compromise.

If you have more than two problem owners, watch the dynamics between them. Ask one of them to make the decision about what is in and out of scope. And spend time discussing ideas that exist on the boundary of your project brief, as it's here you'll gather further insight and context around the project.

Facilitate this session with clear language, and carefully consider the order in which you brief instructions. Stories and examples help, but too many can confuse people and you'll find yourself in an impromptu brainstorm generating lists of 'could do' without discernable output. When delivered well, however, the TISSUE SESSION becomes an intervention that adds immediate value to the project and the team, and leaves your problem owner feeling confident their project is in safe hands and embarking on a successful and creative journey.

Facilitation tip 001
Timings

Timing and clarity go hand in hand.

Facilitators who aren't clear about timings are often pretty lousy when it comes to more complicated instructions. For example: 'Come back at 3:45pm, in this room, with one person from your group ready to share two findings,' is better than saying 'Work on this as a group for 20 minutes and come back ready to share.'

Over a project workshop (let's say three or four days back-to-back) or a series of one-day sessions spread over a month or two, time is going to be mentioned, err, time and again! Get sharp on this. Crisp timing helps creative thinking; contrary to the creative 'experts' out there who say timing is a restrictive factor in the creative process, I say no! This is not the way. Timing is part of the framework from which creative thinking can begin.

Re-learning how to think, for the adult learner, is exposing and can be scary. Adult learners need something understood and familiar as a support. 'The time' can be a support, as everyone knows how it works without explanation. Time can be framed as moments to experiment in, spaces of 'no rules thinking' that people can get to grips with. 'Let's think out of the box' instructions work a lot better when they're phrased with 'and come back at 2:35, which is only ten minutes away'. You're subconsciously letting people know you expect things from them, whilst also setting safe conditions for them in which to perform and respond.

And if you say you're starting at 09:15, then start at 09:15. I have a good friend who talks brilliantly about permission fields – when what is being said doesn't match the behaviour displayed. If you get solid on timings (and start and end things crisply), pace and energy will accompany your project. People will learn. They will trust your instructions more and more, and be more willing to experiment for you when you ask. This is not being a headmaster about time, but using time as an indicator of engagement in the project.

Watch what you say, when you look at your watch.

Interview

Jeff Tan
INNOVATION PIONEER

Jeff is an in-house entrepreneur and Director of Innovation inside one of the world's largest organisations. In the past, he's headed up innovation and marketing services for some of the biggest brands on the planet. And when he's not writing songs about presenting ideas, he can be found running marathons to clear his head.

How do you design and facilitate sessions to help people align behind a common understanding of innovation for their business?

Innovation and 'being innovative' mean different things to different people, all of whom have different lives and experiences. Most of the time, though, people are interested in stunts and tactics instead of innovation. That five milligrams of innovation matters when it's needed for a front cover or a Cannes Award, but genuine transformation, change and new opportunity means much more effort. Innovation is solving a human need and at scale; for example, finding a new use of tech to create a 1% improvement in hospital efficacy – that's innovation!

> *"Change and new are ways the tribe evolves and won't die."*
> — JEFF TAN

You've seen many processes, approaches, tools and language to describe and explain innovation, what has stuck with you?
I like running open, playful games at the start of my sessions; like naming 20 new things you could do with a tomato, make a quick list – go! I can then land the point afterwards that there was no judgement, it was a loose discussion, everyone's perspective was equal. It's far easier to set out the picture of what a project session will look like after playing that game than just asking people to 'be open and playful', assume they know what you mean and then move on. I think games are a great way of making the point that we want people to fail, to be okay when it happens and then move on.

When it comes to innovating where do you like to begin?
I need to define the scope of the problem. I will always want to start with the challenge. And I prefer that to be in a single sentence. Ideally, there needs to be a genuine human need in there. And I'll avoid an ideas factory where we're listing thousands of options. Instead, I need to focus on a small number of ideas and get just as creative about the implementation tactics we need to get our idea done in the business and beyond.

You're often bringing new thinking into huge established organisations. What advice have you for people trying to provoke the status quo?
We humans find safety in the tribe. Safety manifests as people wanting to be risk-free. To counteract that – share what I've said, share the science. Then it's easier to make the case for change given that story. People will want to make contributions and share ideas. It's their way of moving us forward. 'Change' and 'new' are ways the tribe evolves and won't die.

There's bound to be strong opinion the more senior the audience you work with. What tips have you to manage differences of opinion?
Everyone has opinions. In every project. And in every session. When I run sessions, I remind people to question their opinions, as the first comments they share might be reactionary and not that well thought through. When it comes to innovation ideas, I remind everyone that strong opinions can easily crush early suggestions. I ask people to revisit their opinion and turn it into an enabling question – one that seeks more about those starter ideas.

How do you manage any beliefs you develop about your proposals being stronger than your client's point of view?
I've a theory that there's three ways to handle this. Firstly, you might be facilitating a project where you are 'client services' – it might be easier to take the stance of 'whatever the client wants, the client gets'. Secondly, you can adopt a more diplomatic approach and become a democratic consultant. You can offer alternatives; you can coach and co-create alongside. You can offer other ideas, too. Good ideas I believe come from that egalitarian approach where everyone has a voice. Or thirdly, there's the 'hey, guys' let's just do this' and be confident, forceful and clear approach. This theory is all hypothetical of course and every situation is different. But looking back on the work I've done, I've been in all of those positions and many others in between. Sometimes the facilitator is the narrator of a session and needs to put into words what other people are all thinking. Trust yourself.

What is a final nugget of genius you'd like to share?
A good way to make something happen is be public about it. Creating structures around you, such as a promising to deliver an output on a certain date, make it harder to change your mind. Ultimately, as the facilitator, you drive the energy of a project.

Tool 003
Mixing desks & honeypots

Aim: for the project team participants, the sponsor and the facilitator to agree the right ambition level for the project and to arrive at a single brief.

At the start of the scoping phase, you'll likely have one (possibly longer than needed) sentence describing what the business challenge is. During the WHYHAUS and the TISSUE SESSION, you'll emerge with four or five other re-expressions of this starting challenge. They are all of different levels of ambition.

For example:

- Our brands aren't resonating with consumers in northern Europe so we need to re-bottle to create better shelf standout.

- Our brands aren't resonating with consumers in northern Europe so we need to find out what we mean to our consumers and why.

- Our brands aren't resonating with consumers in northern Europe so we need to reposition them and develop new propositions.

- Our brands aren't resonating with consumers in northern Europe so we need to re-design the packaging and pilot a new look in France.

You can't answer all these briefs in one project – it gets messy! A great project answers ONE concise brief. This tool helps you facilitate the conversation to arrive at and align behind one agreed brief.

Here are three imaginary project briefs designed to help a business sell more product. All are different in scale and ambition but on the same topic: coffee. And underneath each one is a reason why it isn't as 'fit and healthy' as it could be. As a result, each brief isn't a good one for a project team to go tackle.

Our brand of smooth-intense-dry-roasted-Dutch-house-fairtrade coffee isn't selling so we need to...

1
...totally re-invent the coffee-drinking occasion with a new innovation in self-serve capsules.

WHAT'S WRONG WITH THIS?

This brief is too **ambitious**.
It might take years of research and R&D to arrive at a new tech to compete against the current coffee capsule market. Also, there are assumptions here that capsules are the key to success. Coffee has forged a place in our culture over many years; changing people's behaviours around coffee, therefore, it is a big ask!

2
...rebrand our product, relaunch in different markets and extend the product range to attract more consumers.

WHAT'S WRONG WITH THIS?

This brief is **over-stretching**.
It's asking the business to do many things. New products, new propositions and new market launches will all take time and money – even if this was co-ordinated, you'd run out of budget long before you got going. There's too much here to answer.

2
...agree a new range of flavours for the instant coffee category.

WHAT'S WRONG WITH THIS?

This brief is **too narrow**.
There's an inherited assumption that the flavour of the coffee is the issue. The project scope is so narrow that the only ideas permitted are just flavour changes – it's likely the answer to our challenge is something else.

At the start of your project scoping, treat the first written articulation of your project brief as if it were 100% incorrect. Remember that someone, somewhere, may have had to type up the brief as a hastily prepared email to you. It's likely they had a picture in their mind of what they thought was the right 'exam question' to answer, but in reality it differs from what's actually needed. The mixing desk tool helps identify the right brief on which to work, and aligns everyone on why that brief is the chosen 'exam question' to answer. 👉

WHAT TO DO & HOW IT WORKS

Using the first brief as a starter, invite your team to write broader and more ambitious project briefs that would sit **above** that challenge on an ambition scale. Then, write narrower, specific and tighter project briefs that would sit **under** that first original brief.

Don't overthink where each brief sits in relation to the others, as your perspective of how well a project brief can be answered will vary to your project teammates and your sponsor: which is exactly what the mechanic of this tool points out. Place the briefs side by side as if they occupied the volume levels on a mixing desk/graphic equaliser*

> For anyone born after the mid-90s, graphic equalisers (and mix tapes) are a thing of the past and such analogies may not work so well, but the concept of Instagram filters lands the sentiment of 'tweaking things up and down' too – in Instagram, you can adjust different settings to change the appearance of the final photo.

A good deal of confusion and 'stall' at the beginning of a project comes from needing to align everyone on a single and consistent story of what the project is all about, and why this is important.

It is key, in unlocking that narrative, to agree in a single sentence (my personal preference) the clear project brief. Using the mixing desk tool you, the project team and your problem owner can now see all the different and potential project brief definitions and choose the best one to answer. This brief will have the right balance of ambition and scope. It is neither so specific that the project team's creativity is stifled ('we just need a new flavour, price point, brand name, etc.') or so ambitious that your project is doomed to fail within days of starting ('we need a chip shop on the moon').

Alternative viewpoints from our colleagues can lead to cognitive dissonance at the start of a project. Just as we're excited about 'making more triangles for the business', new insights emerge that 'circles' are in vogue. We get good at doing nothing. Or certainly good at commissioning more research agencies to send in further field reports and conflicting consumer data. Moving the potential briefs up and down the mixing desk in relation to each other allows people to see in context the merits of one project brief over another. Remember, the aim of the session is to arrive at ONE PROJECT BRIEF. So when looking at a potential challenge, write out the first initial brief and place on the wall – this is your brief 001.

Then ask, 'why does this challenge need answering?' and post the answer(s) from the discussion that follows on the wall, alongside the original brief. This becomes brief 002, which is a different, broader challenge to solve. Follow this by asking the team, 'how could we answer this challenge?' This will lead to another set of options on what to do, which produces brief 003 and then 004, and so on.

Going back and forth with the team like this adjusts the ambition, a bit like adjusting the settings on a mixing desk. And plotting the discussion on the wall allows other people to see project progress and how the thinking has evolved and how decisions are being made.

Asking both 'why' and 'how' enriches the conversation and generates a range of possible briefs for the team and the problem owner to choose from as the 'final project brief' on which to work.

You don't have to use a wall. Sticky notes on a flip chart will work or notes moved around on a Miro canvas if online, but definitely keep all the thinking visual as opposed to verbal only, as this will help everyone see one potential brief and its merits against another.

RIGHT:
A flip chart showing the theory of the mixing desk.

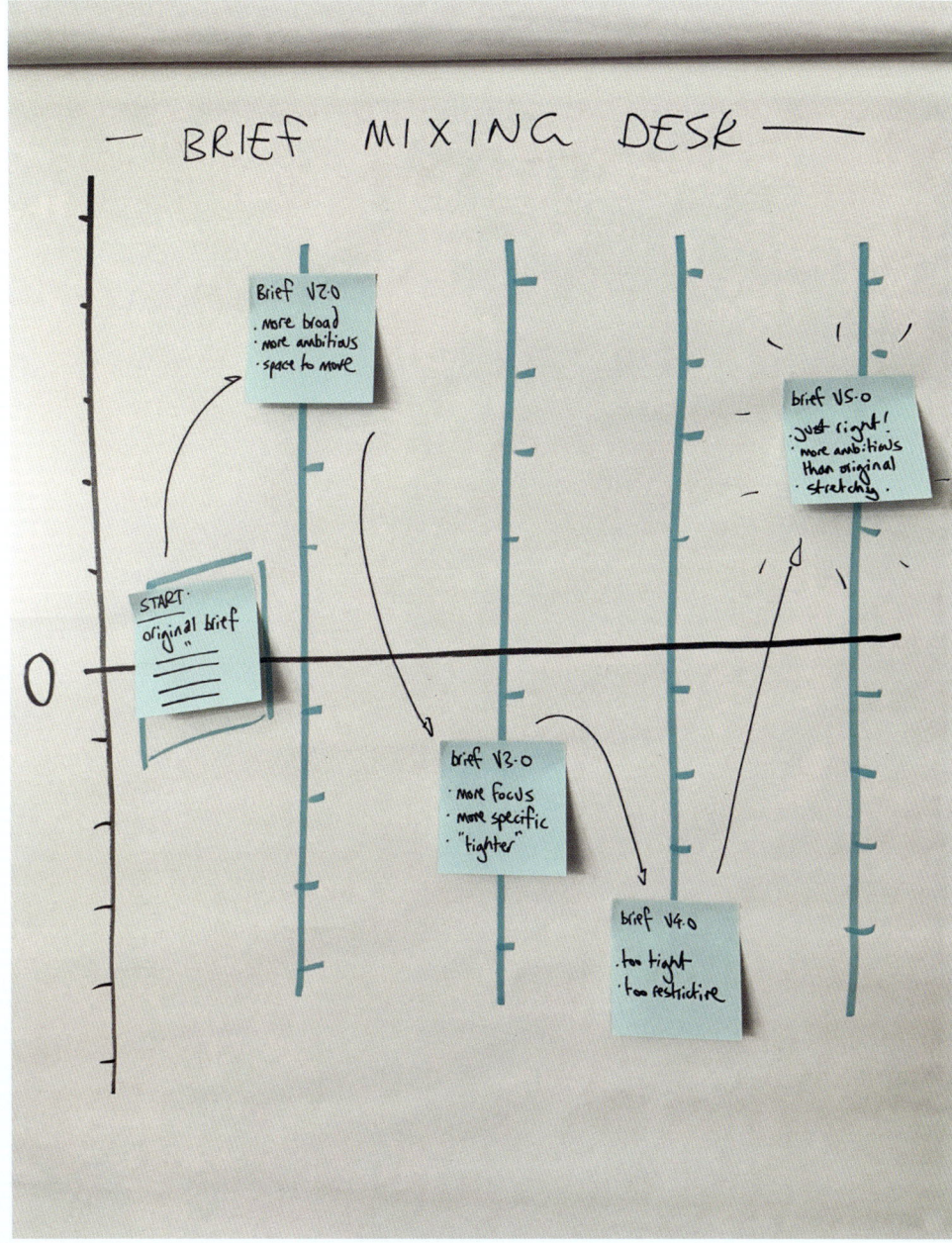

TOP TIPS

In my experience, you need theatre and space for this tool to work well. I was originally schooled to write a starting brief on a flip chart in the centre of a funnel and write two other briefs above and below. But I found that model a little static (see over page). And I noticed project teams struggled to rewrite alternative briefs, as they'd judge their efforts against the first brief and refuse to commit their thinking to paper.

It's far better to ask each project team member (and the problem owner) to consider learnings from previous scoping tools (WHYHAUS and TISSUE SESSION), and then write out the brief they think best for the project to answer. Then as a group, each brief can be discussed in turn and moved up and down the mixing desk as necessary. It might be that three or four clusters emerge from the project team, allowing you the richer opportunity to discuss with your problem owner which one is the most important aspect the project should answer. For example, 'Is this brief about "overall customer experience" as we've got a bunch of potential briefs about that topic or is it about "delighting and surprising" the customer? We've got another bunch of briefs on that theme, too. One might not be as broad as the other, but it will certainly provide us with focus.'

ABOVE:
A colleague of mine went onto the roof one morning and laid out a range of variations on the same brief. The broad ambitious ones were placed at the top of a funnel and the more specific towards the bottom. Seeing the variations all laid out like this helped us decide the right brief on which to work.

HONEYPOTS

An alternative to calibrating the briefs against each other using a mixing desk analogy (sometimes best suited for technical challenges) is to ask everyone to write the project brief as they see it in one sentence, lay it on the floor, and then go stand on another brief that's different to theirs but describes the same sentiment. Remember our System 1 and System 2 thinking (Yoda and Luke)? Like bees swarming around a pot of honey, people will gravitate towards a brief that intuitively looks like it's the same as theirs. Instructing people to 'think on their feet', literally, will get some energy going and force people to move out of their heads and focus on the main thing quickly. Fifteen people in a project team with a sponsor will whittle down to three or so project briefs that the problem owner can take away and think on overnight. They can then report back the following day with 'the exam question'. Neat.

EXAMPLE STORY

My co-facilitator, Joeri, and I were scoping a credit card project for HSBC. We were in Hong Kong, at HQ in Queens Road. We had around thirty people in the room, all somehow involved in the emerging brief of marketing cards.

We used the coffee example (see pages 130–131) to set the scene on why everyone needed to work to the right brief at the right level. We then asked everyone to split into small groups and discuss the learnings from the morning, where we'd heard from various project sponsors, senior stakeholders and other higher-ups who'd taken us through PowerPoint slides of market data and card performance. After leaving the teams to swap perspectives we laid a long line of tape on the floor with different 'honeypots' along its length. Each pot was named to roughly describe a range of potential project briefs (e.g. seasonal promotions, offers or partnerships). We asked everyone to write a one-sentence project brief definition and place it on the line.

The room was equally split. Half of the group wanted to work on a project brief to do with 'loyalty' and the other half believed the brief should be about 'acquisition'. The two briefs were at two extremes of the creative and tactical spectrum. Building brand loyalty won't happen by simply winning customers over through lowering interest rates and offering price promotions. Whilst card acquisition would be in HSBC's favour, such an advantage over other brands would be short term. Competitors could easily offer longer interest-free periods or more aggressive promotions to win back customers from HSBC. The current cycle to own more 'share of wallet' would never be broken.

As the project facilitators, we were in a position to show everyone why there had been an impasse where marketing interfaced with the business. This allowed the sponsors at the bank to reassess their long-term strategy about what to do and why. In the end, HSBC executed a card campaign focussing on acquiring new customers and we we ran a parallel project to develop ideas to complement the brand's long-term strategy to build customer loyalty. By identifying two separate briefs on which to work, HSBC avoided wasting time trying to bring the two problems together.

Facilitation tip 002
Telling is not facilitating

I know of a Senior Brand Leader who went on a 'raise standards' tour with her agencies and stakeholders to a handful of key cities around the world.

Over two days, she and her team sat at the front of the room and talked through a huge PowerPoint from beginning to end. Participants tell me they don't remember the content, other than that there was a great deal of it. They also tell me the whole thing came across as a huge telling off with no guidance on what to do next to raise standards.

'Telling' people is 'lazy schoolteacher' style. And adults don't listen like children, as their context is very different than when in school or college. Telling people great detail won't equal great learning, either, as telling from a PowerPoint doesn't allow for application of knowledge to the task at hand. You can't raise standards if people haven't the opportunity to be conscious of the work they are currently doing. At an objective level, they need to be aware of the new standards expected of them, be instructed on what to do, and have access to the skills and resources necessary to move from one state to the other. Finally, they need motivation supported by feedback loops to help get from A to B. It's not just about information. If it were that simple, we'd all stop smoking, never drop litter and keep under speed limits.

Work with your co-facilitator to map the participants' journey from where they are now to where you want them to be. In our business we take a call early on with the client and agree up front whether the brief is for people to learn or for the business to have a new output. We put things into either a 'capability' or a 'project' box. We can then work together on agreeing the activities that need to be briefed in and how to answer that question. It's rare you can do both at the same time brilliantly – doing and learning work symbiotically. But one will be the by-product of the other.

If you find yourself 'telling' all the time, you're at fault.

Especially if you've travelled the world at your company's expense, and you're muttering with exasperation, 'I've told those people at least five times what I want and they still don't get it.'

Facilitation tip 003
Just eat the strawberry

There's a mindfulness vibe at the moment. Being present. In the now. Truly connecting to what's going on inside us and around us.

I went to a mindfulness session (it's good to experiment). The facilitator asked me to eat a strawberry. I eagerly grasped at her punnet and chowed down a ripe strawberry as requested. So too did my fellow participants. Lots of 'Mmm, delicious, thanks!' from masticating mouths. We were then asked to eat another, but mindfully. We were all briefed to take a strawberry and really look at its texture and shape, and then to notice its weight in our hand and its colour, and our thoughts about how it might taste, and where we expected the taste to be on our tongue.

And then we were asked to place it slowly into our mouths and close our eyes, and then notice all the senses firing off... you get the idea. All very middle class and self-indulgent. It was all going very well; I was indeed tasting a rainbow. I thought it was a great way to stimulate all the senses and get some individual, personal experience around being mindful. It was a brilliant way to get participants to be mindful rather than simply discussing what it could be like. And who doesn't like strawberries, I thought. A really neat idea, and it seemed to be going down well.

It was just a huge shame when the facilitator then said, ' Maybe as you're eating this, think about it being the very last strawberry you'll ever eat, so really savour the experience.' I was being mindful – and then, being asked to think about it being my last strawberry ignited my imagination. The instruction was a stimulus. It could have been passive, careless or deliberate, but I was no longer 'at one' with my taste buds, and instead I was blindfolded in a Mexican jail, awaiting the firing squad with a summer fruit in my mouth. That's what 'maybe think about... ', as a throw away comment, got me to do.

If you want your participants to notice something important to them, allow them to do so. Don't distract people by giving them other things to think about.

If you're going to eat the strawberry, just eat the strawberry!

Tool 004
Rumsfeld's Matrix & Columbo's Question

Aim: for project team participants to individually and collectively exhaust final questions, comments and perspectives about the project brief.

In 2002, the then U.S. Secretary of Defence, Donald Rumsfeld, said at a press conference in reply to a question about weapons of mass destruction in Iraq: ' ...there are known knowns: there are things we know we know. There are known unknowns, that is to say we know there are some things we do not know. But there are also unknown unknowns – the ones we don't know we don't know.'

It's quite a tongue twister! But grammatically and philosophically correct. The web is now littered with Rumsfeld Matrixes. Some of these are worth having a look at as the memes make for good flip charts that get people chuckling.

LEFT:
Discussing Columbo's question leads to further knowledge around an emerging brief.

I use the concept of known unknowns as a way of priming an innovation project team during project scoping, to map topics which they're certain of, feel informed about and confident in. At the same time, we can also map areas of 'unknown' we believe still need to be scoped further, 'just to be sure' we're satisfying our hunches that all has been asked and answered before we move to an insight or ideas phase in a project.

WHAT TO DO & HOW IT WORKS
Have two areas of the room (or a Miro board if you're doing this digitally), one dedicated to the 'known knowns' and the other to the 'known unknowns'. Subtitle these with a bit of context around your project. Take your group to each zone in turn and drop on two to three examples of knowledge gained or knowledge needed that have arisen from your project scoping so far.

During your explanation you'll notice your project team nod happily that they understand. Watch out that they're not being complacent and simply making obvious and high-level lists in each of the two areas. The tool works well if you then split your scoping team into pairs ('Donalds' and 'Columbos'). Group together all the Columbos and ask that they each put a set of questions they've yet to ask the problem owner on the 'known unknowns' board. In addition to their questions, they can also add on a handful of subject areas they still feel need to be further explored. The download doesn't need to be neat or make sense to an outsider – it's just important that the 'unknowns' are captured somehow.

Then, ask their buddies in the Donalds group to discuss all the information they think is the most important to retain and share regarding the current brief. A good way to initiate this is to ask them to prepare a press conference briefing about the project. This creative activity will force people to 'cut to the chase' and rally around a consistent story about what the project brief is and why it's important. As the facilitator you've now created two audiences on either side of this emerging brief.

Appoint a couple of people in each team to speak on behalf of everyone. Ask the Donald team to go first and explain the brief. Then ask the Columbo team to reply with questions and comments about what's missing based on the questions they've just been adding to the 'known unknowns' board. It might be that during the discussion some of these questions are covered off.

Collectively you can then populate a third flip chart with the agreed questions from the group that need to be answered by the problem owner in the next round of scoping in this tool. I like to call that session of Q&A with the problem owner 'Just one more thing'.

This name (and, of course the second team name) is inspired by TV detective *Columbo*, who would pause at the doorway of a crime scene, act on his hunch and ask an innocent question to a suspect. The question would yield a critical part of the homicide puzzle. The overly polite and apparently disorganised Columbo, to the irritation of the suspects and their accomplices, would then piece together the crime and reveal the guilty party – all in a neat ninety-minute episode. Genius.

Taking the problem owner aside a day or two later, and with a smaller team, is worth doing when running the 'Just one more thing' session. You can present learnings so far from other scoping tools, which sets the context for the conversation you're about to have

AND allows the problem owner to hear back what's already been shared. They can calibrate their answers and tidy up any nuances in language, and of course confirm facts, figures, dates and deadlines regarding the brief.

TOP TIPS

Spread your scoping sessions for this tool out over time, if possible. If you're facilitating in-house this might be easier to organise. The nature of business as usual might dictate you only have a handful of meetings with the problem owner as their time is taken up elsewhere. Use this perceived difficulty as a structure to plan your sessions.

If you're running scoping as part of a project off-site and the answer needs to be 'hot-housed' in a week or so, then I advise the session be split over an evening – allowing everyone to revisit the topics discussed in the morning with fresh energy. Remember that a good deal of our processing is subconscious. A great amount of those deeper connections are made as we rest. There's a reason why the older generation would advise big decisions are best made 'having slept on it'.

A MAN WALKS INTO A BAR...

A note about my examples and gender bias. If you're reading this book in a linear fashion, you'll have spotted my analogies and stories are quite male. So far, we've had Luke and Yoda from *Star Wars*, Tom Cruise, *Men in Black*, and now Donald Rumsfeld and Columbo. At the time of writing, I am nearly fifty. My formative years were in the 1980s. I am a product of (and a contributor to) that history. I grew up on a heady diet of American TV and yacht rock. My role models and fantasy idols fought aliens, flew fighter jets and *never put Baby in the corner*.

As we'll see in the Insight chapter, I've used these cultural signposts to help explain how people think and navigate the world. My bias is not a surprise (and certainly ought not be framed as a bad thing). You, too, have your biases and they ought to be explored and used as part of the creative process. It was tempting to replace Donald Rumsfeld and Columbo with female equivalents simply to balance out gender representations. But this is not the way.

Creativity demands that we explore alternatives. In this instance, I think it's brilliant that we use popular culture to help re-express (and, in this case, disguise) an activity that essentially is writing lists on paper. But as the facilitator you must be able to tell a story enthusiastically and authentically. I get an intellectual buzz from discussing the thinking of Donald Rumsfeld. And I feel warm, emotional and nostalgic when I remember watching *Columbo* on Sunday evenings as a family. Those characters have contributed to my map of the world and how I think, present and manage people. Both give me energy, and it's an energy that I can bring into the room. You need, as a creative facilitator, to find and use your icons and stories, too. If they be Oprah, Kylie Minogue or Melinda Gates, so be it. But don't just swap out 'because'. Instead, here are four pieces of advice:

1. Be connective and irreverent
The *logic* of Rumsfeld and the *behaviour* of Columbo are the aspects of the tool that give this activity its magic. The quality of the discussion would be lost if you simply asked participants to list facts on one sheet and questions on the other. It's dull. If we're being innovative, we need to constantly embrace the opportunity to prod people's imagination so they get used to making new connections. When it comes to the ideas phase of the project, your project team (and the output) will be all the better for it.

2. 'Own' your characters – in your story
An old boss of mine, Octavius (yes, quite a name) was fantastic with senior executives. He told great stories – Greek legends, historical allegories and anecdotes about political figures at that time. He could do so as he was expensively educated, incredibly well read and mixed in political circles. No better person for the job. There was no way I could emulate him with the same stories, name drop the same people, and land the point, learning or principle with the same success. My advice then is don't copy the storyteller. Too many people confuse the singer with the song. Columbo, Luke, Tom Cruise and 'Dad jokes' work for me, because that's who I am. I am a living soup of those references and I use them to create an experience.

Given the right set-up we can be unapologetically human about who we are and bring our uncensored experience and approach to life for the benefit of others.

3. Beware borrowed interest
If you swap out a story, example or character from your facilitation toolkit and replace it with another (for whatever reason), ask yourself 'is the learning still there 100%?' I believe you can make almost any character or analogy work if you follow the advice above. However, make sure you rehearse your briefing with someone naive to your project (who isn't the client), so you arrive at the best sequence of instructions. For example, if it involves movement and a series of multi-layered instructions: 'You lot, jump up and down like penguins, whilst this group throw wet sponges at you' without *any* context as to why, it won't win you any favours, and it's likely to end in tears.

4. Ask YouTube
I've yet NOT to find a video short on YouTube that can't bring to life the concept we're sharing in less than two minutes. Movie clips, I think, are far better than a 25-minute TED TALK. And remember that a TV commercial is a story from start to end, in thirty seconds. I think a good scoping session starts off by telling a few stories of times when the right question was answered. To make that task easier, use large visuals from movies and TV, and tell stories about the PEOPLE that solved the puzzle. We remember stories about people and not the process, and this sets the scene for the people in the room with you to begin a similar quest.

Tool 005
Angels & Demons

Aim: to help map the people in the business who will influence the progress and success of the project.

I mentioned earlier in the WHYHAUS tool that people politics is a factor in making a project happen. Anyone reading this who works within an organisation will know this to be true. We've all got anecdotes about projects that died because of people who stopped things before they started. In every business there's a group of 'just so' people who constantly (and perhaps rightly) need to be managed. In pharma there's the 'compliance' team, in banking there's the 'risk' team and, for some of our clients, projects are often sent back to the drawing board because of 'legal'.

No one turns up at work each day to deliberately bring you misery, but I appreciate there are people whose actions, behaviours and emails all add up to putting the 'no' in innovation. When you're scoping a project, you and the project team need to have this conversation with the problem owner. Identify where the angels shine. Find where the demons lurk.

Angels are people who:
- Enter a room accompanied by hope, possibility and wonder.
- Will champion your project when you're not about.
- Will speak positively about the benefits of this project in the context of the business.
- Come to your defence in a room you're not standing in.
- FInd you in the corridor to ask you how it's going.

Demons are people who:
- Enter a room, and all hope leaves.
- Might feel threatened by your project ambition (for whatever reason, the threat is real for them).
- Are gatekeepers to resources who (even without reason) could put on the brakes.
- Become distant stakeholders whose names pop up from time to time in hushed tones.
- Write anonymous emails: 'Brains in a jar', as one of my team says.

There's nothing Machiavellian about identifying who's out there. In fact, objectively and visually mapping the political landscape as you scope a project is key. Consider a project as an object with just two sides – like a beer coaster, for example. One side of the project is the side you see. It faces out. It has a name, a brand, a public reputation. People can point at this project and say, 'Look, there it is, isn't it marvellous, aren't you lucky to be a part of it'. The other side of the coaster sits face down on the table. No one sees that side. It's obscured from view. It's the behind-the-scenes half of the project equation. It's often in darkness. No one sees the actions and activities here. It's the legs of the swan beneath the water, paddling frantically but giving the illusion of calm and poise.

You get the message – we need to love everyone and kill with kindness.

You are often facilitating project sessions in the public world. You book rooms, order kit, make a noise, stick up coloured paper, host weekly town halls and daily stand-ups. People enjoy working with you and it's all rather 'broadcast'. Meanwhile, in the unseen world of people management you're also facilitating the meetings, interactions, reactions and emotions of everyone else's sensitivity. On Monday, you're listening to a nervous brand manager whose sales strategy is under the microscope. By Wednesday you're saying sorry to the facilities team for the unidentified stain on the boardroom carpet. You need to manage it all. And it starts at the scoping stage.

WHAT TO DO & HOW IT WORKS
First, make a list of all the angels. Then, next to their name, give them a superpower. Nothing silly like flying (although that would be cool), but instead a genuine quality you and the project team believe that person brings constantly to interactions. This could be 'always enthusiastic', or 'starts each meeting by asking questions', or 'a source of updates and insights from the marketing team'.

Be clear, the superpower is a behaviour you can spot as a constant.

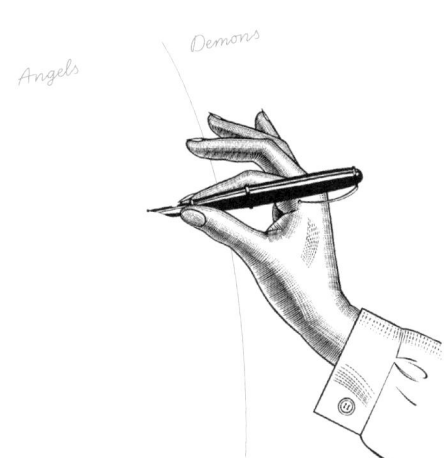

Next, make a list of all the Demons. And next to their name, give them a 'strength overdone'.

A strength overdone is a quality that can stifle progress when there's 'too much' of it. Consider 'likes the details': it's admirable to request the right information in a timely fashion. It's good to ask for clarity around facts and figures. Demanding high standards for quality and precision is a strength. But when overdone, not meeting these standards could be an excuse for not making a decision. Not having all the information could be a reason not to realise a resource. Being late with a report could be misinterpreted as tardiness.

Asking your team to identify the 'strengths overdone' for each demon is a smart way to think about what matters to these stakeholders near and far. When you and the project team step inside the shoes of others, you're all likely to act with more empathy and sensitivity. The project narrative becomes less about what's in it for you and more about how this project benefits others. 👉

Now place all the characters in an 'influence and comms' grid (see example below). This grid has communications metaphors as headings for each square; as your style and format of interaction changes for each audience, decide on your own headings accordingly.

The four box titles don't point to *how* you should communicate with your audiences, that is for you to navigate, as you know the personalities best.

This tool can be a hoot. You can give your angels and demons nicknames along the lines of a common theme, such as the Harry Potter one in the example shown. In the privacy and protective bubble of a project team it's fun to issue superpowers and let off steam about a few 'Voldemorts' but remind everyone that 'what goes on in Vegas...' and remain respectful about your Angels and your Demons; they are just trying to navigate the world of work too. Then, following on from this, the practical learning of how to keep the right people informed to the right level at the right time will be invaluable in keeping the project on track and moving forward.

Involving the project owner, or not, as part of this scoping tool, is ultimately down to you and what your gut is saying. The context of you being an inside or an external facilitator will be a factor. Impartiality or familiarity are both attractive qualities but difficult bedfellows. Truisms exist: 'knowledge is power' and 'familiarity breeds contempt'. That's why you as the facilitator should also be one of the characters on the grid and have the team talk about you and your influence on the project, too.

Condé Nast

Keep these characters informed. 'Information out' communication. A bit like a magazine subscription, regular updates from you, but not necessarily detailed.

Hagrid – weekly updates; email one-pager

Read all about it

These characters need to be managed closely and informed regularly about the project. Seek their advice and counsel, and listen to their concerns and ideas.

Dumbledore – key project sponsor; weekly one-to-one

In the post

A bit like leaflets through the door (or sales emails in your inbox), these characters can receive a lite touch of information about the project.

McGonagall – monthly summary on project learnings

#didyouknow

Speak to these people regularly and keep them informed. The key here is to be engaging but without needing to disclose project details.

Hermione and her team – weekly 30-minute meeting

RIGHT:
Assigning key players their own superhero action figures is another memorable option for this tool.

STORY

When working as Head of Innovation, I reported to the COO. He was time poor, but critical to my world. I was certain he'd be championing my efforts in rooms I hadn't access to. And I knew people I worked with would report back to him on what we'd been doing.

Each Friday afternoon, I wrote a single email as I knew he'd be on the train out of London for a few hours. My email was always a one-page attachment. I'd detail what I'd been up to that week, with whom and what my thoughts were about the following week. It was a simple format that acted as a diary of events and progress for us both.

In each entry, I was careful to signal what, who, when and how, and sign off with something personal. I'm convinced he pulled a few levers on my behalf without me asking. We never spoke about it. But when I left, he took me aside and said it was always the first thing he looked forward to reading on the way home.

Interview
Kirsten Gillard
FACILITATOR, COACH, PROJECT OWNER

Kirsten has excelled as a brilliant project leader and facilitator throughout her long career in the creative industries and media landscape. Kirsten's passion for people and culture has grown over time and she is now a partner in a coaching consultancy dedicated to helping people, teams and organisational cultures to change, grow and thrive.

You've been facilitating projects in the creative industries for many years — what's the immediate advice you can give to ensure creative projects go well?
Bringing an idea physically to life is as vital as conceiving the idea. Keep reminding people about the end point and build alignment. As projects evolve, things change, more people are involved, and the focus can shift away from the initial concept. Therefore, keep contributors honest to the end vision. Create ongoing communication points throughout the delivery: at the beginning, the middle and at the end. Often, many individuals and companies have to collaborate to deliver a concept; ensure everyone is looped in and understands the impact and known effect if deadlines are met.

To secure sign-off on an idea, you'll often need the approval of senior people — what top tips have you got to engage leaders?
You need to understand what the stakeholder really wants from your idea. It sounds obvious but it's often overlooked. And involve the stakeholders in the journey of creation. It is far easier to reach agreement if stakeholders have helped to shape the concept and feel connected to the journey. Ideas won't then come as a surprise! Understand your audience, too — some people are numbers orientated, some are more creatively focused so I tailor my narrative to suit. Sometimes this means putting effort into exciting people. A fond memory I have is of a pitch where we vividly brought a concept to life for the panel of senior decision-makers. We ensured they physically experienced what was at the heart of the idea; the playback of that idea was bold and unforgettable, the audience couldn't ignore the passion and the excitement of the idea or the team. A PowerPoint simply wouldn't have cut it in this instance and they probably wouldn't have signed it off.

How do you tackle negativity towards fresh thinking?
When developing ideas, negativity can sometimes present itself. My advice is to involve the people who at first you might feel are naysayers. Involve, listen and show your gratitude. It's a mistake to exclude them. Listen to their opinions, try to understand where they are coming from and bring them on the journey. In my experience, people just want to help. By ignoring that you might be missing a trick. Listen to all perspectives; they might just add to the power of the end result.

Also, make sure you have a handful of brave people who are prepared to drive projects with determination and use these to set the bar for others to follow. And generate an army of supporters who share the same positive beliefs as you; they will act as beacons when negativity shows up.

Can you tell me why you enjoy working with a buddy facilitator so much?
Although I'm happy running sessions by myself, I really love working with a buddy. You can be more spontaneous when you have someone to spark off. A 'wingman' can help you tackle challenges or any negativity head-on together – we can bounce tactics off each other and prevent each other from taking negativity personally. The diversity of our combined thoughts and approaches in the planning phase can be really beneficial.

I've spotted that when working in a pair we can be reactive and make changes in a relaxed fashion and not feel panicked. The participants get to experience different delivery styles, too – voice, tempos, styles, stories and energy. All that helps keep them engaged and the sessions become more enjoyable for everyone. And, critically, you will get a chance to rest and read the room, whilst your partner is on their feet.

You've told me how fast-paced your world can be – what do you do to prep yourself and the sessions when you're time-poor?
Before I run my sessions I spend time considering the wider happenings of the business at that time. Awareness that people need to be in other meetings, might have important legal emails to answer, and that other deadlines and deliverables are happening all the time is useful. Having a well-defined creative process with clear steps can really help facilitators to plan quickly and cut to the chase. Ideas sessions are a little like decorating, you need to do the prep first to ensure the finished article is pleasing to the eye.

What is a final nugget of genius you'd like to share?
Despite good intentions from everyone, it can be really hard to make ideas happen. For an idea to live in a business you need to make time to see it through. People don't sign off ideas on rationale alone. There's a mixture of the obvious and measurable, and also the feel and instinct behind an idea.

Frankly speaking, for an idea to happen in a big business you've got to doggedly pursue it. If the eleventh hour falls and still nothing is agreed, then you've just got to make it happen. There's a fine line between belligerence and determination and I think the best facilitators know when to step over for the greater good. I love being a part of making things happen. It's a lovely feeling watching others do it, too.

"I love being a part of making things happen."

– KIRSTEN GILLARD

Tool 006
Pirates vs Navy

Aim: using a bit of fun and theatre to help the project participants gather energy and connection around the project brief.

In 1805, Admiral Nelson gathered his ships' captains, lieutenants and junior officers around the captain's table. He fed them a hearty meal and opened the rum... 'Gents, I have a plan. It's a bit left-field, but go with me. Hardy, bring me a flip chart... ' (This isn't historically accurate, but the following is.) Nelson explained that as part of Napoleon's plans to invade England, the combined fleets of the French and Spanish navy were amassing to take control of the English Channel, to provide the Grande Armée safe passage. Boo, hiss.

Nelson's fleet was outnumbered (27 ships to 33). The Spanish and French ships were some of the largest in the world. The British fleet was outgunned, too. Back in the day, the usual 'operating model' of fighting a battle at sea was lining up your ships parallel to the enemy. Opposing sides would fire cannons at each other until the losing side's ships sank or surrendered. It was brutal and bloody. And such was life in the navy outside of rum, sodomy and the lash.

Nelson knew that following current tactical orthodoxy wouldn't beat the French and Spanish fleet. He needed a new plan. He commanded his captains to sail at 90 degrees to the enemy, a bit like a battering ram. Splitting the line of enemy ships into three, the British fleet was to then circle the middle third of the broken fleet and, ship to ship, fight it out on either side.

At the time, the way to communicate orders at sea was using flags. Hence, Nelson's flagship, *Victory*, was positioned at the head of the fleet. Nelson insisted that his plan was to be followed exactly until the line of ships was broken. It was then over to the captains to essentially 'make it up as they went along', as they were in uncharted waters (no pun intended). Nelson explained that because his flagship would be obscured in the melée of battle, it was far better that captains took matters into their owns hands, changing tactics moment to moment, rather than hope to see orders from a distance. 'England expects every man to do his duty' was, in fact, the only signal he issued using flags, while he stood on the poop deck of the *Victory* as battle commenced. The rest is history.

The naval battle resulted in 22 Spanish and French ships being lost, while the British lost none. The Spanish and French lost 4,000 men, the British 400. Poor Nelson got shot in the chest and died five months later of his wounds, which is a bit of a project minus. However, at nearly 60 metres in height, Nelson's Column in Trafalgar Square is a visceral reminder to London's tourists that the British were victorious.

Nelson's design was a bit navy – have a plan, follow orders – and a bit pirate: make it up as you go along. The best of both combined, the outcome of which is still remembered by proud flag-waving Britons (and naval historians) to this day. This scoping tool combines these two different mindsets to help start crafting a plan on how your project should progress as you move towards the end of the scoping phase. 👉

LEFT:
Execute to a plan like the Navy or act first and ask questions later; be more pirate!

WHAT TO DO & HOW IT WORKS

Split your project team into two groups: the navy and the pirates (yes, this is best done with a bit of fancy dress).

The 'navy' are to sit in an orderly fashion, consider the facts of the project, scoping in silence and then discuss as a team what to do. They then write out a six- to eight-point plan (one page on a flip chart) of what the immediate next steps for the project should be. Appoint an Admiral and a Captain to jointly facilitate that group. Embrace the giggles and smirks, and encourage that team to literally march off to complete the task.

Meanwhile, Team Pirate are to thrash out a five-point plan as a team. All voices are equal. No suggestion shall be squashed; encourage your pirates to go wild with their plans of what to do next and how. They're the *opposite* of the navy (where a deliberate project strategy needs to be crafted and communicated). Instead, pirates keep their eye on the big prize (getting to the answer) and will keep that treasure in mind as a motivator whilst they work out their creative tactics. Again, coax out everyone's inner-Blackbeard and set them off to plan the project as a troop of rapscallion swashbucklers – Arrggghhh!

Instruct both teams to present their plans (in character or not) to each other. Each team is to listen and take notes accordingly.

As a project facilitator, you've invited everyone to have input on the plan of 'what next'. Of course, you'll have a design for the next phase of the project, but the team's insight and their collective perspectives is valuable to you. Having run this session over a number of projects, ranging from the technical to the strategic, it always offers something that helps me think differently about 'what next' and 'how'.

I've noticed a handful of starter ideas emerge at this stage that can be safely set aside for later. I also get a sense, from the discussions and presentations, of who in the team is invested in the project. The navy/pirate analogy quickly becomes a shorthand for team members to thrash out thinking. You can ask 'what would the navy do?' if you sense the team is stuck. And invite other team members to 'be more pirate' if you sense they're holding back on their suggestions.

My top tip here is to not get carried away with the theatre of it all. The story told at the start is a good one to set the scene. *A bit of a plan* and *freedom to move* within the plan is what you're after.

Another analogy that works is classical vs jazz. For classical music to move an audience every note must be correct and played at the right tempo, in time with all the other notes from the whole orchestra. A conductor waves a baton to keep everyone working together in harmony. All musicians have parts of the same score and tune their instruments to the same pitch as the oboe. The contribution of many makes the sound of the whole. We cannot fail to be moved by the cathedral of sound when a full philharmonic orchestra is in full swing.

Conversely, jazz musicians open up a piece of music with 'the head'. This establishes the main theme and melody, then after that it's over to each musician to experiment, explore and expand on the head in their improvised performance.

If you'd like to use this analogy, again, split your project team into two groups – team classical and team jazz – and explain that each group is to prepare a project plan using approaches from the two disciplines of music.

Regardless of the metaphor, free discussion is to be encouraged as you and the project team begin to close the door on the scoping phase. You're now almost ready to land the high-level plan of what to do next and which sequence of events will take you on a journey to the answer. Let's look at one final tool to help bring it all together.

Facilitation tip 004
Team names

Big populations of people get more done when put into groups.

Getting the size right, the briefing, the instructions and the timings all matter, but knowing that you belong to a group and that your group has an identity is key.

Team selection ought to involve a bit of fun. I like gathering up people who all have the same colour shoes, or who set their alarms within 10 minutes of each other. Random selection alleviates over-thinking about who needs to team up with whom.

But please, don't give teams numbers once chosen. Instead of Teams 1, 2, 3 and 4, I live to embrace some 80's pop – teams Agnetha, Benny, Anni-Frid and Björn (for example) but you'll find something equally charming. And if stuck, topical names inspired by the morning news feed perhaps. Anything but numbers. No one likes being in Team 4. Because, deep down, being in Team 4 sucks.

Tool 007
Mozart tool

Aim: for the project facilitator and sponsor to agree the plan on how to answer the brief, now it's been thoroughly scoped.

Mozart was a genius, he created fantastic symphonies in his head, with hundreds of thousands of notes all working in harmony. His music moves you. Symphonies are *big* things, made up of *little* notes. Tackling a project, at first, can be overwhelming, as it appears to be a big symphony – large and difficult to take in at once. This is a tool to help break your thinking up at the start of that *big* project so you can handle all the *little* parts of it.

Towards the end of project scoping, and whilst using the other tools in parallel, I'm making a mental note of what's been discussed and agreed. I can then complete the Mozart tool and use it as a focus with my clients to agree the final details and next stages of our projects. This tool is great to capture what's been agreed so far and will prompt creative thinking as you shift from scoping into the next phase of your project.

WHAT TO DO & HOW IT WORKS
Create a big version of the canvas, right, and answer the questions on it:

M: MISSION
What is the big mission for the project? What's the one big thing you're going for and why? (And if you can capture that in one sentence, even better).

O: OBJECTIVES
What are the targets you want to achieve, or what is the current status quo you'll see a shift in, that will prove you're making progress towards the mission? Remember, objectives are something you can measure a change in. What gets measured often gets done!

Z: ZERO
What is the absolute minimum objective you need to achieve for this project to avoid being called a failure by you and the problem owner?

A: ACTIONS
What is the sequence of events that you believe will lead you to securing those objectives? If you were to write a five-point plan on one sheet of paper, for example, what would that be? Do some of these steps need to be broken up smaller?

R: RESOURCES
What resources are needed to make this project happen: People? Time? Budget? Space? Tech? They are all part of the project 'kit'.

T: TACTICS
And finally, what is the first thing that would happen if the project started tomorrow? Who does what, by when and how?

Using MOZART organises thinking. A daunting project doesn't seem so overwhelming now, does it?

Using this tool also allows you to objectively coach another team member on their challenge. Once you've run from top to bottom of the tool as a draft, you can then share your thoughts on some of their responses to the questions and prompts. This fosters a co-creation discussion and further builds on the plan.

The MOZART tool is not to capture ideas. The tool orders thinking and creates a plan, capturing the big ambitious stuff at the top, and the smaller details towards the end. It orders your discoveries and thinking in a hierarchy. Completing the tool by hand and taking the time to connect to the questions and answers, I believe, ladders your knowledge about your project in your mind's eye.

TOP TIPS

Before asking other groups to use this tool on a live project, it's a good idea to pair people up and get them to use it on a personal project they're in the first steps of exploring. This could be planning a family holiday, a birthday party, re-modelling the house or even searching for a new car. Something people already have an affinity with (as they've likely gone on that journey before) that will get their heads in the right space to apply the tool to the project at hand. In addition, my co-facilitator and I have rehearsed

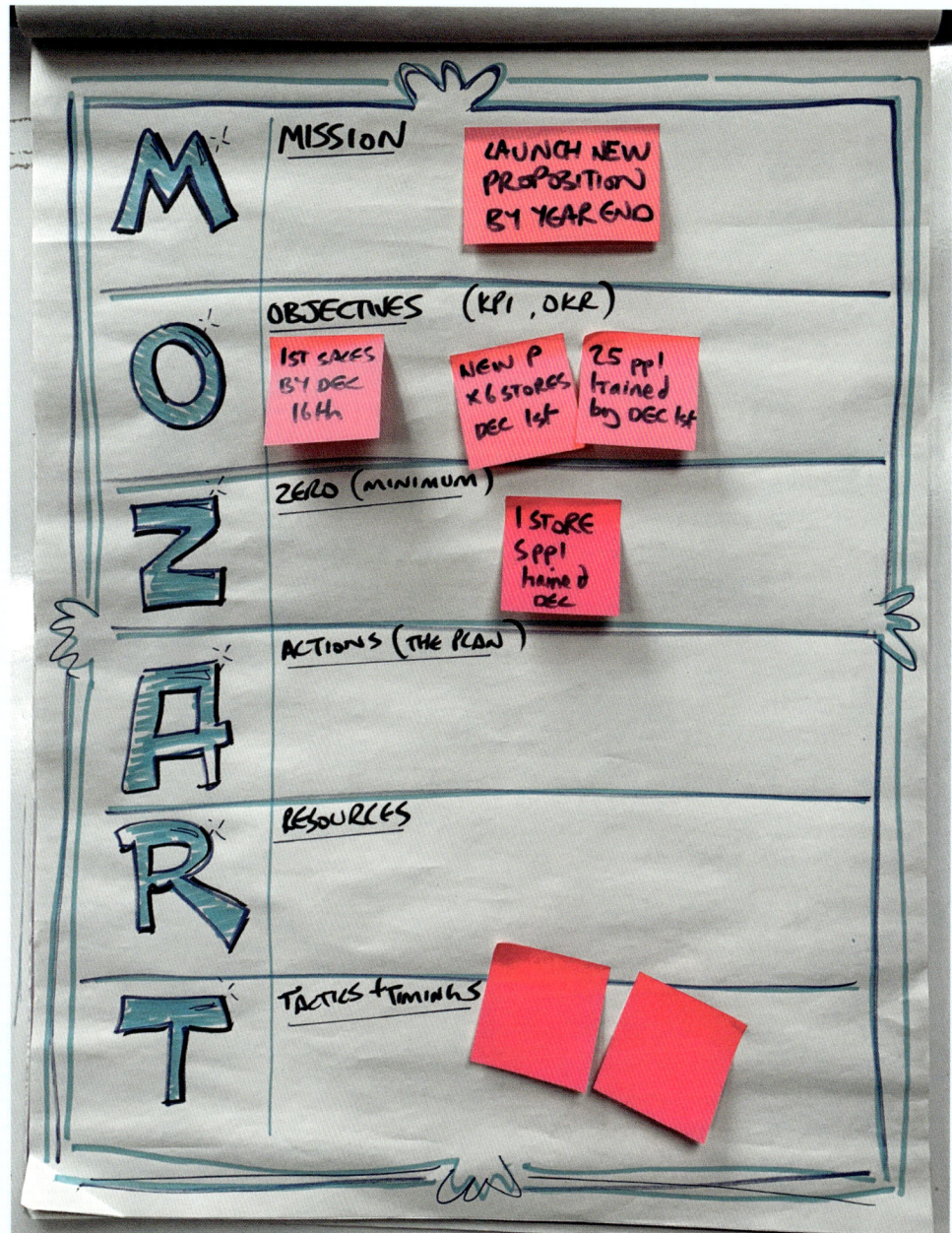

some questions and potential answers relevant to the project in hand ready to populate the tool at speed – that way when we're explaining we can just focus on the reactions of project participants rather than try and make up questions and considered answers on the spot. An example of how the tool works might be as follows:

M = transform cafés closed at night into bars/tap rooms in the evenings
O = sell more beers/wine/lite food, 100 customers per event
Z = pilot with one café by end of month, minimum 20 customers
A = agree date with café, meeting with brewery staff, advertise in press
R = printing shop, local brewery, agreed budget
T = Jenny as project co-ordinator, Sam sort beer, Dave organise press release

You can experiment with A4 copies for individuals and land group discussions on larger versions. I think hand drawn tools look best and feel more creative. So, it's worth asking people to draw their own MOZART chart to coach each other on.

For remote facilitation, the MOZART tool works really well on Miro software. Having the tool locked down and then adding content using coloured post-its is my preference. Those notes and comments can then be copied and lifted into other parts of the project storyboard as you create more content. Always take a photo, however, of the master flip chart that you briefed the tool in from, and save in an area on the Miro board dedicated to the workshop instructions.

Sharing a completed MOZART tool with a project team sends a signal that the project scoping phase is over. Having a copy to hand makes it easier, when asked about the project status, to retrieve useful and clear answers for those who are interested. Be that a ten-second update in the lift or a ten-minute chat over Zoom.

I like to carry a printout of the MOZART around with me after the scoping phase (even if it's a photo of the flip chart on which the team scribbled answers). Then, whenever I'm asked by project sponsors, I've got the story of work done so far to hand. And having the scoping output on one page might make it easier to ask sponsors and stakeholders for additional help in securing some of the structures needed to keep the project moving. At a glance they can see your request in the wider context of the project's big ambition – it's easier for them to say 'yes'

INSIGHT IGNITOR

INFORMATION

What random information does this project team already have about this subject matter that we believe might be immediately useful?

e.g. Consumer feedback, press and web look-ups, company myth and legend, hearsay: 'I saw this the other day . . .' etc.

INSIGHTS

What well-crafted insights do we have already that we can challenge and explore further?

e.g. Insight team shares recent project findings.

INTELLIGENCE

What organised intelligence (intel) do we have in and around the business that can help us with this project?

e.g. Past project outputs, project reports, market research summaries, internal audit information, sales figures.

INTUITION

What do we intuitively feel we ought to explore, both obvious and to the extreme, to stretch our thinking?*

in this situation, rather than to an isolated question in an email that pops up. A final tip is to add a seventh box. Do this in a separate session, one that needn't last very long. It acts as a full stop to the scoping phase and a start to the insight-gathering phase of the process. I call these sessions **Insight Ignitors**.

In this session, ask team members their answers to four questions (shown in the Insight Ignitor panel opposite) and have an open discussion where you record the answers on a chart. The conversation can capture all the information about this project that you and the team believe will help create insights and inspiration for new ideas.

This session provides a brilliant opportunity for the project team to download their unordered thinking in an orderly fashion. Remember the chapter about the brain – we're constantly processing information, most of it subconsciously. You and the project participants will have been generating insights, thoughts and starter ideas about this project from the moment you first read the brief. The scoping tools help identify which project brief is the right one to work on. But, they are not insight-

* Answers to the final question can be identified by using the SUSPECT FRUIT MACHINE tool in the next chapter.

creating or idea-generating tools. You and your project team would be making connections stimulated by the scoping discussions. In your sessions, you may have picked up on people jumping ahead and losing the context of scoping, and instead generating hypotheses and beliefs about how to answer the brief. Use the insight ignitor session as a way for people to decompress their subconscious.

As always, record the discussions visually – allow people to see you write down what they say, and allow them to write down what they think is going on. Have the Insight Ignitor to hand for them to land their opinions, observations and thoughts on.

When people can 'see' their own thinking, and that of others, it becomes far easier to make connections and arrive at new insights. There is a reason we have phrases in our language such as 'joining the dots', 'not seeing the wood for the trees' and 'pieces of the puzzle'. These metaphors and analogies are accurate descriptions of how we join information together to make sense of the world. And when facilitating the next phase of project work (the Insight phase) we must embrace the power of storytelling, narrative and metaphor in order to unlock the mysteries of how people think and feel. In doing so, we can provide answers to their needs with the products and propositions you and your business want to deliver.

SUMMARY

Scoping is about transforming an initial, messy business challenge into a clear and compelling brief that a project team are excited to solve. It's okay to arrive at a brief that has evolved little from the original problem statement as long as you've explored options, scenarios and asked all the questions – never assume a project brief at the start is fit and healthy to work on.

Having a single notion that everyone on the project fully understands is what matters. When you, the facilitator, your project sponsor and the project team participants are all aligned and excited about what the business wants and why, then you're ready to move further on the journey.

During scoping, ideas on what to do will have popped up in discussions. Insights, too, about consumers and the business will have also emerged. And it's here we move onto the second stage of the process...

The Process

2_INSIGHT

The second stage of the process is insight. Insights are the hidden truths driving our mindsets and behaviour. In the context of a creative project, insights are the raw ingredients that power ideas. But remember, process is a misleading sequence of events; and there are hundreds of insight tools out there to choose from.

Instead of focusing on insight tools and data, it's far better you and your project team participants focus on being insightful. When everyone is behaves in a more insightful fashion, it's easier to spot patterns in human behaviour and be inspired to have ideas for consumers' lives.

The intro bit

RIGHT:
Insight is spotting what matters to people and building that into stories we want to act on.

There are three main parts to this chapter. The first sets the scene for insights; what they are and why they matter to the creative process. The second part is a series of 'warm up' activities, all intended to build insightfulness in your teams. There is no 'one way' to generate insights as everyone makes connections differently. But insightfulness is a behaviour we can all learn and develop, and it's far easier to do so reflecting on our personal experiences and learnings from working in a team. The third and final part of the chapter provides you with guidance on how to facilitate insight development in project work. I share our approach – and then leave you with some tips to develop your own approach in the future.

Ultimately, the insight stage of a project is about spotting tensions in people's lives, telling meaningful stories about those tensions and being clear on what jobs people want to get done. Having these components in a compelling narrative that everyone in your project team can share will give you the best springboard for idea generation. For some, insight is about rigorous facts and data – THIS IS NOT THE WAY. Let's first step back from the detail and return to the basics.

Being insightful is something we're all capable of. In fact, we probably act on our insights a few times each day when we need to make decisions around work or home, sometimes without all the facts. There's plenty of marketing speak out there describing insights as deeper truths about human behaviour or penetrating knowledge that speaks to unmet needs. All of this is useful, of course, but too much discussion around what an insight is (I find) can be a bit isolating. When you're a facilitator of a team on a mission to generate insights, the language you use needs to be easy, simple and accessible.

I'd encourage you to read up on the world of customer insights and how organisations have focused their efforts to get closer to customers. Doing so will furnish you with new stories and examples of how and where businesses have employed strong insight strategy to grow. This will keep your insight knowledge sharp. However, whilst there's plenty of literature extoling the commercial benefits of insights, there's not a great deal of information out there on *how* to generate them. My advice, therefore, when introducing the topic is be smart, not clever. Feel free to steal as much of the following language as you wish.

WHAT IS AN INSIGHT?

An insight should inspire you and your project team into action; a great insight will almost point at an idea – it will make the idea so obvious that you feel stupid you hadn't thought of it before! (Go easy on yourself, though.) Great insights can provide rational explanations to human behaviour, and at the same time give you an emotional reaction – an 'aha!' moment, like the eureka moment we ascribe to idea creation.

An insight helps us make sense of the world. And for a project team, insights connect us to the drivers of people's behaviour. Having insights provides us with an edge for our propositions; something that helps differentiate our work from the work of others.

To create insights, we need to piece together disparate data, and form patterns and new connections. As we've learned, our mind has an amazing capacity to do this. To help you and others create insights, it's good to remember we are all consumers and customers, too. We all have wants, needs and desires of our own – therefore, we have all got the capacity to generate empathy with the people who we're targeting when it

- "no-one likes to think they smell"
- "If it's fresh, it must be better for me"
- house is my home (discuss!)
- love the chocolate — NO!
- a treat BUT! want to feel bad about it.
- "It's never as good as the book." "seen shared is better"
- Many of us associate cider with our student days
- SEEING IS BELIEVING — I fear the unknown
- DRINKERS HAVE COME TO EXPECT BAD PINTS...
- ...BUT... now what!
- No-one tells you they need a microwave but they will say they're tired of skipping meals
- LOOK AT ME LOOK AT ME — I'M A HONEY BEE
- DEEPENING INSIGHTS — stuff that explains why the world is ...
- ...TION INSIGHTS
- You too — think the same
- There's enough bad things in my body — show me what good you do...
- In reality I'm prepared to cheat on the big stuff but I can't lie to myself
- give me the guilt free [......] so I can do [......]
- "OPPORT... INS... unmet inspir...

comes to designing products and services for them. I don't believe that insight is a dark art for only special creative wizards in advertising agencies. Let's use an example to bring all that together.

'People love the taste of chocolate.'

'People love the taste of chocolate.' This is not an insight. This is foundation information. Great taste is a category truth about chocolate – who likes chocolate that doesn't taste nice? With insight, you need to capture the more inspiring, stimulating and exciting truth that connects certain types of people to certain types of chocolate. The insight you're after is the ongoing subconscious narrative of people's lives.

Remember all that information about the warehouse of our mind? That information creates a story of who we are and what we want. It's a voice in our head. And if you're reading this and putting the page down to think to yourself 'Do I have a voice in *my* head?' – then hey presto, that *is* the voice in your head! It's a constant companion acting as our guide through life, verbalising our thoughts as we have them and rationalising our wishes as they manifest.

Freud was keen to point out that our 'inner ego' is tormented and distracted by life's tensions and desires. Hence, when part of us wants to gobble down a bar of chocolate, the other part wants to abstain and say 'shame on you'.

We all love chocolate, but apart from taste (a conscious reason we'd offer when asked) there are deeper subconscious drivers that whisper to us as we ponder over our local newsagent's resplendent chocolate offering. Our voice might say: 'that looks nice, but I'd better not'. And what might be driving that voice is an inner belief system held at a subconscious level that says 'Having fun is an expression of living freely. I love to enjoy the indulgent side of life BUT indulgence leaves me feeling guilty. I wish I could treat myself briefly, before returning back to earth and taking charge of things once more.'

That line of text is a bit of a mouthful (pun intended), so we can cut it down to: 'I'd love a treat, but I don't want to feel bad about it'. And if that were an insight that is true for some people, some of the time then we can flip it into a business opportunity that inspires ideas.

In this example, we can answer the opportunity of 'guilt-free indulgence' with Maltesers (the product) and the marketing proposition of 'a cheeky pleasure that won't ruin your appetite'. And that Maltesers (with their light honeycomb centre) are ideal for those who want the thrill of chocolate without the shame of snacking between meals.

Insights are stories that we write to explain human behaviour and the subconscious drivers that we feel more often than we speak.

They help to give us an accurate and deep understanding of feelings related to the brief that we scoped out in the previous chapter. They are about giving external language to an internal world. Insights help you think about what your target audience really wants and needs (and sometimes what they never realised they needed, too). In summary a great insight is:

- Concise
- Energetic
- Neither right or wrong but, for some people, true
- Specific, not comprehensive

Hence, 'I deserve a guilt-free treat' follows those principles and is an insight far more powerful than 'people like the taste of chocolate'.

Notice that the word chocolate didn't appear in the insight. A good insight ought not to mention the project topic or product. People rarely lie awake thinking about products and brands. That's the stuff that matters to you! People are more likely to lie awake thinking about what matters to them. In fact, the 'guilt-free' element of that insight (guilt is often a driver of human behaviour) turns up in a number of chores vs pleasure trade-offs in modern consumer lifestyles. Answering a 'guilt-free *this* for pleasurable *that*' is the insight driving sales of bleach, toilet sprays, floor cleaners and most items on the gondola ends in supermarkets. The guilt-free insight is a driver for propositions that include gluten-free, sugar-free, fat-free, organic only, and almost any ready meal:

'As a parent, I want to give my kids the best, but I haven't time to cook a full meal in my busy life. I feel guilty that saving my time is at the expense of an exotic culinary journey, yet I'm working hard to give them just that.'

Don't worry, El Paso's 'Mexican Street Food in a Box' will scratch that itch.

WHY WE NEED INSIGHTS

Cynicism aside, a strong insight is the creative gift that keeps on giving. From insight comes ideas that add commercial value to your business and bottom line. A great insight-to-ideas strategy ultimately answers the needs of your consumers and helps you and your project team spot the opportunities in people's lives where your product or service (in whatever form) can help.

Here are some further examples of the insight-to-ideas connection. These cases are well-cited consultant catnip, but neatly illustrate the power a great insight has to inspire a great idea.

Dove Their Campaign for Real Beauty rewrote the rules when it came to the beauty sector.

Insight: *Truth is beauty. Beauty is truth. And the truth is: everyone is beautiful.*

Persil Dirt is Good campaign

Insight: *Dirty children are happy children. And happy children means you're a good parent.*

Merchant's Heart Premium soft drink mixers with herbal infusions.

Insight: *People spend a premium on gin, only to flood it down with sugary flavoured tonics.*

Cadbury In the aftermath of PR and production difficulties, Cadbury had become humourless and serious. The ad of the gorilla playing the drums, voted one of the best in the decade, kickstarted people's emotions and love of the brand once more.

Insight: *Eating chocolate is easy, indulgent and joyful.*

And now, to balance the books, here are some product fails and the unaddressed insights that perhaps signalled their ultimate downfall...

✗ The 1985 Sinclair C5 electric vehicle (right). Research showed that people 'felt safer on a bicycle' – which is what they chose instead.

✗ A 1979 shampoo product called 'a touch of yoghurt'. No one liked the idea of washing their hair with yoghurt, and those that did sometimes made the mistake of eating it and got very ill. The insight around powering great hair products is movement, strength and shine – everything that yoghurt isn't.

✗ Maxwell House once produced an instant ready-to-drink coffee in a tetra pack. The problem was that the pack couldn't be microwaved and instead the contents needed to be poured into a mug. If consumers had to pour ready-to-drink coffee from a container into a mug and then go heat it, then it would be easier to simply pour hot water onto instant coffee granules – which is precisely what they decided to do instead.

RIGHT:
No one felt safe driving the C5 in open traffic – and didn't like it in the rain either.

So far, I've described what I'd call 'consumer insights' – the stuff inside the head and heart of everyday people. There are also insights around shopper behaviour and business performance. The business you're in and the project you're working on might categorise insights differently but, again, the basic principles still apply. A good insight is something that gives you energy, and inspires you and your team into action. If you are all excited by something, the chances are the people you're targeting will be excited too.

As insights are neither right nor wrong but instead true for some people, I don't believe you can judge an insight. To help explain, here are some examples from the world of art. For some historians and theorists of the avant-garde, Marcel Duchamp's *Fountain* is a major landmark in 20th-century modernism. For others, it's something you piss in. There are some people for whom Tracey Emin's *My Bed* is deserving of a Turner Prize. Others (particularly those with teenage children) would be all too familiar with an unmade bed and find the piece bewildering – especially when they find out that it sold for £2.5m at auction.

Context, however, changes almost everything in art. Graffiti sprayed on a school wall may well betray the middlebrow judgement of the parent–teacher association. Unless it was a Banksy, at which point people's opinion about 'youths with hoods and spray paint cans' loitering after dark behind the bike shed spins full circle.

If art, like beauty, is in the eye of the beholder, then insight is in the eye of the observer.

Unlike a discussion concerning the arts, which is often debated in public, insight generation is usually a private affair. Commercial advantage is often at stake and businesses will do what they can to protect their insights. Insight sessions happen behind closed doors, re-enforcing the myth that there's only one insight ready to be discovered by one 'clever person' alone. And because interpretation is totally subjective, insights are often misunderstood if they are poorly communicated. The problem becomes worse when insights are typed badly, in vague concepts accompanied by clichéd stock photography, in confusing PowerPoint slide decks.

HOW DO WE GET THEM?

We can't simply ask our customers what they need. We're just not wired to understand what drives us. We develop our own stories to help us navigate our world and we're usually blinkered to anything that doesn't fit that narrative. This is perfectly and fabulously captured by Henry Ford (founder of the Ford Motor Company) who said, 'If I had asked people what they wanted, they would have said faster horses'.

Great insight is elicited from consumers through observation, and developed through creative discussions within a strong creative process.

It is your job as a creative facilitator to create the conditions where you and your teammates can work together in an insightful way to explore a range of observations and information, and to then arrive at insights that your competitors can't.

It might be there's one person with whom you work who is incredibly good at analysing behaviour and arrives at poignant and witty observations about our characters. They're great storytellers and emotionally sensitive. They just 'get it' before other people on the team do and will incubate consumer data and, as if touched by divine inspiration, will leap into the office with 'the insight'.

Here's a story of one such person.

The bestselling statin drug in the management of heart disease is atorvastatin, sold under the brand name Lipitor. It was imperative for Pfizer, the manufacturers of Lipitor, to win in this market. The innovation challenge was 'how do you talk about heart disease to people who are at risk (particularly men) in a positive way?' After many (expensive) months of listening to patient groups, medical practitioners and families of patients, the 'insight' came from one person. She had spotted a pattern in conversations between men as they caught up socially, swapping stories with each other about topics in their everyday lives. She noticed that men talk in numbers:

'How much you lifting? What's your golf handicap? My new laptop's twice as fast. My stocks are up 5%. The kid's only gone and aced his tests. You see the game last night – what a final quarter!'

Everything involved a metric. A move in one value to the next. Men (mostly, in this context) navigate their lives through a dashboard of life information where numbers are directly proportional to performance. A good life well-lived is when things are faster, better, stronger, cheaper, heavier, easier or longer. For men, the insight is: 'It's all about the numbers.'

Now, the efficacy of a statin is measured through its ability to lower cholesterol. That figure is something a patient can monitor over time. The lower your cholesterol number, the lower your risk of heart disease. The strapline for the marketing campaign became, 'Lipitor: the number 1 for getting your numbers down'. In the USA, where prescription drugs can be marketed direct to the consumer, Pfizer spent millions on TV advertising, cleverly dropping in advertisements and, in 2003, Lipitor became the bestselling pharmaceutical in history. In 2008 Pfizer reported sales just shy of $13 billion.

In this case, it was one person who unlocked a fortune. However, hoping to recruit savant insight gurus who can consistently spot an insight isn't a growth strategy. Leaping into the creative session and writing 'it's all about the numbers' is a creative strength, but that talent isn't something the rest of your insight team can share in or support. Having an insight person is not the way. Nor should you farm out your insight wishes to an agency. Far better for your whole team to be insightful.

The good news is that insightfulness is a skill that can be taught. And over time, much like driving a car, it becomes a skill that's far more behavioural and intuitive. Teaching it can be broken into a handful of disciplines and behaviours. Allowing your team to constantly experiment with these behaviours in different ways, before and throughout the insight phase of a project, grows insight capability.

For adults to successfully learn a new skill they need a framework on which to pin new knowledge – they need to receive timely and personal feedback about their performance, and they need time to reflect on and digest that feedback. My analogy would be that of a team ascending a staircase in unison (it's a wide staircase). At each step, everyone shares the same language and common understanding of the skill. The team then steps up together onto the next plane of knowledge and experiments once more. They repeat the process. If at any time the team feel they've lost progress towards an insight, or feel their sensitivity to stimuli has diminished, they can simply move down a step together and recalibrate.

I've noticed my language around insight is constantly evolving and I'm always interested to watch other facilitators run their insight sessions. I realise that there's many approaches – not just one. This part of the book is our guide to help you and your project team participants become fabulously insightful. The more you involve yourself in insight projects the better you become. The coaching of other team members in insight work will make you stronger in your facilitation skills and give you deeper knowledge behind some of the science and psychology that underpins the creative process. Let's start by gently warming up. 👉

> *"If I had asked people what they wanted, they would have said faster horses."*
>
> — HENRY FORD

10 Tools to insight utopia

Here are ten tools you can use to teach people to become more insightful. In our GENIUS BOX insight workshops we link all ten together, taking time to debrief one in readiness for the next, and taking teams step-by-step on the insight journey. And remember that creating the environment for an alpha state of mind (see page 70) at all times is critical.

Some of these exercises work better in the evening, some are best done in pairs. Some work well when people can walk outside, and some are more suited to groups huddled around a table. Much like an insight, there is no 'right' or 'wrong' here, but I've set up what I think is a good briefing for you. Over time you'll tweak your instructions and stories, as I have. The real learning comes from the discussions and the synthesis of your participants after each activity. We obviously can't land all those years of feedback here, so instead I've outlined what we're trying to achieve and what to look out for.

If you're designing an insight course to build insight skill within your business, then spend a few days with people to embed that learning. It's not something you can 'do' in 60 minutes, squashed into a busy week, or worse still in lunchtime 'bitesize' sessions – I think that sends all the wrong signals. If you're midway through a project and you're using this book as an injection of stimuli, then pick a few activities and use them as warm-ups before you task your team to review the consumer information you've gathered so far.

Insights can 'pop up' like mushrooms, unexpected and unannounced – just as they can emerge in a steady fashion over time. Your insight 'radar' needs to be calibrated to spot both.

Finally, an insight is rarely parcelled up in one piece like some lost jewellery that's discovered when moving a rug. Insights are the language we're using to describe the many voices that exist in many people's heads.

Social science selection bias (or survivorship bias) is a phenomenon where we reach conclusions from concentrating on people or things that made it past some selection process whilst overlooking those that did not. We're schooled to spot things that change – it's easier to measure what we can see. However, in matters of insight the absence of activity is also a data point. Miles Davis, the jazz musician, said he played the notes that weren't there. Remember to piece together not only the things that people say and do but also what they don't say and do.

Here are some warm-up games I encourage every project team to work through in advance of any insight sessions. The first five are all about connections. To be insightful we need to make connections between facts and topics; sometimes like with like, sometimes like with 'not' like. The second set of games are all about metaphors; spotting connections in the 'hidden meanings' in what consumers say. To be insightful requires us to build different stories employing different words.

Creating an insight story is a bit like joining up stars in the sky to reveal a constellation. Play the games in sequence; each builds upon the other. Set aside enough time to do this (an afternoon perhaps) and allow for plenty of discussion and reflection. Everyone on your team sees the world differently, so there's tremendous value to be gained from exploring everyone's perspectives and experiences. 👉

Insight Tools 001–005

Connection games

Being aware of human behaviour.

① What comes next

This is the type of brain teaser some people may have on a phone app. They're found online in IQ testing games or pub quiz packs. The brief is to spot which object in the sequence comes next. Hand out a set of five or six such puzzles to small teams. You can give the same puzzle to all teams or a different set of puzzles to different teams. What to do will be dictated by the group size and access, or not, to a photocopier!

WHAT TO DO
I'm sure you've seen these pattern- or sequence-spotting games before. Have a go – this is nice and simple. What comes next in the sequence?

You can start off with easy ones and then progress to harder ones. If you've got the luxury of a few days of training, you can turn all these games into an 'insight reminder pack'

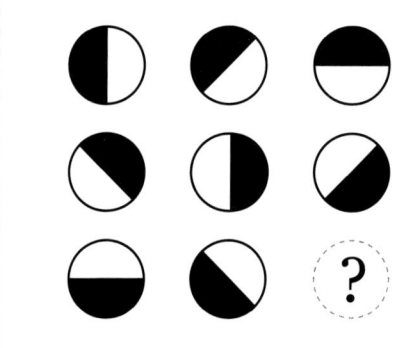

EASY

Choose answer:

for your participants to take away and share with their friends.

HOW IT WORKS
Our brain can spot patterns when we ask it to. Sometimes, it'll do that without our asking – phone numbers one digit out from our own leap off a page. Where lots of the same sort of behaviour is happening over time, patterns are there to be discovered. What came before is a clue to what might come next. We're using the past to help us accurately predict the future.*

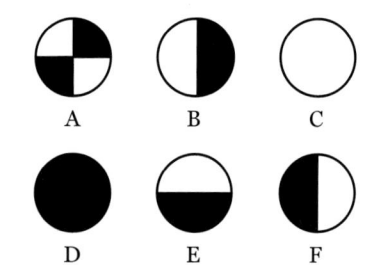

(ANSWER: F, as it's a circle spinning clockwise 45 degrees each time.)

HARDER

 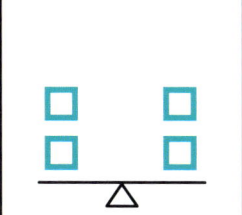 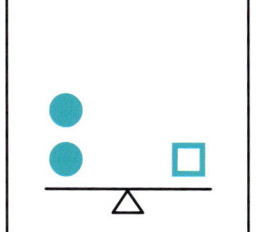 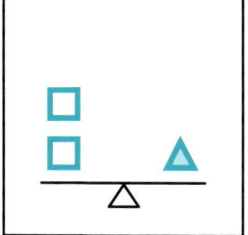 

Choose answer:

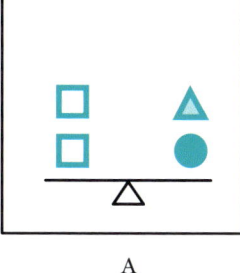 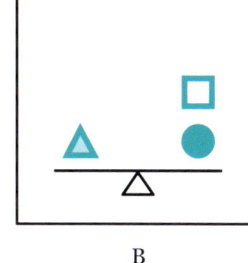 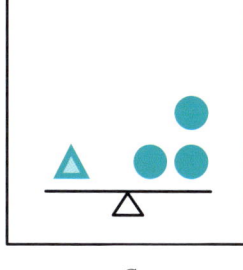 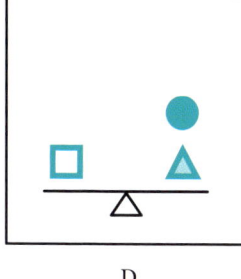 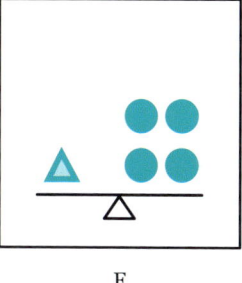

A B C D E

---

* Interestingly, despite all the decades of statistics gathered across all sports, it is still impossible to 100% guarantee the outcome of a sports fixture (be that a horse race, rugby game or cricket match). The only instance of us getting better at predicting future events using previous behaviour and patterns as our guide is the weather.

(ANSWER: E. The shapes are on scales, and a circle is half the weight of a square, and a quarter of the weight of a triangle.)

② Linking words

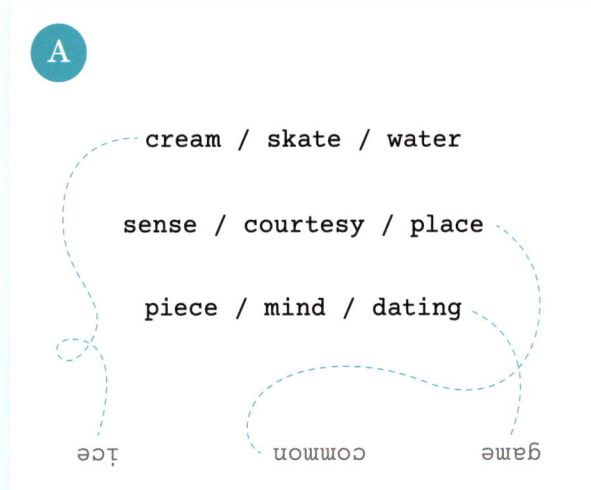

A

cream / skate / water

sense / courtesy / place

piece / mind / dating

ice   common   game

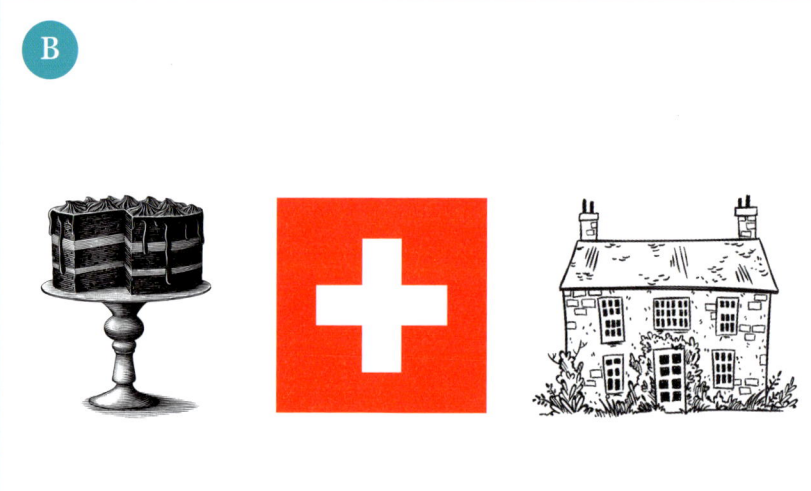

B

These two games are about connection-making, the next step on from pattern-spotting, and getting better at doing this in groups. We mix up pictures and words to give the brain a full workout. It's also interesting to see how people whose first language isn't English play this game, as some idioms don't translate – which is a good topic to discuss, as many external agencies from one 'place' are often asked to elicit insights about another 'place'. Things do get lost in translation.

WHAT TO DO
Split your project team participants into groups of three. One person in each team is in charge of managing the energy of the group and talks out loud about the images and words they see. These team facilitators encourage the other two members to keep talking and thinking out loud too – this keeps the thinking 'in the open' and helps teammates make connections as a group. What one person says out loud might help another team member make a link and find a connection.

Here, we have pictures AND words to test your brain. The first part of the game is to find the word that links all three previous words. Then, the second part of the game uses pictures, too. Which word links 'cake', 'Swiss' and 'cottage'? The answer is Cheese!

HOW IT WORKS
Some regions in the brain are stimulated by pictures rather than words. In playing this game, the mind has to work harder to find those connections because they're not obvious; they require our wider general knowledge to fill in the gaps. The pictures teach the brain to look at one layer of information and then invite our deeper subconscious to get involved, and to strengthen its ability to forge links as a result.

❸ Spot a theme

This game asks participants to spot patterns and make connections within topics of conversation. We're asking teams to do the same activity, but this time instead of the input being shapes, words or pictures, they are mini stories presented in verbatim quotes taken from real (or imaginary!) projects. This one is about chocolate (since we covered that topic earlier).

WHAT TO DO

Issue small groups (three to four people) with around ten 'clues' from a consumer session, such as the chocolate examples here. It works well if everyone is familiar with the topic. Ask participants to spot any themes emerging from the quotes, and capture those themes and discuss them. You can do this by having each clue printed separately on its own slip of paper, manually grouping them and then sticking them on another piece of paper on which you write the theme. Then place all this output on the floor or a desk for other groups to see and discuss too.

You don't have to wordsmith the themes you spot, just jot down the main elements. You can start your theme by stating 'there's something here about... ' to help tell that story to each other.

'Oh yes chocolate. Who's ever going to turn down a cheeky bite of chocolate? No harm in that at all!' *Gemma, 32*

'My friend and I took loads of chocolate on holiday when we passed through Duty Free. We gobbled most of it up on the plane and sat there like sick children for the rest of the flight.' *Corrin, 30*

'Chocolate – a moment on the lips, a lifetime on the hips – that's what my aunt would say.' *Charlotte, 34*

'I add a little chocolate to my chilli. The taste smooths off a little and makes the chilli sensation last more.' *Simon, 43*

'Chocolate is simple to understand. Fancy and exotic for the girls. Big chunky bars for the boys. Easy.' *Ryan, 32*

'Oh there's something secret and dirty about scoffing a piece of chocolate up without telling anyone its there.' *Deborah, 43*

'I don't eat chocolate. More of a savoury guy. I just lost the taste for it a while back.' *Xav, 31*

'I love dark chocolate most of all. It's much classier isn't it? Not like milk chocolate.' *Amy, 28*

Here, Gemma, Corrin, and Deborah have said something on a similar theme. This is: there's something about eating chocolate quickly, as it's naughty!

HOW IT WORKS

If there is something important to be found that will contribute to an insight, it will 'float' to the top of conversations and emerge through the many consumer interviews and observations you make. However, this will only happen if you're sensitive to each other's thinking and if as a group you're all 'in phase' with each other – a bit like being in tune and on the same wavelength.

This is a lovely warm-up exercise to get a group working 'all as one' and spotting themes. It also allows people to practise spotting and communicating a theme to others, too.

Sharing themes with each other might spark conversations about how these people were thinking and feeling at the time.

We're now starting to open the door to their world and what matters to them, rather than focusing on what we want to tell these people with our propositions and brands.

④ A bit of mind reading

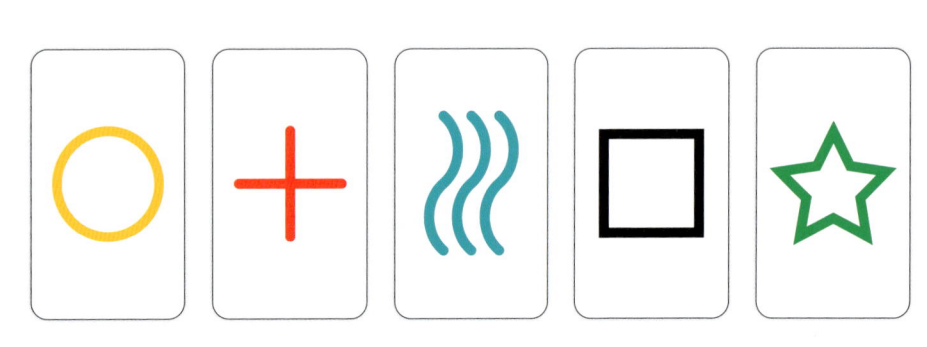

These are the famous Zener cards, used by magicians, mentalists and hustlers (depending on your point of view). The quest to find people with extrasensory perception still eludes us, but there is always merit in embracing the irreverent during the creative process.

WHAT TO DO
Buy a couple of packs of cards (it's probably easier than spending time at the office printer making your own set). Split your project team participants into pairs. Give one person in each pair a handful of cards, say 15. Ensure this is a mix of all five card symbols. The second member of the pair now has to 'guess' each card their partner is holds up in turn. Of course, this is total bunk and there is no way they'll get it right each time.* However, invite people to spend time considering their answer. Without simply racing away with guesses, ask them to spot what it is they're thinking and feeling each time. And ask them to use that information to help guess which card their partner is holding. You want people to spot what they're doing with all their senses and arrive at an answer that is more than just 'thinking quickly' and guessing; it's a process of chance, probability and elimination.

If they do, please get in touch!

HOW IT WORKS
Insight requires us to use our intuition and imagination. We need to 'feel' our way to an insight just as much as we think our way logically through facts, figures and associations. At some point during this game, people eventually give up on one strategy and switch to another – we need to remember that moment when we intuitively felt our first approach was reaching a dead end.

We're all capable of being intuitive. For some it's a sensation in our body – often in the stomach, hence why people talk about a 'gut feeling'. Our intuition is linked deeply to our subconscious and our survival systems. We have echoes in our DNA that hold pre-programmed responses to certain sets of threatening conditions. Extreme heights, the cold and darkness don't bring out the best in our behaviour, as those environments were very bad to our forefathers – particularly those who fell, froze or got eaten. In our modern lives, we've changed our immediate environment so we live longer and more safely. We have to go out of our way to deliberately leap off high buildings. However, our intuition is a powerful biological heuristic. It's there to say to our conscious brain 'hey, this looks a bit odd to me, take a second look'.

Our intuition knows when someone we care about isn't being honest. Our intuition knows there's something odd about that Rolex on eBay for only £20. It knows the figures are lying. It spots things our conscious mind can't. When it does, listen to it. There's something there to be discovered and it'll take a change in your energy and awareness to articulate what should be visited again.

⑤ A brilliant insight game

This game is great as an energiser before any insight session and is certainly one for your training retreats. It gets people moving and connecting.

WHAT TO DO
Issue a pack of sticky notes to everyone. Ask them to walk around looking at their fellow teammates, taking in all of who they are. But do this in silence. Invite people to take time making observations about their colleagues and to tune into their intuition about everyone's personality.

After a few moments of walking and thinking, ask everyone to write on some sticky notes answering these questions about the others: What is this person good at? What else do you believe about this person? (Give some examples using your co-facilitator, such as 'good at thinking on their feet', 'doesn't like rom-com movies'.) Mention to the group that they should listen to what their intuition tells them about their colleagues – not simply guess, (or be insulting!) but genuinely tune in to the vibes they believe their teammates are giving off. The aim is for each person to have written several notes and to have stuck them (gently) on their colleagues, and to have several notes stuck on them by their colleagues.

Wait until everyone has finished sticking things to each other to review all of the comments. Ask your participants to spot any themes about themselves that have emerged from the 'data' they've received. Is there a connection (or disconnect) here between the personal brand they want to project to others and the actual perception and impact of who they are to each other?

HOW IT WORKS
Some of the answers people receive will be based on acquired knowledge from being a good colleague – 'we believe that Sarah is brilliant at strategic thinking and she's famous in the team for doing just that'. However, we're actually all incredibly poor at measuring other people's performance. Our assessments and ratings of how others perform in a discipline is totally subjective.

Consider that it is only us who know that the pain we're experiencing from a broken collarbone is registering a 10/10. It is not for the doctor in the emergency room to twist your arm about and say 'nonsense, that's clearly just a 6/10 pain injury'. We're notoriously poor at rating other people's performance and experience. The only thing we can be 100% accurate on is how we *feel* towards others when they interact with us. This internal bias and judgement towards our lives and our perceptions has become a bit of a 'thing' in recent times. Our bias is often seen as a negative, and great effort has been spent on eradicating bias from the workplace.

THIS IS <u>NOT</u> THE WAY.

We're all (thankfully) different, and each of us brings a unique view of events and happenings. It's an unavoidable consequence of being human. It's antithetical to want cross-functional and diverse teams when at the same time peddling a narrative that bias is bad and needs inoculating against. If we extrapolate unconscious bias training to the extreme we eradicate

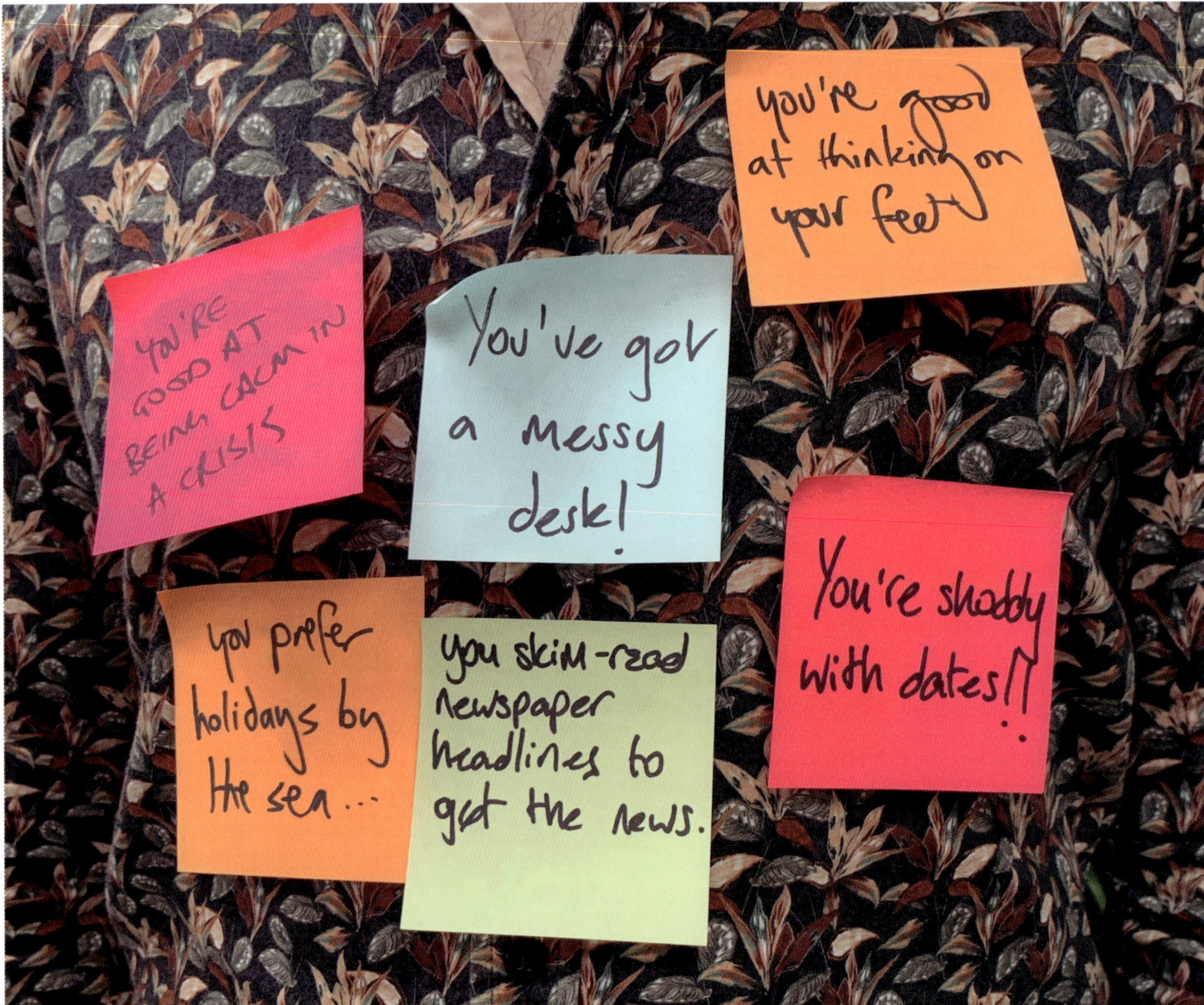

all misconceptions about each other and arrive at a homogeneous, insipid and unoffensive end point. The human equivalent of magnolia paint and vanilla envelopes. There is no colour, texture or tension to explore if everyone has the same view of each other. Remember that insights apply to s*ome people some of the time*. There is no unifying theory of human behaviour that we can latch on to that will help all businesses sell all sorts.

Placing a sticky note on a stranger that says, 'I think you're good at cooking without a recipe' may say very little to people about their impact on the team, but portrays far more beautifully to others what you yourself value. Sharing a moment of playfulness and irreverence together is one of those tiny touchpoints that builds trust in a team. We've been imaginative with each other. We've tried something out that might not work, and we've come through the other side safely and without injury. We've both given and accepted feedback unconditionally. And we've even laughed at the surprising truths some people may have been able to guess about us.

In Part One of the book, I spoke about how we form immediate impressions of someone's character based on extremely brief snippets of their behaviour. This leads on to attribution theory – the way we attribute someone's behaviour to the person themself (their personality traits) or to their situation (other people, stuff that's happened that day). Both concepts are at work here when we play this game.

Debriefing this energiser allows you as the facilitator to make the point that our judgements and preconceptions make us who we are. And as we're all prone to making these judgements, we're all equally flawed – or should we say equally special. If we're to build successful insights, and from those insights be inspired to build products and services that are desirable, then they need to be desired by 'humans'.

These connection-making games work. They highlight the differences between how each of us interprets the world, and show us that those differences create combined team strength. The collective power of many minds is more powerful than one or two smart people thinking hard. Spending time playing the games, and setting aside time for quality discussions after each game, dispels the very negative view that if we're to be successful, our unconscious bias is a bad thing and needs to be eradicated. This is not the way. Creativity needs the opposite philosophy. For a team to be insightful, exploring and amplifying our bias and resulting interpretations will actually power more penetrating insight and stronger ideas. By playing the games you as a facilitator will be attuned to the differing personalities in the project team. And all of the participants will be more sensitive to making multiple connections that they couldn't do before.

We're now ready to use these skills as we face into the second set of more challenging and creative insight activities: the metaphor games.

OPPOSITE:
When playing this game, don't talk! What do you believe to be true about your fellow teammates?

Facilitation tip 005

One instruction at a time

Piling on instructions distracts your project participants from the task at hand.

For example: 'Take this platform and use these three steps to arrive at two starter ideas' is better than 'Take this platform and use these three steps to arrive at two starter ideas for the campaign. Then after lunch we'll share your suggestions with the other groups and then have an ideas session followed by a session in the afternoon to narrow the ideas down to a winning three. Your group will develop one of those executions.'

I've seen things like that happen. Instead of overwhelming their audience, great facilitators keep the project journey in their heads, and over time, step-by-step, brief the participants to solve the problem.

Giving too much away can stifle the creative process – or, worse still, will lead to people crushing starter ideas too soon, as they start judging their output too early. Explaining all the process in one go isn't your job.

My first driving lesson was reverse gear and clutch, first gear and clutch. That was it. In the context of a ten-day course, it was a given that there was more to learn in lesson two. Lay off the lengthy instructions, take stuff out and stick to one instruction at a time.

Facilitation tip 006

Don't be neutral

I've read too many clever papers from academics on the role of the facilitator being that of an impartial adviser or a neutral observer, who smoothes operations and gently coerces the group from A to B.

I'm at a loss! How do you do that while remaining neutral? This is not the way.

As you're reading this, you're already forming an opinion about what I've written (and you're welcome to it); it's human nature. Share your opinion and then we can make use of it by embracing the sentiment and using your perspective to stimulate debate, discussion and, eventually, decision-making. Such a stimulus helps people get from A to B, or we all sit in silence.

Being neutral isn't being positive. And the creative process needs positive intention to get it moving. I'd argue that if you're actively avoiding getting involved and sharing opinions, then your actual impact is negative.

Think about it. People are happy to share opinions in social occasions where they're not being paid. The context is different and perhaps their opinion isn't even welcome. Why remain neutral when your business clients have commissioned you to facilitate? Signalled, up front, personal opinion, is a powerful tool that unlocks 'the stuck' and spikes up creative sessions. Opinion is at the heart of most conversations – there is no need to censor your mind.

Facilitation is not coaching, so asking 'what do you think you should do?' time and again, really won't move things on. And given all the things a great facilitator has to do in prepping projects and training sessions, opinions can be offered freely and take no time to plan. Importantly, opinions, thoughts and perspectives are an extension of who you are and what you stand for – and that has value for any creative process. Moreover, being consistent with that over time builds a credible brand for your skill as a facilitator. Your audience will fill in the gaps – they're bright people, they'll work it out. If you stay neutral with nothing to say, then you're simply warming a seat.

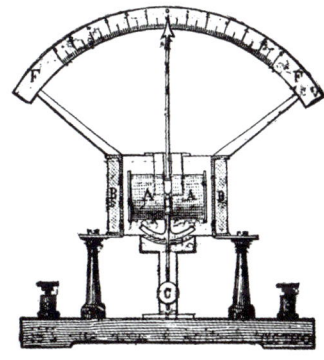

Interview

Henrietta De Souza

HEAD OF CUSTOMER EXPERIENCE AND DEVELOPMENT

Henrietta has been developing customer insights and enhancing customer experiences for over 20 years. She coaches teams in building their insight and human-centred design capability, and works within large organisations uncovering the insight that powers propositions and brands throughout the world.

You're passionate about insight – what's the secret to creating insightfulness in teams and generating great insights for business?

For an insight to work, it has to be inspiring. It's not easy to convince people the first time round. And building insights isn't a skill everyone has total command of. It's about looking for all the puzzle pieces to reveal the big picture and then stepping back so you can see it. Even then an insight, and the ideas it inspires, needs to galvanise people into action. I believe that customer-centricity is an experimental mindset, one that means the team and I can never give up, and it's the key is to understanding what works best for your organisation. Being insightful is all about persistence, demanding more investigation, curiosity and blending perspectives together.

Tell me about the value a great insight has to power a strong idea.

You can't have ideas without an insight. I see myself as an ideas person, but that's because I'm connecting the dots: I'm reading from a variety of sources. I love data, I wonder what people are up to, I'm asking myself all the time 'what might their motivations be?' and I'm searching for a deeper understanding. That behaviour triggers ideas in me. People don't buy ideas, they buy into people who are telling the story about those ideas. I believe insight also has the power to bind people together and create like-minded teams, too. It's often the way in the pitch that we start with a problem. You've got people on the hook, but it's the insight that gives everyone the relief – that 'aha, here's what really matters' – and then the idea you propose makes sense.

There are many roads to insights – how much of it is following process and how much is it using feeling and intuition?

It's all largely feeling. The more you do, the more you can trust your gut. Instead of slavishly following a process, I can feel my way in a faster and more fluid fashion to an insight. However, process has its place. It allows people to be brought along on the journey that you did in the moment, and it gives them comfort that there's a robustness to it. So, more speed is great sometimes, but not so great if you're new to a team. Having a process allows me to tell people where we are on the insight journey and how that insight fits into the context of the larger project story, too.

Connecting the business to a customer insight is critical – what pitfalls need to be avoided?

Running too fast can actually hinder things. Whilst it's a skill to be quick to an insight, I've realised over my career how important it is to take stakeholders on the journey one step at a time. They will challenge you, but my tip is not to hold your position, but instead ask them about theirs and ask them 'why?' I've found that this teaches me far more about the perspectives and beliefs of my stakeholders and the wider business. I gather insight about them as individuals, and of course if there are further valid perspectives that might strengthen our insight, I gather those too. I have found that the people who feel like detractors at the start of a project soon become my most enthusiastic advocates. Overall, it's about being brave enough to be open to other people's points of view and embracing those perspectives.

There's a lot of talk about 'putting customers at the heart of our business' – what does this really mean beyond the platitudes?
This is genuinely about teams within a business working together, listening to customers to understand their evolving needs and then having a clear process by which you can make change and design to those needs. I've helped businesses to realise that our customer and business goals always align, they are simply two sides of the same coin. Take mortgages, for example – people don't want a mortgage, they want to buy a home. That's what the motivation is. And it's a deeply emotional and personal moment in people's lives. For a bank, we want to build trust and retain customers. So, if we make that purchase as easy as it can be, we take away stress rather than adding to it; we build loyalty and advocacy at the same time.

Facilitating a team to be more insightful needs certain skills and behaviours – what are you looking for in your facilitators and project participants?
I'm looking for curiosity, and a passion for people and the world. I like people who are creative problem solvers and who can think differently. It's important

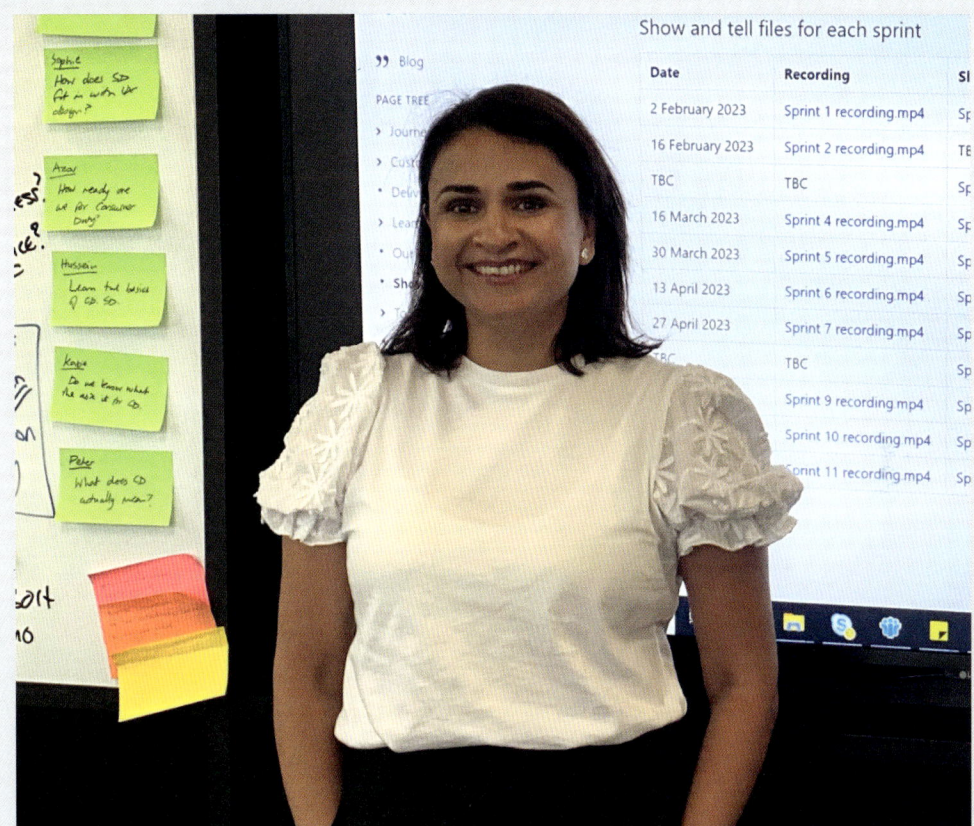

to be courageous to find and tell a compelling story that drives action.

What is a final nugget of genius you'd like to share?
Love what you do. People remember your passion because of how it makes them feel – energised, inspired, motivated. They want to jump on your train because they believe in you. Believe that you're going to get them to the vision, the destination, the deliverable.

"It's about being brave enough to be open to other people's points of view and embracing those perspectives."

– HENRIETTA DE SOUZA

Insight Tools 006–009

Metaphor games

Unlocking the deeper layers of human behaviour.

Disney are brilliant at telling stories. *Frozen* is, of course, a masterpiece. The film works as it's based on the insight that sibling love is enduring and unconditional. This is a neat break from the usual 'fall for the one true love' plotline, and the film challenges a handful of other fairytale tropes, too. One that's quite a twist is that the handsome prince (Hans) turns out to be a nasty piece of work (how could you do that, Disney!) However, near the start of the movie there's a catchy little number sung by Ana and Hans: 'Love is an Open Door'. Check it out. My favourite bit of the animation is the silhouette of the two characters dancing in the candlelight. All cheery stuff.

Now, love isn't *literally* an open door. Love is not a slab of timber swinging on a hinge – this is a metaphor. It's alluding to the way a door opens and that you go through it from one space to another. And love, like an open door, is an opportunity to leave one stage of life and join someone else to start a fresh new stage. A metaphor, therefore, is a powerful insight tool that helps us directly refer to one thing by mentioning another. Additionally, our language is peppered with similes. Similes (you'll remember from school, I'm sure) are figures of speech where we highlight the similarities between two things. Being 'as brave as a Lion', 'as sharp as a tack' and 'as bright as a button' are a few examples.

We speak in these re-expressions all the time. Similes and metaphors make up a high percentage of our language, and as much as six metaphors/similes/analogies can be found in one minute of spoken word. Metaphors are the keys that unlock our understanding of what's buried deeply in the realms of other people's subconscious. If we shine a light on what people say, we can navigate the mind and find the hidden treasures that are the psychological drivers of people's thinking and behaviour.

Let's take a look at that those last two sentences again and identify the seven re-expressions:

'Metaphors are the **keys** that **unlock** our understanding of what's **buried deeply** in the **realms** of people's subconscious. If we **shine a light** on what people say, we can **navigate the mind** and find **hidden treasures** that are the psychological drivers of people's thinking and behaviour.'

These games tune people up (see what I did there) to listen out for the metaphors in people's language. Strictly speaking, the phrases aren't all metaphors, and the following exercises are not English Grammar tests. The skill here is identifying the re-expressions and spotting the patterns in people's behaviour.

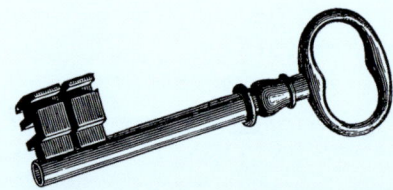

6 It's a bit like…

This first game shows project team participants how often we use metaphors in our everyday language without realising it. Some of our behaviour is automatic. We can't accurately describe how we feel or why we're motivated to act a certain way, so when asked about it we might say 'Well, I guess it's a bit like…' and the metaphors that follow are particularly useful to us. They are figuratively highlighting what's really going on for people at a subconscious level. Whilst a considered answer to a question may give us surface level intelligence, the deeper and more useful information may come from exploring the metaphors.

WHAT TO DO

Issue teams with a set of situations (see example ideas and responses, right). You can either print these on cards and make a pack or, as I prefer, hand-write them on coloured paper (which keeps people in alpha state). Ask one person in the team to read them out nice and clearly, the way a good game show host would, and then give each team member a moment to write out a metaphor for that situation. Sharing team responses in turn and at speed is great fun. It's a lovely energiser to play for around five minutes or so.

HOW IT WORKS

This game warms up our brain to metaphors because we have had to create them. Next, let's switch our focus to spotting these types of signals in other people's language when they're describing situations and decision-making in their lives.

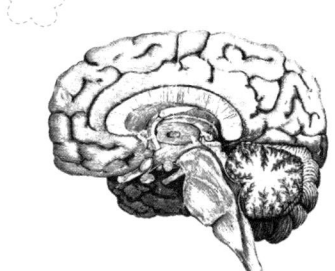

Going to the dentist is a bit like…

The first date is a bit like…

Negotiating a pay rise is a bit like…

Paying by credit card is a bit like…

Going to the dentist is a bit like… the long walk to "Shame Town."

The first date is a bit like… three hours of sobbing inside; I wish I'd said that instead

Negotiating a pay rise is a bit like… an immovable object meeting an unstoppable force

Paying by credit card is a bit like… a magic trick but the audience sees what you do!

⑦ Metaphor spotting

Run this activity as an individual exercise first, and then pair people up to swap their notes and observations. There's no right or wrong – people spot whatever they have energy for and what resonates with them. Importantly, at this stage everyone should be looking beyond the obvious responses to questions in consumer interviews to also see the hidden messages, inferences and suggestions, and what's not being said. A bit like the phrase 'reading between the lines', this is all open to interpretation and it's those interpretations the activity is designed to explore.

WHAT TO DO
Issue everyone in the team with a sheet of at least ten 'verbatims' (exact quotes from consumers) from a project. You might want to write up a number of these sheets with differing levels of 'obvious' metaphors as a resource for the future. All ten quotes need to be a mixture of people discussing the same topic. You'll notice how these verbatims are mini stories and should make sense in isolation. Ask participants to spot the metaphors/re-expressions in the quotes first, and then to discuss with their buddy what themes are emerging. There is not just 'one' big theme waiting to be discovered, but instead a handful of possible insight areas that range in intensity and energy. What the group spots is the insight they believe is the most pertinent. In the holiday example in the panel above, the themes could be:

- No one size fits all
- A good holiday is when you split things up
- Lots of small things, not one big thing
- Movement for some; stationary for others
- Surprise vs predictable

"I can't stand beach holidays – why would I want to stare out to sea all day? It's so boring. I can't help but think I'm using up my life by sitting still. I'd much rather jump into a city and go exploring." *Corrin, 30*

"Holidays for me are about compromising. I lose out on all I want, but I gain a few surprises along the way." *Ryan, 32*

"I'm saving up for a holiday for me and my mates. We're off to Itay. The lakes I think. We chose it because it looked nice on the website. A bit like how I had imagined things to be when it was much older. Like a lost world." *Izzy, 20*

"A holiday is a marker, isn't it? A sort of break in the rhythm of things. I look at my work diary and I like to see the boxes for holiday coloured in really easily. It reminds me I've something to look forward to." *Amy, 28*

"Planning a family holiday. Oh it's tough work, isn't it? It's like a pizza where you all want different toppings. I wish we could divide the week up like that so we'd all get what we wanted." *Simon, 43*

"Holidays are a state of mind. I can be lonely in a busy place if I need to be. You've got to be open to possibility I suppose. Turn new street corners, follow your nose, sniff out the opportunity." *Deborah, 43*

HOW IT WORKS
Metaphors reflect our deeper motivations and drivers. When topics matter to people they have energy. This is a different energy than the normal narration of everyday life. Consumers will use language that hints at their self-talk. If we attune ourselves to metaphors, and where we see and hear them, it's an indication that we're close to uncovering what really matters to the people we're researching.

8 Write a story like Don Draper

There's a brilliant scene in the TV show *Mad Men* when our anti-hero Don Draper manages to convince the product team guys from Kodak that their new innovation shouldn't be called 'the Wheel', but instead 'the Carousel'. It's worth checking out. The writers and art directors of the TV series must have worked tirelessly to make both the script and the setting for the scene work so well together. In it, Don starts off by telling a story (a lie about his first boss being a Greek called Teddy). He explains that in Greek the word for nostalgia literally translates as 'pain of an old wound'. Don continues to use other metaphors such as 'twinge in the heart', and explains that the new device isn't a spaceship but a time machine allowing people to see the world as a child would – travelling backwards and forwards through time until we reach a place in our hearts where we ache to go again. The scene is brilliantly written given the subplots about Don's character and how his stoic, external genius is a far cry from a man wrestling with deep personal demons.

WHAT TO DO

I mention it here as showing the clip is a good energiser with which to start or end the metaphor activities. Show the clip and run it through end to end. Just ask the team to watch what happens, and pose a few questions about the kind of emotions that are in the room at the end of the scene – specifically, what are the emotions of the Kodak team and Don's colleague. Then show the scene again and, as Don says them, write on a flip chart the metaphors, similes and re-expressions in his storytelling (see example, bottom left).

You can then point out how the original brief of 'sell a wheel' is lacking insight, but the proposition of the product 'the Carousel' is far more compelling. The power of an insight story, then, is critical to our insight development.

HOW (AND WHY) IT WORKS

Showing a clip like the one from *Mad Men* sets an overall scene that shows how insights are all part of the story that is our lives. Our own personal narrative exists in the story with neat little characters – us and those we interact with. Our minds join up the dots and make patterns to fit those narratives. As a result, we're driven by subconscious forces far deeper than we realise. For example:

- Buying soap at a gondola end in a supermarket might appear to be a routine purchase, but there are deeper reasons for what brands we choose that connect to our feelings of safety and hygiene. These will be linked to nostalgic memories of laundry days with our parents or grandparents.

- The smell of fresh bread is a trick every estate agent knows; people don't want a house they want a home. And fresh bread reminds people of growing up, unconditional love and nothing but fond memories. The very things a good home should be.

- It's not obvious, but swimming pools are tiled blue to give off subconscious signals of cleanliness and purity.

- And to this day you still need to add an egg to ready-made cake mix, as you're less likely to feel guilty about cheating in the food prep.*

This insight was discovered by Sigmund Freud's nephew, Edward Bernays, who suggested the egg was a sign of fertility and that baking is a sign of love. Women who were making cakes out of boxes didn't feel emotionally invested enough just adding water. Adding eggs would make it feel more like baking. And to this day that's what you still need to do. Remember, insights apply to some people, some of the time.

⑨ The Generation Game

Greek philosopher Aristotle is attributed to saying, 'give me the boy until seven and I shall show you the man.' This sentiment captures nicely what many of us know intuitively to be true: that what happens in our early lives shapes our outlook on the future. Our map of the world and our place in it is very much influenced by the happenings and impact that life has upon us. It's important to keep this in mind when generating insights. There are clichés in business about 'getting closer to our customers', being 'customer-centric' and 'walking in our customers' shoes'. All this rhetoric needs to translate into activities and systems that truly help us understand and see the world from our customers' point of view*.

Because an insight need only be true for some people to be of value to us, the more we can do to understand the world as others see it, the better. A sentiment enigmatically captured by writer and diarist Anaïs Nin: 'we don't see things as they are, we see things as we are.'

When musician Billy Joel turned forty he listed all the key events that had happened in the decades during his life. That song became 'We Didn't Start the Fire' and is a whistle-stop tour of 20th-century American culture. Inspired by the song, this game is designed to help your project participants become even more sensitive to the underlying stories we're all telling each other about our lives. It starts the foundation of being able to (ahem, clears throat) step into the shoes of our consumer by looking back at significant events in our own lives.

WHAT TO DO
Remind everyone of the Billy Joel song (although it's from 1989, so it could be the first play of it for many!) The point is that there's a lot that goes on in our lives, and when we take time to remember what has happened to us and around us we might spot beliefs that are common to us all, as well as the things that make us unique.

Now, create a big cross on the floor with tape, to make four zones (see over page). These zones are where we can tell stories – by printing out pictures and writing notes on coloured paper to put in each zone – that teach about our past and the events that have shaped our lives.

All of this is a rich psychological and sociological backdrop to decision-making and behaviour. If we're trying to understand why certain people choose Nike over Adidas, or Hendriks instead of Gordons, and we're focused on that topic alone, then we'll struggle. Our choice of sports shoe or gin is part of the story we tell ourselves in response to the world we live in. Everything we do is in the bigger

---

*I remember working in a bank and sitting in on a loans project. I observed that **everyone** in the room at that time was a seasoned long-timer at the bank. They certainly knew the workings of the products. And were all probably paid handsomely for the jobs they did. It was unlikely that any of us had needed a loan for (I guessed) at least 20 years or more, and six-figure mortgages didn't count. And yet there we were, sipping lattes, trying to 'step into the shoes' of people with fluctuating incomes. A loan only has utility when it enables people to do something they need to do. Without that, it's just more debt, the very thing people want to avoid being in.

POLITICAL/SOCIETAL
What things were happening at global level in terms of geopolitics having an impact on society?

POPULAR CULTURE
What was fashionable and trending at the time. What did people get up to?

WORLD OF WORK
What were your perceptions of what work would be?

TECHNOLOGY
What tech at the time would have been impacting people?

context of the lives we lead. Don't just focus on the tiny details. As anyone with an aquarium will tell you: 'Look after the water, not the fish.'

As the facilitator, you go first and demo the tool. Pick an era – perhaps simply your 'formative years', or a particular decade – and talk through each of the four areas in turn, sharing at least two examples of 'big things' that you remember from your past. The events can't be something that happened in the press that week. Nor can they be fictitious stories. They need to have had significant impact on you to become a lasting memory. They are likely to be the topics that other people of your age will also remember. For each example, you'll need to tell a concise story about what that happening is all about and why it had an effect on you. And, at the end of your storytelling, you need to share what you believe.

These small stories that bring to life a belief are what we call 'drivers'. Drivers are far more nuanced and useful than values. 'I value people and friendships' isn't something that provides help when generating insight or ideas as it's too generic; who doesn't value their friendships? But the driver of 'I believe magical things happen when people connect' puts what I value in a context that is meaningful to me and that others can understand more readily.

Insights aren't facts. They're stories about what matters to some people some of the time. Your stories are best told with a picture as a prop. A picture paints a thousand words and will help fire off

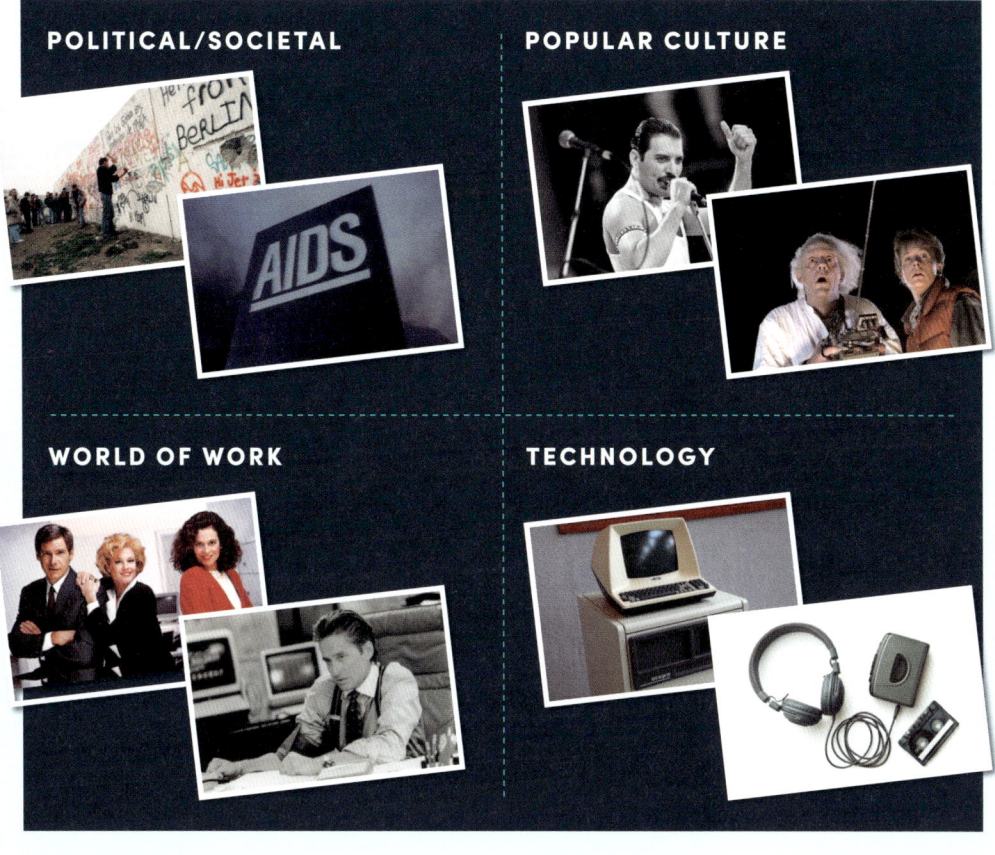

being challenged and resolved. This was the time of leaders Reagan, Thatcher, Gorbachev. It was also the time of 'fear' as I remember vividly the AIDS commercials on TV, the leaflet that dropped though our letterbox and the topic of AIDS being hugely misunderstood at school and at home. From these two 'big things', I could say that, **I believe there will always be things bigger than me that fall outside of my control.**

POPULAR CULTURE: On 13th July 1985, I watched Live Aid on TV, and to this day I still think it's cool. I have fond memories of watching it on tape on the school bus when we went on trips months after the event, too. And *Back to the Future* was a film I remember being excited by (it still holds up as a classic) and my friends and I would do the best we could to emulate Marty McFly's mannerisms, as he was incredibly cooler than anyone I knew growing up in leafy suburban Britain. **I believe magical things happen when people connect**.

WORLD OF WORK: I was very aware growing up that there was a 'work life' outside the home that Mum and Dad went to. And, indeed, all the other adults I knew also had these things called 'jobs'. School was different – that was where I went every day, but I knew that would eventually end. I had a sense of 'I need to get a job as there is no alternative'. And, despite my messing about in class, I privately worked out that I needed to

the memories of those in the room, too. It also helps set the context for folk who aren't as familiar with these events as you are. When you've told your stories, allow people to think individually and take time to reflect on what you've said, before adding their own stories to the grid. Ideally, this game is best briefed as an overnight assignment to really allow people time to identify their personal stories. Here are mine: I was born in the early 70s, so my formative years were from the mid-1980s on and into the 90s as a young adult.

POLITICAL/SOCIETAL: The late 1980s were governed by the fall of the Berlin Wall and the possible end of East–West tensions. The Cold War had been in play during the time my parents grew up and there was now a feeling of hope and connection as a result of old prejudices

work hard to get on in life. As an adult I can look back and see that I grew up in a time where 'greed was good' – the excesses and spoils were there to be taken. And there were the first glimpses of equality for men and women in the workplace. The two pictures I show are from the movies *Working Girl* (1988) and *Wall Street* (1987). In *Working Girl*, Tess McGill (Melanie Griffith flirting with Harrison Ford) memorably said, 'I've got a head for business and body for sin!' And in *Wall Street* I looked at Michael Douglas and wondered was this the working world? From these two stories, I could say, **I believe that work is a part of life. I don't subscribe to the work–life balance philosophy. I need, therefore, to be my true self at work to be happy.**

TECHNOLOGY: And finally, tech at the time was pretty rudimentary. We had one (!) computer in my first school. Everything on the TV programme *Tomorrow's World* somehow connected to a green monitor. Unlike today, it was tech you could 'fiddle' with more readily; I could fix my cassettes with a pencil, if they got caught in the machine. I could 'break' a computer programme and enter some code from a magazine to make the games easier to play. We could help our geography teacher, who was struggling with the VCR machine, operate the remote. Tech was something you could be more hands on with. **I believe tech isn't the answer, it's simply another tool. You're the genius.**

Below, you'll see a summary of my beliefs as a visual, and what it looks like in an actual session. Depending on your group

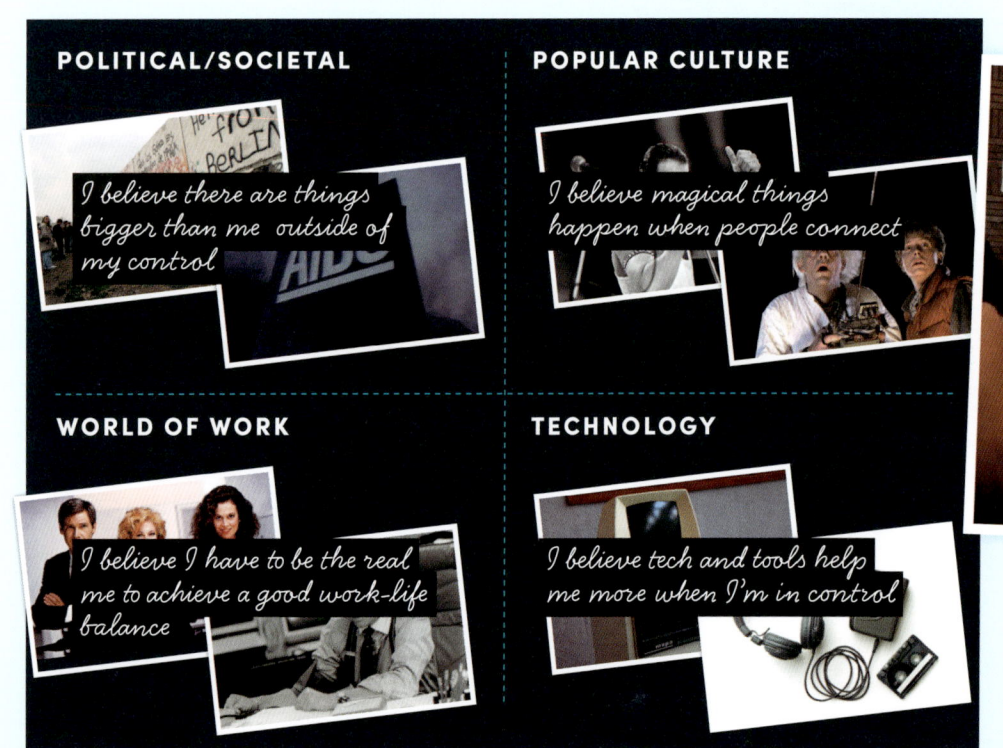

ABOVE/LEFT:
A summary of my beliefs (*left*) and what that looked like during my storytelling about them (*above*). The coloured notes indicate where participants shared their memories too.

size, you can split everyone into small teams (three is good) to fill in grids of their own and story share.

In this instance, as I've told my stories I've invited people to drop down into each box the kind of things they feel were influential in their lives, too. On the flip chart, I've set a bit of context about the bigger drivers in our lives, other than the conscious immediate needs of 'let's get coffee'.

This activity takes time, and I think is much better if you share your example at the end of the day and then give the other people in the group until the next morning to think about their own stories. Inviting them to drop down a few starter examples as part of my story effectively 'primes' their minds for the task later in the evening, and sets conversation off in the right direction should they also be heading to the nearby bar.

Be specific about the time period from which you'd like people to recall their stories. Of late 'the 2000s' is a good one. This is the sort of thing I've got so far (see table, above right).

HOW IT WORKS

Your insight team need to spend time telling stories, discussing what they believe as a result, and listening to each other. They need the time to ask questions and go off at tangents — in doing so they will share much more about what they think and feel. They'll forge closer connections to each other, and they'll 'own' that moment in the project. An energy will come from something that they generated from the stimuli they shared. I think this is critical if they're to become more empathetic and sensitive to the short stories they'll mine when reading through consumer data.

Bring this activity to an end by hearing the 'big themes' from each group and their 'generation grid'. Ask if there were overlaps and commonalities. And importantly, ask how closer do team members feel to each other and potentially people 'out there' in the real world after their discussions.

2000s–2010s

POLITICAL/SOCIETAL
· 9/11: War on terror
· Social media: impact on facts/truth
· Climate change
· LGBTQ+

POPULAR CULTURE
· Move from CDs to digital downloads
· *Friends*
· YouTube

WORLD OF WORK
· Globalisation
· Financial crisis
· First email address
· Working from home/work-life balance

TECHNOLOGY
· Internet
· Digital cameras
· Electrification replacing fossil fuels
· Apps on our devices

There is no 'big reveal' here — there isn't one universal truth about all humanity. You'll likely have quite an interesting (and potentially rambling) conversation. Allow time for this, as you're finally starting to walk in the customer shoes.

However, great insight teams don't see 'customers' as annoying vessels who don't do what they want and refuse to buy what we're selling. Instead, customer behaviour needs to be seen in the context of a more colourful world of which we are just a part. Running this activity builds empathy and neatly sets things up for the final 'warm-up' when it comes to teaching groups how to be more insightful. 👉

⑩ The human drivers & spot the tension

Let's summarise the insight journey we've been on so far. The list of questions below are what each of the nine previous games have asked your team, each task building up the complexity step by step.

1. What happens next in the sequence/spot the pattern?
2. What connections and links can you see?
3. What themes do you spot?
4. What are you feeling, where are you feeling it?
5. What emotions are present?
6. What metaphors describe what's happening?
7. What deeper themes are emerging from the metaphors?
8. What stories do we tell ourselves about the world in which we live?
9. As a result of those stories, what beliefs do we have?

Too often on insight projects, teams are quick to fill in the empathy maps (I'm coming to these later in the chapter) without warming up each other's minds. If we were to throw ourselves into the local gym as a team and start hurling iron around, it wouldn't be long before one of our teammates had an injury. Hence, in sport we warm up.

When learning any practical skill we establish some foundations. In music, for example, we learn the scales by practising them and creating muscle memory. A professional pianist once told me he no longer sees the notes on a page but instead changes the shape of his hand over the keyboard as he hums along to the melody he's reading – playing the piano has become intuitive for him.

Similarly, the power of 'the team' affects performance. Studies have shown that if you sing in a choir you're more likely to remain in tune than if you're warbling alone in the shower. And that if you row, you're more likely to pull harder and more consistently in a team boat than puffing away on a machine in the gym. I want you and your insight team to all behave in tune with each other. The collective 'wisdom of the crowd'* will be far stronger than any one clever savant. I believe these warm-up activities are essential. Skipping over them is not the way. They lead somewhere. And the final warm-up is to spot the human drivers being challenged in any situation.

HUMAN DRIVERS
Consider queuing for coffee at your local Costa or Starbucks. It's something you've done many times before. While

---
*In the mid-1800s Francis Galton (Charles Darwin's cousin) spotted that a crowd at a county fair accurately guessed the weight of a cow when their individual guesses were averaged. The average was closer to the cow's actual weight than the individual estimates of most crowd members. The 'wisdom of crowds' theory proposes that a diverse collection of independently deciding individuals is likely to make certain types of predictions better than individuals alone. Something worth noting next time you and your mates are guessing the number of coins in a jar.

you're three or four people away from the counter, you've enough 'dwell time' to fiddle with your phone, spot a potential seat and ask yourself if you fancy a cake (or chocolate!) – funny how those treats are positioned 'just so'...

Then the critical time comes. You're in the 'me next' moment. Shopper behaviour consultants (yes, that is a job) know this is not a good time to try to speak to people, because they're preparing what to say and how to respond to any questions the server may ask. But, just as you think it's your turn to order, the person in front orders five drinks for the audit team. It's the most complicated order the staff have ever heard, including a frosted-almond-syrup-decaf-frappuccino-with-fairtrade-organic-oatmilk – oh, and a charcoal vegan croissant, too.

That's it. Your body is consumed by rage. Your shoulders tense, your chest pounds, your hands sweat and you're shouting inside your head at the top of your voice 'you bastard!' Of course, when audit man turns around to apologise, you reply with 'that's fine' and a forced smile. Beneath our polite exterior, however, is a seething mass of repulsion towards audit man and his tribe of bean counters. Why?

Because all you want to do is **get out of there** and **get on with your day**.

And in that statement are the clues to the human drivers that are being challenged in that moment.

- 'Get out of there' is a reference to *containment*.

- 'Get on with your day' is a reference to being in *control*.

Control and **containment** along with **transformation**, **balance** and **connection** are deeply rooted psychological drivers. These are the foundations on which our character is built, and in any given moment will act as a filter in our decision-making and subsequent behaviour. Again, metaphors (see Insight game 006, page 180) are often clues as to which human driver is being challenged. When we spot these types of metaphor we're likely to be very close to the powerful energies that are influencing the behaviour of those we observe. These drivers will be easy to spot when we revisit the storytelling from the Generation Game (see page 185) and the beliefs that everyone has shared as a result of it.

The drivers that will ultimately boil down to wanting:

- Control
- Containment
- Transformation
- Balance
- Connection

WHAT TO DO

Remind everyone of the generation game activity. Revisit your stories and the drivers* that were revealed in your beliefs. Issue a fresh set of verbatim quotes from some market research (see example over page) to your team and ask them to spot the metaphors that point to a tension being created. Where there's tension there's a human driver being challenged. We're not here to be psychologists and name the actual driver, life isn't that binary, and although the coffee story works as an example it's one built as a teaching aid. In reality, all our drivers are constantly being challenged and our personality and sense of self is constantly massaging our ego and self-control, so we don't lose our temper publicly in coffee shops. That said, tension exists, so spot it and you're one step closer to articulating an insight.

SPOT THE TENSIONS

"Hunting for birthday presents is torture. I'm always worried they'll have what I find already, or that they'll not like what I choose. That would be a total waste of time for me if it came true." *Gemma, 32*

"Birthdays can sneak up on you, can't they, like take you by surprise. All that shopping for people. One moment I've got money and the next, it's all vanished!" *Corrin, 20*

"I received a really smart tie, pen and bag for my birthday. I felt all grown up. I felt excited about my new job and that people had spotted what was important to me." *Ryan, 32*

"It makes me laugh watching dads trudge around shopping malls like they don't belong. It's so obvious they feel obliged to be there. Maybe we should give them a 'get out of shopping free' pass." *Izzy, 20*

"When I see the present, it speaks to me. I can feel it in my bones. I walk past it in the shop and I just get a shiver. There's a voice in my head saying 'that's it' and I buy it right then." *Helen, 28*

"Finding a birthday present for my wife isn't that hard. I don't need to be a genius or rely on magic. Sometimes we walk past a shop close to her birthday and she'll say, 'Oh, that's pretty', and I make a mental note, and then sneak back into town later in the week. I feel like a spy, and it feels really good when I get home and I've completed the mission." *Simon, 43*

"Each year, shopping for the birthday present gets harder. Like another exam to test how much your really love your partner. If you buy a rubbish present it means you've given up!" *Chris, 34*

"My sister and I buy each other our birthday gifts together. It's a ritual each year. A joint adventure and we love doing together. I don't know why more people don't do it. We have loads of fun." *Deborah, 43*

"But the act of going out to buy a present is much more rewarding than the gift itself. I know that sounds cliché, but it's true. It's the same with journies and destinations isn't it." *Xav, 31*

"I sometimes shop in the malls and then go home and buy what I saw online. I don't feel under pressure to buy things when I'm at home. I can put things in the basket and checkout when I'm ready." *Amy, 28*

In this example, I've highlighted in the first quote two possible tensions. If I were to ask Gemma's subconscious what's going on, I think she'd be saying something like:

'I have fear of losing connection with people, which manifests in worry over my gift choice. And I fear that I've wasted my freedom and/or control over my day by spending time on a task that resulted in disappointment.'

To prevent this activity becoming overly complicated, ask participants to complete a simple formula for each quote, by just filling in the following blanks:

I want to do this _____ , but I need to do that _____

In Gemma's example, one answer could be *I want to* **buy a gift quickly**, *but I need to* **invest in my friendship**.

From now on, I ask that our starter insight is captured in the first person. I've spotted that doing so connects project team members far more closely to the people they're researching. No longer are we observers making measured and scientific investigations, but instead concerned citizens on a quest to help the needy. For example:

I'm lonely
vs
Some people get lonely

Using the first person like this will help to focus in and isolate the tensions. Where there isn't an obvious tension you can't write: 'I want to do this but I need to do that', as it won't necessarily fit what teams have spotted or discussed. Instead, start by asking your participants 'what's going on and why does it matter?' – then ask again after they've had a discussion. Then you can capture people's opinion in the first person.

As an example, Ryan says:

"I received a really smart tie, pen and bag for my birthday. I felt all grown up. I felt excited about my new job and that people had spotted what was important to me."

What's going on and why it's important could be: Ryan's at a pivotal life moment (new job and birthday coincide) and he is in a moment of reassessing what's happened before and what could happen in the future. Written in the first person this could be, *'I need public recognition every now and then as this helps me remember the important moments.'*

And when Izzy says: *"It makes me laugh watching dads trudge around shopping malls like they don't belong. It's so obvious they feel obliged to be there. Maybe we should give them a 'get out of shopping free' pass."*

So, Izzy has observed that some people get fazed by shopping, as there's so much going on they don't know where to start. Written in the first person (the voice of one of the shopping mall dads) it could be *'I get overwhelmed, I'd love an easy path to take.'*

This is a multi-layered activity. You're asking your team to spot something in the quotes; discuss and agree their findings. They need to identify if there's a tension and, if there isn't, then identify what is going on and its importance; and finally capture it in the first person.

To do so will require a final bit of imagination – it's essential, then, for this and all activities, that you show your team examples of what you're looking for. Showing people the required output of an exercise helps clear up any of your language people didn't quite understand. Say the brief once and show 2–3 examples of what you're looking for to land the point.

HOW IT WORKS
Let's look back at my Generation Game beliefs and the human drivers behind them:

I believe there will always be things bigger than me that fall outside of my control. This is a direct signal that being in control matters to me.

I believe magical things happen when people connect. I value connection. Whilst I enjoy my own company to recharge, I do enjoy being with other people. So much so that I started life as a teacher. In fact, I was helping 'run sessions' in my late teens and it's become a way of life ever since.

I believe that work is a part of life. I don't subscribe to the work–life balance philosophy. I need, therefore, to be my true self at work to be happy. We don't seek things to excess. Having balance instead of extremes is a driver – for example, working long hours for other people without reward is something we'd all avoid, I'm sure. I don't resent working into the wee small hours on a project if I wish to, as I know I can grab that time back at a time of my choosing. I have good balance in my life as a result.

I believe tech isn't the answer, it's simply another tool. You're the genius. Again, this is a reference to the driver of control. I hope that people on my projects feel they are at the helm of the discoveries we make and the ideas we have.

My beliefs point out that the drivers CONTROL, BALANCE and CONNECTION are important to me. If I'm in a situation where these are compromised, I tend not to be my full self and disengage. Looking back at jobs, situations, relationships and moments when I wasn't at my best (putting it politely), I realise my behaviour was shocking. Behaviour is a symptom of an attitude. If I like something and find that topic engaging, I'm more likely to behave positively towards it. And my language in describing my attitudes and behaviours will likely point (metaphorically) to those deeper drivers.

As masters of insight, you and your team will look at people's language and the metaphors they use to spot the tension in moments of their lives. When you spot this, it's far easier to connect to what's driving behaviour. Then we're just one small creative leap away from connecting the dots and articulating the insight that will hopefully yield fruitful innovations.

Human drivers

She's a team player	Connection	*He's a loose cannon*
I am centred	Balance	*I feel slightly off*
I've turned over a new leaf	Transformation	*A bit like Jekyll and Hyde*
On the same page	Containment	*Out of our hands*
In a good mood	Control	*Out of my mind*

ABOVE:
It's hard for people to articulate what they value if you ask them directly. It's better to listen out for cues in their language that imply what drives their behaviour. There's a degree of interpretation by the 'listener', so constantly discussing and exploring possibilities within the project team is key.

Facilitation tip 007
Deliver positive instruction

I went to the swimming pool with my kids. There were lots of signs telling me what I couldn't and mustn't do.

No running. **No** shouting. **No** diving in the shallows. **No** entry. **No** sitting on the side. **No** more than three people here. I didn't see signs telling me what I *could* do, nor any instruction or information to help me get the best out the experience either. Hmmmmmm.

It's the same with your signage on a project or training. Emphasis ought to be on 'what you want people to **feel**, **think** and **do**' and not on 'what you want them to avoid'. We process negatives differently than positives. This is a neurolinguistic thing (technical), but our brains dismiss negatives and focus goes into what immediately follows. A bit like the pub trick 'don't think about a packet of crisps'.

The same is true for physical instructions. 'Don't run!' exclaim all parents, just before their children trip over in the playground. 'Don't go too fast!' my fellow ski instructor would plea to an over eager teenage group at the top of a mountain.

We ignore negatives.

At teacher training, when it came to using tools in the design workshop, I was told **not** to demonstrate to a class the behaviour you *didn't* want to see. (Oops, see what I did there?) For example, 'Don't hold it like this' should be replaced instead with 'Hold it like this.' Likewise, 'Don't forget…' is better expressed as 'Remember to…' These have proven to be great pieces of instruction for adult facilitation. 'Work in pairs' is a clear positive instruction rather than 'Don't work alone' which is negative and lacking any instruction.

Look through your notes for your project briefing and check the bullet points of instruction you'll be giving. Spot where you're being specific about an activity, and write out and say out loud the positive re-expressions of that instruction.

You'll be coaching yourself to be a positive instructor – someone who gives positive instructions.

It's a lovely way to build trust and to show you love your participants.

Facilitation tip 008

No rules in golf about club selection

My old boss, Seb, told me this one. There are no rules in the game of golf stipulating club selection.

Players know which club is meant to be good to use for certain shots, but the best golfers are creative and innovative about selecting different clubs for different shots.

For your project session design, there's no need to be wedded to a specific tool for a specific job. We've all got favourite stories, examples, anecdotes and analogies, but take care not to fall into the trap of over-using an old favourite.

I've seen the same story being offered time and again when giving feedback to participants and groups. On reflection, it was more about a story the facilitator wanted to tell than actually helping the participants land their personal learning. I understand how a well-told story is a teaching tool, but not all teaching tools are right for learning; could you play another shot or use a different club?

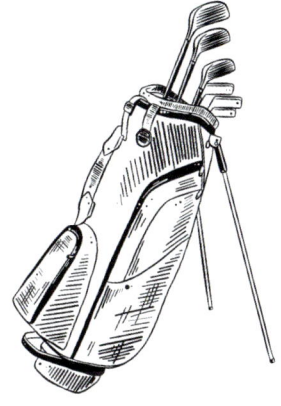

Insight framework

My father was a policeman – I grew up in a house of suspicion. He was, for a time, a detective.

The analogy of acting as a detective (ah, Columbo again!) is a useful one. However, the job is nothing like TV, where crimes are solved in neat 50-minute formats. Instead, solving crime took long hours, piecing together disparate and seemingly unconnected events until the crime was solved. Dad explained that first, officers start with information – facts and evidence collected at a crime scene or as part of an ongoing investigation. Over time, the information develops into intelligence, a far more structured story of what is going on and why, until finally that intelligence becomes a case, and the case is brought against someone.

This sequence of events is a useful analogy for the work you and your project team participants are to do in building up an insight case to fuel your ideas sessions. The stronger the case, the stronger your ideas. Bland ideas are probably not powered by enough energy from the insight stage. So, articulating an insight in a clear and concise way is critical if we're to innovate. For that to happen, we need a framework on which to hang our insightful efforts. Using the detective analogy, our seven part framework is:

1. Collect the information
2. Use the Suspect Fruit Machine
3. Build a crime scene
4. Build the case
5. Create empathy maps
6. Identify the pains, gains and jobs to be done
7. Ask the final question (who dunnit?)

Let's take a look 👉

❶ Collect the information

This part of the framework is about collecting the raw data, facts and information surrounding your project topic. This will include customer interviews, observations, shopper data, material from home visits, web pages, reports, leaflets, product samples... anything that's associated with the customers you're researching and the context in which they're behaving.

In our detective analogy, information can be shortened to the word 'clues'. Clues are pieces of information that we have seen, read, heard or experienced first-hand. When collecting clues, we must be careful not to jump to conclusions, but instead simply capture and collect. Clues are best captured in the first person (as that builds empathy, remember). In addition to the clues from people, it is also essential to collect clues from the lives these people are living. This sets the context for the behaviours and mindsets that we're trying to capture, and will help you and your team be more successful in articulating your insights.

As a rule (a very loose one), I ask that two-thirds of 'clues' are from people we speak to* and the remaining third are from the context in which those people are found.

Two examples:

If I were on a loans project for a bank, two-thirds of my clues would be from people who have taken loans, are considering a loan, or have paid off a loan, and one-third would come from literature around loan products. I'd have examples of loan leaflets from banks, spam 'loan' emails, screenshots of 'payday loan' propositions, etc.

If I were on a beer project, two-thirds of my clues would come from beer drinkers, bar staff, non-drinkers, etc., and the remaining third of the clues would be photos of the beer aisles in supermarkets, a variety of beer packaging and some food and wine magazines.

A good mixture is what to aim for.

> * The type of people we speak to and how we interact with them is a critical and therefore creative moment in the information gathering phase. The 'suspect fruit machine' (see page 200) is the tool to help you collect information from where your competitors can't or won't go.

② Use the Suspect Fruit Machine

This part of the framework is a tool that helps you secure a rich mixture of different types of people (suspects) to talk to and describes how you can gather information from them in a variety of creative ways.

Before online gaming, fruit machines were a great way to lose a weekend's wage packet. At college, the jackpot in our fruit machine was £250 – in the early 90s, to an 'impoverished' student, that was an utter fortune. Cast your eyes on the key feature of the fruit machine: the three spinning drums that needed to align in order for your £2 investment to double, triple or go all the way. We can use the fruit machine analogy to help an insight project team think of a range of different people to speak to in order to inject the necessary creative edge an insight project needs.

There are three types of people who will have a connection to your project topic. First are the types of people you'd naturally gravitate towards to speak to – they have a very clear and obvious connection to your topic. The second group have a deeper and more specific connection to the topic – they may have technical knowledge that 'Joe Public' doesn't; they may have years of experience in that topic or work with people who are affected by it. And finally, there are people who have a wild and extreme connection with your project topic – think of 'opposites', 'negatives' or 'naive' to help you think creatively about who people in this category might be.

The first task in using this tool is to list the people ('suspects' if you continue to use the detective analogy) in each of the three categories. A rough split for the volume of your discussions is 70/20/10. So, 70 per cent of your time should be spent speaking to people in the obvious connection category, whilst only 10 per cent of your time needs to be spent speaking to those with a wild and extreme relationship to your project topic. I've completed here (below and over page) the suspects list for the loans project and then the beer project to give you working examples.

To build a suspect fruit machine, draw three columns on a large white board. At the top, write clearly what's at the heart of your insight investigation. The output of the fruit machine tool becomes far more useful when you start asking creative questions about what the inputs are. You want to understand more about people's relationship with something. As a result, your insights will be far more interesting and certainly move away from obvious surface level truths.

If the project were bank loans it would be about people's relationship with risk. If debt is about balancing, then who else knows a lot about balancing? You could speak to trapeze artists (they balance), or accountants who have to 'balance the books.' Loans often require regular payments overtime. Who else knows a great deal about keeping things 'regular'? How about the conductor of an orchestra?

When speaking to these types of people it's important not to let them know you're asking them for knowledge about bank loans as they'll try to solve the problem. Instead, you're keen to find out all there is to know about 'how to keep things regular'. This might furnish you with an edge to your insight and inspire ideas, too.

Let's switch to beer (hooray!). During the alcohol projects I've worked on in the past, a good deal of time was spent discussing what the first sip is all about. This is particularly exciting when there's a practical element to the work! The first sip is often broken down into stages:

LOANS

Obvious connection	Deeper connection	Extreme connection
People considering a loan	Debt collectors	Trapeze artists
Those who have paid off a loan recently	People who've declared bankruptcy	People with no bank accounts
People in good credit who had a loan once	Accountants	Orchestra conductors
People who have taken a loan and are struggling to make repayments	People who work in banking and are familiar with the product (likely to be on the project team)	

BEER		
Obvious connection	**Deeper connection**	**Extreme connection**
Pub regulars	Bar tenders/publicans (what do they think given their experience in serving people beer?)	Teetotallers (what do they drink and why?)
People who buy beer in the weekly shop		Builders – know about the perfect pour (mixing and pouring concrete)
Anyone who says they enjoy a pint at the end of the day	Beer producers	Yoga instructors – know about moments of relaxation
	People who brand beer for a living (likely to be in the project team)	

(i) leading up to the purchase, (ii) the pour, (iii) the first sip and then (iv) the moments afterwards. Who knew it was such a complicated affair? However, breaking down these moments into isolated *stories* makes it easier to spot the more lateral and creative opportunities to speak to more interesting people – all of whom have a relationship with that beer-drinking moment.

If 'the pour', for example, was seen as a critical moment for the perfect serve, then speaking to a builder about mixing and setting concrete might yield some interesting insight material.

The 'first sip' is obviously key – I wonder if speaking to a relationship counsellor about the importance of making good 'first impressions' would be a beneficial chat?

The fruit machine provokes thinking.

If you and your team keep approaching the same sorts of people with the same sorts of questions, then it's unsurprising that the same sort of insights are crafted. Use this tool to have a knockabout session with your insight team and you'll guarantee something far from the norm. And, if in doubt, jump in a cab as taxi drivers have an opinion about everything.

EXAMPLE STORY

I worked on a tech project, where the ask was, ultimately, to find out more about people's relationships with technology in decision making. I spoke to an airline pilot as I figured they'd be using tech all the time to make decisions. Interestingly, when the conversation shifted to 'what you do in an emergency', the pilot told me that the drill is for everyone to sit on their hands.

With a cruising height of 35,000 ft, it takes about 45 minutes for the aircraft to descend through the sky if it lost forward power. That's enough time for the pilot and officers to take a breath and run through the checklists, which are written out on laminated flip books. No technology involved. They sit on their hands to prevent themselves being caught up in the instinctive behaviour of pressing buttons and fiddling with knobs to rectify the situation – which is exactly what *not* to do, as you're likely to make matters worse.

An unexpected and interesting insight, and something to ponder next time you're on board...

③ Build a crime scene

This part of the framework is about building a physical space to 'see' all the different types of clues you've gathered so you can spot connections more easily. In the same way the games at the start of the chapter were about seeing patterns and joining up information, building a crime scene enables you and your project team participants to do this with your consumer data.

In our detective analogy, the crime scene is a place filled with evidence. For your insight project, you and your team need a dedicated space that becomes 'a place where the insights happen'. I believe this space NEEDS TO BE PHYSICAL. We listen with our eyes. We process information with our whole body. We cannot expect people to reach insightful and creative epiphanies if customer data (information) is lost in CRM software or PDF reports on a shared drive. We need to get close to the information if we're to fully understand it.

Consider that if you're redecorating your house you'll buy some tester pots and dab the walls with colours to choose from. If you're more adventurous you might create a 'mood board' with photos and swatches to build a picture of what the next environment will look like. When we buy a new car we take it for a test drive.

And when we buy clothing we try it on. The nuances, metaphors and human inferences that signal life's rich tensions are lost if they are typed up in Excel sheets. It's hard to ask your subconscious to wander around a shared drive. Instead, when information is visual and accessible we're more likely to spot what's ready to be discovered.

So, build a crime scene. Stick information up on the walls. You need to be able to move each item (a clue) separately, draw circles around clusters of interesting snippets and have the space to take a step back and see the bigger picture. This is a team activity. You, as facilitator, and your project team participants should all be involved. This takes time, too. Build the crime scene in parallel with team members returning from their consumer interviews and safaris. Spend an hour at the end of each project day building the crime scene and discussing your discoveries. There's a reason TV shows and movies have the detectives in an incident room making connections as they pin clues on a wall – it works.

④ Build the case(s)

This stage is essentially creating big themes out of the information you gather. At first these themes will be nebulous, out of context and perhaps contain just a few words, such as 'guilt free', or 'help me win', but over time and further discussion, those themes will become more specific and nuanced; closer to the insight examples at the opening of the chapter. For example, 'guilt free' becomes 'I want to be free from the guilt I feel when I gobble down a bar of chocolate on the morning commute' and 'help me win' could evolve into 'life's a game, and I can win if I have a few shortcuts'.

To build those cases, I advise consistently asking your team two questions when reviewing the information they gather: the first is: **What's going on and why?** You're asking your team to tell you (and themselves) a story about the theme they've spotted. It can start with, 'there's something about… ' and then expand into and 'and this is interesting because…' This is an extension of the skill they learnt in the 'Spot a theme' game (see page 171).

The second question is: **So what?** (a shorter version of 'why does this issue matter in people's lives?'). I like having these questions up in the crime scene for people to see and refer to; it's a simple nudge that recalibrates conversations. The themes can be called 'cases' – the emerging stories that may or may not be pertinent to your project. Some will have more energy than others. Some may apply to greater numbers of people than others. Some may evolve into insights that are true for some and not at all for others.

At this stage, therefore, there is no judgement about which story is better or stronger – and certainly no 'right' or 'wrong'. What we spot and discuss is all potentially useful. I believe that if there is an energising and inspiring insight to be discovered then the team will spot it, but only if they approach each other, and their discussions, with the right behaviour. If insightfulness comes from following the framework, then the behaviours are the creative energy that keep that framework adding value. Insightfulness, therefore, manifests when people are:

Playful – not being wedded to an outcome.

Curious – constantly asking questions and developing hypotheses and explanations.

Nurturing – being positive and exploratory towards each other's suggestions.

Interested – looking at the world 'with eyes open', not being satisfied with the first answer or the obvious. This is about digging deeper, and asking (like Columbo) 'just one more thing'.

Good-humoured – a relaxed mind is in alpha state, open to possibility and free to make new connections.

As always, keeping things visual reminds people of what to do and how to be. And two film references make re-expressing this stage of the insight framework all the easier. In *La Luna*, Pixar's short film about a trip to the moon, the young boy and his two grandfathers use brooms and a rake to push tiny stars around, so when seen from a distance their work gives off the light and shape of the moon. It's a lovely metaphor about 'the big picture' being made up of smaller parts. Similarly, it is only when Neo fully accepts his place in *The Matrix* that he can see a world beyond the code. Prior to that all he could see was isolated data bits – nothing made sense, it was just noise.

Advise your project team to constantly zoom in and out of the information, calibrating output from one discussion against outputs from another. If you spot a piece of information that interests you, trust your gut – it may indeed be the missing piece to the broader puzzle, which reveals the insight that will inspire project ideas.

⑤ Empathy maps

An empathy map is a pre-designed canvas (the larger the better) where you can place your project clues in a way that enables you to tell an emerging story about the 'tribe' of people you want to focus on and have fall in love with you (and your product offer).

This stage of the framework enables everyone on the project team (facilitator, project team participants and sponsor) to build a clear and compelling story about what's going on in and around the lives of the target consumer. Populating each part of an empathy map helps develop an overall story about what this consumer wants and needs, and helps you as a team agree on the most important aspects of that consumer's life. A great empathy map will start to inspire ideas.

I like empathy maps, but they are often brought out too early in a project. Worse still is when they're handed out to complete overnight without the team having any chance to incubate thinking, discuss themes or share stories about the topic. This is not the way. You can't complete an empathy map without having any information from your discussions to hand. And completing the map won't then give you an insight. An empathy map, I believe, is best used to tell the story to people outside the project team about the consumers you're interested in and what's going on in their lives. This sets context for the shorter insights you'll craft later. In any insight story you tell, there's a degree of context setting and establishing a status quo. A typical insight story might present as:

'Ordinarily, *this sort of person* has *this sort of relationship* with *this sort of moment* when they're doing *this sort of activity* in their lives. We've spotted that when *this new thing happens* what they *actually think is this*, and they *probably feel like this* about it, too.' 👉

GOAL

1. Who are we empathizing with?
Who is the person we want to understand?
What is the situation they are in?

2. What do they need to do?
What do they need to do differently?
What job(s) do they want or need to get done?
What decision(s) do they need to make?
How will we know they were successful?

6. What do they hear?
What are they hearing others say?
What are they hearing from friends?
What are they hearing from colleagues?
What are they hearing second-hand?

What do they think and feel?

Pains What are their fears, frustrations and anxieties?

Gains What are their wants, needs, hopes and dreams?

3. What do they see?
What do they see in the marketplace?
What do they see in their immediate environment?
What do they see others saying and doing?
What are they watching and reading?

5. What do they do?
What do they do today?
What behaviour have we observed?
What can we imagine them doing?

4. What do they say?
What have we heard them say?
What can we imagine them saying?

There's a before, during and after to an insight story – something that 'People like the taste of chocolate' fails to deliver. Similarly, 'Beauty is truth and the truth is we're all beautiful' is an 'insight story fail' when the sentence is taken out of context. Had you been a part of the *Unilever* journey when *Dove* first acted on that insight, you'd be all the more connected to the consumer and better prepared in telling the world about their lives. This is what an empathy map helps you do, but it won't tell the story for you. It's still just a tool, and is only as valuable as the content that goes in and the story that comes out. On the previous page there's a typical empathy map lifted off the web. Interestingly, the website that I copied this from stated that an empathy map 'analyses and describes behavioural aspects of the ideal customer.' An empathy map does nothing of the sort! It is for you and your team to analyse and describe the behaviours and mindsets of your customers. The empathy map (like many of our tools) is just a set of boxes on a page. It is the briefing about what content goes in and the story told thereafter that matters. The empathy map is for the team to order their thinking and case-building, so the stronger insight story starts to emerge. Below is our adjusted map, which I think is more useful.

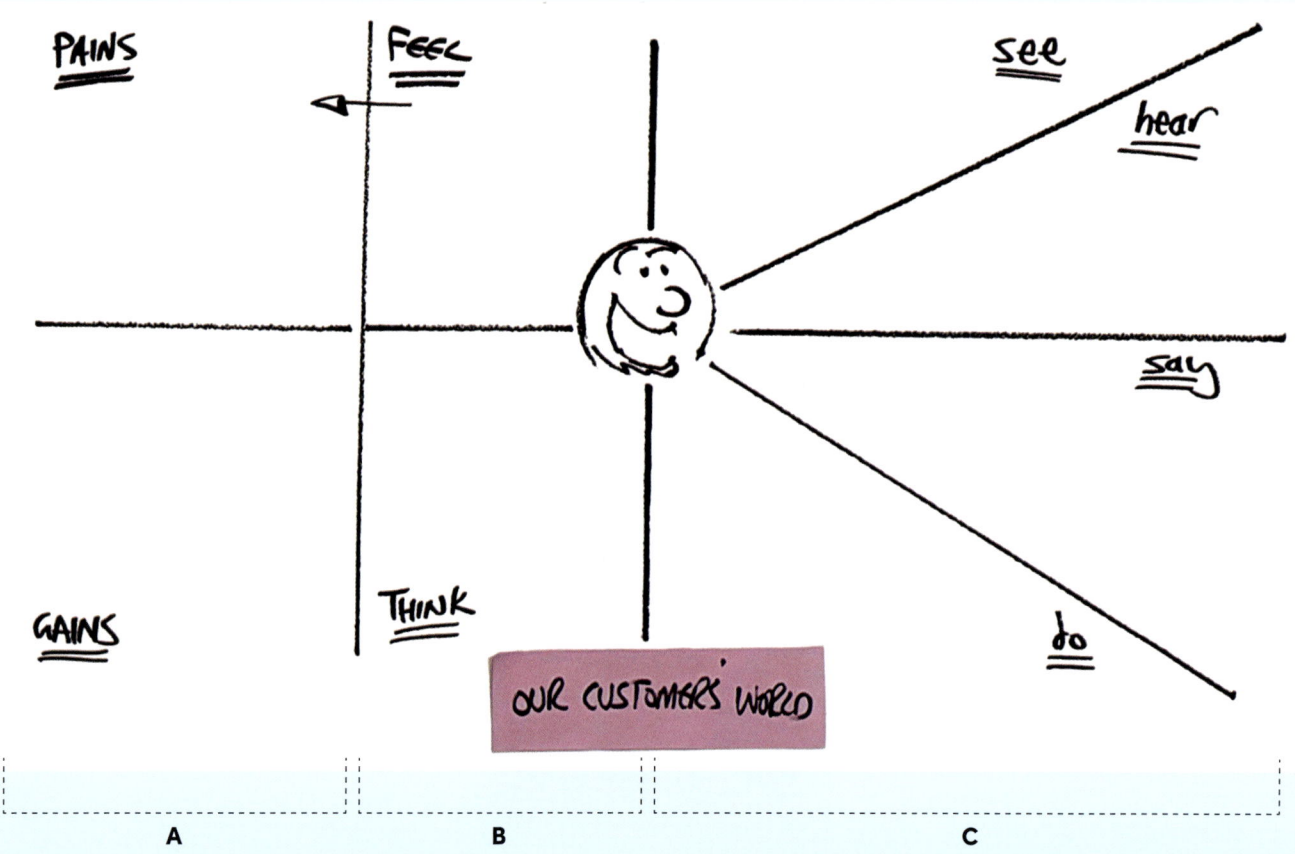

A   B   C

Our empathy map captures two customer worlds: the external and the internal. The external customer world (C) is one we share with them, thus making it easy for us to capture exactly what the customer sees, hears, says and does. These data points are on the far right of our empathy map.

The customers' internal world (B) is a lived experience for them alone. We can hypothesise what they think and feel, and sometimes we can collaborate our conclusions when discussing topics with customers. But ultimately, their thoughts and feelings are what we (as a project team) put language to. We capture these topics in the centre of our empathy map. And on the left of our map, we capture emerging customer pains and gains (A). These are subjects that we are crafting in parallel to our information gathering.

Gone are the days of giving customers a demographic (age ranges and social settings being the norm) but instead 'customer needs' are what an empathy map is going to help you articulate. For example, a male aged 25 may not have much in common with a woman of 42, but they can both be of equal interest to a bank when it comes to obtaining a loan.

A completed empathy map needs to be a large canvas for a team to stand around, plot stories and discuss what's going on in people's lives. I prefer to have a separate area in my crime scene for the empathy maps – on an opposite wall, for example.

Have as much as you can up on the walls for the teams to read and absorb. The brain is constantly searching for patterns. It will spot 'what's next' from a sequence of information and develop an acute sense for when there are 'gaps' to be filled. Building the story of why customers behave in certain ways will develop as a result of subconscious processing, just as much as from conscious discussions. When team members leave conversations and focus on other tasks, the brain will still be thinking about the topic. So, over time you and the team will develop a selective attention to the insight subject you're investigating.

It's important, then, to ring-fence your team and dive into the insight topic for a solid and unbroken amount of time for

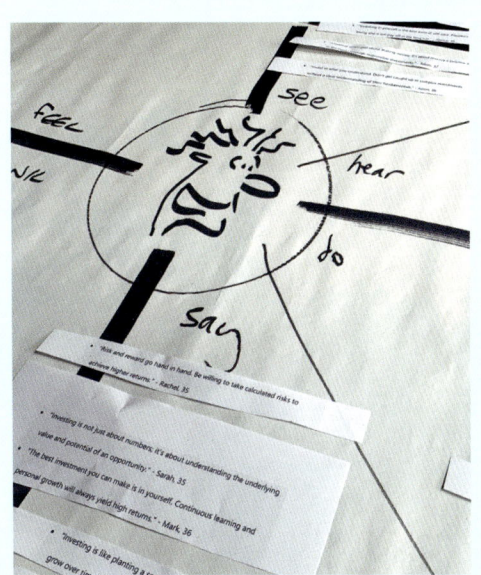

the subconscious incubating power to grow. There is no perfect timescale here as projects vary in size, ambition and commercial risk. I'd advise keeping a core group of people consistent throughout the insight stage for the overall customer stories to grow and strengthen over time. Once those stories are getting easier to tell, you can use the handful of empathy maps which have the most energy to help craft your final insights. And it's the 'cases' and empathy maps you keep referring to most that are likely to be the ones that have the magical energy.

Build ONE empathy map each time your project group believe they've spotted a distinctly new human story. It's far easier to navigate emerging insights if they're on separate maps. You may have copies of the same 'see, hear, say, do' from time to time, but your conclusions for 'think and feel' will be different.

Discussing your consumers' pains and gains is a critical part of the insight framework. Identifying and putting language to what your particular consumer feels and thinks in both positive and negative ways is key to your overall story about this 'tribe' of person. Writing a compelling story at this stage makes it hard to ignore them! If well written, we want to help this person by having ideas for them. Being clear about the pains and gains draws together all the work you've done so far and sets things up for the final two elements of the insight framework.

⑥ Pains, gains and jobs to be done

In this part of the framework, we expand on the work already done with the empathy maps by reviewing the consumer story. By adding or highlighting specific details about what your consumer finds frustrating (pains), what they want more of (gains) and what specific activity, action or help they need (a job to be done) we help them achieve a shift from pain to gain. In some insight projects, this might not be necessary as you've covered enough in your empathy maps so far to be inspired for ideas. But in other projects, being very specific about a participant experience (no matter how small) can yield inspiration.

Let's start by recapping the stages in our insight framework so far.

1. Collect the information. Customer interviews, observations, shopper data, home visits, web pages, reports, leaflets, product samples... anything that's associated with the customers you're researching and the context in which they're behaving.

2. Use the Suspect Fruit Machine to ensure your information gathering is cast far and wide (and a little weird). Doing so injects the creativity necessary for differentiating your findings from others.

3. Build a crime scene. Build a physical space where the information can be collated, filtered and grouped into buckets of interest. Stick it on the walls – make a mess!

4. Build the case. Discuss the connections and patterns you spot. Those groupings become insight cases, stories that start with 'there's something about... ' and continue with 'and this is interesting because... '

5. Create empathy maps. Once you've identified some insight cases, use an empathy map to write the information gathered into a compelling story about what's going on for that particular type of customer in that particular moment in their lives. This story will connect to your business brief and the insight project you're running. Everyone at this stage needs to agree this story – if not, return to the crime scene and start spotting other connections.

Now you and your insight team have arrived at a handful of insight cases that need one final creative push to inspire idea generation – and we have a final activity that will help you and the team craft the insight story from which ideas will come. We're now going to articulate, as clearly as we can, the tensions in our customers' lives, by pointing out their pains and their gains and, as a result of these, some jobs that need to be done.

Customer pains are synonymous with the struggles, challenges, and difficulties people face. Pains are swirling around in our subconscious self-talk. The pains are likely to exist where human drivers are challenged (whether real or imagined*) by life's little upsets.

> * My college professor would often quote Dr John Lilly (an American psychologist who was famous for hanging out with Tim Leary, experimenting with LSD and talking to dolphins): 'Whatever appears to be true, whether real or imagined, becomes true in the power of one's own mind'. It's a truth I share at the start of my insight sessions to remind the team (and myself) that we're trying to step into other people's heads. And what's going on for them is their reality and their truth, and not our reality or our truth. Far out, man.

Conversely, gains are what people would like to have in an ideal state. They are not the opposite of a pain, but they are the ambitions people have for their desires and positive emotions. Life's surprises (those we like) can be classed as gains, as can the obvious 'fixes' to any friction.

WHAT TO DO

1. Rewrite tension statements. We can identify the pains by first reviewing the tension statements we may have already written in our insight cases. Written in the first person, they'll be captured as: 'I want to do this, but I need to do that' or, as we've suggested, a first-person response to: 'what's going on and why does it matter'.

Revisiting these statements will help you identify what your customer's pain points are. Be specific. The more focused the better.

You're effectively creating 'think bubbles' that capture the inner voices of your customers as they're describing their lives moment to moment – as if you're eavesdropping on someone's conversation. Imagine being able to hear a shopper's thoughts out loud, '…ooh, I like this dress, but I don't want my friend Alice to be jealous I'm getting all the attention at her party… but I do want people to look at how fabulous I'll look!' Place these in a THEMES area on your canvas.

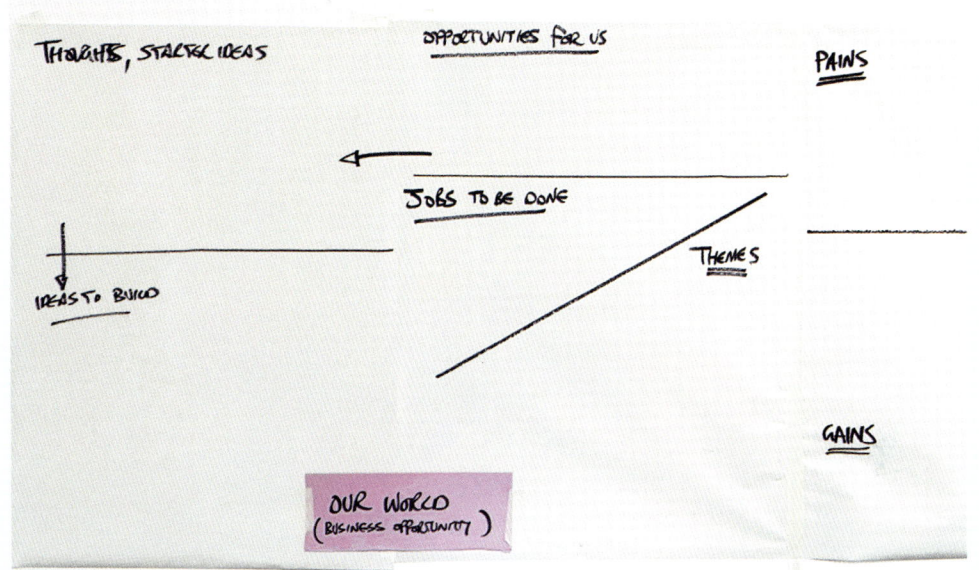

When complete, step back from the insight cases and discuss which ones feel more energetic and interesting. This might help whittle down a shortlist of what to pursue in your project.

2. Identify the pains. To do this, split your team into pairs – in group work nuances can get lost, and two people can more easily spot a pain in the tension statements. It might be that pains fuel tensions statements and vice versa. Pains are reasons why the tensions exist so there's plenty of overlap here. Again, after discussing the customer pains, re-write using first-person language: 'I need this… ', 'it doesn't work when… ', 'I don't like it when people tell me… ', 'I hate it when… happens'.

ABOVE:
For every insight case we think has energy, we build an empathy map. Here, an expanded version has space to land the pains, gains and the jobs to be done. When complete (see p214) each team can tell a compelling story to inspire idea generation.

3. Identify the gains. Take care not to just list the opposites to customer pains. Instead, imagine your customer already in a pleasant status quo and not negative about anything. Now imagine them in an amplified state of positivity around the situation they're currently in. What does that state look like? Put a mindset and a behaviour to it: 'I feel amazing because I now have… ', 'I want this feeling of… to continue', 'Now I feel… things are so much better'. 👉

(product), they need to make a hole in the wall (job to be done). Let's retrofit that sentiment to a handful of the other insights we've discussed in this chapter:

People don't want a bottle of wine (*product*)**, they need to feel like good hosts/guests** (*JTBD*)**.**

People don't want cosmetics (*product*)**, they need to feel beautiful** (*JTBD*)**.**

People don't want microwave taco shells (*product*)**, they need to feel like good parents** (*JTBD*)**.**

JTBD theory is a switch in the toolkit we use to understand customer needs. **The job, not the consumer, is now the focus of our analysis.** The late Clayton Christensen, famed for his books, *The Innovator's Dilemma* and *The Innovator's Solution*, described this concept back in 2006 in a paper he wrote with Intuit founder Scott Cook – the theory just asks: 'What job is your product hired to do?'

To understand what job our product or service is being hired to do, we need to identify what progress the customer is trying to achieve in a given circumstance. We can look at the pains and gains we've identified to establish the context for this question. We're then far better equipped to spot exactly what the customer hopes to accomplish.

This will require team members to discuss findings playfully and openly. Instruct teams not to worry about capturing the perfect words to describe the pains and gains. They needn't worry about the sentence structure of these emerging insight stories as long as they are agreed and aligned on what they believe is going on for the customer. Completing the empathy map with these missing elements of the insight story allows you to discuss and identify the 'jobs' the customer needs doing.

JOBS TO BE DONE

People buy products and services to get specific jobs done; and while products change over time, the underlying job to be done (JTBD) doesn't go away. For example, people don't want a drill

This growth or accomplishment is the JTBD. We all have endless 'jobs to be done' in our lives. Some are small (how do I pass the time while waiting in the coffee queue), others are big (find a more rewarding career). Some are regular (clean myself head-to-toe in the shower before going to work), some show up unpredictably (find some first aid quickly as I've just cut myself).

The creative trick of language is to swap out 'buying' with the word 'hiring'. When buying a product, we're mainly 'hiring' it to help us complete a certain job. If the product does the job well, we're more likely to hire that product again when we confront the same job. This behaviour would be part of the loyalty and connection we have to a certain brand.

To this day I still choose Axe deodorant. When I'm travelling away from home and I need deodorant, I'm always searching for Axe first before reluctantly buying another aerosol in its place. When we hire a product that doesn't satisfy our hopes of answering the 'job to be done' then we 'sack' that product/service and go look-about for a replacement.

Mostly, everything on Amazon is a potential solution to a JTBD. Some will do that job better than others. Similarly, everything on a supermarket shelf is answering food shoppers' jobs to be done. Interestingly, however, when looking at supermarket growth over the years, the underlying needs of customers may not have changed that much. In the mid-1970s the average supermarket stocked 9,000 unique products, today that figure is closer to 40,000. However, the average supermarket shopper acquires 80–85% of their needs in only 150 different supermarket items. A scan of your own backdated regular supermarket trips will support this finding, which means we're all ignoring 39,850 items in our local store.

Most of us have adopted a strategy to get along through 'satisficing' – a term coined by Nobel Prize winner Herbert Simon. For things that don't matter to us critically, we make a choice that satisfies us and is deemed sufficient. You don't really know if that face scrub, car battery, floral gin, floor cleaner, aftershave, cereal bar, bank loan is THE BEST, you only care that it's good enough – and that's how we tend to get by. It's our brains finding shortcuts and efficient ways of pattern spotting to ease cognitive load.

Our minds, therefore, will be searching for the 'answer' to the JTBD in a super-fast subconscious way. It's only later, when asked to rationalise our behaviour, that we craft a personal story for our decision making. I guess I've never really thought about why I choose Axe, I suppose as it was the first deodorant I used as a teenager I've simply maintained that 'hiring' commission ever since.

Our rational explanations are often dull.

THE MILKSHAKE EXAMPLE

The famous example used by Christensen to explain JBTD theory is the McDonald's milkshake. Some years ago, McDonald's were trying to increase sales of their milkshakes. As you'd imagine, they interviewed milkshake customers and asked them if they would like bigger milkshakes, or new flavours, or thicker milkshakes, etc. However, after improving the milkshakes with the interview results, they found that customers didn't buy more milkshakes.

Remember, nothing's right or wrong here, but some things are true for some people. To understand which job arose in the lives of some customers that caused them *sometimes* to 'hire' a milkshake, Christensen and his team studied a McDonald's restaurant for 18 hours one day. They found that half of the milkshakes were sold before 8:30 in the morning. Often, the milkshake was the only thing the customer bought, and the milkshake customers were alone. And they always got in a car and drove off with it. To identify what 'job' the milkshake was answering, Christensen returned the next day to speak to the customers. He asked them: 'What job are you trying to get done

that causes you to come to McDonald's to hire a milkshake at 6:30 in the morning?'

As that's an academic question, likely to cause headaches and nosebleeds in humble everyday commuters, I imagine the questions were far more carefully crafted – likely to be about their drive to work, the story of their morning so far, the morning they had ahead of them, and their weekly routine. Remember, everything we do is in the context of our lives, nothing is in isolation, and is influenced by all things.

It turned out that the commuters interviewed all had the same JTBD, and it had several component parts:

1. Each morning had a familiar routine. They had a long, tedious drive to work.

2. They just needed something to have while driving to stay engaged with life and not fall asleep at the wheel.

3. The customer wasn't hungry, but they knew if they skipped breakfast they'd be hungry at their desk later.

4. They were short on time, but couldn't afford the luxury of sitting in a restaurant to order a sit-down meal.

5. They needed something they could hold with one hand while driving, and something they could keep for the whole commute.

6. And finally, whatever they chose to eat couldn't drip, spill or drop crumbs on their clothes or car.

The milkshake, when hired, ticked all of those JTBDs. McDonald's milkshakes were not competing against Burger King's milkshakes. They were competing against bananas, chocolate bars, donuts or crumbly bagels. Milkshakes performed far better than their competitors as they were easier to consume, only one hand was needed and they were viscous, meaning it would take the whole commute for the consumer to suck up the milkshake through the straw. Let's look at this in terms of pains and gains.

Here are the pains:
- I've a long boring drive
- I'm in a hurry, I'm time-poor
- I've only one set of clothes, I can't get them dirty
- I get hungry if I skip breakfast

Here are the gains:
- I like an interesting or productive drive (taking a phone call, listening to music)
- It's lovely feeling full after a good breakfast
- I want a good start to my day
- Things that save me time put me in a good mood

You'll notice that the actual product doesn't feature in the pains and gains. Customers didn't care about the ingredients or flavours. All customers cared about was to still be full at 10am and have something to entertain them throughout their commute. They would be 'satisficed' with any milkshake. Unveiling this explained the reason why McDonald's milkshake sales, after improving the milkshake on dimensions and flavours, hadn't changed – it was irrelevant to the JTBD.

To improve the milkshake for the morning JTBD, McDonald's moved the milkshake from behind the counters to the front of the desk by the tills. To help customers not be late for work they also gave people a pre-paid swipe card so they could just dash in, fill up a cup and go without being stuck in line. They also made milkshakes thicker to take longer to suck up through the straw. When McDonald's understood that they were competing against bananas, the sales of the milkshakes increased by seven times. And milkshake-sipping consultants like me enjoy telling the story (in McDonald's branches) to land the point that spotting a JTBD is the final keystone that completes the 'insight temple'!

❼ Ask the final question

The walls of your crime scene were once bare and empty, but are now littered with notes, sketches, photos, verbatims and thoughts. Part of me believes if the room were empty and you listened hard enough you'd hear the walls whisper faintly the inner dialogue of the characters you've created. It's a fait accompli at this stage: your team intuitively knows what matters to the lives of these consumers and, if given space to do so, I believe they will be very clear and perceptive about the consumer (tribe) Jobs To Be Done that need answering.

The final element of the framework is to ask the final question: who dunnit? This last element of the framework pays homage to the detective who assembles everyone in the drawing room at the manor house and through cunning storytelling, theatre and aplomb reveals the perpetrator of the crime. 'It was Mrs Lavashom, with the candle stick, in the pantry...' (cue final chase, shooting, tears, pithy comments, take a bow, credits). In this instance, however, our big reveal is 'and the thing that our customers really feel is this ____, so the opportunity for us here is to have ideas to help them do this:_____' (take a bow).

WHAT TO DO
Invite the project sponsors/stakeholders to an insight storytelling session with you, your project team participants, and other influential characters in the business who all have an interest in your project. In advance have a call to remind them about the learnings from the SCOPING stage of the project. In your insight storytelling session you, as project facilitator, can remind everyone about the project, the learnings from the scoping phase and a headline of all your insight investigations using the Suspect Fruit Machine.

As project facilitator (ideally one of two) you may both want to lead the storytelling session, but at the same time, this session is a great opportunity for your project team participants to take turns in telling the insight story to everyone in the room. This sends the signal that 'we're all innovating around here' and 'this has been a team game', and dispels the myth that insights are only for special people with 'insights' in their job title.

Start at the beginning. A great who dunnit story follows this rough format:

Set the scene:

1. Remind everyone of the brief/key scoping learnings.
2. Describe your consumers/the tribe you think you want to go after.
3. Explain your perceived wisdoms about their behaviour and habits – and how they relate to your current business issue.

Share the methodology:

4. Briefly explain the suspect fruit machine.
5. Share some stories and charming anecdotes of how it pushed creative thinking.
6. Give 6–8 interesting facts that make the assembled crowd coo, 'ooh and ahh'.

Move to the empathy map(s):

7. Share key elements of what your tribes say, do, hear and see in the world, and what they think and feel.
8. Share what you as the project team believe are the pains and gains.
9. If applicable, state clearly (in the first person) how your consumer 'wants to do this ___but needs to do that ___ ' clearly describing the tensions here.
10. Be specific about the Jobs To Be Done – remember that Don Draper talks about a consumer 'itch' that is answered by a calamine lotion (your product proposition).
11. End your insight story with the areas where you're excited to have ideas (some ideas may already have emerged).
12. Take questions, be gracious and thank everyone.

This session signals the end of the insight stage and the shift to the ideas stage. It ought to be a celebratory moment for you and your project team participants to enjoy. You've worked hard. I now recommend giving the team a break from the project to allow time for the insight story to 'sit inside' you all, so that when asked you can tell it succinctly and energetically. It's this story that inspires you to have ideas. And it is the ideas stage you're ready to prepare for next.

SUMMARY

Sitting at a desk late at night thinking hard is not the way. At its heart, the insights stage described in this chapter is about the human character and telling stories. It's about laughing at our own idiosyncrasies, habits and routines.

At the start, creating insights can feel overwhelming. However, in reality, this is not so. I've run several projects where my co-facilitator and I asked our project team participants to think about a tribe of people overnight. We told them to make notes of assumptions about their tribe's behaviour and also what that tribe of people want more or less of (pains and gains) in their lives.

We asked everyone to share some of their thinking over morning coffee and then sent them out 'on safari' for a few hours in the city in which we were running that project. People returned brimming with fresh observations and perspectives. That activity alone was enough to inspire new and powerful ideas.

Interview

Esra Demir

STRATEGIC TECH PARTNERSHIP LEAD

Esra leads strategic tech partnerships for one of the world's largest financial institutions. Her work involves the design and delivery of a number of partnership projects between tech firms and the bank, all on a mission to make it easier for customers to manage their finances and lead their lives. When she's not running projects, she's likely running up a mountain to get a different perspective.

You've been facilitating projects in one of the world's largest organisations, how do you secure the support and resources your projects need?
I take judgement calls based on the big risks. Risks about whether I ought to spend my time reacting to incidents and firefighting immediate projects or carving time away to build long-term programmes. I am part of a chain. But that's not to say I am at the mercy of forces outside of my control. No, I have responsibilities to deliver on our organisation's long-term plans – to futureproof it.

To secure sign-off on an idea, you'll often need the approval of senior people – what are top tips to engage leaders?
Senior stakeholders often, understandably, have fixed ideas about levels of risk – especially in areas where you don't have data. If there's an opportunity to demonstrate an idea, in use and as an experience that a current customer is having, it's a far more powerful argument to present. Senior people are not going to argue when a customer shares a story of the benefits they've had.

I also listen out for people's language. There's a subtle, but definite, difference between a person saying 'I can't', 'I can't just yet' or 'I want to, but…' If you listen out for these mini stories in what stakeholders say, you can almost hear what it is they need, and how to secure their support.

We first met during the global lockdown, when all projects had to be run digitally – how did you change your facilitation approach to keep successful?
I became incredibly conscious of the subtle loss of inference and nuance in our communication. I had to look for anything that could be a clue to the world of my other team members. I needed something we could connect over, not only as teammates but also as humans. Even spotting a sports watch on a wrist would be a beacon to me. I could ask someone about it and then we'd discuss a shared enjoyment of running and being outdoors and suddenly we're getting back the quality of human connection in conversation I think digital risked taking away. This is especially important in my world with multi-cultural, multi-language teams; we lose a great deal in translation, especially over work. We need shared experiences and stories to create a shared understanding.

Many of your project participants live in different countries and only meet online – what do you do to create a strong and positive project team culture?
Icebreakers are always an agenda item for me – although I don't call them that. We always start our Monday meetings by offering gratitude to people in the team (a thankathon). By pointing out other team members' actions we become far more conscious of the impact we've had on each other in the week. Over time this

drives stronger engagements within our teams. Storytelling is also key. We can use pictures, scrapbooks and even Lego kits to hold up to the screen. All these are powerful ways to help tell a story and offer far more than words alone.

I encourage storytelling as it allows people to bring their personalities to life and to reflect at the same time. Our time is precious in our profession – it's important, then, that my teams are using it purposefully. And spending time like this is worthy investment. I've noticed I'm far more aware of the differences in my teams because of this and we all appreciate each other too.

Your organisation partners with many firms, agencies and individuals to deliver projects for you. What is it you look for in a facilitation team?
Running projects is like herding cats and it's difficult to do it alone. I'm looking for people who can command a room – even in digital space. I need people who can think flexibly, and on the go. Great partners do that. Great facilitators also need to be engaged in the material. I want them to see the end horizon of a project and work backwards, thinking about all the parts of that project that could arise, problems and opportunities alike. And finally, the team needs to have a sense of fun. I want to learn new things and go on a journey. The promise of laughter is essential.

What is a final nugget of genius you'd like to share?
You've got to find a way to fall in love with the problem. Remember that a solution might be something you might use, and something a customer will use. But also remember that sometimes a potential solution might be the thing that limits you, and you need to let it go to open up to bigger opportunities. Never lose sight of why you're part of a project. Short-term thinking and making small gains keeps your head down. Look up and you'll see where you're making a difference.

"The promise of laughter is essential."

– ESRA DEMIR

The Process

3_IDEAS

We're at the ideas stage. In reality, ideas don't 'wait' politely in people's minds until scheduled sessions; they can pop up out of discussion at any time during the project process. However, this chapter will help you facilitate ideas sessions — or 'brainstorms'. A great facilitator needs to set the agreed standards of what an idea is, align and nurture idea-growing behaviours, and finally, capture ideas so they can be communicated and assessed against the criteria agreed at the scoping stage. Above all, a great creative facilitator will spot and capture ideas in discussions where, ordinarily, people are too quick to capture thoughts alone.

The intro bit

We're now at the third stage of the creative process: ideas. Having identified consumer pains and gains and specific JTBD, you and your project team participants will be charged up and inspired to have ideas. During the insight stage, the same starting idea may have cropped up time and again in conversation. And, in some instances, ideas may have popped up during the scoping stage. It's now the time to formally create the environment where you and your project team participants focus all your creative energy on growing ideas. It's time to hold a brainstorm.

We've all been participants in ideas sessions. The good ones are well planned and well executed. The bad ones spontaneously pop up during other meetings. As a result, people aren't prepared for them and rarely behave well. Remember our minds are constantly processing thousands of signals from the world on a moment-to-moment basis. Access to our subconscious is shut. Brainstorms are just cognitive overload. It's far easier, and more efficient, for our minds to disengage. We endure these sessions, happy to survive them and, with luck, avoid the next invite. Perhaps you've experienced the following:

Emma, an overly enthusiastic member of the internal communications team, invites you to an 'ideas for strategy' session in room 22b. A laminated table sits in the middle; hard-backed chairs are neatly arranged around it. There is no natural light. There's a sideboard hosting some copier paper, a whiteboard eraser, and a tape dispenser missing the tape. A whiteboard is stained with red and green ink marks from previous meetings. Both colours of pen rest on the shelf below – without lids. A creased flip chart loiters in the corner. The room is stiflingly hot, but the air-conditioning controller doesn't appear to do anything. You look at your watch – there are three hours dedicated to 'ideas for strategy'.

About eighteen people shuffle into the room; some sit, some stand. Those who got seats around the table open their laptops nervously. The last person to arrive is Emma. Without establishing any context in her set up, Emma starts describing how great ideas in the business will help everyone 'move forward' and be 'one team'. Among the platitudes, Emma states that ideas for the strategy are the most important priority in the business right now. 'Worth at least three hours,' you think, as you glance at your watch again. A few people ask questions about the strategy, but Emma doesn't have the answers. Three or four conversations spark up across the table but it's among pairs, rather than the group as a whole. A minute or two of low-level murmuring ensues. Emma grapples with the lopsided flip chart and brings it to the corner of the boardroom table. She picks up one of the whiteboard pens and writes the date in the top corner, then double underlines it. "So, who's got any ideas then?" There's a bit of a quietening in the room, but two people are still muttering to each other whilst also typing emails.

"We need a better framework," says someone.

"Yes," someone else agrees. Emma writes the word 'framework' on the flip chart – the pen's green ink fading sadly on the letters O, R and K. "Have you got a marker?" she whispers to the person sitting closest to her. "No, sorry."

"Strategy roadshow," says someone.

"Might be hard to fit in the end of Q3," is the immediate retort.

"Strategy roadshow for business unit managers then. They do it. But remember those guys are busy, too." Emma writes the word 'roadshow' on the flip chart, only to cross it out after listening in on the conversation.

This goes on for nearly two hours. Some people remain standing, others keep wedded to their seats. You have a starter idea about a simple document, mostly photographs. On each page would be a one-liner about the business strategy. It's for team leaders to use in meetings with their team when the new strategy is finally cascaded. When you suggest it, the room finds three reasons why it's hard to do, and Emma writes the words 'photo album' on the flip chart.

Finally, the session is over. Emma rips off the flip chart paper, folds it up and stuffs it between the screen and keyboard of her laptop. You're the last to leave, realising you'll never get those last few hours of your life back.

A day or two later an email arrives in your inbox from Emma. The title is 'Ideas output from brainstorm session'. She's written to you and everyone who attended – and cc'd all department heads, some other names who aren't part of the project and Claire in accounts (who everyone knows left earlier that month). You open the attachment and there's a two-page PowerPoint. Page 1 is a low-res stock photo of a small sapling in a pair of cupped hands. The title is 'Ideas for strategy'. On page 2 is a list in Comic Sans font; there are thirty bullet points, and you recognise only a couple of comments. Disappointedly, you spot that 'photo album' is in a shorter sub-list titled 'Ideas not selected'.

The ONE TEAM logo of internal comms occupies the bottom third of both pages. You stare out of the window, catching a glimpse of you own reflection, saddened to think that across the country, and perhaps globally, on that same afternoon thousands of other brainstorms (equally as ineffective and wasteful) were happening – opening their sessions with those immortal words: "There's no such thing as a bad idea."

THIS IS <u>NOT</u> THE WAY.

The story is, of course, fictional but is based on real events with which we can all empathise. There's a cluster of business organisations around the globe who are famous for their creativity and innovation. And ideas sessions are at the heart of their success, growth and fame. However, despite the allure, it's understandable why the internal facilitating of innovation gets a bad reputation – ideas sessions

are the worst culprit: badly designed and badly delivered.

The good news is that ideas sessions, I believe, are the easiest to fix, and it's definitely possible to engineer positive experiences for people. The main failings stem from two issues:

- Not establishing clear standards for **ideas** (as opposed to thoughts)

- Not establishing standards in **behaviour for ideas**

And while easy to fix, we at team GENIUS BOX are clear on this: if brainstorms are going badly, it's 100% the responsibility of the facilitator!

No excuses. All roads in a chaotic and unproductive brainstorm lead to the facilitator. In this chapter, our focus is on explaining the standards you must protect in ideas sessions. When you've established those standards, ideas will fall naturally from people's conversations. You can take with you the book of '101 Lateral Thinking Techniques for Innovation', but nothing will happen if you skip over the standards.

Let's take a look at each of these points in turn and then bring those two components of great ideas sessions together into a powerful approach that will guarantee better output.

Thoughts vs ideas

In creative sessions you'll often have people make suggestions, treating them as 'ideas' when in fact they haven't had an 'idea' at all but a 'thought'.

It's hard to 'do' a thought in business. Thoughts don't get very far commercially or impact the world in the way ideas do. It's critical to navigate people's language and conversation, and to ensure you capture only ideas – not thoughts – in creative sessions, as it is ideas that will fuel your innovation pipeline.

Now, all this might seem a question of semantics, but not so. It's essential that people in your creative sessions are super clear on what will stand as an idea and how this differs to concepts, insights, platforms and creative briefs, and so on. There is a great deal of language out there in 'innovation land'. Although people may be vehemently aligned on the same topic, it only takes a small misunderstanding in nomenclature (words) for chaos to come along and slap the teeth out of a great session.

Here's the way we at GENIUS BOX suggest you treat ideas and keep them separate from everything else in an ideas session. Get clear. Get *really* clear on the difference between what you and your project team are going to call an idea and what you're going to call a thought.

The word **idea** is used in our language very liberally:

- I've an *idea*, let's go out for dinner tonight.
- I've an *idea*, we've got twenty minutes, let's grab a coffee before we go into the next meeting.
- I've an *idea*, I'll call the brand manager and ask for her opinion.
- I've an *idea*, let's... (fill in your own example).

However, in these instances the word *idea* is really shorthand for 'I've a starter suggestion on what we do next, but I need you to agree with me, and then add the missing details.' Consider that the subtext to the above is actually:

Dinner: 'I've a starter suggestion on going out for dinner tonight, I hope you like that suggestion and you'll join me, have you got another suggestion of where to go? I was thinking Thai?' (The conversation needs to also agree the time and travel arrangements, and only then have you something you can *do*).

Coffee: 'I've realised there's a 20-minute break. I feel I need to do something about my energy, I've a starter suggestion of getting a coffee, how do you feel about that?' (The conversation needs to agree which coffee shop, given the time available, and who else is invited or not on the trip. Only then can you *do* it.)

Brand Manager: 'I've been thinking about the project and realised the brand manager's input would be really useful. I'm not sure what questions to ask her yet, perhaps you can help me craft a few? I wonder, is this a phone call, email or face-to-face?' (You need to agree what you're going to ask, when, how, and finally, who is going to do the asking. Only then can you *do* this idea.)

The beauty of our language and the workings of our brain (adapted to live in social settings) is that the word 'idea' does *a lot* of work in these types of conversations. We intuitively and speedily fill in the gaps and understand what we want from each other, and what to do next, to make our suggestions happen. But in ideas sessions, when we say 'idea' to describe what it is we're thinking, what we actually have *isn't* an idea, fully formed and ready to go. We're sharing our thinking. And that thinking isn't something that everyone understands to the same level as us.

Remember, when you think of an idea a series of (billions of) electrochemical signals flood your mind and create something unique and personal inside your head that no one else knows of. In that instant you've only a simple story to describe that idea. You create a picture in your mind of what that idea is and does. Some people *feel* their way to this moment and form a coherent image and story as a result, whilst others *see* the idea in their mind's eye and then react to it emotionally. We'll then immediately and unavoidably experience a degree of self-judgement about whether our idea is feasible and worthy of more attention or not. Consider how you must first conceive of a 'chip shop on the moon' before dismissing it as ludicrous. These moments may be fleeting, but whatever you conceive in your head is unique to you – fragile and certainly only one part of a potential solution to an issue.

So, the word 'idea' must only be used in an ideas session when the following conditions apply:

An 'idea' is something you can 'do' – and everybody in that creative session has the same quality of understanding about what that idea is. Anything and everything else are what we'll call 'thoughts'.

Warm-up games

Before any ideas session spend some time aligning people's language around what ideas actually are – so you can all agree the standard for what constitutes an idea. The example we use is this:

Thought = As part of company wellbeing, I think it'll be good if the team eat more healthily.

Idea = Let's provide a complimentary fruit smoothie for everyone each morning. It can be mixed up fresh each day, and served from a handful of jugs into glasses. If you're in the office that morning, smoothies are free from 09:00–10:00.

Suspend judgement for now!!

Providing a free fruit smoothie every day for each employee in a large office might not be a good idea but we'll discuss idea *judgement* later. For now, it's important as a facilitator to have high standards for what to expect and demand from people when discussing, building, landing and communicating ideas. All we need focus on is 'that the idea *could be done*'.

The **thought** about 'eating more healthily' can be answered by the **idea** 'have a fruit smoothie on the desk each morning'. We could also answer the same thought by:

- Providing a hamper of 'help yourself' vegetables in the foyer.

- Giving staff pre-paid debit cards that can only be redeemed for healthy food options in the canteen.

- Hiding the fizzy pop and chocolate bar section in vending machines by frosting the glass.

Interestingly, you might be reading the above list of ideas and thinking 'hang on, I need a bit more detail...' Which is exactly the point! If you're still struggling to align with my descriptions, then I am only communicating a thought to you, and it's not yet an idea about which we both share the same interpretation.

Play the following three games with your project team participants in order to get the team you have in front of you all aligned around their understanding of what is a thought and, crucially for the project, what is an idea.

Game 001: The basics

Game 001 is easy – split your project team participants up into groups of three. Issue each group with the 12 statements shown; each one on a separate sheet of paper. Ask each group to place each statement in one of two piles. One pile is THOUGHTS. One pile is IDEAS. Once complete, discuss with each group how they decided what statement went where.

This game is less about navigating the nuances of thoughts and ideas and more about getting used to looking out for what people in the project team believe an idea needs to be. Everyone will have a set of criteria in their head about what an idea is. When you play this game with others, the group will discuss their answers and norm around that 'standard'. Hence, there is no right answer for which is which!

> Use my list to start. Over time, you'll write your own statements inspired by ideas sessions you're part of. In the photo you'll see each statement is on an A5-sized coloured card. The game works best like this as groups have to physically move cards and thus commit to a decision. If your statements are simply a list on a sheet of paper, the game won't work so well as one person ends up doing all the work.

- An easier to operate pushchair
- A 5-minute beauty treatment
- **A better recruitment programme**
- A treasure hunt based within an amusement park
- Build your own cocktail kit
- **Self-heating coffee**

- **A 2-for-1 offer**
- A banking app that does savings for you
- Fancy dress Tuk-tuk after party
- Hot chilli version
- **Reusable spray with lemon scent**
- Self-cleaning brake callipers

When running an ideas session for the first time with a new group, it's essential to play this game. Similarly, on the next project you might take 50% of your team with you and they'll know what an idea is, but then they need to align with the new recruits on that next innovation project, so again – play the game.

DEBRIEF

Ask these questions (and expect/discuss these types of answers):

1. **How did you *know* what was an idea and what was a thought?**
   Thoughts are shorter in length, less detail. Ideas seem more concrete – you can see where they're going.

2. **When you disagreed with people in the group, what did you do to resolve the conversation?**
   We'd discuss the thought a little longer and people would add more detail or come up with more answers to the questions – filled in the blanks a bit more.

3. **Are there any that you're still not sure about, and why?**
   For some of us this makes sense, but some of us still need detail.

4. **What advice are you going to give to each other to keep looking out for ideas?**
   Keep asking questions to get enough clarity so we all agree on what the idea is.

Game 002: Live outputs

For game 002, use the output in the box below that's from actual project brainstorms during real project sessions in the GENIUS BOX past. In the future, you'll save some examples of your own output, too, to play this game. Doing so allows you to give more context behind each thought/idea to enrich your debrief. It's good to build a 'pack of past output' to help you play both games 001 and 002, and also to show the standards of what good idea capture looks like.

Again, ask groups to place each example onto either a **thoughts** or **ideas** pile. It's always good to play these games to warm people up before ideas sessions, so everyone is attuned to the kind of language that pops up in such sessions and the standards we want to establish and maintain. It only takes a few poorly captured conversations to get stuck up on the wall as 'ideas' for the clarity and quality of output to drop very quickly.

DEBRIEF

Ask these questions (and expect/discuss these types of answers):

1 **Did you notice what was different between the first game and these actual statements from live ideas sessions?**
A bit harder as the content isn't as obvious as in the first game. Lots more interpretation needed.

2 **Have you heard or said these types of things before?**
This happens a bit more in business. We can sometimes feel productive if we keep capturing output, as that's a sign of a good session – but it might be a quantity of poor instead of quality ideas.

3 **What will happen if we keep capturing vague and broad – albeit positive-sounding and seemingly productive – output like this?**
Capturing lots of thoughts and starter thinking but still leaving a great deal of detail unanswered. It'll be hard to assess ideas when compared to the brief. It's hard to tell the good ideas apart from those that are potentially better but poorly captured.

4 **What can you do to 'sniff out' the idea a little more?**
Constantly ask more questions, no judgement, but ask for detail – and where there isn't detail we need to build with suggestions/details of our own.

- Last-mile EV charging: home owners make money by lending their charge points out to companies who've signed up

- Coaching clinic: hold one-hour coaching clinics within the business for project teams

- Banking app: have a cartoon style 'saving pots' feature within the app that allows you to allocate your weekly or monthly budget into different categories

- 'Book of me': personalised feedback system for staff development, perhaps in a physical binder

- Internal project plan timeline: create a visual timeline with dates for the project

---

If there remains one person in an ideas session who still doesn't understand what's being described, then what you're all discussing is still only a thought. You'll need to keep discussing it until everyone in a group shares the same understanding of what the idea is, what it does and how it works. Only then do you have an idea.

Game 003: Descriptions

This game can be played on the morning of a brainstorm as a final tune up for the ideas day ahead. It's a good one to do in pairs as it creates energy and humour.

Split your group into pairs. Ask Player One to think of five well-known man-made objects and/or social occasions, e.g. a desk lamp, a camping trip, the Olympic Games, a watering can, a jazz club*. Each 'thing' should then be written on a separate card. Player One flashes the card and Player Two has to describe the 'thing' without *saying* the thing. For example, desk lamp: "a small metal frame, with a bulb on it, a shade, like a small umbrella and it does the job of someone holding a torch above your hands whilst you work". (Not, "a lamp that sits on your desk".) Swap over a few times so both players get to think up 'things' and do the describing.

DEBRIEF
Ask these questions (and expect/discuss these types of answers):

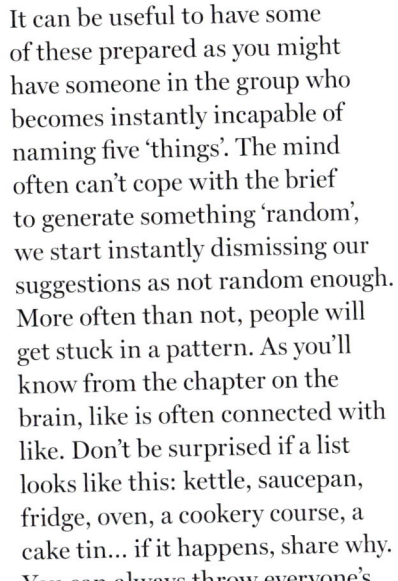

*It can be useful to have some of these prepared as you might have someone in the group who becomes instantly incapable of naming five 'things'. The mind often can't cope with the brief to generate something 'random', we start instantly dismissing our suggestions as not random enough. More often than not, people will get stuck in a pattern. As you'll know from the chapter on the brain, like is often connected with like. Don't be surprised if a list looks like this: kettle, saucepan, fridge, oven, a cookery course, a cake tin... if it happens, share why. You can always throw everyone's five things into a hat and take them out randomly.

1 **What was it like when you were first describing the ideas?**
Hard work, my brain froze, stumbled over my words, mind went a bit blank.

2 **What happened after a few rounds and you relaxed into it? (This last part leads the witness a little!)**
We relaxed, and the words came far easier, our descriptions became a bit more detailed but more specific, too.

3 **I heard laughter towards the end of the game, why was that?**
Some of our descriptions were smart and clever, and often a play on words, or just made us giggle because they were inherently funny observations about what those objects were.

Playing the game over a few rounds helps people become more deliberate about the language used to communicate to each other. Language is critical when it comes to communicating thinking and translating thoughts into ideas. An idea is hard to process if language such as 'make it easy' is in the description. And broad concepts such as 'simple', 'sustainable', 'digital' can creep into idea discussion and still confuse. It only takes a few misplaced words, hurriedly scribbled on a sticky note to confuse people. At the same time, a few particular words in idea annotation can bring clarity to a thought and make it an idea. A group that plays this game before a brainstorm is likely to work at the same level and maintain a similar standard of idea description and annotation as a result.

A variation of the game is to ask people to think about descriptions for the 'things' overnight. You can debrief in the morning, and compare the differences between descriptions that were incubated over time to those created spontaneously in the moment. Ask people to describe the energy and focus they had in each situation. And have a discussion about what impact that energy might have on the quality of thinking, idea capture and communication.

Facilitation tip 009

Avoid gotchas

There's a lovely scene in the first Harry Potter film where Professor Snape starts his class like so:

"Mr Potter, our new celebrity. Tell me, what would I get if I added powdered root of asphodel to an infusion of wormwood? You don't know? Well, let's try again. Where, Mr Potter, would you look if I asked you to find me a bezoar? And what is the difference between monkshood and wolfsbane?"

Harry sits, dumfounded, exposed and rather crestfallen as Professor Snape sneers down at him. It's a great scene – and a good example of 'gotchas': questions to which your audience can't possibly know the answer.

If they don't know the answer to the question, then why ask it? It's not fair. It's the same as setting extra homework as a punishment for the child who didn't understand the first batch. Posing a gotcha creates distance between you and your audience. Awkward silence, anyone?

Please don't do that; it's bad for you and worse for them.

Questions change the dynamic of a class or session, of course. They fire off different parts of the brain. Recall is triggered, giving other parts of the mind a rest – great for learning. But get creative on how you ask the questions to change pace and shift direction between one phase of delivery and the next. You can hide a question in the theatre of delivery.

If you're keen to share knowledge, facts, figures, trivia and put a few myths to bed then set your questions as a quiz, a multi-choice, a peel-and-reveal, a team game, answers out of a hat. Get participants to write the quiz. There is always a better alternative than a cold 'gotcha'.

Facilitation tip 010

THE BEST TOP TIP EVER

After briefing in the instruction:

Say 'It's that simple.'

Don't say 'Everyone got it?'

It's that simple.

And for those needing more of an explanation… When we ask a question, we invite a response. You're inviting people to ask a question requiring you to explain things again. The problem with doing that is you'll use different words in a different rhythm and use up more time – it'll lead to confusion: yours and theirs.

Don't say, 'So, did everyone understand, or do you want me to explain again?'

Far better you step away from the flip chart, click your fingers and give thumbs up with a confident and expectant tone in your voice stating 'You can *only* do this right. Enjoy yourselves, and see you at 3:20 with your answers. **It's that simple.**'

Interview

Sue Woodley

INNOVATION DIRECTOR, INTERNATIONAL MARKETING

Sue has over 20 years working within FMCG (fast-moving consumer goods), with businesses and brands including L'Oreal, GSK, Coca-Cola and Suntory. She's led insight, strategy, and pioneered new innovation ecosystems within business. When not running sessions with her project team, Sue will be on consumer safaris opening kitchen cupboards, visiting stores or exploring new technologies – but always relentlessly asking herself what drives human behaviour.

You run innovation projects end-to-end, what part of the process challenges your facilitation the most, and why?
Running any part of the creative process digitally has its challenges, especially if you've not met or worked with members of the project team before. It's no longer the case that we'd hop on a plane and workshop concepts for three days on the ground. It's very much the case that I can be given a brief on a Monday that we'll be workshopping digitally on the Thursday, with ten people all dialling in from different locations. It's hard to ensure we get the right quality of discussions online – partly due to technical challenges but also because people arrive with all sorts of agendas and it's only when you get going you spot what's really on their minds. Of course, it's too late then as the clock is ticking.

You've high expectations for what ideas should look like, have you any tips for people to meet your exacting standards?
We're too quick to capture thoughts and then try to run with those – I don't see many ideas. My advice is don't capture the first thing that people say. An idea needs to be real. It needs to be sharp, and easy to explain to people. I think ideas are what you need to build prototypes that you can then go test with consumers and out of those experiments will come the answers to the project. You can't just have the answer in one session.

What do you do when you sense that something's not going to plan during a creative session, in any part of the process?
We're social animals. We pick up on tiny signals. Side conversations, rustling with the food bags or stationery, fiddling with the phone, being late. All these are tiny signs that something is 'up'. The trick is not to carry on regardless. I prefer to call it out and ask everyone what is the

"We need to embrace risk, give things a go."
– SUE WOODLEY

main thing our session, or that part of the session, is there to achieve and ask people for their perspective. Rather than stick to the process, it's important to keep sight of the main objective. If people can leap ahead or get to the end differently, and we're all in agreement, then I'm happy to let go of the process we thought we should follow to get there. I remind myself it's not my responsibility to have the answers, but instead to get to the answer with other people. The group will have far more suggestions than me alone. So my advice is call it out, ask and be open to an alternative plan.

You've also commissioned many agencies in the past – what is it you look for in creative facilitators?
Business is ultimately about people, so above anything else, will they keep me and my team safe and motivated? During a session I want to feel like they are in control and we're all heading in the right direction, safely. I need someone who I can trust not to get stressed. It's a given they'll have obvious energy and passion for the process, but it's their self-awareness that matters. Being able to read the room, pick up those who've fallen down, bring people back when they've gone too far, reading the situations and adjusting their own style in the moment. That's great facilitation. That's what makes a great partner.

You've seen many processes, approaches, tools and language to describe and explain being innovative – which are the ones that have stuck with you the most?
The tools I've seen and those I use have evolved over time but aren't dissimilar to ones I first used many years ago – because they work. What you can't do at your desk is lead a creative process. Get out there to see and interact with people who are facing problems so you can design better answers for them.

What is a final nugget of genius you'd like to share?
Keep things simple and agile vs sticking rigidly to one particular approach. If you're going to design solutions with consumers in mind, start with the consumers. We're too quick to jump to answers. Answers are not the way. For me it's prototypes – tangible things we can share with consumers to test our hypothesis and then get better at developing solutions. To do that we need to get out and try new things. We need to embrace risk, give things a go. Both individually and in our teams. The value of experimenting, testing and learning is paramount. As a mantra in our team, we say 'failure is an option, but fear isn't.'

Best behaviour for ideas

As mentioned at the start of the chapter, there is a common and immortal cliché – there is no such thing as a bad idea.

This is nonsense. There are thousands of bad ideas, and I've had a great deal of them myself. Some of the ideas I've pitched to businesses where I've been laughed out the door include:

- A fondue-themed restaurant chain called 'FOND-OF-U', with the strapline 'It's a bit cheesy'. The feedback was candid and direct: 'That's the worst idea I've ever heard'.

- A syringe-based energy drink for teenagers.

- A nappy and three baby wipes sold in packaging that becomes the disposable bag. This is dispensed in airports, newsagents, bus stops and train platforms for parents whose babies have a surprise 'accident'. The brand is called 'Bum on the Run'.

- A mobile physiotherapy service operating out of a van called 'Silence of the Hands'.

- An investment vehicle where you float the capital of your outstanding mortgage on the stock exchange for the time you're away from your house during the working day.*

Ideas are rarely (if ever) fully formed when we first conceive them. They're fragile, and, as we've discussed already, they're likely to really be a collection of thoughts and the potential beginnings of ideas. What usually happens when we share ideas with other people is we invite immediate judgement. We do this because of the way our brains are hardwired.

We are all incredible, conscious animals who, from the moment we're born, exist in an elaborate social network – more complex than any other living organism. We're collectively aware of our world-changing achievements throughout the centuries. Our global societies and civilisations have extracted energy from the Earth and shaped our physical environment to meet our needs. We've conquered the sky, harnessed the power of the sun and created technologies that liberate us from danger and others that provide education and entertainment. We are an enlightened species.

*I still think this has legs, by the way. But you'll see in the limitations of writing a book, the copy doesn't do the idea justice, and I've really only shared a starting 'thought'. I also believe I invented iTunes when I was a teenager, as I had an insight that I only really liked one or two songs in my CD collection and figured I could make a huge mixtape with all of my favourites, but needed a special machine where I could simply type in the ones I wanted to listen to. What can I say – genius.

OPPOSITE:
For successful ideas sessions, we need small groups, positive intention and great energy. Fancy dress is optional.

At the same time, however, we're astonishingly poor at listening to each other and growing ideas. This is because we're still, at our core, pretty primitive when handling creative thought. Ideas are the embodiment of 'new', and 'new' represents either 'friend' or 'foe' to our prehistoric operating systems.

Remember, we have two operating systems: System 1 and System 2 thinking (see p51). Both are inextricably linked to protect the body from harm and to maintain energy efficiency. When a new idea taps on the door of our subconscious (metaphorically speaking) and asks to be let in, it is accepted and catalogued in the warehouse of our mind.

At that same moment our brain says 'Actually, if I can't fit those ideas into my neat story of the world and my place in it, I'll dismiss it as a foreign body, because frankly, I've other things to deal with right now – so it's a no from me.' This happens in microseconds. We feel a dismissal before we think about it. Our subconscious super-fast brain calls the shots and judges the idea as a 'non-fit', so protecting our deeper held beliefs and drivers of what good looks like.

If you're reading this and thinking 'such nonsense'. Boom! You're doing it right now. We can use our learnings from earlier in the book as stimuli to help us realise why we're so quick to judge and dismiss ideas. Let's start by looking at our default – often negative – responses in relation to the brain, scoping and insight before looking at how a creative facilitator can unlock potential in these same fields.

BRAIN: Remember our default 'busy' beta state of the brain? Access to the subconscious is shut. You're operating on only a fraction of total brainpower capacity. If your beta brain was an Intel chip, then a new idea would come along like a fresh new computer program and 'crash' the operating system. It's a sensory overload. When we're relaxed and in a suitable environment, however, our minds are likely to be flooded with alpha waves – we've more access to our subconscious, we're more likely to make patterns and connections, and therefore more receptive to external stimuli. A starter idea from someone else is just a stimulus. When we discuss that idea and both take ownership of it then an idea is shared, and we'll subconsciously want to look after and nurture it.

SCOPING: A badly understood brief is difficult for people to connect to. An un-scoped 'exam question' is hard to answer. When we scope project briefs, we're increasing our attachment to the question that needs to be answered. Otherwise, when new ideas come along, fresh out of nowhere – in a rushed, badly run and ill-timed brainstorm – we might ask ourselves, 'Hang on, where does this idea fit with the project brief we're answering? There's nothing here on the walls to remind me of what we're doing or why. Arrghh! This is awful – and therefore that's a bad idea.'

INSIGHT: We all carry an internal story with us about who we are and our place in the world. That narrative is formed by deeply rooted values, beliefs and motivational drivers. Our actions, decisions, purchasing behaviour, choice of friends and daily habits are all linked to the story of the life we believe we're living. A new idea comes along and it's alien. But it needs to fit in our story. If this idea looks like it'll result in 'more work for me on this project' then we'll do all we can to avoid signing up for it, unless it's in our personal interest to do so. We make these assessments in seconds. Judgement is unavoidable and inevitable*.

However, judgement is just people's energy manifesting itself in negative form. And a great facilitator (now, you!) knows that you can use people's energy to build ideas and nurture them, rather than find fault and kill them. Now we've established the 'standards' for what ideas are, we can run some games to align everyone's energy positively.

BRAIN: The facilitator is responsible for the physical environment of ideas sessions. They can design the space and flow of the sessions so that critical factors such as natural light, hydration and sustenance are catered for; participants will remain in alpha state.

SCOPING: The facilitator is responsible for setting up the ideas session in the context of work done so far and for connecting people to the brief. They can ensure that the brief to be answered is constantly on display during the ideas sessions. When participants inevitably become distracted, they're brought back into focus by the exam question to be answered being right in front of them.

INSIGHT: The facilitator is responsible for issuing participants, in advance of the session, with the insights that have been uncovered during the project so far. This insight ought to be inspiring. Insight is just a stimulus to inspire ideas. And along with other forms of prepared stimuli, it's part of a toolbox of material designed to energise and engage participants throughout the session.

And finally, it is the responsibility of the facilitator to establish and agree the language standards to be used when navigating between thoughts and ideas. It is their responsibility to describe, model, demonstrate, encourage and lead the right creative behaviours for ideas to live and not be judged. To reiterate: If brainstorms are going badly, it's the responsibility of the facilitator. And during the opening of this chapter, Emma hadn't checked all these boxes. It's likely the same for many brainstorms you've been a participant in, too. 👉

> As a personal experiment, challenge yourself to 24 hours without judgement. Monitor yourself. Look out for your self-talk. Every time you have a negative thought reset the clock.

It's 100% the responsibility of the facilitator to set the standard for the positive energy needed in ideas sessions.

A good facilitator should always be reading the room, looking out for and aware of the potential damage negative language can do in an ideas session. Of course, it's not always intended to kill ideas – it's part of our survival instincts, as already mentioned – but it won't help.

In the box below you'll read some commonly heard phrases that are all incredibly efficient ways to kill an idea. They are filled with predictions about the future, and loaded with judgement and negativity. After spending time with someone who responds to suggestions like this, you're likely to walk away with a bruised ego and deflated self-esteem. You probably wouldn't like to work with that person again. In fact, you both have the same output from the conversation: nothing. No ideas at all. And you've learnt the behaviour of judgement and assessment.

To an extent, business traps us in this way of thinking. We're encouraged to mitigate risk and make speedy decisions. Some of us are rewarded with ever larger salaries to do so. Eventually, a small and lucky few secure the top spots in the organisation and perpetuate the myth that work needs to be rigorous and serious. And in order to succeed, the next generation of employee needs to emulate the conservative risk aversion extolled by their leadership team.

In order to grow ideas, the ongoing cultural norm needs to be flipped and opposed. We need to consciously seek out all that's good in a starter idea and actively suspend our judgement. To do this, I strongly recommend that all facilitators state the following:

All ideas need to be discussed as if budget and ridicule weren't a reality. Build as if everything is possible.

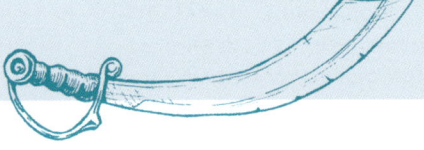

LANGUAGE WE USE TO KILL IDEAS . . .

We're polite, professional people. It's unlikely you'll be in an ideas session and colleagues will outwardly state 'your idea is shit' to your face. Instead, we're likely to say:

'That won't work because...'

'Yes, but...'

'Although we ought to check with compliance that we can...'

'We tried it before, it didn't work...'

'I don't think people would go for that...'

'It'll cost too much, though...'

'Can we park it for now...'

'That's all very well in theory, but in reality...'

Idea-growing behaviour

We're huge fans of improv comedy at GENIUS BOX and want to encourage its use in sessions with the following games that demonstrate idea-growing behaviour. These sketches can last a few minutes or over an hour. All players abide by the same rules, whether a seasoned professional or novice performer. They 'agree' with whatever statement is offered in the performance and embrace all comments as opportunities to grow a story; it's a lovely demonstration of how an idea is grown over time by aligning behaviour. These games are much like improv warm-ups and align your project team participants on idea-nurturing behaviour. But first, let's flip this and take a look at what killing an idea looks like with our game: Simon's Picnic*.

Split your team into pairs. One person is going to go on a picnic and suggest a starter idea for what to take. Their partner is going to say, 'No, because…'

 A big shout-out to fellow GENIUS BOX facilitator Simon, who is a fan of this game. If your co-facilitator happens to be called Glenda, the game can be called *Glenda's Picnic*.

SIMON'S PICNIC

I'd like to go on a picnic and take some strawberries.

No, because… that'll bring out the wasps, and we'll get stung. Let's go on a picnic and bring sandwiches and pre-mixed gin and tonic.

No, because… that's boring, and not everyone likes gin. Let's send out a list and encourage everyone to bring their own dish.

No, that won't work, because… it's too difficult to organise. Let's go on a picnic and order a pizza delivery.

No, that's a bad idea, because… the pizza people won't want to bike out to where we're sitting.

and then give a reason, and then they will make a suggestion of their own. The original picnic goer then models that exact same negative behaviour, and so on. Allow the teams to indulge their most negative selves. A typical conversation can be rehearsed in advance with your co-facilitator and demonstrated as above. You get the principle. Allow enought time for each player to offer up at least six starting ideas for a picnic, and to kill six suggestions for their partner too. A few minutes is usually plenty time to play this game. 👉

SIMON'S PICNIC DEBRIEF

Ask these questions (and expect/discuss these types of answers):

1 **What did it feel like to find fault with people's suggestions?**
Easy, and quite enjoyable!

2 **Did the game feel good then?**
Yes, we had a sense of power and authority when it was our turn to find fault with ideas. There's no shortage of reasons why things wouldn't work.

3 **Do you want to work with the person again?**
Not really, no.

4 **How many ideas have you actually got for your picnic?**
None!

5 **How many starter ideas did you kill?**
Loads!

Now, demonstrate an alternative picnic brainstorm with your co-facilitator, where one person suggests an idea and then the other person says 'Yes, and…' to build positively on the idea.

Yes = giving agreement and energy to the starter idea.

And = adding in the detail, makes things more complete.

THE 'YES, AND…' GAME

"So, I'd like to go on a picnic and take some strawberries.

Yes, and… some fizz, they go well together.

Yes, and… we can pack them in smart-looking hampers.

Yes, and… they could also be packed in classic British summer themes such as Wimbledon, Henley boating regatta and 'a day on the pier'.

Yes, and… let's add fancy dress, too, so people can eat, drink, dress up and then take photos that get shared.

Yes, and… we could put all those photos in a coffee table book for everyone to remember what a great day we had.

Yes, and… let's…

A quick demo, like the one in the box above, allows you to add a little more theatre (without over doing your enthusiasm and losing credibility).

Again, you get what to do and how to behave. Once you've demonstrated the game, ask your pairs to play it too. Remind them to very clearly 'agree' with whatever suggestion is offered by their partner, to suspend judgement about that suggestion and to say 'yes, AND!…' (to signal positive energy and good intention) before then building upon that suggestion. Allow the pairs to play this game for slightly longer than the negative game, allowing for laughter and energy to grow in the group before debriefing the activity.

'YES, AND…' DEBRIEF

Now ask the group the same questions as before, but with a slight tweak (and expect/discuss these types of answers):

1. **What did it feel like to build on people's suggestions?**
   Easy, and quite enjoyable!

2. **Did it feel good then?**
   Yes, we got carried away in the moment and ended up somewhere we hadn't imagined.

3. **Do you want to work with the person again?**
   Yes, I believe I would.

4. **How many ideas have you got?**
   One really good one – likely to be rude, no doubt.

5. **What advice would you give people who want to grow ideas in brainstorm sessions?**
   Be positive, be playful, be open to possibility.

At the start of introducing the Simon's Picnic game, most people will leap to conclusions about what the point is. They are likely to have encountered this type of ideas growing game before and nod enthusiastically that they need to 'be positive' and 'not judge ideas' in the brainstorms. What tends to happen is the theatre of the game is overdone and the point about suspending judgement is lost. The game becomes a distraction at the start of the session – and is sometimes briefed in poorly – taken seriously or worse, not played at all. Then, as the live business topic is introduced, the behaviours are immediately lost and the group continues to capture only thoughts – and worse, resorts to judgemental behaviours. The net result is a poor idea output and a memory of an awkward and embarrassing game at the start of the session.

Spend time in the debrief pointing out that 'accepting offers without judgement' is necessary when building all types of ideas, no matter how hard it is to fight our natural tendency to judge and criticise. If we judge ideas too early, groups develop that capacity as a collective skill. This will lead to the behaviour of bringing in judgement earlier and earlier as ideas are suggested. The outputs of creative sessions will be fewer and people will start to harbour false truths about which ideas are (and are not) possible in their business. 👉

At this stage in the process, as the team facilitator, you're becoming the ideas coach. You're training your project team participants in the behavioural standards of what is and isn't expected for ideas and elevating the standards of what to be captured from now on. Remind your group that Simon's Picnic part one was pointing out how easy it is to find fault with ideas and kill the energy. And the second version of the game, by saying 'yes, and…' acknowledged the power of good intention and positive energy. A final version of the game brings these learnings together with the knowledge of what to look for between a thought and an idea. Playing this game will raise the team's 'ideas-growing' skill level higher.

GROWING STARTER IDEAS

Issue the same pairs (as everyone ought to be in a groove now) with a small stack of 'starter thoughts/start ideas' (see examples, right). Explain that these statements, made of just a few words, will be somewhere in that fuzzy zone between a thought and a starter idea. We all interpret these statements differently and, for some of us, they are very clearly ideas whilst other people need more information about them (it's also good to remind people about this). Ask each pair to choose one starter idea, and then go back and forth in picnic fashion at least seven times with 'Yes, and…' replies to grow that starter idea into something more fully-formed. Do this for a total of three starter ideas. Pairs should return to the group having grown three starter ideas, about which both people have the same understanding.

Five minutes is usually enough time to do this, but allow more time for this activity if needed, as the learnings will be richer.

Starter thoughts/starter ideas

- Pop-up cocktail bar at a festival
- Christmas decorations with a twist
- Portable sink and shower unit
- Brilliant 'first day at work'
- Brand new type of job interview
- Child's toy to help with maths
- Pet spa for when you're on holiday
- Make crazy golf sexy again

DEBRIEF

Ask the same questions as before, but with more discussion. The 'yes, and… ' game is easy to play with a fictitious picnic (likely to end in implausible outcomes) but in this instance pairs are genuinely having to grow an idea that could be realised. And when doing so they'd probably have had to fight their inner voices about what is likely to be real in the world. Hear from each pair. The stories will help build a collective experience in your project team – one that helps support and secure the overall standards in idea-growing behaviours from now on.

1 **What did it feel like to build on people's suggestions?**
It took longer. A bit trickier now we're discussing business ideas rather than fictitious picnics.

2 **How did it feel?**
A bit tiring. We feel like we've 'earned' the idea and had to work for it.

3 **Do you want to work with the person again?**
Yes, we both have the same memory of the chat and we're now in a good place to describe that idea to others.

4 **How many ideas have you got?**
We've got three. But we chose those starter ideas we thought would be easy to grow.

It's very easy for our fast-paced (and well-intentioned) brains to judge any starter thinking as we're still connected to learnings from the scoping stage and inherited beliefs about what's possible in the business. In a live brainstorm, we can't afford the luxury of judging ideas and choosing to nurture only the ones that make sense to us. That approach cripples innovation. This is not the way.

For example, it's easy to grow ideas for soft drinks and beer as at the centre of those product propositions are the sentiments of joy and fun. It's harder to connect to pharmaceutical, banking or software projects as perhaps the driving forces of ideas are safety, compliance and efficiency. Therefore, the same 'yes, and…' behaviour is needed to grow ideas in this context. And, in fact, you'll need to emphasise all the more that people should not 'judge' suggestions at all – no matter how wild. Some of the most ridiculous suggestions in our creative sessions have led to commercially successful ideas.

> **EXAMPLE STORY**
>
> When I worked in a bank I took part in someone else's brainstorm (although the meeting didn't start out that way). The topic to answer was roughly 'ideas for a better culture'. There had been round after round of restructures, whilst the whole office was also being kitted out in snazzy new furniture. Someone, somewhere, had decided that there needed to be an 'agile' mindset from now on, and we were all being asked to suggest what this looked like.
>
> My suggestions were fragile and incredibly nebulous, because I'd had little time to think. I quickly thought of activities I'd like to enjoy, and I reworked some examples of 'agile' things I'd read, seen and heard about from other businesses we'd all like to emulate. We were asked to capture our ideas on sticky notes and stick them to the flip chart. Just like the story at the opening of this chapter, a day or two later I received an email with a bullet list of suggestions. I noticed all of mine were missing. I asked the facilitator who'd run the session what had happened. She replied that some didn't make sense to her, so they hadn't been taken to the next stage, and the remaining suggestions were thought to be too controversial so they weren't taken forward either.
>
> Her answer illustrated neatly the two reasons I've been discussing in this chapter why brainstorm sessions can fail: standards and behaviours. Not having a set standard for what an idea is and then poorly capturing half-baked output led to some of my sticky notes being dismissed. And, not nurturing positivity but instead judging starter ideas accounted for my remaining suggestions being ignored. The result of the session, as far as I could see, created some rather benign rules about keeping meeting rooms neat and tidy – something anyone with a modicum of respect and common sense would have the decency to do anyway. The ONE TEAM logo took up the bottom third of the PowerPoint list.

When facilitating idea generation in groups, you might want to use the analogy that creative sessions are a bit like making pancakes; the first few will be dreadful, but when everything is warmed up, the outcome is going to be far tastier and far more rewarding.

PART 3 — THE PROCESS: IDEAS

THIS IS NOT THE WAY

242

The 'Big Six'

At GENIUS BOX, we have six distinct aspects of group work that we believe provide the best environment for idea generation.

It is not true that 'there is no such thing as a bad idea'. There will be some terrible ideas in your ideas session. These will be mostly at the start, as people 'get into the groove'. What is true is that, at the start, no idea is fully formed enough to be assessed against another idea, nor against the original project brief. Only after time will the merits of ideas present themselves clearly enough to be assessed, scored and judged. Until then, all ideas (even in the knowledge there will be some howlers) must be given equal attention and equal love.

We've discussed that an idea is something that everyone in a group shares the same understanding of, and that to grow ideas all group behaviour needs to be aligned positively (remember 'yes, and...'). We can combine these two standards into a powerful mechanic that will allow you to capture ideas in a consistent fashion time and again. The picture opposite shows a project ideas session. The idea emerged within a few minutes. From the outside this looked like a relaxed knock-about session where conversation flowed. Looking closely, we can see all the key aspects that would differentiate this session from one where someone clutching a flip chart is simply shouted at by a crowd of people. We call these key aspects the 'Big Six'.

① Small groups

The group shown opposite comprises of three people. They are sitting opposite each other and, importantly, everyone is at eye level. Everyone can be standing around a high table or crouched over a coffee table – it matters not – but being at eye level with each other sends the message that: We're all equal. We're all expected to contribute, and we all have equal voice. This is a team. A small group is ideal. At GENIUS BOX our facilitators will always engineer ideas sessions with pairs, threes or fours, and no more. This makes it less intimidating for those who are naturally reserved in larger crowds* and makes it far easier for the facilitator to see when everyone is making contributions. 👉

About the myth of introversion and creativity: introversion is not about being shy, hating big crowds and hiding from brainstorms and the world of creativity. Nor is extroversion solely about people enjoying leaping about on stage and needing to be the centre of attention. Both are about energy and how our minds are stimulated. Some thrive off the inputs from others, whilst for others energy and stimuli come from within. Well facilitated, *everyone* can enjoy an ideas session. It ought to ebb and flow allowing for periods of reflection as well as group animation. A session that's just chaotic and noisy is likely to disengage everyone. It's your responsibility to include everyone rather than let people opt out because of preconceived ideas about who does and does not suit brainstorming.

② Facilitator and participants

It is the facilitator's job to ensure the energy is right, that the environment is good for alpha state, and that the pre-agreed standards for idea capture are maintained. Importantly, they lead and maintain the standards in idea-growing behaviour. It is not for the facilitator to be the only one having ideas. When observing ideas sessions and brainstorms, the facilitator is easy to spot at a distance; it is they who are holding the pen, they are asking lots of questions and they're clearly responsible for what's happening in that group.

Creative participants are those who are responding to the brief and taking it in turns to share their starter ideas. The facilitator invites the other creative participants to grow the starter ideas against the scoped brief (or a Job To Be Done from the insight stage) until ideas are fully formed. The idea is then captured (see p247, Capturing the idea correctly) and the group moves on to the next starter idea. If, at any time, the facilitator becomes excited by the idea conversation and wishes to offer input then they are free to do so, but without losing context that they must ensure the 'thoughts' are translated into ideas and safely captured for the future.

Remember, when an idea is first offered in conversation it's still only seconds old. Even if someone had been incubating the thought overnight, that fragile idea was still, until recently, electrochemical signals in someone's head. They're doing the best they can with the language they have to describe the idea. Sometimes (and the more you facilitate, the more often you'll spot this) people are describing not the ideas but instead the benefits of the idea as if it existed. You'll hear people say 'I've got an idea. Wouldn't it be nice if we had *something* that made that thing we did *easier*.' This is a thought. It's actually someone putting words to their thinking...

Rarely (maybe it's impossible) can one person alone have the idea; the fully formed business plan, the brand name, details on manufacturing, distribution, marketing, operations, cost management, quality control and the comms plan. No. Ideas are built by the team. Here are some questions and comments that GENIUS BOX facilitators say when running ideas sessions that we sense have become people just forming ideas and sharing thoughts. Use these as a guide (as every ideas session is different) to progress such thoughts into more fully formed ideas:

"You're moving your hands as you describe [the starter idea], tell us more, what's going on there?"

"If I walked into an empty room and [the starter idea] was sitting there, what would I see?"

"If I wanted to sign up as a member to [the starter idea], what would I do first?"

"How could that aspect of [the starter idea] work? What does it look like?"

"That's interesting, don't skip over that bit of [the starter idea], tell us more."

"That's lovely, tell me why you like that part of [the starter idea]."

"What else does this part of [the starter idea] do and how?"

The facilitator never judges ideas, and calls out the participants who do.

3 Considered positive energy

In *The Lego Movie* everything is awesome. And (of course) life isn't, and neither are all the ideas. Too much positive energy is actually negative.

People can smell disingenuous positivity.

You may have been on a phone call where your answers are 'excellent', 'awesome', 'fantastic' and 'amazing'. Such superlatives aren't appropriate when describing your responses on an insurance renewal or when booking a table for two. Instead, in ideas sessions, we advocate being positive in a 'considered' fashion. Reserve the 'amazing' and the 'awesome' (which are sort of judgements, really) for things that truly make you stand up and take notice, and instead give praise and positive encouragements with 'thank you', 'that's interesting', 'that's thought through well', 'I like how that aspect of your idea links to that part of the idea', 'nicely done'. If everyone adopts the mindset and energy of a coach – rather than a cheerleader – the ideas session will be less exhausting.

The best ideas sessions I've attended are those where I've walked in and a gentle murmur of people 'in focus' and 'on task' was evident. Few people were looking up from their group; there was a palpable level of activity. The noise level was that of an animated dinner party rather than a crowd at a rock concert. Of course, there was laughter. And arm waving. But these were the exceptions that stood out – and could be discussed in team debriefings – rather than a constant.

MAINTAINING POSITIVE ENERGY

Apart from the obvious 'no, that won't work', the facilitator needs to have their radar up for many types of judgement. Hopefully, having played the Simon's Picnic game (and its follow-ups), everyone remembers how to behave positively and what it feels like to do so. It becomes challenging, however, when people are working on actual live projects. It's only natural for System 1 thinking to hijack System 2 thinking and fast forward to possible traps in a starter idea. This type of judgement can creep through in conversation. Here are some judgy-sounding comments, their potential effects and what you can do about it. People are judging ideas when they say things like:

"But remember we will need compliance to sign it off."
This is a prediction. The final idea isn't yet formed. You're inviting the constraints of existing processes to hinder the potential of a new idea.

"It would be easier if we did this instead…"
This kills the suggested idea and replaces it immediately with another starter idea.

"I'm just saying it could take time…"
Watch out for offhand remarks like this as they signal a disconnect from the conversation. Such comments may appear helpful, but are actually more in the, 'I don't want to be the person who said I told you so' camp.

My top tip is to listen out for comments that involve time, scale, legal, cost, approval. These are all reasons to stop an idea before it has time to circulate in a conversation. If you hear any such judgements, 'use the difficulty'. Like this…

Legendary actor Sir Michael Caine says that any time we are faced with a difficulty or a problem we can use it to our advantage. He uses the great story of a misplaced chair during his rehearsals to illustrate this:

"I opened the door, and I said to the producer – who was sitting out in the

stalls – 'Well, look, I can't get in. There's a chair in my way.'

He said, 'Well, use the difficulty."'

So I said, 'What do you mean, use the difficulty?'

He said, 'Well, if it's a drama, pick it up and smash it. If it's a comedy, fall over it.'

This was a line for me for life: Always use the difficulty."

Sir Michael goes on to say there's never anything so bad where 'using the difficulty' can't be applied. If we use it only a quarter of a percent to our advantage then we're still ahead. Bearing this in mind, we don't let negative statements in a session get us down. When someone presents difficulty in a session, turn what they say into a stimulus for others to build up the idea:

"But, remember that we will need compliance to sign it off… "

– 'Great spot, what could we do to this idea that would make it easier for compliance to sign off?'

"It would be easier if we did this instead… "

– 'That's a good spot. Let me make a note of your suggestion. And now let's return to the original idea, how could we make this idea easier to manage?'

"I'm just saying it could take time… "

– 'We don't know that it will take time yet, as this idea isn't fully formed. Time sounds important to you though, tell me part of the idea that does excite you when it comes to saving time.'

Negativity is just energy. Our role as facilitator is to use energy in the right way for the task at hand.

In scoping we'll often need considered energy. During our insight work we'll want a reflective and relaxed energy.

And for ideas sessions we need intensity and focus; a positive energy to nurture positive thinking. There is always a way to use any perceived difficulty (judgement) as a way of growing the idea.

Finally, ideas can also be killed by a yawn, a smirk, or a grimace – even sarcastic laughter. These negative non-verbal behaviours need to be called out by the facilitator, too.

④ Grow one idea at a time

In our story at the opening of the chapter, Emma wrote every suggestion on the flip chart, and on one occasion crossed out an idea (judging). As we now know, these suggestions weren't ideas but instead were people's thoughts. Each word or starting headline signalled the beginning of a starter idea that needed help. In order to truly see what output an ideas session creates, it's essential to grow one idea, and give groups the time to do so, before moving onto the next. An oft-told riddle helps illustrate the point:

You are handed two seeds. One is for a rose and the other a weed. How can you be 100% certain which one is which? The answer is to plant both, water them and give them sunlight. After a while the two seeds will germinate and grow. And once that has happened, it'll be clear which is which.

It's the same for ideas. They need time to develop. And ideas develop in a conversation, but only when everyone is building on that one idea at a time. A group of participants calling out a range of starter ideas and having each of those comments captured on a flip chart is just creating a list of thoughts. It's a bad method. Is it any wonder people are usually reluctant to stand and field those types of conversation?

In order to grow just one idea at a time, invite one participant in your group to suggest their starter idea. Have everyone add to that idea positively. Eventually, there'll come a time when everyone has given some input. The idea is now formed a little more – it's no longer something captured in one or two words (often thoughts) but instead is a story of several parts, made up from a handful of specific details. The idea's DNA is clear (what it is and how it works), as are the handful of parts giving it enough detail so that a stranger could have the idea explained to them in one pass, without needing to ask too many questions.

What's critically important is the ability for everyone in the group to share the same common understanding of the idea and the same common language when describing it. Once you're at this stage, you can safely call your discussion the 'end of that idea', write the idea down on paper and then move on to the next starting idea from the group.

⑤ Capturing the idea correctly

When it comes to capturing the idea, do it last. The shorthand phrase to express that discipline, that I was taught, is 'sit on the pen' – literally if need be. Acting too soon stifles an idea. I was part of an ideas session for Next, the retailer, many years ago. The facilitator leading the session invited people to share their ideas; the focus was teenage accessories. After a few coughs and shifting in the seats, someone called out 'a new bag'.

We now know that 'a new bag' is just a thought. However, the word 'bag' was written on the flip chart. Then there was an uncomfortable pause. And then the facilitator nervously *underlined* the word 'bag' as she *said* the word 'bag' once again to the group. Next didn't launch anything new on that occasion.

Successfully capturing an idea is clearly critical to the entire process. When you are ready to do so, only then grab a pen and some paper. We suggest these three stages to capture an idea:

First – draw it. Stick people, arrows and basic shapes are all that's required. This image should capture what the idea is. 👉

Second – add some annotation to that image. These are little details that describe how the idea works. For this reason, ideas need to live on A4 size paper minimum and never, EVER trust them to sticky notes!

Third – give your idea a title (do this last; don't waste your creativity in wordsmithing). Naming your idea gives your efforts a mental 'full stop'. And when it comes to sorting through the ideas, it will give you a shorthand to help navigate your way to one particular idea amongst all the others.

ABOVE:
An idea, on A4, captured in a café in London. Whilst it makes little sense to you as the reader, it's got a picture, some annotation and perfectly captured the conversation we were having at the time.

6 Work in an alpha-state environment

When we're in alpha state, we've got far more connection to our subconscious where we access a rich source of stimuli and information – vital for making new creative connections that help us generate better ideas. So we need to look after our brains, as creating those new connections uses energy. It will be more tiring sitting around a dark and gloomy table in a dark and gloomy room, for participants to be reminded of the problem we're answering or some of the insight stories we've uncovered. It won't take long for people to start behaving in a way that matches their environment.

When facilitating ideas sessions it's essential that the facilitator keeps their radar up for the impact the environment is having on the group energy – and sometimes a new environment may be required. After only a short while, even the most inspiring space can become distracting. There is no 'rule' of when to do this. Each group will have its own unique energy. The subject matter will also impact how tiring ideas are to generate. Ideas for marketing an over-the-counter painkiller require a different focus than ideas for a TV channel wishing to sponsor the World Cup.

A common belief is that an environment needs to be filled with colour and stimuli, soft furnishings and plenty of toys – the opposite of a grey meeting room. This is not the way. It gives creative facilitation a bad name. Instead, link the problem you're solving to the environment you choose. The environment can amplify the experiences of the audience you're solving for or indirectly stimulate thinking by providing an extreme experience. My advice is simple: environment is mostly about *how* you are rather than *where* you are. Monitor energy and change things up at least every hour; even if that's just a walk around the block.

At a great ideas session groups are small and the facilitator moves between them after landing a few ideas so others within each group can take turns at facilitating. As head facilitator, you are playful and relaxed, creating a considered and positive energy for idea generation. No judgement; all comments are welcome and all invited to contribute. Teams grow one idea at a time before capturing it and moving on to the next idea-generation conversation. Don't make lists, don't judge ideas and keep changing the environment to keep it fresh and energised.

EXAMPLE STORY

We were running ideas sessions in Dubai for the Jumeriah group – famed for premium coastline properties including the iconic Burj Al Arab. We'd spent the day at the Burj hearing from management on how the hotel had to compete against other properties now that it was no longer the only option for discerning global travellers. This type of tourist was looking for something even more exclusive. We'd spoken to staff in all the behind-the-scenes workings of the hotel and even had time to sample the delicious food, 'be a guest' and have a dip in the pool, if only for a few hours. We had plenty of insights inspiring us to elevate the Burj proposition. Our task was to leave the client with a handful of provocations and ideas to stimulate debate and influence strategy. But we couldn't translate those insights into ideas.

There was too much good stuff to see sitting in the Burj. We were surrounded by what many hotels aspire to become. Everything around us was (literally) glittering with gold. The distraction was real. We made the decision to check-in at a downtown hotel, a humble affair with little to offer – the Burj it certainly wasn't. But it was easy for my co-facilitator and I to enjoy a cool beer and talk about the experience we wanted to have when looking around the cheaper hotel. We arrived at a series of ideas for the Burj that were inspired by the environment of the downtown hotel and how it had impacted the way we felt and thought.

To keep the energy going, we also played a game by giving ourselves only two minutes to sketch and annotate an idea before sharing it with each other. This forced everyone to stick to the core idea and not capture fine details.

Interview

Sarah Christensen
INCLUSION PIONEER

Sarah lives and works in the UAE. Her consulting practice specialises in diversity, equity and inclusion. She designs and delivers programmes, training, mentoring and coaching for senior leaders and leadership teams who want to develop their diversity agenda. When not in the classroom, Sarah can be found in the ocean, unwinding under the waves teaching others how to scuba-dive.

You ask all kinds of people to make creative connections — what do you do when facilitating your workshops to ensure the sessions are successful?
I am relying on my energy. Great facilitation is energy transfer. Be that found in coaching, training, mentoring, problem solving – you're constantly measuring the energy. I want people in my company to be energised, inspired and motivated. There's nothing worse than a dull facilitator never changing the tone of voice or moving from the spot. Energy is what matters. Movement, voice, body, facial expressions – it's a physical job, so you've got to lead with energy.

People from all around the globe tackle making creative connections in different ways — what are the consistencies you've spotted in this inconsistent world?
I've seen people build upon each other's suggestions when we're aligned and I've seen people break down ideas when we're not. There's no definitive answer, but what makes ideas grow, and creative connections form, is that building behaviour. That committed, patient, deliverable build of one suggestion on top of another. Once we've all agreed the ground rules, then it's easy for me to ask gentle questions of people to unlock their thinking and push things further. Asking people 'how does that suggestion apply to you', for example, creates advocacy and empathy. Ultimately, creative connections come from listening and building.

You never get a second chance to make a first impression – what do you think are the important first moments for participants when being facilitated by you?

I need everyone in the room to contribute to the project and for that to happen they need to know I have energy for them and the task – and that I'm here to facilitate a journey. I'm here to help people form their story and not impart mine by talking at them for six hours at a time. Facilitation is not about talking at people, it's about creating that space where insights and ideas can be formed.

Tell me about teamwork – what does that concept mean to others?

Teamwork exists when there are no boundaries in the way of collaboration. I'm thinking right now of a client session just recently where a small group of us were building on suggestions from each other. There was no negativity in the room, we seemed to have been caught up in a world of possibility, the energy was palpable, infectious even, and when it was over and we agreed our outputs we were so alive. I wasn't tired, I was in a better state than I was at the start of the day. Teamwork should deliver that. I can't know the finer details of my clients' business culture, so instead I create a space where that culture can be explored collaboratively so that we arrive in new places.

Facilitating creativity needs clear communication – have you any advice here about landing the right message?

Be clear in your communication. I know that sounds obvious, but I think people are quick to get into the topic without establishing clarity on what to expect and how in the beginning. I will say that my role is not to give the answer, it is to help the group arrive at an answer together. I invite people to be respectful of each other's contributions big and small. And finally – let's go! I've got to create an energetic beginning, an expectation that we'll arrive at something powerful.

Diversity of thinking is essential to a creative project. But diversity can mean different things, too. Is there an elegant way that facilitators can navigate diversity?

You can't leverage the power of diversity without inclusion. And I favour a layered approach. Diversity is at the bottom, to unlock that you need to be inclusive first. And by that I mean include everyone in the room carefully and in a considered fashion. It's about taking time to look people in the eye, let them see you, give space for quiet moments to linger and for people to reflect on your questions and instructions before asking them to respond. To give people the space to do all of that there needs to be a layer of belonging. Where people can belong, they can bring value. So right from the start I am keen to ask everyone two questions: what mood do they choose to bring to the session and is there anything that might be holding them back from being at their best? When I allow time for us all to have that discussion then we belong to each other, our needs are included and we're ready to explore and release the power of diversity.

What is a final nugget of genius you'd like to share?

Don't shoehorn your agenda into the lives of others. Don't be wedded to outcomes right at the start. Allow big and powerful learnings to be discovered. Great facilitation should feel like a powerful massage – when someone finds a tough knot and kneads it really hard with an elbow! You need to find the knots and spend time there. Unleash perspectives and ideas from others.

> *"Great facilitation is energy transfer. Movement, voice, body, facial expressions – it's a physical job, so you've got to lead with energy."*
>
> – SARAH CHRISTENSEN

More on idea capture

Capturing and preserving an idea with precision and clarity is a facilitator's core skill.

A picture paints a thousand words – so, practise drawing ideas! Between us, the team at GENIUS BOX have run over 10,000 creative sessions. Many have involved generating ideas. Therefore, we've spotted some immediate tips and tricks to help capture ideas using pictures. This advice is extremely useful if you find yourself facilitating people who say 'they can't draw':

- Most ideas involve people. An idea happens to a person. Or a person interacts with an idea. Stick people are very useful to master.
- You can show how people interact with an idea by using arrows.
- Interaction happens over time and ideas have impact over time. Time can be shown by drawing a clock face.
- Ideas usually need supporting structures to make them happen – usually people, with some money and a bit of time. You can label your ideas easily with these three bullet points: People. Money. Time.

If the idea in your idea generation session is a new product then this is relatively straightforward, as it's a shape of an object that sits on a shelf in a store. If it's a pot of yoghurt or an electric car you're still drawing a shape (90% of the time made from boxes or cylinders) and labelling the features.

However, most ideas in business brainstorms are changes in strategy, processes/systems or customer journeys. It is rare that these ideas are made of just one element. Instead, the idea is a new way of working, a 'thing' told within a story of many scenes. It's easier to draw a series of sketches, a bit like a cartoon strip, of what the idea is and does.

Another option is to see the idea as if it were being assembled over time – like Lego or IKEA instructions, most people have hands-on experience with both. Therefore, have to hand some examples and show that these visual guides use symbols and icons instead of words.

As explained previously, when we capture an idea we follow the three-step process of drawing it, labelling it and naming it. Let's expand on this further.

When **drawing** your idea, invite comments from the participants to ensure you've captured all of the key details and important aspects of the idea.

Add labels to the idea or list the sequence of events that the 'user' of the idea would go through when the idea is up and live. A good way to land this language is to ask 'If I was describing this idea to people on the phone, and they couldn't see it, what would I tell them that's important?'

When **naming** your idea, make it short and pithy – something that captures its essence or benefit. A name makes it easier to remember one idea over another so you can quickly find it and add builds and amends when those moments arise.

Similarly, at the assessment stage, named ideas are easier to remember than descriptions: 'Hang on! Where's TUK-TUK-TEA-BOY? That idea really stood out'. This shows how a name gives the idea energy, a personality and a character that we feel obliged to connect to and nurture.

If you can't think of a catchy title for your idea, then imagine being involved in it if the idea was alive and well. Then use language to describe to someone what that idea felt like: 'New banking onboard induction journey for graduates' could be renamed as 'BIG DAY OUT'. If you're still stuck, just name the idea after a popular film or a news headline from the day.

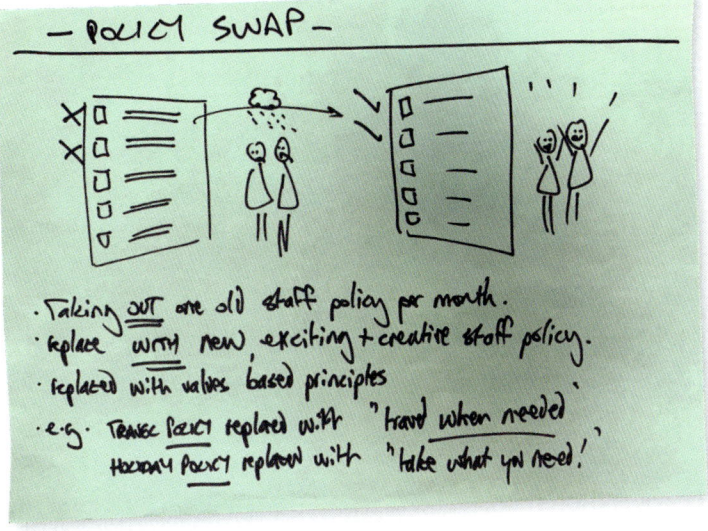

LEFT & BELOW: Every idea is made of many details. So go for the important stuff – focus on capturing how the idea works and what people will see and do.

Ideas coaching

Most ideas are made up of lots of little 'idea-ettes' that combine and link with each other to create an overall 'big idea'.

This is particularly the case when it comes to ideas for strategy, change and transformation, or anything to do with culture within an organisation. Critical, then, is the language people use to describe ideas when capturing them. As part of our ideas sessions, we spend time 'ideas coaching' to hone people's understanding of the power of description and bring everyone up to the same standard. The more ways you find to describe something, the more likely you are to hit upon the perfect descriptions of ideas (as opposed to thoughts). Play this game to help your group work on their powers of description.

IDEAS BUZZCOCKS
Create a list of descriptions of ideas, and ask people to work out what real things those ideas are. You can do this in 'team pub quiz' style or give out sheets for people to complete individually. For example:

A bit like a big school sports day. It's held every four years. There's one country that hosts it in the summer and builds a big stadium. All the other countries turn up for a few weeks and play lots of sports against each other. The winners in each sport get medals.
Idea: the Olympic Games

Usually spread over several fields. Lots of bandstands and stages. Tents with activities. Food stalls and live music for people to dip in and out of.
Idea: music festival

A quiet space. Lush furnishings, low light, private bar, gives off an exclusive vibe. Only travellers with special tickets are allowed access. Wifi, showers, food, etc all free with ticket.
Idea: airline lounge

This activity teaches people that specific language is important to describe an idea and keep it from being just a thought. You can land the point that a number of sentences are needed to describe an idea. It is a myth that ideas can be described in a single sentence. This is not the way!

Idea DNA

There is merit in finding common factors in one idea and adding them to other ideas.

For example, any 'event' idea will likely have a website or app where tickets can be bought. This element of the event idea can be copied across to different events. Similarly, a 'change programme' idea will likely have a 'kick-off', some 'comms' and 'measurements'. These elements will likely be common components, regardless of the scale and ambition of any change programme.

However, these are ancillary elements to an idea and don't differentiate between ideas. If you take the ticketing website away from the event – what is the event? If you take the kick-off and comms away from the change programme – what is the change programme going to change and how?

When growing ideas, you need to listen out for the idea DNA. I've alluded to the 'core idea' and the 'essence of an idea' – this is what we can call the DNA. When you identify the DNA of an idea, you're then clear on what the idea is and what it does differently when compared to other ideas. This prevents a cluster of ideas getting combined into something that becomes too broad and therefore difficult to describe succinctly.

Idea DNA is the unique and distinguishing feature of your idea that you protect, regardless of how many other elements are added. When you've protected the idea DNA, it's easier to adjust other elements of the idea to fit a brief or in response to feedback at a later stage.

DNA: WHAT TO DO

When growing the ideas in your ideas sessions, allow time for everyone to have their discussion until you're satisfied that it's an idea being discussed and not a thought. When ready to capture the idea, ask clearly 'what is this idea and how does it work', and allow time for participants to answer. Then state 'so, I'll capture that like so.' and get it down on paper. Read out what you've done and then ask 'what else have I missed?' We don't use printed templates at GENIUS BOX, as people capture images and annotations inside the boxes but leave white space around what they write. This leads to images being quite small. It's also harder to remember one idea from another. The creative energy, so important to ideas sessions, soon evaporates when handling lots of same-looking templates. Instead, coloured paper and fat marker pens keep reinforcing the messages of 'no judgement, ideas only, keep things simple'.

Whether the idea is a good idea (answers the original brief) is up for debate later. What matters at this stage is that you and your project team participants have captured your ideas clearly and not simply captured thoughts.

Ideas cannot be readily understood if they are captured by only a few words on a sticky note – that's really just thoughts! A well-captured idea will have an illustration of what it is, a description of how it works (bullet points are great rather than long paragraphs) and a title to help the group remember it for the next stage.

Idea trees

At the start of this chapter, we learnt that ideas are something you can do, *and that anything else we believe is a thought.*

At GENIUS BOX we believe this is the one and only key differentiator to focus on when facilitating ideas sessions. If you only take one thing away from our advice, it should be to keep focusing on growing ideas and not thoughts.

Another tool to help you coach and facilitate others in understanding the difference between thoughts and ideas is an idea tree.

Some ideas can be small and simple, and implemented for little investment whilst taking only a small amount of time and involving a few people; for example, 'a pop-up café selling coffee and cakes in the foyer of the company HQ, that turns up every second Wednesday of the month.' Other ideas might be something that will cost millions of pounds and require thousands of people to complete – such as 'a privately funded rocket for rich people who need their next big adventure'.

The comparison is extreme but deliberate. Great facilitators are brilliant at assembling in their mind's eye what people are discussing and then grouping that content into either briefs, thoughts, ideas or tactics – this is what I'd call an idea tree. It is in an idea tree that the elements of a conversation are laddered up on top of each other. And a great facilitator plays back those conversations to the participants in the session, so those people focus better on growing ideas in place of having distracting conversations all about thoughts.

Splitting the conversation up into groups will also help you spot when people are talking about the benefit of having an idea. You don't want to talk about benefits – you want the **idea** that gives you the benefit! People will list lots of reasons why an idea would be a good thing and get caught up in the theatrics of such a conversation. The energy is enticing, and people can easily mistake the conversation as productive. But lists

ABOVE:
Remember the standards for idea capture: picture, description, title.

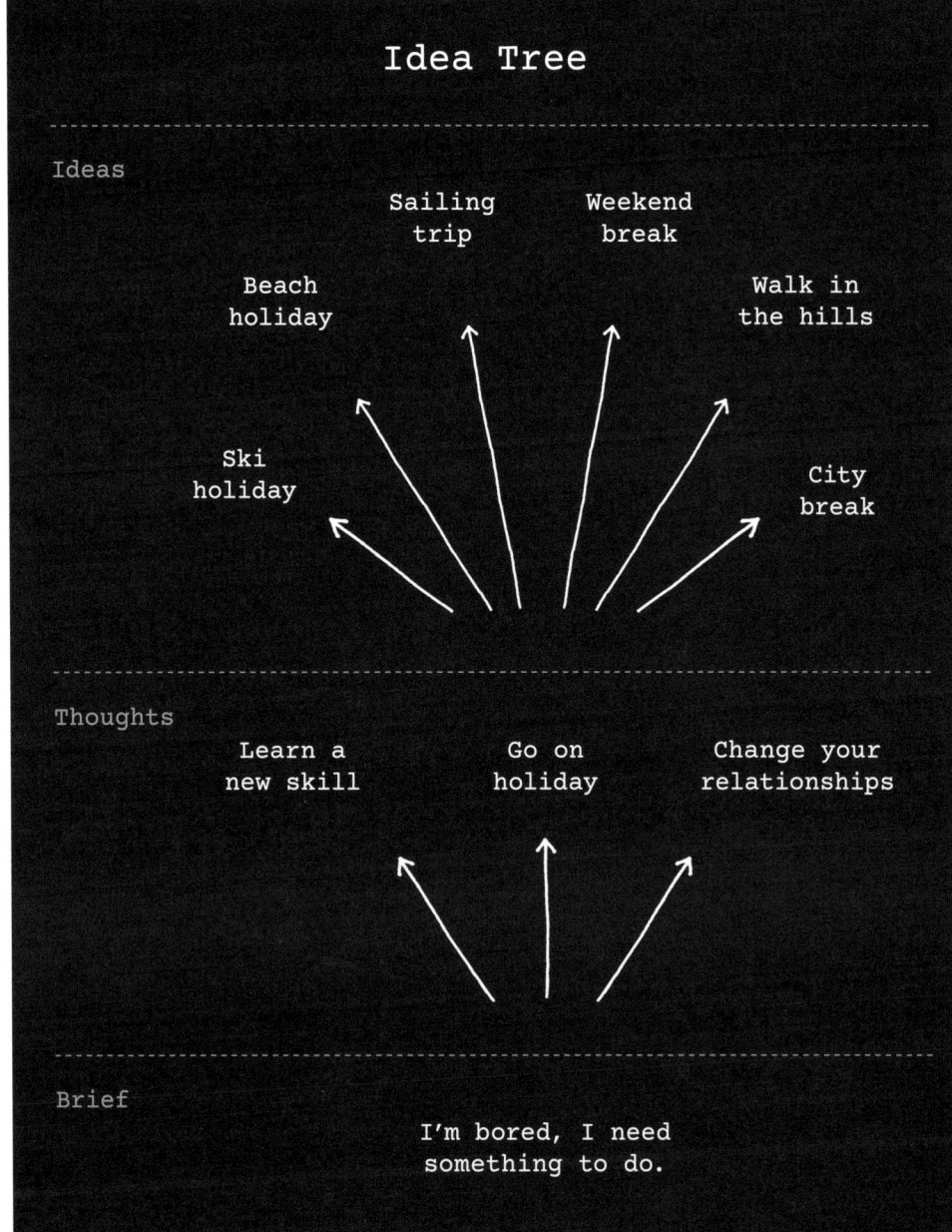

of benefits can't be *done* and, therefore, you're not capturing ideas. Idea trees help you spot where the chat needs to be.

- From one brief, many thoughts can come
- From one thought, many ideas can come
- Each idea will need a series of tactics to make it happen
- Sometimes lots of other smaller ideas are all needed to come together to make things happen and work – and in these instances, confusingly, that first idea is essentially the starting brief for a mini project

Let's look at the ideas tree tool, using a handy illustration and a personal issue as a starting point.

Brief: I'm bored, I need something to do.

Thoughts: go on holiday, learn a new skill, change your relationships (other thoughts can be listed).

There are lots of ideas we can have off each thought:

Thought: Go on holiday.

Ideas: Ski holiday, beach holiday, sailing trip, weekend break, walk in the hills, city break, and so on.

And if we took one idea – the weekend break – we can get narrower still and plan an itinerary with lots of detail and smaller ideas from which the main weekend is built: take Eurostar to Paris, book into a hotel, have lunch in the city, river trip, afternoon drink, music concert and dinner. Breakfast in bed, trip to the artist quarter, fly home...

All these components are in one topic: being bored and going away, but they sit at different levels (literally on your paper or in your mind's eye). This is how facilitators funnel down conversations. The broader levels are wide and open to possibility. It's here that thoughts, suggestions and concepts belong, as nothing is fully formed. It is here facilitators place starting ideas, concepts and topics that keep recurring in conversation. At the top of the idea tree are the more specific and tactical aspects of ideas being discussed – it's here you'll find all the detail.

Great ideas sessions guide conversations through this process so people put their creative energy into things that can be done.

Now, let's look at an issue in business.

Brief: We need a better induction programme.

Thought: A 90-day journey

Starter ideas: mini ideas to group together to best answer the brief:

1. Welcome pack
2. Tour of the business
3. Team dinner
4. New joiner specific projects
5. One-month review

Idea detail: Different stages on a 90-day induction journey that a new inductee experiences as they join the business. Each stage is a week or so long, and contains a set amount of new content for the new joiner to absorb. In turn, the business slowly 'upskills' the new joiner, and the new joiner gets to slowly become part of the organisation. At the end of the 90 days the new joiner has had a decent 'dipping into' the business, and we can celebrate with a proper 'welcome' ceremony.

This example neatly illustrates that most projects aren't solved by just **one hero idea**. No, the big ideas in business (especially internal process ideas or strategic programme ideas) are usually made up of lots of small ideas that come together to ultimately satisfy the brief.

Too often that context is forgotten in ideas sessions and people, when faced with a blank sheet of paper, unconsciously think they have to write down the 'one clever catch-all solution'. As a result, their unconscious minds take over and drive a great deal of *thought* that is captured and discussed. It feels quite productive, but on closer inspection it's not really clear what the *ideas* are that could solve the brief.

The structure of funnelling ideas through an idea tree system will help avoid such pitfalls and enable you to see which (smaller) ideas work well together to answer the brief. Do this as much as you can with all of the ideas arising from your sessions so you have some solid work to take forward to the assessment, selection and implementation stages, as outlined in the next chapter.

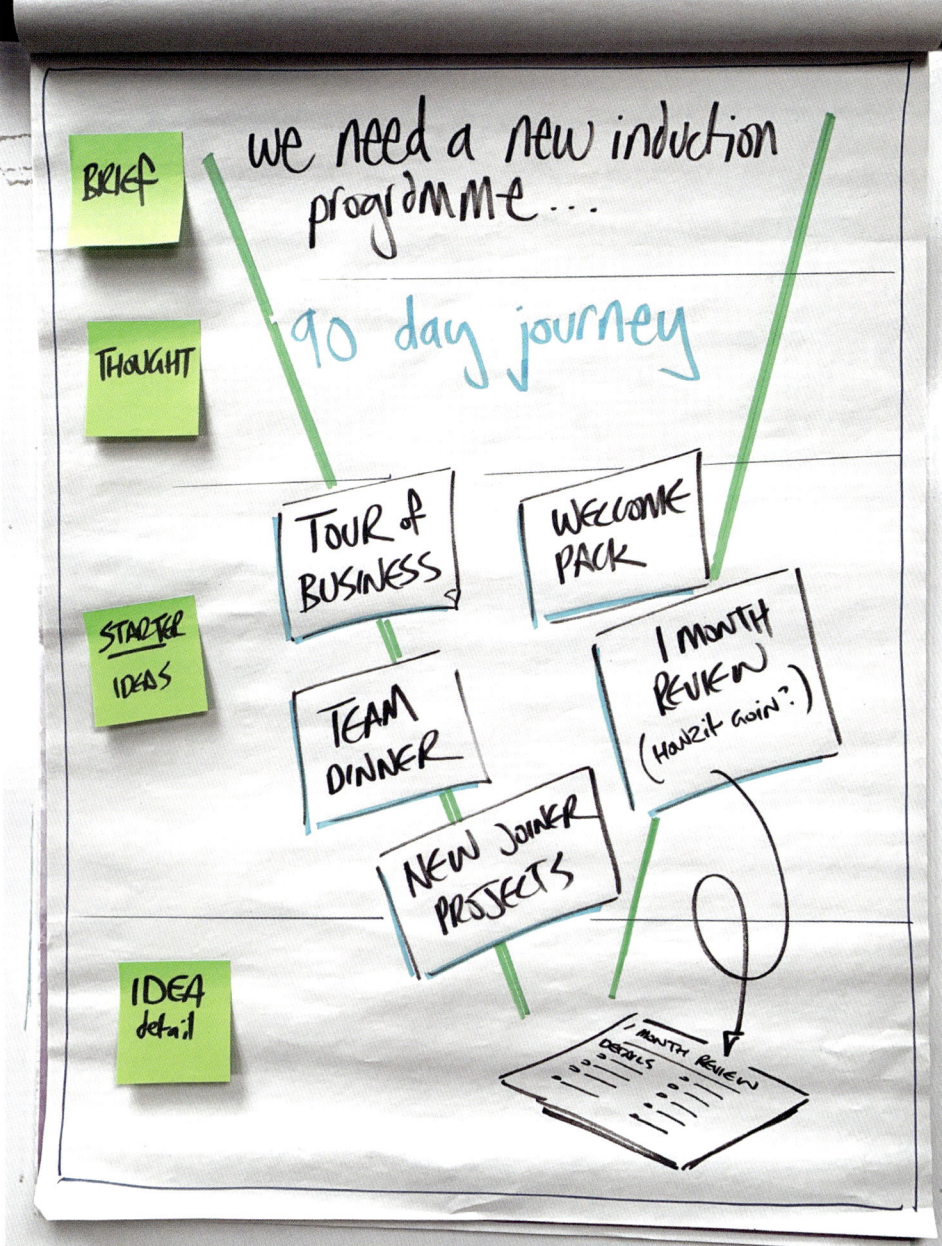

SUMMARY

Ideas are the output of your creative endeavours. Scoping the brief correctly and uncovering insights will power great idea generation. Once you have a range of ideas, it's then time to move along the process and start selecting the ideas that best answer the brief. This requires a brand-new batch of tools and accompanying behaviours.

There are masses of 'idea generation' techniques out there in books, websites and downloadable videos – all of which are potentially useful and value-adding. But if there's just one thing to take away from this chapter it's that you need to **capture ideas and not thoughts** for your projects to be successful. I've mentioned this time and again throughout this chapter and pointed out the nuances in technique, language and behaviour that garner strong idea capture and understanding.

Now you've got the ideas – let's choose the ones that work best.

LEFT:
An idea tree helps to navigate the difference between the brief, thoughts and starter ideas.

The Process

4_SELECTION

The final part of our process is idea selection. There's little point creating ideas if some aren't chosen to be embedded into your business or launched into the world. At the start of this stage all of your ideas are assessed for selection. You'll score and audit them so it's easier to choose which idea or ideas are put forward as the solution to your original project brief. Facilitating this part of the process presents more challenges as you'll be wrestling with what ideas are chosen or not – but you've got this, you're a genius!

The intro bit

A great deal of the selection stage is choosing how many ideas will be chosen and recommended to the business. It is a scoring and auditing process, during which ideas get better as the details on how they'd be supported and project-managed into the business are discussed and explored.

For too long choosing, refining and auditing ideas has been perceived as hard work; it's not seen as a part of the process that allows for much creativity – and instead, people think that 'blue sky' thinking should step aside for rigorous decision making. I disagree. There's a real need for this part of the process to be just as creative and colourful as generating ideas. Idea selection demands that you and your project team participants switch mindsets in the moment from assessment (judging ideas) to building (growing ideas) as conversations unfold. Therefore, this stage is as much about remaining positive ('yes, and...' behaviour) as it is about being considered and decisive.

Your challenge as a facilitator will be to keep everyone incredibly clear on what to do (as an activity), why they are doing it (connecting the activity to the project context) and, finally, how to behave (as mindsets and behaviours are critical). Remember the monorail metaphor? Whilst your project team is in the last part of the process, you are keeping your 'radar' up and listening out for further scoping learnings to help make decisions, insights to help strengthen ideas and 'plussing' (see p287) to make ideas better. Above all, remember that you're likely to select a handful of ideas to recommend to the business; rarely is a project solved by one magical answer alone.

Ideas at the selection stage need a bit of help from time to time to get them across the line. To do this you need to run impromptu idea-building sessions. Similarly, no project can commission *all* the ideas as an answer to a brief, therefore, choices have to be made about which idea is selected. This requires a different family of mindsets and behaviours. The skill is being able to switch between the two mindsets *and* bring your team along too. Selection sessions absolutely have to be facilitated. And the facilitator needs to be super sharp on aligning everyone's behaviours, so they're either in 'assessment mode' or 'build mode'.

This chapter gives a set of tools to help you and your team whittle down the idea outputs from your ideas sessions into a handful of well-captured and fully formed ideas. Importantly, these ideas will come with the instructions and structures to help embed them into the business.

The selection phase should be seen as a creative session in and of itself, where output becomes ideas that are unavoidable and inevitable.

In summary, selection requires a good deal of auditing and scoring that helps filter and group ideas. It's then a far easier task to choose which ideas to take forward and hand over to the business to project manage. This chapter offers up five auditing tools, six scoring tools and other top tips to help you choose what output to recommend. Let's first start with where you left off at the end of your idea brainstorms. You're likely to be looking at a big pile of ideas... 👉

OPPOSITE:
Me again! Adding final details to a batch of ideas ahead of an idea selection session.

Auditing

At the end of an ideas session, you will have a range of ideas. Intuitively, as you've been facilitating, you'll now favour some over others.

It's natural. You'll have been part of the generation of those ideas as you ran those ideas sessions. Similarly, your co-facilitator will have ideas they are attached to that are equally as charming. And discussing ideas at the end of each session starts to build an emotional bond between you and your output. This will also be the case for other members of the project team. Creative projects become a significant part of your working world. You cannot be wholly objective and neutral when facilitating a project, nor can members of your team. So you need a way of selecting ideas that allows you to look after the idea you love, as well as looking after all the other ideas being generated by the team.

GOOD IDEAS AND BAD IDEAS

Let's revisit the cliché of 'there is no such thing as a bad idea'. Asking people to make decisions on whether output is either 'good' or 'bad' creates nothing but a swirling mess of subjective discussions. This is not the way. Instead, successful selection is about **focusing on the ideas that best answer the brief**, combining them to create stronger propositions, and also creating the structures needed to help embed them into your business. All other ideas are potentially useful for other projects, or parts of those other ideas can be used to strengthen the chosen ideas as they journey though the implementation stage.

My analogy is that of Lego bricks. There are no 'bad' bricks, only bricks that don't suit the model you want to build at that time. Similarly, there's no such thing as 'bad wallpaper', it's the issue of people's taste in decor that's up for discussion. However, when it comes to innovation projects or strategy programmes, we don't need to be subjective as there is always the original brief to refer to. Having scoped that brief thoroughly at the start of a project, we're certain that our output from those scoping sessions stipulates the types of output our problem owners were looking for. And because you've run brilliant scoping, you'll be all the clearer on the specification of ideas that will answer the brief. Therefore, you and your team are constantly looking to save and bolster ideas that best fit the brief. To help, you must first navigate the output and whittle it down into manageable chunks.

It's time to sort through the ideas that were produced from your ideas session. Ideas of value will be rescued, as will sickly ideas needing a new lease of life – and ideas that don't satisfy the original project brief will be quickly weeded out. There is no need to overthink the decision per idea, as each pile will be revisited in turn and each idea will be examined multiple times as it journeys through the assessment process.

Audit Tool 001
Piles of purpose

Let's start by grading your ideas and sorting them into categories to make the selection process easier to navigate.

The first stage is for you and your buddy facilitator to sort through the output of all of your brainstorming idea sessions and put each idea into one of four categories (see right). There may have been a few days – hopefully not weeks! – since your last ideas session. And whilst you will have good memories of the session, the finer details of all the ideas will have been lost in time. Reconnecting to the ideas reminds you and your co-facilitator of the output you've got; and grouping that output into four 'piles of purpose' will help reconnect you to the project. You'll also get a sense of the scale of auditing and scoring work that lies ahead. For the purpose of explaining our auditing tools, I've assumed that you've garnered the nice round number of 100 ideas from your brainstorming sessions. Well done!

WHAT TO DO/HOW IT WORKS
The team will sort the output ideas into four piles. Over time we've worked out the rough percentage of ideas per pile as follows:

- Good quality, good clarity ideas – approximately 40% of your output
- Good quality, poor clarity ideas – approximately 30% of your output
- Good clarity, poor quality ideas – approximately 10% of your output
- Poor quality, poor clarity ideas – approximately 20% of your output

Use this as a guide, but there are always exceptions. A big brainstorm with sixty people over two days will yield very different output than a focused afternoon with eight people who are deeply embedded on a project.

Give the team a clear instruction on each of the piles and which idea outputs should go into which pile. (We colour-code our piles, too, as the descriptions become a bit of a tongue-twister!) 👉

The pile categories are:

✓ Good quality
✓ Good clarity

✓ Good quality
✗ Poor clarity

✓ Good clarity
✗ Poor quality

✗ Poor quality
✗ Poor clarity

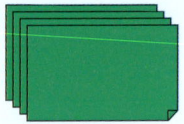
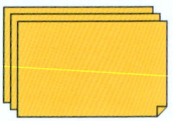
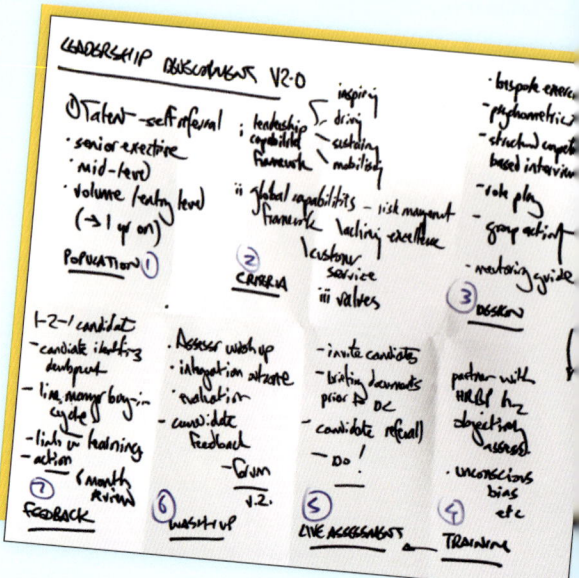

Good quality : Good clarity
Green pile – about 40% of your ideas output

This is an idea that could be done and is well captured. People understand this idea when they read it. It needs little or no further explanation than what's captured on the page. The idea description could be popped in a brown envelope, posted to someone, and the receiver upon opening would 'get it' and understand what to do. This is the gold standard. This is what you want to head into the implementation stage with. When shared across three people, everyone understands the idea consistently.

Good quality : Poor clarity
Yellow pile – about 30% of your ideas output

This is the family of output that requires a bit of attention. The DNA of the idea is relatively easy to spot. There is a consensus, when passing the idea around, on what the idea is and how it works. However, the quality of the capture is letting it down. If not addressed, this type of output could have easily been dismissed, and some potentially brilliant ideas for your project might have gotten lost in the recycling. These ideas need a tiny bit of creative effort and a further round of brainstorming and creative attention. A sign that you've got this type of idea is that when shared with three different people, all three 'sort of get it' but have three different explanations of what the idea is and how it actually works.

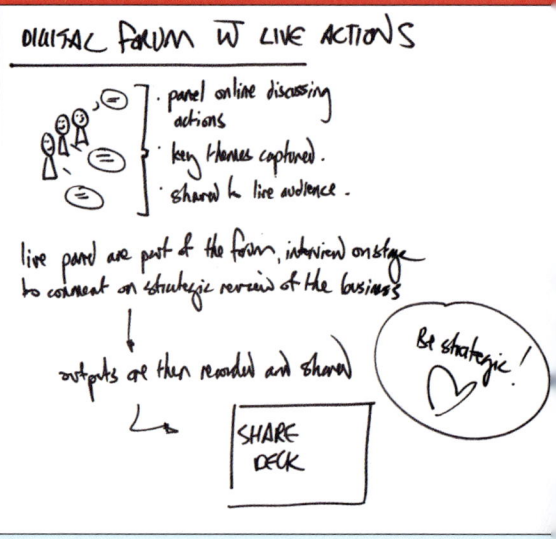

Good clarity : Poor quality
Red pile – about 10% of your ideas output

At first glance the idea ticks all the boxes. There is a clear description that makes sense to you and the project team. There are accompanying images and diagrams that bring the idea to life. It is well-annotated and has a title. This type of idea may be easy to remember amongst the huge volume of output because of key features or even the colour of paper it's on. But on closer inspection, there isn't much of an idea there at all. You could argue that you've got 'well-captured nonsense'. It doesn't feel quite right, and the group largely agrees it won't cut it as an idea to answer the brief. These ideas need a solid revisit if they are to be understood and then succeed in the selection stage. A sign you've got this type of idea is that people just repeat what's written on the page when asked to describe it, or they start to make something up on the spot and not refer to the idea at all.

Poor quality : poor clarity
Black pile – about 20% of your output

Despite all your coaching, advice and repeated instruction on capturing ideas and not thoughts, there will always remain a percentage of ideas that are poorly captured, totally illegible and make no sense to anyone. This amount goes up when you have big groups. Hackathon-style events that are great for engagement and 'team bonding' (shudder) are notorious for producing poor quality, poor clarity output*.

Even after another discussion on these kinds of ideas, where you've had someone redescribe it, you and your project team will know intuitively that it's a dud. It's for this reason alone that people may have lost the energy to feed it the creative attention it deserved at the idea generation stage. Proof indeed that there are such things as bad ideas. A sign you've got this type of idea is that when you show it to people they just look at it and pull faces!

* My experience of hackathons: great for energy and engagement, but outcome is a secondary consideration. Any good ideas that came from a big event were likely nurtured by a small team after the event, who took the hackathon output and scoped the brief further and built the idea(s) up over time.

In summary, this initial round of sorting and auditing your bundle of ideas will start to shift the narrative of the project away from idea generation and into idea selection, and feels like you're really starting to get somewhere. But there is plenty more to do! 👉

Audit Tool 002
Kill your darlings

The American author Mark Twain was famous for saying that killing off a key character in a story is crucial if you're to build tension and drama. You can't have all the characters living happily ever after with no loss or grief. We need tragedy to create space for the good stuff in stories to happen.

The same sentiment is true for ideas – we can't do them all. Only the ideas that best fit the brief ought to be chosen. To start slowly filtering out the better-fitting ideas, we first need to kill off the weakest links.

WHAT TO DO/HOW IT WORKS
Start with your black pile: the **poor quality: poor clarity** ideas. Ask your team to adopt the most positive of mindsets (for the project) and the most objective of mindsets (for the ideas). Then taking each idea in turn, ask, 'do we save or let this one go?' We've had some hilarious drama at this stage by treating ideas as puppies and dressing up as vets in white lab coats, deciding which idea needs to be 'put down' in order to do 'what's best for the project' so that there isn't anymore 'suffering'. Granted this is a potentially upsetting role play.

We choose to do the role play from time to time with the right client, who enjoys our kind of humour, but a bit of theatre does help. A dustbin with a sign on it, a 'room 101' box, a Viking funeral pyre… all these scenarios help maintain the conversation's pace and remind people that this stage of the process can be enjoyable. The ring of a bell or a honk of a horn when an idea is 'saved' are also nice touches. The project brief may also provide a metaphor to experiment with, too. In the past we've also appointed a decision maker (Dr Zero, the Grim Reaper, Madam Happy, etc.) who can have final say if we're stuck on what to do.

If there is anything worth saving from the black pile it may be an aspect of an idea that could be added to an idea in another pile. If this is the case, simply staple those ideas together with an accompanying note and move on. Also, by looking at these ideas one by one, you may come across one or two that people do not want to kill – in getting a bit of proper attention at this stage, they might get fleshed out and resurrected and therefore miraculously become good quality/good clarity and qualify for the green pile. You never know. It's only going to be one or two of the ideas, I promise, but this is why it's worth working through this stage systematically.

Exhausting the black pile ('killing your darlings') will enable you to get rid of up to 20% of your output.

Audit Tool 003

Grey's Anatomy

Next, it's time to look at the yellow pile, **good quality : poor clarity**. We call this 'Grey's Anatomy' as the ER is not a relaxed, knockabout environment for growing ideas or playfully experimenting with creative thinking. Emergency rooms in hospitals are fast-paced. Smart, qualified and experienced surgeons, doctors and nurses work with each other at speed, sharing their knowledge to work out what is best for a patient. It's the same energy needed here. Focused, precise, cut-to-the-chase energy. The ideas, and how they might be saved, need to be discussed quickly – they might only need a few tweaks to make them fit and healthy.

WHAT TO DO/HOW IT WORKS

Split your team into pairs. Issue each pair with a different idea from the yellow pile. Each pair has just four minutes to read the idea, discuss what they think the idea is and does, and make notes about this on a 'lifeline slip'. You can tell the group that four minutes is the amount of time the brain can live without oxygen before cells start to die, and it's the same with the idea they're discussing.

A lifeline slip is a slip of paper where the pairs summarise in bullet points any missing information they believe will help other people understand this idea. Sometimes all that's needed is a short (but clear) description of additional detail to breathe life into an idea that wasn't 'quite there'. Pairs can either add to the idea to bring up its quality or ask a question they believe needs answering if the idea is to survive to the next stage.

Once all your pairs have worked through their small selection of ideas you'll have two piles – a set of ideas that were once yellow, now lifelined, and as a result, now have good clarity as well as quality. Those ideas can now join the green pile. Your second pile will likely be smaller, but is still a set of ideas that raise questions in the team – even after having some lifeline attention. That means these ideas are actually captured 'thoughts'. My advice is to bin them. Be brave and decisive. There is little value finding yourself in an impromptu brainstorm at this stage. It's far better you move on to the next pile and then the SMILE tool, which will tidy up any remaining confusion.

ABOVE:
Lifeline slips. Capture here the missing details still needed for people to understand what an idea is and how it works.

Audit Tool 004
Jazz session

Now look at the red pile. This is the **good clarity : poor quality** pile. If you're a jazz musician, you'll know that a jazz session has some rules and it's not all 'just made up'. You start with the main melody (the head), which establishes the basic structure of the piece, and then all the players have their go at improvising on that theme. Then everything and everyone comes together as a final full stop to the piece. It's the same for this crucial audit session for this pile of potentially useful ideas.

WHAT TO DO/HOW IT WORKS
As the project facilitator, read out a red idea – so you've provided 'the head' to the team. Ask each member of the group to then add their immediate (improvised) input to that starter idea. They can either 'build' the idea themselves, by sharing something they've been inspired by, or can ask a question about the idea to the rest of the group so someone else uses that as a stimulus to build on the idea. Those are the rules. A build can follow a build and thus the idea will get stronger. And a question must be answered by a build before another question is asked. Make notes of these builds and attach them to the idea (literally).

And be aware that too many questions will simply (and quickly) kill the idea. If the idea is tough for the group to improve and build upon, and they are instead asking lots of questions, then you're dealing with 'neat nonsense'. See that as a sign the idea is a dud and bin it, you no longer need it.

At the end of your jazz session, your red ideas will be in either the bin or the green pile as you've made note of the builds that have improved them and made them worthy of saving. Again, as a rule of thumb, expect most of your 'neat nonsense' to go in the bin with a small percentage going into the green pile.

Let's take a moment to summarise where we are at the end of this fourth activity. Using our example of your ideas session having generated 100 ideas, once you've worked through the audit tools so far you will have whittled this down to, say, between 60 and 70 ideas. We now have one final auditing tool before we move on to scoring, assessing and selecting the ideas that you'll choose to take forward.

THE STORY SO FAR...

		Keep	🗑
✓ Good quality ✓ Good clarity	40 →	40	0
✓ Good quality ✗ Poor clarity	30 →	20	10
✓ Good clarity ✗ Poor quality	20 →	5	15
✗ Poor quality ✗ Poor clarity	10 →	2	8
100 ideas		67	33

Audit Tool 005
Smile

I have to thank a brilliant client on my first ever project for sharing this tool with me. The tool and its accompanying claim has stuck with me ever since:

"A good idea should make you smile."

When explaining this idea, I have a large A2 version of the SMILE chart that forms the basis of this tool (see over page) and then complete each section on a live project idea with the group. Everyone then knows how it works and can be set off in pairs or small groups to take turns in running a SMILE coaching session.

WHAT TO DO/HOW IT WORKS
Using our example numbers (left), we now have 67 ideas that everyone agrees are good quality (they make sense to everyone in the room and are captured well enough for those outside the room to understand too). Mix these ideas up and issue small groups (of no more than four people) with 7–10 ideas. The groups will then discuss and SMILE each idea. One person in each group needs to read out the unfinished statements on the SMILE sheet to the other participants, and after a quick chat should write the agreed endings to the 'SMILE aspects' in the six boxes. There is no quick way to do this. Be disciplined, methodical but relaxed and working at pace. The six boxes are:

S = Simple
A good idea is simple, elegant and clear. It can be described in a series of connected sentences that help build up a consistent picture of what it is and how it works. It is clear and easy to explain. By completing this box, the idea commands a common narrative that the whole group knows and understands. If what you have is more of a thought than an idea, filling in this box will be a challenge.

M = Memorable
A good idea is memorable. It sticks in your mind. You think about it after the ideas session. You tell your friends and family about it. And when asked about the ideas you created, good ideas are the ones you share first with colleagues. Memorable ideas evoke emotions. They may make you laugh, roll your eyes, shake your head or point and call it out. They have a memorable quality that encourages you to share them with others.

I = Interesting
Good ideas are interesting. They literally make you think, 'oh, that's interesting!' and command your attention. Interesting ideas are often linked to an insight. This idea is an answer that will satisfy the insights you've uncovered during your project journey. An example of an interesting idea is Fever Tree tonic water. It's interesting because it commands a premium price based on the insight that if 'two-thirds of your drink is mixer, then why wash down your nice gin with low grade tonic?'

L = Linked to brand
A good idea also has a strong link to the project on which you're working. Importantly, a good idea will be something that only *your* business can do as this idea is 'on brand'. Other businesses *could* do this idea, but if your business made this idea happen, people would remember you for it. Sponsorship activations are an obvious example of where linked ideas exist, especially for beverages. Pimms for tennis, Guinness for rugby and (I still remember) Carling for football and Bailey's at Christmas!

IDEA NAME:

SIMPLE
Sum up in a couple of sentences for someone I don't know:

MEMORABLE
This is the only one in the world because…

INTERESTING
'Hey! Look what the guys at [insert company name] have done.'

LINKED TO BRAND
It's [insert company name here] because…

EMOTIONALLY POSITIVE
We feel better about [insert company name] with this idea because…

CHERRY
It's already a great idea, we could make it better if we did this too:

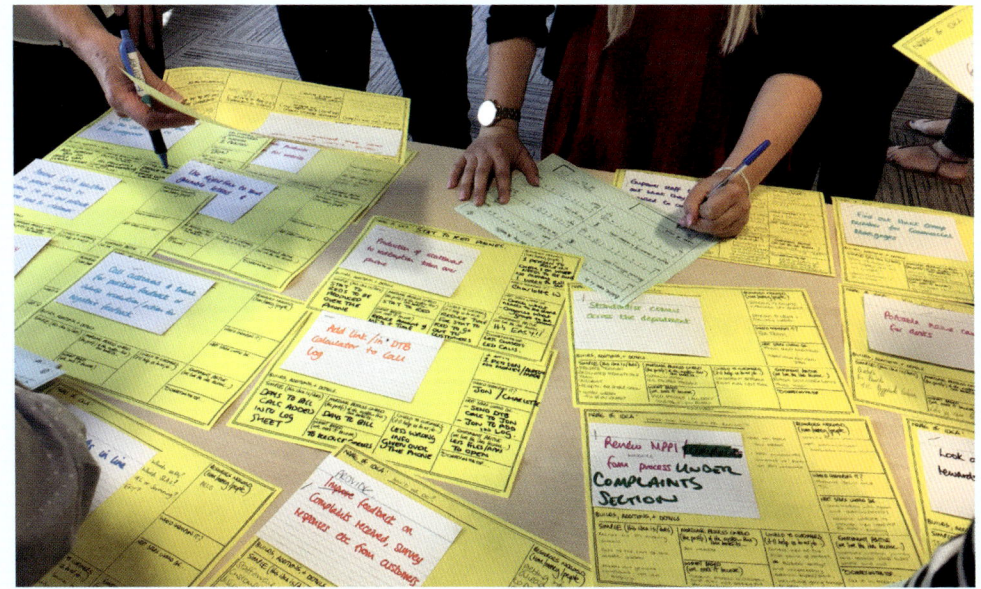

project team with a strong story of ideas. To use a metaphor, the problem becomes wrapped in an ideas blanket. A bit like the way that many neurons firing makes a neural cloud (a thought within the brain), many ideas all joined up make a compelling project output. And, as a result, a handful of ideas are more likely to get sign-off into the business as they combine and create a compelling case.

During this SMILE process, some ideas, no matter how easy they are to describe, will stand out as weaker than others. Project participants will agree that whilst the SMILE 'boxes are ticked' there may be some particular ideas that are intuitively felt to be duds. You can expect to lose up to 10 or 12 ideas here. The rest will now have been brought up to the same standard in clarity – and will all be at home in the green pile*. You can now take these ideas forward to start scoring their quality.

E = Emotionally positive

A good idea makes us feel good that it's in the world. We'd be delighted to know that this idea is out there enriching people's lives. Conversely, watch out for the opposite! Remember I mentioned an idea for an energy drink in a syringe? That's simple, interesting, definitely memorable, linked to the brand – but no one should feel good about anyone injecting anything through a needle into their bodies! Ideas that have a strong emotionally positive vibe can last longer in the assessment process even if they score lower in other areas. If people love the idea and feel good about it, it's more likely to get done than something that scores highly in other aspects, but is overall frankly bland.

You'll notice a sixth box in the tool. This was the happenstance of photocopying, as five boxes didn't look good on a page. Box six is called 'Cherry' – the idea is already good, but completing a 'what would put the cherry on the top' box invites one further build to the idea. Having options in box six also provides a stimulus for other ideas and possible links from this idea to the next.

As we know, rarely is a project ever answered by just one hero idea. Ideas (like the neurons in Part One of this book) link to each other and form networks. Linking one idea to another can provide a

> As you work through the auditing and scoring tools, your physical output will be growing too. One idea (originally captured on a sheet of A4) may now have a 'lifeline', a SMILE sheet and other sticky notes of comments and amends. Take care to look after your output, keep your stapler to hand and don't work outside on a windy day!

Interview

Joeri Schilders

CREATIVE YOUTUBE CONTENT CREATOR & ONLINE FACILITATOR

Joeri Schilders is based in the Netherlands, but has lived and worked in Beijing, Shanghai and Singapore for the last 20+ years. He can facilitate in a number of languages and enjoys facilitating groups 'in the room' as much as he does digitally. You can find him championing better ideas at the YouTube channel 'The Magic Sauce'.

You took the move a long time ago to switch to online facilitation – as a facilitator, what changes took you the longest to get used to?
There were many, but the big one that comes to mind is not having people in the same space. There's an energy missing. Heat, the sounds, the aura, the vibe, the impact of having someone lean over a table and get closer to you – all those senses we talk about and take for granted. I missed those at first. But in new groups that I now meet online only, of course I don't miss that energy, instead I've spotted we create a different energy.

The other change that took me a while was living in what I thought was a 2D world. How could digital really replace what happens in a room – but actually you can do all of that and, I believe, so much more using technology wisely.

Compared to facilitating a group of people in a room, what do you think are the most important factors affecting someone participating in a project online?
In a room, you as the facilitator are driving the engagement. Online I think you need to facilitate the content so it's engaging. You have to use photos, different types of text pop-ups; you need to switch between shots of you and shots of something else. I think people need to use their emails, and WhatsApp, and text and calls during the sessions. When

we plan our sessions we'll send gifts to people's houses, too, to open up on our cue. I've got assistants moving stuff on Miro boards and someone handling all the dial-in connections when we run the workshops – you can't do it all. Working hard on this makes what could be a sterile experience so much more.

Can I run 'as good a session' with just my webcam or do I need decent kit?
I think it's less about the kit – all the gear and no idea – but your bandwidth needs to be good. People will forgive a glitchy picture from time to time if they can hear great quality sound. That's why radio and podcasts still work but watching TV with the sound down is a struggle. I think it's also important people step away from the screen. I'll instruct people and then say go away for 20 minutes, leave the room where the camera is and work elsewhere, then let's all come back and discuss our work.

What's something that online facilitation has over face-to-face facilitation? What does online do better?
It's funny you've asked this question. We had a low bar to start with. I watched for months in 2020 as LinkedIn filled up with really bad or obvious advice about how to work online. It took a while but eventually some really ingenious tech emerged, with people using it in creative ways. There are software platforms where I can hover my mouse over participants having conversations and listen in to what they're saying, and ask questions and drop hints. I couldn't do that as easily if I sent project people to different rooms in a hotel. If people are stuck, I can instantly find an image from the web and send it to them – I can't do that as quickly face-to-face. I can mix music and videos and drop that to teams – again, something really hard to do in the moment in traditional ways of working.

Digital allows 24/7 working, too. We've had teams send output from one session over to another team as we sleep, and then we wake up and my co-facilitator can brief me in on what's happened and we pick it up again. Like a baton. That's infectious. And something I've noticed is that group work is much better. Before, one or two people would do the work and other people might just watch it all happen – when everyone is watching everyone else's effort online, I think the output is better; no one can hide.

Let's get your advice: give me some classic online facilitation traps to avoid.
Oh, so many to choose from. But seriously, get your camera at the right angle. I don't want to look up your nose all the time. And, importantly, don't just sit there. Be animated. Show me movement. Zoom in on stuff. Have your props and visuals at the ready. If you're going to mention something, make sure that you have it to hand.

> *"I think a lot about how we'll need to change the way we facilitate as more and more Gen Z enter the workplace."*
> – JOERI SCHILDERS

What is a final nugget of genius you'd like to share?
Not so much an insight but a thought really. I think a lot about how we'll need to change the way we facilitate as more and more of Gen Z enter the workplace. They're always, and I mean always, using two or three screens to absorb or work on content. Their attention span is short. If you're not engaging in a few seconds – boom you're gone. What does that mean for complex content? What does that mean for details? And at the same time these people are creating so much material and sharing it, building upon it, mixing up ideas in a way we can't keep up with. There's no way we can see and know everything out there that's being shared. So how do we keep attention? It's just something I think on.

Scoring

Taking the ideas through a rigorous scoring process is the next stage in making a final selection.

It's great to have many heads in a room for creating the ideas, but as you move through the selection phase, it's important to minimize numbers. This avoids lots of 'group think', or as one client said, 'we talk so much about finding the consensus, we end up with a camel and not a horse'. Nicely put.

Idea selection is more about decisions than options. You want to be creative about how you make decisions. And the tools we use for 'scoring' the ideas that have made it to this stage of the process are all designed to engineer positive experiences around decision making.

Up to this point, you've used ALL members of your project team. They who contributed to the generation of the ideas, and they all understood the context behind the ideas so were able to make them better and ask each other to help fill in any missing details or correct poorly captured output. But now it's time to say goodbye to around two-thirds of your project team, leaving a core group of 'you and decision makers'. During the project's journey, the people best placed to be part of decision-making will have been decided. The question of who this might be should have been asked in the scoping phase. Perhaps part of your weekly project-management discussions with the sponsor will also have decided this. Those project participants who remain can also be joined by one or two newcomers. Fresh, objective eyes are useful at this stage. Scoring can be a troublesome topic.

IT'S RESULTS DAY!

Every year in the UK, around the last week in August, thousands of students find out how well they did in their end of year exams. And by the time the evening news is broadcast, the headline story is usually about how standards are falling and how easy it is to pass exams. Predictably, reporters will find an old schoolmaster who's found a GCSE question in an A-level paper and run a piece about whether trigonometry or Latin has its place in the modern curriculum. It's a regular and predictable cycle of media reporting each summer.

LEFT:
For the final stages of scoring and selection work with a smaller team. Less is more!

Getting back to the point – grades are set *after* all the exam papers are in, as no one knows how hard people will find that exam when it's written earlier in the spring. If students find that the paper is hard, then low scores would be expected; setting pass marks for A, B and C at 85%, 75% and 65% won't work if everyone is getting less than 50% of the paper right. Similarly, a project team setting hard boundaries for which side of 'good' and 'bad' (chosen and not chosen) ideas should sit – before the ideas are scored – is a flawed approach.

The other issue with scoring is that humans are notoriously poor raters of other people's performance. We feel we can rate someone's abilities using a set of criteria, and that using the criteria as if it were a lens or filter enables us to attribute a score to a particular disembodied quality – such as 'creative thinking'. And we act as though applying the same criteria to someone else will give an accurate score of them, and so on.

However, we all have our own idiosyncratic behaviours. Some of us are naturally more generous and find the good in people and their efforts, others are more critical. And, importantly, some of us would embrace all the numbers on an assessment scale, whilst others would score people using only 5, 6 and 7. The 'idiosyncratic rater effect' means that we each have a unique pattern to the way we rate other people's performance, and it follows us wherever we go. But the lens we carry around with us to rate other people (and score their ideas) is, in fact, more of a mirror that reflects back at us our own patterns of thinking.

Many people believe that combining and somehow averaging 'my rating of you' with many 'other people's ratings of you' will somehow reveal the 'real score' of you – but that is just wrong. The output will be more bad information. The same is all true for when people score ideas. We each carry an idiosyncratic pattern of leaning towards generosity or slavish attention to detail. And whilst we may be issued with criteria to score ideas against, we're still not mitigating against the idiosyncratic rater effect. The point is that asking people to score ideas out of 20 and then choosing the top 10 per cent is not the way!

At GENIUS BOX we use the following scoring tools and 'tools for getting unstuck' to further whittle down our bundle of ideas and help us decide which ones to take through to the 'grand final'. 👉

Scoring Tool 001
Save in a fire

During the ideas sessions, people will fall in love with a handful of ideas. These are the ones they would save in a fire. The first scoring tool selects these ideas so you can put them to one side. Until we do this people will be totally distracted with worry about whether their favourite idea is safe. This tool enables you to dissipate that energy by allowing your team to 'save from the fire' the ideas for which they have most passion.

WHAT TO DO/HOW IT WORKS
Lay out all the ideas on the wall (or floor). It's important people can SEE the ideas clearly. Explain that everyone can take this moment to save their favourite ideas based on nothing more than emotion and energy – how people feel about the ideas guides whether they can select them. Give each person a set number of stickers (*see right*) and ask them to wander around the ideas (we play relaxing music, obviously) and soak up the output.

Ask them to make a mental note of where they're going to place their sticker and then step back to the far end of the room (or for a bit of fun, walk around with their finger on their nose) so you know they're ready. Then 'all as one' ask them to go and stick their stickers on the ideas they would save in a fire.

Some fun suggestions for types of stickers you could use might include:

- Fake money (we issue $1-million notes!)
- Heart-shaped sticky notes (we love a cliché, too)
- Green dot stickers
- Or some other project-themed sticker

The volume of ideas and number of people in your 'choosing group' will help you decide which of the next two methods to use. Either ask your team to:

- Choose their top three ideas (three ideas per person) and place a sticker on each

or

- Have six stickers and place them anywhere across a maximum of six ideas for wherever their energy goes. For example, that could be one sticky dot on each of the six ideas, or maybe two stickers on one idea and four stickers on another – to show the comparative 'strength of love' they have for them.

Make a note – it's probably easiest to snap some pictures – of the stickered ideas as you might need to refer to the number of stickers on an idea to help 'trump' a decision later. Then collect up all of the ideas in preparation for the next scoring tool and thank the group.

It *might* be that the idea(s) to take forward as the solution to the project are now staring you in the face and there's no need to use additional scoring tools or have further discussions. For example, if everyone puts all their stickers across **only five ideas** (it can happen) I recommend that you, your buddy facilitator, your sponsor and a few other project stakeholders have that conversation now; it might be all you need.

Scoring Tool 002
Comparative assessment

As described earlier, we're not very good at rating other people's performance, as our pattern of scoring – which reflects our personal approach to assessment – will follow us around. It's the same when it comes to marking an idea against a set of criteria. What I may believe is a 'creative 10 out of 10' could be someone else's lowly 4. Assigning an exacting metric to something is hard for us to do. Consider how we're unlikely to know the *exact* weight of the car below:

Even if I help and give you some options, we're still unlikely to be 100% accurate. Although, giving a range of options at least increases the chances of people being roughly right.

I could present you with three options, one of which is exactly the right weight of the car, but then I've essentially made a multiple-choice activity and you could easily work out the weight by looking at the answers and establishing which two options are clearly incorrect.

☐ 50kg   ☐ 800kg   ☐ 4,500kg

This is really interesting, isn't it? Without having *any* knowledge about the weight of the car, you've arrived at your answer by making comparisons. And humans are *really good* at making comparisons.

I'm confident that 100% of people would be able to answer this question. Which of these two cars is heavier?

Whilst we don't know the exact weight, we can assume with a high level of confidence that we can comparatively assess which cars are heavier than others and place them in order. This is the theory

A

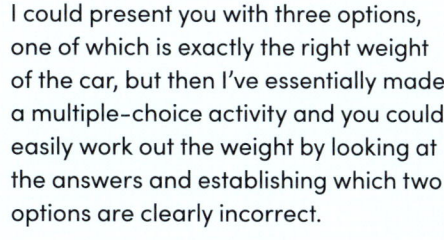

B

of comparative assessment, which was first mooted back in the 1920s. It's been used in risk management and project planning for decades, and I believe we can use it to help assess ideas. 👉

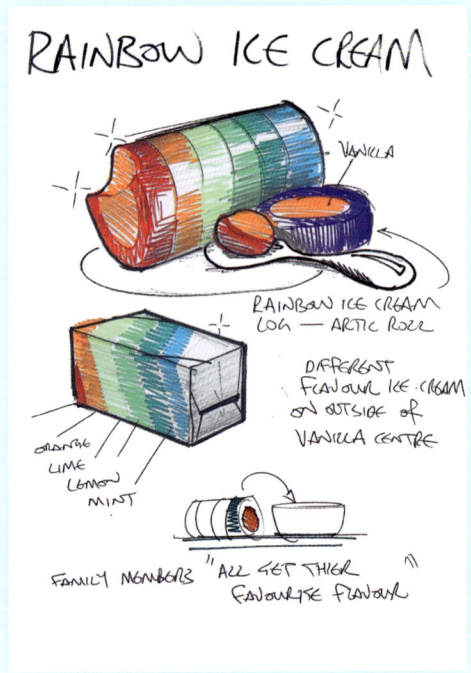 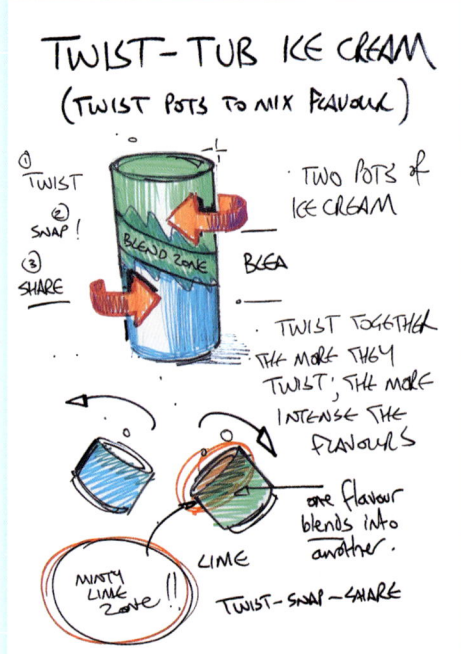 

Look at the rainbow ice cream idea above and give it a score out of 50. You can't, right? And if I gave you some criteria to follow, your idiosyncratic pattern would apply – and your scores would be no better or worse than anyone else's.

However, if I gave you three ice cream ideas (*above*) and asked you simply to choose which is the better idea, then your decision would be easier (and quicker). Remember that our System 1 thinking is a near-instantaneous process, happening automatically, intuitively and with little effort. System 1 thinking is driven by instinct and experiences. So, at times in the past when you've needed to make choices about one thing over another, you've built unconscious heuristics that help you answer questions such as 'which is better'. This ability may have been honed whilst choosing ice creams or sweets as a child. In these instances, your data points aren't singular (like when I was asking you to assess only the weight of the car) but multiple. The 'best' ice cream is going to be a choice your System 1 brain makes by assessing the imagined benefits of taste, texture, longevity in the mouth and a host of 'flavour' attributes you weren't consciously aware of as a child – but could just 'know'. Even complex factors of friend-envy and look-at-me-walking-out-the-shop-with-the-coolest-looking-ice-cream-ever would have been part of your unconscious, super-fast, System 1 decision making. Therefore, we *do* have the power to make choices when presented with complex and multifaceted options – such as people's unique ideas.

If you, your co-facilitator and your project sponsor haven't arrived at any winning ideas after the 'save in a fire' activity, then it's time to run this comparative assessment activity.

WHAT TO DO/HOW IT WORKS

Prior to the session, you, your co-facilitator, your project sponsor and one or two project team participants, if appropriate, agree approximately five 'criteria' against which you'll judge ideas*. These will be heavily informed by the scoping session tools (WHYHAUS and TISSUE SESSION, for example). Resist having more than five or six criteria as too much time thinking about the ideas will make people tired. You're there for a good time and not a long time! Let's assume our sample size remains around 70 ideas. First, prep the tool as follows:

- Remove the stickers from the ideas identified in 'save in a fire' (as obviously that might influence people).

- Randomly mix up the ideas from 'saved in a fire' with the other ideas.

- Then sort that big group of ideas into seven random groups of 10 ideas.

- Name each pile after a famous duo, such as Fred & Ginger, Bill & Ben, Hall & Oates, etc. Name them anything but Pile 1 & 2, or A & B, because being in team '2' or 'B' sends subconscious signals to our brains; team 1 is always going to be better than team 2 – right?

- Split up your now smaller project team into pairs and issue each pair a group of 10 ideas. (It's likely that a couple of pairs will need to repeat with a second round of ideas.)

For example, if the ideas were for 'Ready-to-drink gin-based cocktails', project specific criteria could be:

✓ Interesting flavour combination
✓ Alcoholic content
✓ Sense of premium
✓ Celebrating our brand of gin
✓ Seasonal or long term

Next, ask each pair to follow these instructions:

- Take two ideas at random from the 'Fred' pile and decide which is the better idea based on your criteria.

- This 'better' idea becomes the 'best' idea – place it on the floor next to a large sticky note called 'best'.

- Place the other idea to the side next to a sticky note that says '3'.

- Take a third idea from the 'Fred' pile and ask: is this idea better than the 'best' idea? If it is, swap that idea out and push the original 'best' idea next to a sticky note that says '2'.

- Take a third idea from the 'Fred' pile and ask: is this idea better than the 'best' idea? If it is, swap that idea out and push the original 'best' idea next to a sticky note that says '2'.

- Repeat this process for ideas four and five in the 'Fred' pile and you will have ranked the ideas from 1–5 comparatively against each other.

- Now do the same for the 'Ginger pile', in a relaxed fashion allowing for a bit of discussion within the pairs.

This game will give you 14 'best' ideas out of the 70, and 56 ideas that are 'good quality : good clarity'.

Now place the stickers from the 'save in a fire' round back on the ideas, and see if that furthers debate on which ones get taken forward. Revealing these stickers will show everyone where the passion is, in comparison to the sorting of 'good' and 'not so good' ideas. Move a few ideas around if necessary, and move on. It might be that everyone is now aligned behind a clear five or six ideas. If that is the case, again have the discussion with the project sponsor about whether or not to end the selection stage there. If you decide to carry on, move on to Scoring Tool 003.

Scoring Tool 003
Sheriff badge

This is a dead simple tool. We use (and trust) the wisdom of our project team to assess the chosen ideas. We need a set of figures that helps *quantify* the elements of the chosen 'best' ideas, so we can make further informed comparative assessments.

I've seen primary school teachers ask children to mark their own work in this way. I believe in putting decision-making in the hands of the people who are closest to the information. Doing so provides your team with far more agency and the belief that ideas will get done. Additionally, this activity imbues the team with the culture of 'we're innovating around here'. It is they, after all, who will shepherd these chosen ideas into the business and could well be part of the initial project management of them.

As a facilitator, remind your team that they are the genius. It is they who came up with the ideas and it is they who are best placed to work out how they all score. Your activities and exercises are simply helping them navigate those mighty decisions with ease.

WHAT TO DO/HOW IT WORKS
Create a 5-point star (or at most a 6-point star*) like a sheriff's badge. Each point of the star represents a criterion from the scoping sessions where project output and success were discussed. Each of these is to be scored out of a set number.

However, if all the star points are scored out of 10, people can easily give each one a '7' if they get lazy or remain undecided on a score. So, mix up the maxi values – have some scored out of 5, some out of 12, for example – as it forces people to make more conscious decisions about how well an idea scores. Alternatively, you can use horizontal bars. Your team can shade up to a score value, or circle a number. What matters is committing the scores to paper.

- Split up your now intimate project team into pairs or threes.

- Distribute the ideas equally across your groups. In our example, 14 ideas are taken forward initially, but it's likely there will be as many as 20–25 once you embrace the ideas 'saved in a fire'.

 Scoring needs to be an accessible task, and something people enjoy. If there are lots of ideas and a scoring 'cloud' of 19 criteria per idea, that's hundreds and hundreds of discussions that need to be had and people will become tired. Remember, System 1 thinking conflicts with System 2 thinking. We want people to make deliberate and conscious decisions and not just whittle through the scoring by 'thin slicing' available information and scoring in a hurry.

- First, ask each participant to score ideas in their allocated pile individually. Then get the pair/group to discuss each idea in turn and calibrate the average for the ideas they've been issued.

At this stage, as facilitator, it's time for you to build a master chart to plot the scores. Then, at the end of the scoring, pause. This is another opportunity to step back and see if there are any contender ideas that are clearly popping up time and again as strong options.

Assuming your group scored around 25 ideas, your output at the end of this stage comprises this bundle of scored ideas, some also displaying special love from the team as they have 'saved in a fire' stickers on them too.

Scoring Tool 004
Grade boundaries

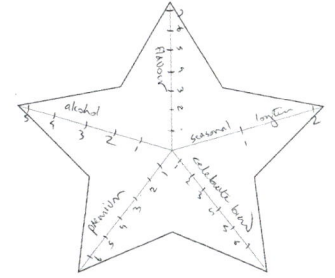

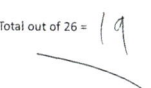

RIGHT:
Scoring ideas using the sheriff badge in readiness for final selection.

It's now time to decide how many ideas are recommended as lead 'solution' ideas for the business. It might be the project only ever needed one idea (unlikely). More common is that the project needed 6–8 final concepts to be presented to senior sponsors who decide which to pilot, launch or further invest in.

Often, ideas are grouped into families of 6–8 ideas and then given an internal wrap, and listed on an innovation pipeline or backlog of system launches for the business. Your project may have been asking for a shortlist of 12 (to be launched one a month). Perhaps your project sponsor may have needed one idea be launched in the USA and one in Europe, and they've requested a final list of four from which to choose the final two. You will know what's needed from having completed the scoping stage. Ultimately, you'll need some form of 'red line' across which ideas are either chosen to go forward or not. We need, then, the grade boundaries.

WHAT TO DO/HOW IT WORKS
Lay out all the scored ideas on the ground so you can see them in context and in relation to each other. You might

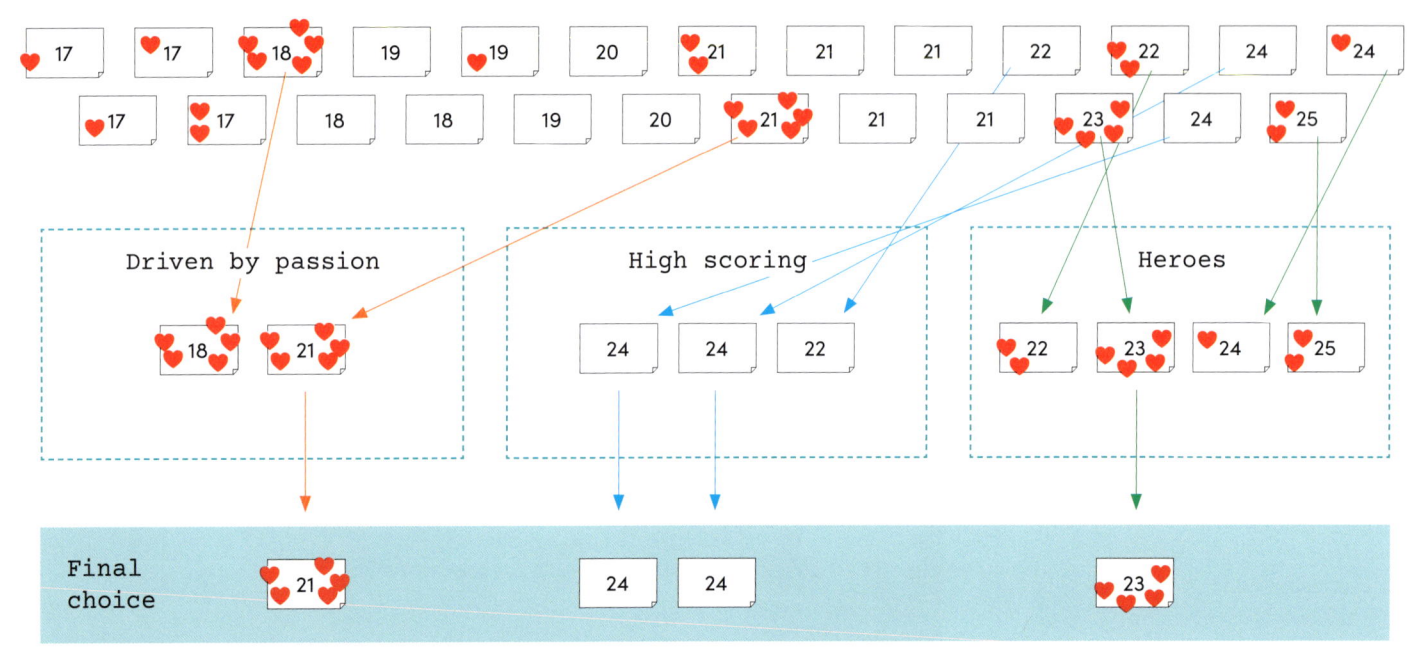

need to double up the rows if space is tight. This is where a lot of space helps. Arrange in score order (I have lowest on the left to highest on right). As you'll see in the illustration above, the spread of those scores won't be much. The highest and lowest score will differ by only a few points.

Create three 'zones' that you'll drag the ideas into:

- The first zone is for your 'hero' ideas. These ideas score the highest ('technically' good ideas) and show they've ignited passion within the project teams (indicated by 'save in a fire' stickers).

- The second zone is for your 'high scoring' ideas. Those ideas that emerged as 'bests' (or close!) in your comparative rounds and when assessed against criteria, score highly.

- The third zone is 'driven by passion'. These ideas might not score highly, but they have attracted love and attention from the team as indicated by the 'save in fire' stickers.

And it really is as simple as dragging down the 2–4 ideas that meet the criteria in each of those three zones.

As the facilitator, explain the three zones, pull down ONE idea into each (to help you explain the difference between the three zones). Remember to then return those examples back into the main sample!

For this final decision, the size of your project team will now be even less. It's likely to be you, your co-facilitator, a couple of members of the project team and the sponsor – less is more.

Tools for getting unstuck

Occasionally, you'll get stuck on an idea. The team won't know whether to keep it or bin it and move on. You'll need some tricks to get things moving.

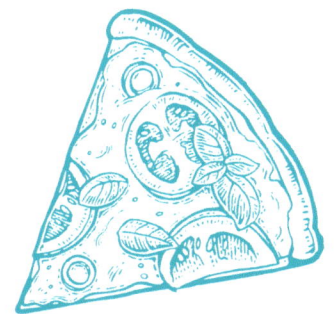

Being utterly fixed to a 'process' approach when the choosing ideas to implement is not the way. For example, deciding which features live on a banking app is a very different project to creating a new brand story for a gin-based cocktail. Understanding what's technically feasible will influence decision-making for the app, while considering marketing executions will influence the cocktail project. Therefore, as a facilitator, the activities you design and deliver for auditing, scoring and ultimately selecting the ideas to recommend to the business will need to be flexible.

Ultimately, decision-making is a mixture of head and heart. If you get stuck at any time during the selection process, we suggest you try some of the approaches on the following pages to get going again.

Pizza toppings

Ask your project team if there are any surprises in the ideas currently in play. It might be that you've got one or two ideas that scored well despite not being loved in the 'save in the fire' activity. Similarly, there may be an idea that had love from the team in 'save from a fire' but aren't present in this shortlist of 'best ideas'.

To help answer this question, look at the interesting and memorable aspects of the ideas and, if needed, you can:

- Score them again (to fudge an idea into selection). This is a quick cheat, and might be all that's needed. If all the team agrees – then that's fine.

- Alternatively, you can build up a particular element of the idea so it scores higher.

To build up the idea, you can try taking elements of other ideas that haven't been selected, or combining them with aspects of ideas that have been selected.

As this conversation has now evolved from an assessment chat to a creative conversation – take a moment to recalibrate the behaviours and the agreements in your session.

Imagine the ideas you're currently 'stuck on' as pizzas. Now imagine all of the other ideas as pizza topping ingredients from which you can pick and choose elements to make your current idea more 'spicy'. You could:

- Swap out an element of an idea and replace it with another.

- 'Halve' your idea and shore up the low scoring elements with higher scoring elements from other ideas. 👉

There may also be a way of taking each attribute of your current high scoring idea and making those attributes even stronger by adding attributes from other ideas. The context of the project and why you're stuck will help you decide what to do. For this creative activity to work, it is essential you see all the ideas. You'll need space to pin up, review, observe and handle them in order for team members to discuss and refine the attributes of the ideas they want to polish up.

Facilitating the pizza-topping session will require you to tailor your instruction and put people in pairs, groups or to work individually. You can't 'broadcast' the same instruction to everyone each time you get stuck. Instead, work with your co-facilitator and between the two of you, one can 'map progress' of ideas as they get 'bettered' against a project criterion whilst the other manages the energy of the participants and what they do.

BELOW:
It's worth adding bits of one idea to strengthen another if people intuitively feel an idea is worth saving.

Plussing

While working on your pizza toppings or looking critically at your best ideas to address any remaining weak spots, always encourage your participants to use the behaviour of plussing.

Plussing refers to the general rule that you may only criticise an idea, or any aspect of an idea, if you add a constructive suggestion at the same time. It's a behavioural term first coined by Disney Pixar and is a useful standard to set for your remaining project participants as you fine-tune your offerings.

During idea selection, you and your project team participants will switch mindsets between 'assessing' an idea and then responding to an invite to 'make the idea better'. Navigating the two mindsets is key. You cannot criticise and grow at the same time. Plussing is an instruction to the group and a signal you can use to remind people about how to behave when discussing aspects of an idea.

WHAT TO DO/HOW IT WORKS

Give the group time to wander around re-reading the selected ideas and letting them soak in. The ideal time to do this is first thing in the morning, over a coffee, after a night of having 'slept on' the topped-up ideas. Or at least, your team should return to these ideas after a break. Remember how our minds make better connections when rested and in alpha state! Each idea will likely be taking the form of multiple pieces of paper stapled together and annotated with new comments. Your role as facilitator is to make it easy for people to reconnect to these ideas so you may need to give everything a good tidy. Rewriting a few headlines on coloured paper, for example, helps you signpost what people need to look at.

Next, guide the conversation by taking a look at each idea in turn and inviting discussion from the group. It's a small group now, so you ought to be able to build off each other, remembering to:

1 Accept all offers (accept the idea, don't reject it)

2 Use 'yes, and… ' instead of 'yes, but… '

3 And make your partner look good.

You'll remember that the Simon's Picnic game from the Ideas chapter also follows the same principles.

By adding constructive suggestions to an aspect of an idea, you'll build up that idea's strength in small increments. It's easier to add builds to a part of an idea than rebuild a new idea from scratch.

Of all the three principles in plussing, 'accepting all offers' can be the hardest to stick to as it's fairly counter-intuitive. People try to defend their own ideas and reject other people's new idea builds and suggestions; they personalise feedback they perceive as negative more intensely than feedback they perceive as positive. Remember how our brains are hardwired to be efficient to protect our own interests. We have deeply embedded codes of self-preservation. Comments that don't 'fit our story' are dismissed and ignored. Having worked hard on an idea, we see parts of ourselves in it. When that idea scores a 6 out of 10 we naturally feel bad, and will be all the more sensitive when we find that aspect of our idea being critiqued in a team discussion.

In the end, the group might not accept all the builds and suggestions during the plussing conversations, and I think that's okay. There's the moment people in your team receive the feedback, and the moment the team (or individual) acts on it. These are two different moments. It is likely that two different mindsets will be present. Our minds make their best creative connections when in alpha state and not beta state. This conversation around spotting 'fault' with an idea can easily get 'busy' and people will resort to beta thinking. Suggesting an element from another idea to embed in another will also create reactions ('that's no longer an idea I recognise or love!'). Remind people to smile, listen to each other and keep relaxed. If everyone agrees, plussing will help unlock a few people and ideas from being stuck.

How to get things moving

I'm also an advocate of stepping away from the assessment stage if the conversations remain hard or heavy. If you're still undecided on what ideas to take forward, here are some final solutions to help things along. All of these work:

1. Stop!
Come back in the morning. Allow overnight unconscious processing to work its magic in your sleep.

2. Change the team
Bring two people in, bring them up to speed; ask them to join in the conversations. A different point of view (even only a couple of voices) will change the dynamic. Think about the impact of a little cordial in a glass of water.

3. Run a silent/anonymous 'general election'
Ask the team to take photos/notes of all the ideas in the discussion and make a 'choice' each. You can have a ballot box, voting slips and add a bit of theatre to this. Use the output as the final decision or a stimulus for a round of discussion.

4. Take turns at 'just a minute'
People have to talk passionately about the value of an idea. If they can't talk for a minute then is the idea any good?

5. Build a deck of 'Top Trumps'
For the final selection of ideas, write a new set of overall project criteria (a mixture of criteria from the scoping output and team love criteria) to build a new attribute list. In a smaller team of participants, ask team members to apply a fixed set of points across the Top Trump ideas and see if the same 'strong ideas' emerge as in previous sessions.

6. Take the leap
Go with your gut. Issue a final round of big sticky notes printed with 'FINAL CHOICE' and run 'save in a fire' one more time.

7. Bring in the project sponsor
Explain you're at an impasse with so many great ideas and ask if there is a hierarchy to the criteria they gleaned from the scoping. Rating the criteria might just tip a decision to choose one idea over another.

8. Question the problem owner
Ask them for specific information about time, budget and implementation factors from the business. One or more of these aspects might quickly cross off a potential idea choice, for example, *'We love the JELLY JANE idea, as it scores highly in all aspects of the brief, but it'll cost twice as much as the budget allows, and we feel it would take twice as long to implement as the time we have readily available.'*

"Never underestimate the power of a small group of committed people to change the world. In fact, it is the only thing that ever has."

– MARGARET MEAD

Embedding

Your role as a facilitator (on this project) is nearly at an end. But there are a few more activities the business needs of you and your team before they can embed the chosen ideas.

Embedding is about fixing the ideas selected firmly into the company that needs them. The way to do this is to present the best ideas to the business with all the detail needed for them to be adopted into established ways of working and ongoing project management systems. This might mean completing templates and software portals; you can expect a bit of 'admin', too. In the context of our GENIUS BOX process, the role of you being the creative facilitator is almost at an end. But there are two more tools to help signpost the exact route of ideas as they face into the business. These are our Transformation Maps and 'C-suites' (see pp292–297). But first, let's recap how we got to this point.

1. Out of our notional sample size of 100 ideas, you filtered out 40 ideas immediately that fell into the category of good quality : good clarity, and put them to one side. Where needed, idea lifelines were used to flesh out missing detail in the remaining ideas, resulting in another 30 being saved, and you dismissed the remainder.

2. This left around 70 ideas in total. You and your project team participants completed a SMILE tool for each idea, securing consistency in clarity and quality across all the ideas. This made it far easier for everyone to understand how each idea worked.

3. You then ran the 'save in a fire' activity to identify the ideas people in your project team had passion for. It's this passion for an idea that will help see it through any internal quality gates and sign-off stages present.

4. The team then ranked all of the ideas using comparative assessment tools. This identified the top 'best' 14 ideas. You then brought back the 'save in a fire' stickers to enable you to take forward a final 25 or so ideas.

5. This was followed by a quantitative scoring tool using the 'sheriff star' to attribute a measure of how well ideas ranked against project criteria from the scoping stage. A further round of 'pizza topping' (process) and 'plussing' (behaviour) would have strengthened up a handful of ideas.

6. From this spread of 25 ideas, you selected the hero ideas (high score, lots of passion), the technically sound ideas (high scores alone) and those ideas that people just loved regardless of their low score. The final, let's say, nine ideas were a mixture of these categories. And from this shortlist, the project sponsor and problem owner can select what will be embedded into the business.

It's now time to give the project sponsor and project managers all they need to help embed these ideas into ongoing, monitored programmes of project activity. And to do that we'll start by using some Transformation Maps. 👉

LEFT:
A pre-session tidy of the ideas before the final selection.

Transformation maps (T-maps)

Transformation maps (T-maps) enable you to gather all of the relevant elements of the chosen ideas into a consistent format; to identify the tactical aspects to make those ideas a reality, and finally to plot those tactical 'make happen' aspects into a timeline. T-maps are used to brief in and 'hand over' output from your facilitated innovation project to the business who commissioned the brief. Essentially, they are a visual implementation plan.

Creating T-maps is a two-part process. Firstly, each idea is discussed in detail and the major elements of how it works and what are needed to make it happen are identified and logged on a MAKE IT HAPPEN sheet. Second, those sheets are then placed on a large T-Map canvass (see p294) and the tactical aspects of how to make that idea a reality are plotted

**MAKE IT HAPPEN
IDEA NAME:**

What is this idea?

What does it do/how does it work? (Describe for people who are going to experience it)

How do we communicate to people who will experience this idea that it's happening?

What are the perceived commercial benefits for this idea?

If we started this idea tomorrow, what's the first thing we'd do?

What resources do we need to make this happen?

People

Time

Process

Budget

What's this idea called? (For business planning purposes)

on the timeline. This set of activities is facilitated by you and you're assisted by a small number of project team participants who are familiar with the ideas and the wider operations of the business to which these ideas are now being offered.

PART 1: MAKE IT HAPPEN
For each idea complete a make-it-happen form, like the one opposite.

However, the form you complete may look different as different projects obviously create different ideas at the end. To make a 'hotel booking app' idea happen will require different information than is needed to launch a range of breakfast cereals. Additionally, your business may provide its own version of this form as part of its project embedding process.

It is worth noting that although completing these forms and plotting ideas on a T-map may be the last activity you as a facilitator do in your project journey, for your project sponsor and business, they signal the kick-off (and scoping!) of a project management journey. One where the idea changes from a 2D concept on sheets of paper,

to realised, living outcomes. Whilst filling forms about ideas isn't as exciting as having ideas, they are essential if the ideas are to be understood by other staff, project managers and external agencies. Make-it-happen forms ask questions about the idea that focus on time, people, resources and other structures needed to make that idea happen.

I spoke earlier in the book about ideas being a bit like coasters in a bar – we see only the top side and not the underside. It's the same principle. The ideas being discussed and evaluated so far have been through the lens of those people 'seeing' or 'benefitting' from the idea.

From now on, we're no longer discussing what the ideas *is*, but instead what is *needed to make the idea happen.*

Adapt the boxes on our suggested make-it-happen from as needed. Not all the information will be known – the exact product pricing, or the actual size of packaging, for example. Brainstorms don't really elicit that type of detail. But at this stage, there is enough of the idea captured across sheets of A4 and A3 from your project sessions for people to align behind a common understanding of what the idea is and how it works. Remember that the purpose of the make-it-happen form is to identify the elements needed to

RIGHT:
A project team building a T-map. All actions are colour-coded for extra clarity.

change an idea captured on paper into something that could actually exist.

PART 2: PLOTTING THE MAP

Next, on the floor or wall find a large space, and a large piece or roll of paper, and draw the following:

This is your T-map canvas. In the top-right is where your organisation wants to be, or where the department needs to be, or what the team wants to achieve in a defined timescale. Explain to the group that the ideas, when implemented into the business, will act as the stepping stones that create the envisaged end state for the organisation, department or team. In order to *do* the ideas, they need to be embedded in a plan with a sequence of events and support structures. And if the T-map is used to monitor progress, then the ideas will inevitably get done.

Around the border, stick the make-it-happen form of each idea and a visual of the idea from the brainstorm sessions. In the example below, the T-map has space for five ideas.

Completing the T-map requires you to identify the resources, and actions needed to secure those resources, in order for those ideas to happen. It is that sequence of events that are plotted on the T-map. Completing the map forms part of the 'hand over' to the business, so your project team participants will now be a small group of knowledgeable people who between them know the ideas *and* the workings the organisation.

You can facilitate a whole group and take each idea in turn, or split your group into pairs to take an idea each – at this stage, you'll know what makes sense. For each idea identify where in the future the resources to make it happen will be managed. As an instruction for the project team, ask these questions:

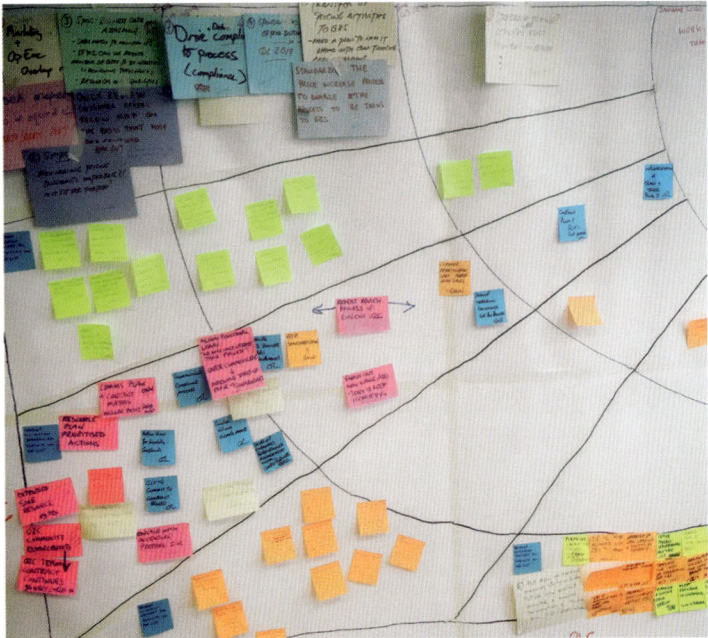
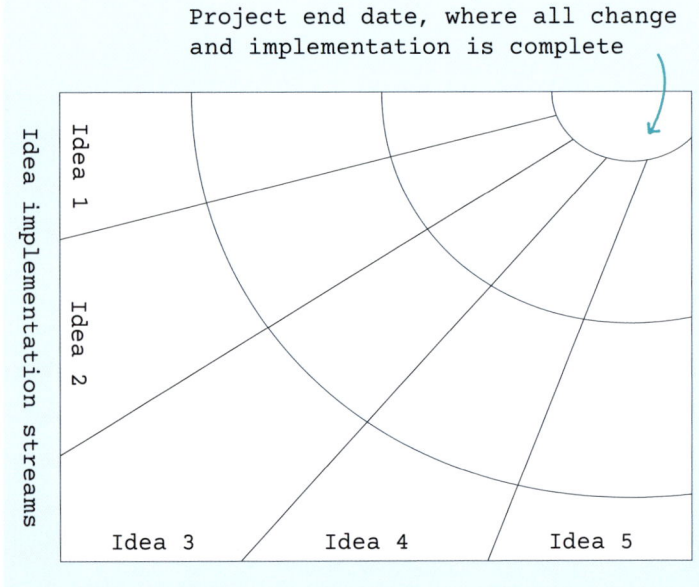

1. **What** are the resources needed for this idea?
2. **Who** has access to these resources and **who** must be approached first?
3. **Where** in the business will those resources come from?
4. **Why** are these resources needed for this idea over others?
5. **How** will we secure those resources?

The answers to these questions (and others you and your co-facilitator discuss in advance) are written on sticky notes by the team. They are then plotted on the T-map in each idea's 'swim lane'. Effectively, you've mapped out a project plan as a series of activities 'to do' within the business.

When a T-map is completed the idea moves away from a concept everyone has agreed to support to something that is live, present and real. As an output to a creative session, a T-map 'secures' ideas in a story of the future. There's a palpable sense of 'these will happen' when ideas and their implementation plans are mapped in this very physical and illustrative way.

Completing a T-map and then having it on display for a day or two allows you to brief in project managers, idea 'owners' and other people in the business who'll take charge of the ideas from now on. It's both a tactical tool for idea implementation and a prop for you to share project output as part of your project story.

A PICTURE PAINTS A THOUSAND WORDS

We also believe it stimulates a thousand thoughts. The nature of creative sessions means that the language used is rich in insight and metaphor. Visualising this language by having illustrators 'live scribe' these conversations is a fantastic method of capturing the re-expressions falling in the room during our work.

Having a team of illustrators in our network is a strength. GENIUS BOX has been partnering with a freelance network of illustrators since our very first project. Everywhere we go, they go. And, obviously, asking illustrators to draw up the ideas 'properly' will help other people in the business who weren't part of the ideas sessions connect to the ideas generated.

If you don't have internal capability to draw up ideas then seek out freelancers. There is no shortage of talent out there, just a few clicks away on a web search. It's an immediate way of raising energy and interest around project output.

Build a C-suite

You've now facilitated people through a creative process. Well done. The business has ideas. And what's needed to make those ideas happen is now plotted on a T-map. Project managers and junior account executives are dividing up the work into neat to-do lists. We now need one final creative people push to get ideas truly embedded into the business. It's time to build an ideas C-suite.

There is a saying (there is always a saying!) that 'what gets measured gets done'. For project implementation it is hard to 'get done' an idea. But it is easier to measure whether a small action that contributes to an idea's implementation 'is done' or not within a fixed time.

At the project end, there's a sense that project implementation becomes a huge enormity for the team to overcome.

Well, now is the time to build and facilitate a new team!

In the past, GENIUS BOX has worked with a different team to embed the idea than the team who had the idea. The embedding team translates your project output into content that people working in the wider business will recognise in their ordinary work flow.

As part of the handover, we've encouraged a team – made up of original project members and also those of newly appointed idea embedding – to choose three important characters for embedding the idea. The embedding team might only exist for a few weeks until ideas are in 'workflow' and have become part of ongoing business as usual. To spearhead that embedding team, identify three important characters who'll look after the ideas and their progress over the first few critical weeks:

CEO, Chief Enthusiasm Officer
This person is the champion of the idea. It is their role to talk positively about the idea in 'town hall' meetings, internal presentations and, when asked by other departments, to go visit and explain what the idea is and how it works. The CEO will gather feedback and reactions from the business and feed that back to the embedding team. The CEO will also help build the internal narrative for everyone in the business to use. It is the CEO who works with the sponsor when it comes to generating the public story about the idea and the story of what your business tells the world. When people talk about the idea, they need a story. The CEO is responsible for that story.

CTO, Chief Technical Officer
This person is responsible for securing the resources needed to make the idea happen and reporting back to the CEO and CCO on all matters associated with how the idea is developing from page to production. The CTO will work with a number of stakeholders in securing people, time and budget to solve aspects of implementation and realising the idea.

If the CEO is holding a box of Lego and describing the picture on the front, then it is the job of the CTO to build the instructions for the idea to happen (and help people follow them). Lego works when the parts come together with the plan – that is the job of the CTO and their team.

CCO, Chief Commercial Officer
This person is 'the numbers'; they look after the flow of budget and manage the costs needed to make the idea come true within the business, and achieve the projected return on that investment for the business. To build an idea takes time. Time costs money. Building an idea will need experimentation with prototypes, piloting the idea with focus groups, or running test-and-learn sprints with agencies, creative partners, consultants and other specialists.

The CCO needs to work with the sponsor, as they both secure the finances to fund the idea. The CTO informs the CEO that the idea is making progress against the project ambition. The CCO works with the CTO on when to release further batches of resource. Together, this C-suite becomes a powerful internal team that know, understand and 'can do' what's needed to make the idea happen within the business. When partnering with our clients to help embed ideas, we build these C-suite teams and align their objectives to those of the project sponsor and the business strategy. In doing so we create a network of responsibilities that creates the necessary support for ideas to happen. And, as a facilitator, when you are at this stage of the project you can be satisfied that the journey of the idea is at an end and can decide, if appropriate, to accept a new commission or carry on facilitating the project management meetings and help watch those ideas become reality.

SUMMARY

In this final stage of the process, I've shared the techniques we use to select a small number of premium ideas from a large pool. I suggest you mix up your approach so you're inviting project team participants to use both their head and their heart when making decisions.

At all times, use plenty of space to lay out the ideas; people need to see what's going on. When we see decision-making happening, it drives progress and creates value.

Remember to praise people every time ideas are killed or selected. Brave decision-making adds value to the business. Remind everyone that the project is near its end because of their hard work.

Now that we've worked through the four stages of our process, let's take a look at the other factors in our GENIUS BOX model that will impact the success of your creative projects.

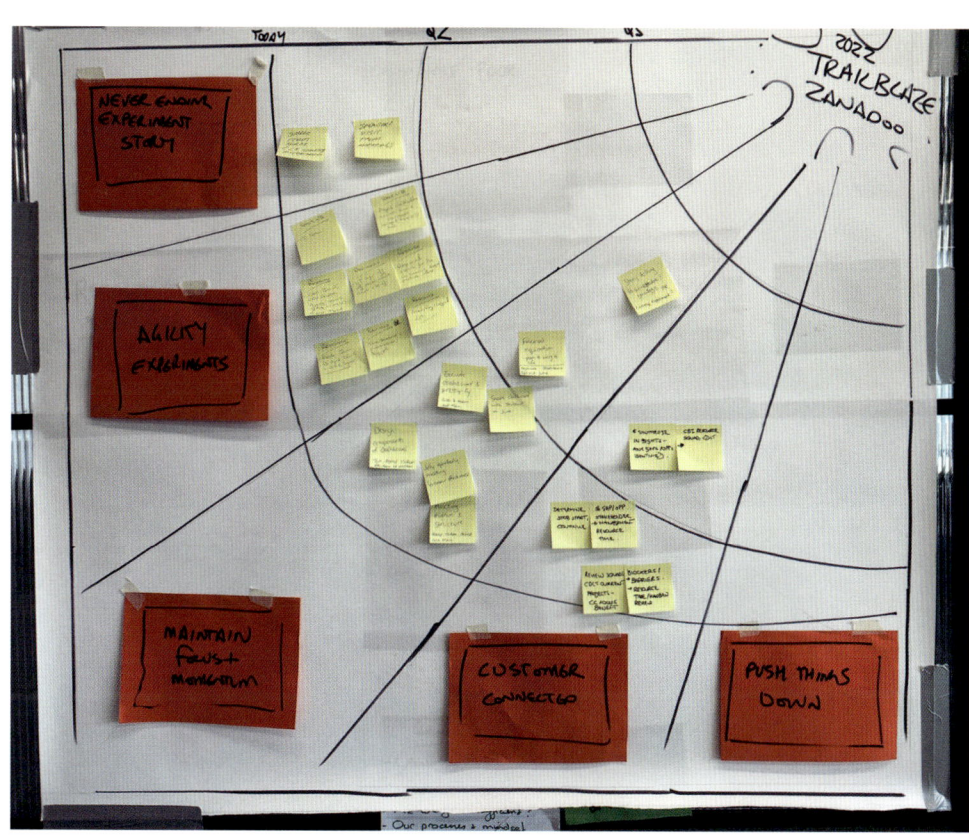

LEFT:
A T-map plotting five different projects; an at-a-glance resource for the ideas C-suite.

Part 4

FINDING THE WAY

Now you've got the tools to use alongside the GENIUS BOX model, you're nearly ready to get out there. In this final part of the book, we'll revisit some of the key aspects of the model you need to remember as you prepare for, and work through, your facilitation journey and get started!

Developing your way

Business isn't deliberately designed for conflict, but most people are fighting over limited resources, restricted budgets and tight timelines. Project delivery, for many, is hard. So, having confidence in a project facilitator who can creatively and confidentially hold a room, brief in instruction, surprise and delight project participants and, importantly, secure useful output is incredibly valuable. Being able to do all of this in a way that energises you raises the brand of facilitation and ought to be a rewarding and authentic operating space for you to shine and grow.

Our time exploring tools and skills is at an end (for this book at least) and in our final chapter we are switching your attention away from what to do, to how to do it. Remember, the quality of your behaviour is what creates impact. Repeating instructions using the same language and relying on the same examples over and over is not the way. It's dull for you and boring for others. It's essential you experiment briefing in the tools and using the skills in different ways each time you're faced with new challenges. This will keep you fresh and bright each time you're facilitating a group of people. And as a result, your energy will be all the more vibrant and engaging; exactly what the business world needs.

Let go of the concepts of 'right' and 'wrong' and instead embrace every session you facilitate as a new opportunity to try things out.

If things don't turn out in the way you had imagined, move on and give something else a go with the same hope and ambition. If you run a session and it goes 'just fabulously', ask your co-facilitator precisely what they saw you do – grab all the detail you can paying particular attention to how you behaved more than what you said.

There will always be a series of inter-related factors that impact you, your project participant team and, of course, the project output. Let's take a deeper look at those factors once more to help inspire you to consider your design and delivery in new times, time and again. For that we need to revisit our GENIUS BOX model from earlier in the book. Using the model keeps you creatively sharp so you can deliver on what matters for the project for it to be a success. Don't see the model as something designed to trap you and restrict your thinking. It's not a box you put creativity 'in', but instead a powerful way to set your particular style of delivery free.

The cube revisited

Here, again, is our GENIUS BOX 'cube'. We use this model before, during and after the design and delivery of a creative project. It keeps our facilitators mindful of how all six elements of the cube influence each other and therefore keeps us conscious of our project team participants' needs during sessions. I invite you to use this model (until you develop your own) as it will help you to land learnings, reflections and ways to improve quality in your further sessions and subsequent project commissions.

In Part 2, I introduced the cube by describing its six sides in two groups of three: the 'individual inputs' of process, behaviour and competency, and the 'aspects impacted by your inputs' – strategy, environment and culture. In this part of the book, we look at its six aspects in three groups of two opposing pairs, to highlight the subtle inter-relationships between all six factors. The key message here is that nothing you do when you facilitate sits in isolation; you're constantly impacting the other five elements. Great facilitation is being mindful of all these moving parts so you can take decisions confidently in the moment when things change – which is inevitable if you're truly leading a creative journey.

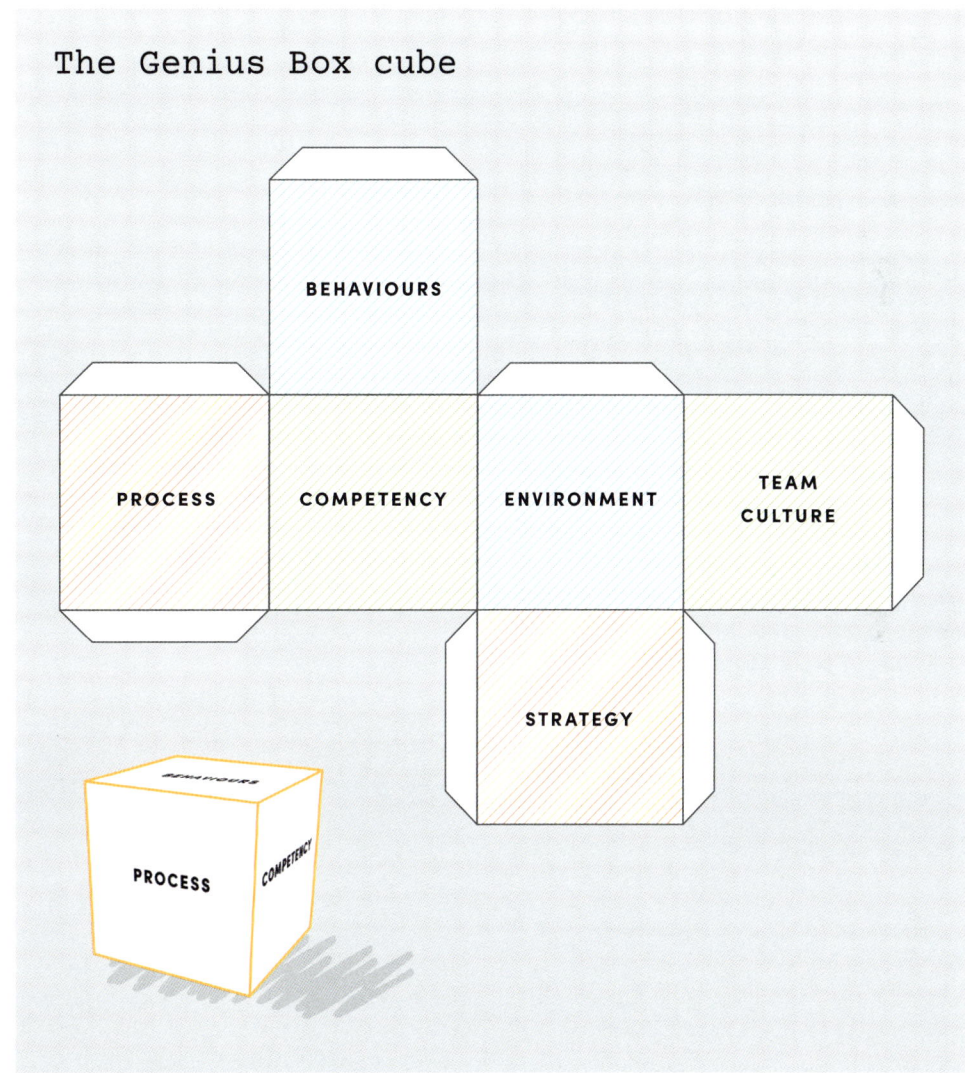

The Genius Box cube

Process and Strategy

These terms mean different things depending on the type of business in which you're working.

In the context of facilitation, strategy is about your high-level design and delivery of the creative process to answer a specific business brief. Ultimately, process and strategy are about being crystal clear on what you're doing and why you're doing it in a certain way. To help secure the best strategy for your project, let's revisit each step of the GENIUS BOX process through the lens of two concepts mentioned earlier, the 'radar' and the 'monorail' (see pp104–105).

When planning your projects, you can use the monorail and radar to build a picture of how your creative journey will unfold and to see what areas may need further attention. This will give you a greater sense of preparedness and excitement; after all, it's important to build positive energy and confidence about facilitating a project.

You – radar: You are at the centre of the process. You see all the stages and what's coming next. You're aware of what you are thinking. Use that personal awareness to think 'what next' for the project and the project participants.

The team – monorail: The project and the project team are on a track. Each stage of the process (scoping, insight, ideas and implementation) is to be visited in turn. You're at the helm of the monorail – looking ahead, seeing what's next.

ABOVE:
Keep listening out for the signals that let you know which part of the process people are thinking about.

LEFT:
This monorail image was used in a project that had a slightly different process. But the principle is the same; always signpost to the team where you are and where you're heading in the process.

The team – monorail: In planning the scoping sessions for a project, consider where that first conversation will happen. Is there space to have material up on the walls to be seen and referenced? Can the 'starter brief' be summarised in a one-pager and be sent to your team in advance? Is there enough 'theatre' to distinguish one tool and stage from the next? Have you and your co-facilitator (if you have one) agreed what scoping tools make sense for the project kick-off and who is briefing in each one and for how long? And remember that every participant in your project team also has a series of reactions to the brief on first exposure. Unlike you, they won't know how to map their thinking. So, use tools and activities such as the 'WHYHAUS' (see p120) and the 'CAR WASH' (see p122) as opportunities to land all the topics and questions your project team participants mention and ask. These tools allow you to 'coach' your project team on improving their creative thinking as well as land content that will help everyone arrive at answers – nicely does it.

SCOPING PHASE

Let's start exploring your immediate responses on being handed a business challenge.

You – radar: On being given the brief, you will have a number of reactions. Being mindful of the radar concept, you'll likely be able to spot and discretely list several areas for your immediate thinking. You'll have questions you feel need to be asked and answered during the scoping phase. These questions will be asked by you or you'll want your team to ask them. You'll have a couple of hypotheses that could be tested during the insight phase. You may have immediate ideas – it's only human nature to do so, remember your System 1 brain (Yoda) will have already made speedy and intuitive connections. Have those ideas ready to use in the scoping phase with the TISSUE SESSION tool (see p124), and/or draw them up in a little more detail and see if they are still valid come the ideas phase.

INSIGHT PHASE

Insight is all about inspiration. We want to find out what matters to our 'consumer tribe' and why. To facilitate insight, you need to behave insightfully, always keeping your personal radar attuned to be curious and playful. Above all, tell stories about consumer tribes, all the time.

You – radar: I think it's important that you plan your own insight journey and carry it out in parallel with the activities you help design and deliver with your project team. You need to make observations of your consumer target in the environment that best allows you to understand their behaviour in the context of the project. This helps you tell stories to the group, and becomes stimuli and inspiration for them. Additionally, your clue-gathering from observations and interviews provides you with a greater sense of empathy for the tasks you're asking of your team. Furthermore, your insight development contributes more content to the project, and from this further insights will emerge. Remember to constantly be asking 'what's going on for this consumer and why does it matter?'

The team – monorail: Think about the number of insight assignments you'll send your team on. Using the fruit machine tool (see p200), for example, will help assign challenges to different participants. Remind them that gathering information is not the same as arriving at 'the insight'. Take care that your instructions don't use language such as 'go out in teams to discover the insights'. It's easy at this stage of the process for participants to believe they will uncover 'an insight' neatly packaged along with the answer all ready to go. But this is not the case. Remind your team that the focus is to listen to your consumers without judgement, and to listen out for their tensions, pains, issues and problems.*

The insight stage is about wonder and possibility, not searching for 'the right' answer – it's unlikely that anyone will tell you precisely what idea they want. To be successful here, keep your team curious, playful and relaxed.

IDEAS PHASE

Ideas don't pop up, fully formed, ready to go. Ideas begin in the realms of the subconscious as feelings or fleeting images. We describe ideas with words, but what we actually communicate to other people, are usually thoughts.

You – radar: As I've mentioned multiple times, when you're facilitating a project you will have your own ideas. The process is *designed* to help generate ideas. And the scoping and insight phases will inspire you to think up ideas – so, don't try to ignore them, capture them. Use your co-facilitator to help land your thinking so your ideas are of the highest quality

> 'No one knew they wanted a DVR, a microwave oven or a minivan, but what they could tell you was their pain: they weren't getting home in time to watch their favourite show; they didn't have time to cook a healthy meal; and they were having to cart an ever-increasing number of kids, dogs and sporting equipment to a myriad of places. In other words, customers can tell you their pain, they just can't tell you the solution. That is your job.'
>
> —LINDA YATES, CEO OF MACH49

and clarity. Co-creating, communicating and capturing ideas will keep your idea generation abilities high. You'll be better at coaching others in your project team as a result. Keep in mind that your project team participants will also be thinking up ideas, too. I think it's good to have an 'ideas I've been thinking of' conversation from time to time during the project. For example, you can leap back and forth across the process and validate an idea as part of the insight phase.

Additionally, if project participants are struggling to form starter ideas, then your own starting ideas may be just the stimulus they need. Your ideas can be framed as starter suggestions on which they are free to build. I've found that ideas shared this way are often made better by project team members. You can then concentrate on facilitating the group in the knowledge that your creative input to the project is being nurtured.

The team – monorail: Critically, the ideas phase will only work when you set the standards and shared language to define what is a thought and what is an idea. Most ideas sessions fail because it is still only thoughts that are being captured*.

Always agree the standards as a team for what an idea needs to be. And to do that, always play the Thoughts vs Ideas games (see pp224–227). It's also worth having on the project room wall somewhere an example of an idea's

growth from thought to sketch to rough mock-up and then as it journeys through the implementation tools before final adoption into the business. And even better, a version of the idea drawn out by an illustrator as a final worked up concept. Preparing all this, allows you to signal progress during the ideas stage. Idea generation is very much a visual activity, so this storyboard on your wall becomes a great teaching aid to your facilitation signposting and keeps your project participant team aligned, excited and maintaining the same standards.

SELECTION PHASE
The final phase of the project process is, of course, selecting the ideas to go forward into the business. It's here your role as facilitator may be at an end as you

*Do not ever try to capture a whole idea on a sticky note – there is no room for anything but a thought to exist on that tiny space.

ABOVE:
A starter idea being worked up into a more concrete idea with plenty of details.

hand over output for others to implement in the business. But this is no reason to believe creative thinking is at an end too. In fact, your mind has already been working hard on selecting ideas whilst you've been busy focusing elsewhere.

You – radar: Remember from Part One that System 1 (Yoda) thinking is much better at determining comparisons *between* things and is very good at working out the *average* of things, not the sum of things. This means that during the project your unconscious is assessing output and arriving at points of view on the comparisons between ideas. This explains the reasons why we might favour one idea over another. So I advocate using comparative assessment (see p279) to sort ideas first and then use a score card (see p282) to gather the hard data you need for making decisions.

You can trust your personal radar in choosing the ideas you think best answer the brief. Your mind will have been constantly assessing comparisons throughout the project, and at this final stage in the process you're putting that decision-making front and centre of the conversations in the project team.

Choosing a final idea from a range of different options is much like the Best in Show decision being made at the end of the Crufts dog show. There may be a set of common criteria for all the dogs but all dogs are different. Like cannot be compared with like (ask any Dachshund standing next to a St. Bernard). An overall winner is selected even though it is nothing like any of the other finalists; each dog is judged against its own breed's standard. It's the same for ideas. If you're intuitively gravitating towards something, share with the team and use your point of view to help make decisions.

The team – monorail: This stage of the project can often be seen as an anti-climax. After many weeks of work, a handful of ideas are taken forward. The energy in conversation is less about 'building things up' and more about 'drilling things down'. It doesn't feel as exciting as an insight or ideas session. And, naturally, there is disappointment when certain ideas aren't taken forward.

When facilitating this part of the process, remind everyone that they still need to make creative connections. In fact, a 'poor idea' that is about to be culled can be saved when people take elements from rejected ideas and apply them to it. To do this you need to remind your team that the behaviours required to 'build' an idea need to switch to another set of behaviours for 'assessing' the idea. If groups are struggling to do this, you could split teams into 'growers' and 'assessors' and place them in different rooms. This reinforces the behavioural mindset in each environment. Everyone will have been working hard over the last few weeks with you. They will have easily fallen into a 'groove' and to arrive at an answer quickly and get 'an idea over the line', they may rush decisions. So, a little 'theatre' goes a long way at the idea selection phase. That's why the 'Save in a fire' activity, the idea lifelines, the SMILE sheets and all the team check-ins during the selection phase, help break up group thinking into small chunks with more energy and focus.

In summary, the monorail and radar concepts help you and your co-facilitator craft a solid process and strategy ahead of all your session delivery. As a pair, take time ahead of the project to share what's on both of your radars. Will that immediate thinking hinder the attention you give to others or inspire them to make new connections? Make a note of specific questions, ideas and concerns that you've both been thinking of and decide what could be used as stimulus for the project. Agree as a pair how you'll support each other during the facilitation of sessions, who briefs in which activity and if there are specific tools or debriefings you both want to experiment with in new ways. Importantly, agree who does the scribing, paper collection, stapling and all the administrative 'sticking up' and tidying up – don't assume this will 'just happen'; a great deal of successful creative facilitation needs order, discipline and prep behind the scenes. Work hard on this and you can enjoy your time with your project participants in the room.

Interview

Sanjay Patel

PRODUCT SPRINT FACILITATOR

Sanjay has been working within the FMCG (fast-moving consumer goods) industries for over 25 years. He's delivered award-winning innovations for packaging, proposition and prototypes for some of the biggest brands on the planet. His style mixes deep technical knowledge and insight with playful irreverence. And he's managed to deliver global Sprint experiences in a digital online format too.

You've been working within businesses creating your own unique version of a Sprint. Tell me what that offering is compared to other versions people may have heard of.

The original Sprints were pioneered in the software industry. Intense periods of time (a week or so) would be allotted to a core group of people to focus on one or two issues. That team of people would be ring-fenced to write new code or trial a new website to get feedback from customers.

Product Sprints are different, though, as we want to test a product *with* consumers, and not a hypothesis *about* consumers. Software Sprints help validate an insight about what consumers might think to help generate new ideas. Our Product Sprints translate already existing ideas into live prototypes that we can test in the market.

So, compared to a Software Sprint, what does a Product Sprint look like?

You can test software without harming people, it's completely different when you're asking people to ingest a product. For food and drink we can't just cook up something in a kitchen and give it to people in the street the next day. It's simply not like a tv show. Physical products need to be safe; we've got legal obligations to adhere to.

Our Sprints translate 2D concepts into 3D prototypes, so that's the branding, the packaging and, importantly, the actual liquid or food that people consume. Whilst we can facilitate that journey in a week, it takes a great deal of planning in advance to align all those parts of the business to work with us in an intense few days.

What are the particular conditions of a Sprint that differ to those in other types of innovation projects?
It's not about speed. A Product Sprint is about arriving at *better business decisions* sooner. We can only do that when we have a clearly defined brief as our input and agreement with a partner on what output should be. We need tangible products and use quantifiable data during the Sprint. We can't launch a new food or drink product based on the reactions of 12 people in a bar. Access to live surveys, where we can quickly gather feedback at scale, are important.

Are there any facilitation differences you've spotted in your delivery style that have changed as you've delivered more Sprints?
Oh, I've definitely become more punchy in my style. The commercial exposure is huge on a Product Sprint. You're not just suspending normal work for a handful of people to sip coffee and play with laptops. There are dozens and dozens of people behind the scenes who are all involved. We're sharp on time, and we don't wait around for people. It's soon evident to the groups that Sprinting means putting in the effort. But I'm also deliberate about the fun. We need to be able to let off steam, play with our food, and sing and laugh together.

How do participants react to a Sprint vs a series of sessions spread over time?
I remember at first how some senior people were nervous and almost negative about the Sprint approach we proposed. I guess in business we can all get comfortable with soft beds, business class flights and reliable broadband. I've been working within large corporations for years and, in truth, they move slowly not because of lack of willpower but because of the sheer volume of work to do.

For a Sprint to work, we needed to totally immerse people away from home, the office and other distractions. It's a huge risk. Our first Sprint meant sharing dormitory bedrooms with colleagues and taking it in turns to help with the catering, in addition to actually solving the business problem. That's a totally different way of working. Going on a Sprint became a badge of honour. People were fired up about it. A real career highlight. It's something we can all be proud of.

What is a final nugget of genius you'd like to share?
There's a big difference in facilitating the creative process and running a Product Sprint. To take people through a series of design stages from insight to ideas requires skill, of course, but to run a Product Sprint you do need specialised knowledge on product, packaging or manufacturing. Without that, you're ultimately creating something that isn't legally or ethically viable, and most importantly, not creating trust and credibility in the Sprint teams. The idea might look good and you might feel very pleased with your efforts, and consumers hold it in their hand and give you positive feedback – but if it's not safe or costs too much to manufacture, then it's a fail.

"We need to be able to let off steam, play with our food, and sing and laugh together."
– SANJAY PATEL

Environment and Behaviour

When you're facilitating, you'll be in a space, and will be monitoring and reacting to how that space affects everyone's behaviour.

Environment and behaviour are inextricably linked – when people are in a poor environment it'll affect creative behaviour, and behaviours affect the quality of the creative environment. Keep connected to the learnings about the brain and alpha state that are necessary for your mind and the minds of others to make connections. Let's remind ourselves what we learned from Part One.

- Your brain is like a gigantic warehouse that stores all the information about you and the world. We each create a personal story that we use to navigate life, and we also use this story to compare what's going on for us compared to what's going on for everything and everyone else.

- As a creative resource, the more 'stuff' there is in your head from experiences you've had, the better.

- Accessing all of your brain content can be tricky, as a good deal of your brain's processing works at the subconscious level – you're unaware of the thinking you're thinking when you're thinking about things!

- When you're busy at work, rushing about, focused on emails and typing up your PowerPoints, the 'door' to your brain warehouse is shut – it's rare you'll have creative ideas at these times.

- When you're occupied with something almost mindless (like washing the car), or being out in nature, or letting off steam with colleagues, the door is open. It's at these times you find you'll have ideas more easily.

- This state of mind is found when our mind is flooded with alpha waves (see p60) – and alpha waves are present when we're more relaxed.

More alpha, more ideas.

Therefore, our choice of environment needs to be deliberate as choosing a particular place in which to hold your sessions will help to keep everyone in an alpha state.

Keeping everyone in alpha

Your task as a facilitator is to generate and maintain an alpha environment during your project sessions, so your group are more likely to arrive at creative breakthroughs. However, unless you can ringfence people for a week at a time, it's best to assume that everyone arrives to your sessions straight from other meetings, frustrating commutes or other mental distractions. Don't just assume their energy and focus is immediately aligned with the work you're going to ask them to do. And certainly don't choose meeting rooms that look like the one pictured here.

It's essential to have fast, knock-about, easy, relaxed and irreverent conversations with each other if you're to solve problems. Having people arranged formally around a ghastly slab of oak laminate won't accelerate conversation, but will, instead, hinder and stifle it. And, if there's no natural light that means there are no natural environmental changes to indicate the passing of time – the room will look the same at 3:00 in the morning as it does at 3:00 in the afternoon. There is nothing in the room to help you or your fellow project participants connect to the challenge. This room is a creativity killer.

Much has been written about the best designed environments and spaces for innovation, but when you are facilitating the creative process, it's essential that you create a space that helps the mind switch into alpha state. That's why the environment is such an important part of our model. 👉

LEFT:
A dull working space with no natural light will unsurprisingly stifle creativity.

Too often, the need to create an alpha environment is misunderstood*. Instead, look no further than your own surroundings at home as inspiration for a suitable place to run a project – soft furnishings, natural light and plenty of space and stimuli. A good deal of offices and off-site meeting spaces are still locked into a formula where sleek lines, cleanliness and order influence the aesthetic. I've been trapped in innovation rooms that were the most hideous of spaces. Hot, stuffy and clinical. One even had a sign saying 'do not stick anything up on the walls'.

Creative connections need flexible spaces, so keeping things organic and simple (and where everything is easy to move) is a must for you as facilitator. The best innovation environments aren't created through the facilities team and management, but instead develop spontaneously and are often self-organised. As the facilitator of strategic sessions or innovation projects, you can accelerate the design and delivery of a physical space that creates the right 'mental space' for connections to be made if you follow a few simple rules.

DAYLIGHT

Natural light is essential. Windowless basements are only good for storing the photocopier paper; they are not appropriate for a project basecamp. However, when you're just getting

My sister-in-law still teases me that I live in a world of overstuffed beanbags and lava lamps. She works in corporate banking. And I reply that given the economy over the last few years, her environment is probably the same. Touché. Family rebuttals aside, please don't contribute to the cliché by insisting that the only way to innovate is to sit everyone on beanbags.

started on a project and scoping the brief for the first time, a quick trip to a room without natural light might be worth it to land the point about the power of the environment. And on the odd occasion when you do have to move a room without windows, remember that your personal energy and reaction can help dictate the impact the environment has on your team. Stuck in a basement once, we drew windows on the wall showing scenes we wanted to see...

DRAW

Whenever possible, literally *build* the topic of conversation and make it as big as you can. Large paper sheets stuck on walls provide living canvases where project participants can 'draw on the walls' and make connections from one topic of conversation to another. This is especially useful at the insight stage. Remember, we can't see into the workings of our heads – but we can see each other's thinking if we draw stories, draw our conclusions and draw the arrows of our logical thought. Creating large canvases on which to see collective thinking frees up cognitive load in a project group – there's no need to take as many notes when it's all on display.

And *always* use paper, not screens! And lots of colour, with big fat marker pens! Flip charts are your friend – they'll need to be prepared personally, allowing for client nuances, stories and inferences as part of their design. All these things keep people in alpha state. They are anchors to our childlike selves and echoes of how we worked in our early school years.

Don't use PowerPoint to brief instructions to your project team. Whilst it's a great tool for large events or stage work, it's still one used to broadcast fixed content at people – the very thing a creative project cannot do. Drawing pictures, in the moment, and using flip charts encourages interaction and playfulness. Your images invite others to draw their thinking too. 👉

BELOW
Flip charts are your friend. Keep copies of the images that work well for you.

"I am a man of fixed and unbending principles, the first of which is to be flexible at all times."

— EVERETT DIRKSEN

SPACE

You need space to 'see' thinking and to physically move around and be animated. When you create space, you can engage project participants; you can see who is involved and active, and who isn't. Space makes it easier to manage group work, too, as you can assign different teams different parts of the space to run different activities. Being able to move any stimuli around will make it easier for you and the group to see patterns. And when you see patterns, your processing powers will be heightened and energised – and you'll make creative connections.

Remember that the floor is also a useable surface. A meeting room floor or the corridor outside can be used as a surface on which to build storyboards, canvases and tools. This photo is the 'WHYHAUS' tool (see p120) at scale on the floor, allowing for multiple people to ask questions, place down answers and add further comments. When participants interact physically with material, they remember content far more easily.

MUSIC

Finally, play music. Music is sound. Sound is moving air. Moving air is energy. Background music can help individual reflection, and an appropriate playback of a tune someone mentioned earlier in the day might be a great way to bring people back into the room and connect to you. No need for over-thought playlists. Just play. Given the choice, music over silence.

In summary, your chosen environment affects your project team participants' behaviours and vice versa; behaviour impacts the immediate working environment for everyone. Be deliberate in your choice of environment. If you really don't have an option about what room to use, you still have a choice. Every space can become a create space with a little thought paid to lighting, the amount and position of furniture needed, the use of the floor and the imagery that's around the room and up on the walls. If all else fails, use your room as a 'base' and send people outside to work – the world is one big canvas to be stimulated by; rarely will we have a creative breakthrough sitting in a windowless room thinking hard.

Competency and Team Culture

However you deliver your facilitation sesssions, the team culture you create is a vital component.

Team culture needs investment. You and your project team participants will quickly form a particular way of working with each other (a culture) that's different than the rest of the business in which you're operating. It's only going to take a handful of sessions for this team culture (and your project reputation) to evolve.

Whether you're running large sessions with a co-facilitator or an intimate coaching session on your own, that team culture will become forged; it's inevitable and unavoidable.

The choice of whether to run a session with a buddy is a competency call. Some activities and ideas can be facilitated by you alone in a relaxed fashion over a coffee. Others, especially when working with large groups, will definitely require a co-facilitator. With a good deal of advance prep, two of you can manage a large crowd for a day or so by mixing up the energy and taking turns with the activity briefings. Use the YOU/TEAM/TASK competency framework (see p92) to help decide what to do and why. Establishing a habit of using this framework in your discussions as facilitators reinforces the standards you're elevating as part of your culture.

A positive, can-do attitude is a must for a facilitator and team. As you facilitate more and more projects, you will find that the 'can-do team culture' is stronger each time. Repeating project cycles gives you the ability and mastery to think ahead of the project's team members

LEFT:
Your team. Your culture. You set the standards for what's expected.

and to make connections at speed and with great confidence. The Greek word for this concept is *phronesis* – loosely translated as 'practical wisdom'. You can rely on *phronesis* in sessions where you don't need to prep the content with your co-facilitator. Welcoming people to the session, joking about the news, swapping stories of the day, referencing what people said earlier in the session to make a point later are all examples. *Phronesis* gives you the in-the-moment confidence to share a story or not. It helps you decide what tool comes next, how long the breaks need to be and what ought to be shared in the summary at the end of sessions. You develop that ability over time. So too will your participants if they become part of your regular team on a certain project – this creates a strong creative culture.

However, this strength overdone can lead to what's known as the 'Einstellung effect' – our predisposition to solve a problem in a specific fashion, being reluctant to countenance alternative ways of thinking things through. Our approach at GENIUS BOX is to,

always leave at least 15% of our facilitation and session design to chance.

Knowing 'the answer' on day one of an innovation project is not the goal. If you're truly being creative then you and your team will work in harmony with the process, and along that journey the right insight will inspire the right type of idea that will answer the brief. You cannot possibly know what or when that moment will be. So, leave space for it to happen.

Jotting down the plotline of what you *think* the project story *could be* is a good way to calibrate the design and delivery of your creative sessions. Sometimes the inputs and outputs of your sessions will closely match what you envisaged and sometimes the project plotline of your team will diverge. A good project may be a combination of what you believed the answer to be and what the project team arrive at. For example, when dealing with different sources of data on an insight project, give your project team options – this empowers people to make choices. By putting project decision-making in the hands of the lowest appropriate person, you create expertise. You also reinforce the message that you aren't the one responsible for having the answer.

Culturally, this means reminding everyone to be comfortable when lost and to trust that not having all the detail about every stage is an active part of the process. And remember that, as a facilitator, you cannot afford to be wedded to a particular outcome in order to facilitate a truly creative journey.

In summary, team culture is in our GENIUS BOX model as it reminds us that our way of working is something we have intimate knowledge of and feel passionate about. But anyone on the outside of a creative project/process isn't aware of the tools and tricks and methods of the mavericks – or the competency required to facilitate them well.

It's worth noting that, culturally, your role as a facilitator can be divisive. The business you're working in or for wants you to make creative connections, solve problems and bring the best of maverick thinking into the organisation. At the same time, it needs you to be reassuringly professional and have detailed plans for your creative sessions. The different types of mindset, attitude and behaviour often don't mix well.

Your project team culture will be measurably different to the established culture in the business in which you're operating. This creates opportunity for learning and development. Over time, by involving more people in the business in creative projects, you'll be elevating creative capability. Work closely with senior leaders who are responsible for 'people' and their development. By involving both people and product conversations in your ongoing facilitation work, you'll be raising the internal brand of creative facilitation and embedding proof points of 'we're innovating around here', which is a critical business need.

Creative session planning

> *"Perfection is achieved, not when there is nothing more to add, but when there is nothing left to take away."*
>
> —ANTOINE DE SAINT-EXUPÉRY

In your project session planning, it's easy to get carried away in your own world. Great facilitators are motivated to do a good job. But, always remember it's the facilitator's job to create the conditions where other people arrive at output they build together. The following tips work in harmony with the delivery tips scattered throughout the book.

1 KISS MINTS

When reviewing sessions in your projects, use this simple two-word memorable mnemonic to coach yourself and your fellow facilitators on session design:

KISS = keep it simple, stupid! This reminds us that the design of instruction, the content of a story and the briefing of information need to make sense first time, every time. Never assume everyone in the room knows all about all of the moving project parts.

MINTS = materials, interaction, numbers, time, sequence.
This breaks down as follows:

Materials: consider what materials are needed. Instead of just talking about a moment in a movie, could you show the movie clip (or a big screen shot of that moment). Instead of mentioning a product, could you bring it? Additionally, having 'kit' implies participants will need to 'do something to it' and therefore the session becomes interactive.

Interaction: This is essential to engage adult project participants. Sitting still is good for watching Netflix, it's not a good behaviour for solving problems. Interaction is happening when your briefings become quizzes. Interaction is happening when participants are drawing, walking-and-talking, or moving sticky notes around on a canvas. Mix up the interactions, don't repat the same activity time and again.

Numbers: Mix up individual, pair, group. A great session invites participants to reflect individually, calmly and in silence. There is plenty of pairs work, where participants meet other people and generate output. This leads to more 'ownership' of output. And finally, groups need to be managed – threes and fours are ideal. Remember to appoint one member of each group as facilitator (with a small 'f') for that small session. Small is great for sorting content, making decisions and building energy.

Time: You now know your brain is thinking about several topics in the background whilst you're working on other tasks. My advice, therefore, is that three 30-minute sessions throughout the day on the same topic, is better than one 90-minute sitting. However, time is also affected by attitude; if you leave it to the last minute, it only takes a minute to do!

Sequence: In what order of events should the session run? On one hand, it's better

 ×  ×   =

to get people doing something first and then debrief. But flipping that order around allows you to hear knowledge from the group first, enabling more 'before' and 'after' comparisons in your discussion. You may also want to canvas perspectives and opinions prior to an activity and then 'draw a line' (metaphorically) after using a tool to signal a shift along the creative process. So keep it flexible and take care to always read the room.

② TAKE OUT THE KITCHEN SINK
You want to coach your project participants on their project journey. It's only natural to be excited by project content. We've dozens of tools to share, not only from this book but also from our back catalogue of experiences. It can be tempting to add *all* this 'good stuff' into project session design. But don't. To engineer at least 15% of unplanned space, you need to take content out. Put simply, everything and the kitchen sink doesn't belong in your design.

Sometimes insight sessions only need one game to align everyone's energy before participants are tasked with going out to hunt for clues. Sometimes that's enough to build playfulness and create a bit of laughter before the ideas session. Think about **you**, the **team** and the **task** at any given moment. Ask 'what's needed here?' and then consider options in your design.

③ THINK UP AND DOWN
Ask yourself the following questions when planning your facilitation sessions:

• Consider a creative session lasting an afternoon. What does your design look like?

• Consider that afternoon could be one of a few days back-to-back. What does the design look like now?

• If those afternoons fall in a four-week project, and it's now Week Two, what does the design look like now?

• And finally, your team (on that afternoon) is one of three teams who are in parallel project groups within the business. Your other co-facilitators are working with those teams and you'll swap over later in the project. What does the design look like now?

Thinking up and down means leaving the session in isolation and seeing what else came before and what else will come after that session. To do that you need to lift yourself up and out of the session and review the project from a high altitude.

Give the same questions to your co-facilitator as part of your first planning meeting and explore each other's responses. A shared and agreed plan is something you can both take ownership of and as a result, enjoy briefing in and facilitating. 👉

④ DAYDREAM AND INCUBATE

This is a picture of my daughter taken when she was a lot younger.

It's a long-haul flight and unlike Mummy (who'd taken the opportunity to nap) my daughter sat on the seat armrest and gazed out of the window. She listened to music and sat for what seemed like hours as we flew high above the clouds. I cherish this photo. It captures beautifully the behaviour of daydreaming.

Daydreaming is an example of being in alpha state. We are semi-focused on one thing, removed somewhat from the conscious passing of time and energised simply by the topics that pop up in our attention. Children are good at daydreaming. And children don't have trouble having ideas. It's unlikely we'd be rewarded at work for daydreaming, so I was delighted to capture the photo (top, right) once of a client working on a problem, but in a similar fashion to my daughter. He sat alone, in his own little world, making notes on the issue the business faced – as I recall, it was an insight challenge. The room, as you can see, wasn't that inspiring – plastic office plants against magnolia walls. But there was space. Loads of it. And the height of the windows added to the sense of scale. After an hour or so he popped off the windowsill with a big smile on his face. 'Cracked it', he said.*

Give yourself time to think.

---

* Incidentally, it started to snow at that moment; perhaps the universe was showing us there is such a thing as magic 😌

"If you can dream it, you can do it."

— **WALT DISNEY**

(5) **BUILD IN SURPRISES**
The 'peak–end theory' is a psychological rule in which an experience is evaluated and remembered based on the peak (the most intense) point of the experience and/or the ending of the experience. When people assess an experience, they tend to forget or ignore its length. Instead, they seem to rate the experience based on two key moments:

1 **the best (or worst) moment, known as the peak**
2 **the ending**

At first glance, this could mean that, despite your best efforts, your innovation project will be famous for when it's over!

Your project participants' recollection of events will be impacted greatly by their interpretation of what happened rather than, for example, the actual experience of a brainstorm (or, indeed, the entire project process) as a whole. Like it or not, it's inevitable that your project team will remember a different experience of your session depending on their levels of engagement and involvement.

To mitigate against peak-end theory, build surprise into your design and delivery. A surprise can be a special guest. This is great for the insight stage, for example. Instead of imagining what it's like to be a professional musician, why not invite one in to talk to you.

A surprise can be a visit (to the factory, or theme park or even a trip on an open top bus). A surprise can be revealing instructions in coloured envelopes, or asking participants to 'open a box' with a new activity inside. Every TV game show

is essentially a 'pub quiz' dressed up in surprises. There is always a different way to instruct people to follow your instructions, complete a task in a timed window and report back their findings. Whilst it's (likely) impossible to guarantee that everyone in the sessions will engage 100% with the tools and activities during their time with you, it's important to design and deliver the sessions with the intention that everyone will. Remember that people only like surprises they like, so keep surprises positive and enjoyable.

❻ ONE, TWO, GROUP

Good project sessions have time set aside for individual reflection, pair work and group activity.

Individual reflection is an important tactic for embedding learning. If, for example, you're running an insight project, there will be opportunities for people to incubate their thinking and arrive at insights. People will need time to make connections and indulge in possibilities and hypotheses about what's going on in the heads and hearts of potential consumers. Even a 20-minute session in silence is enough for people to calm down, make notes and connect to material.

Pair work is powerful. If a project team is stuck, split them into pairs, send them on a 40-minute break to discuss the issue and come back with a point of view. This will also give you time, as the facilitator, to consider what to do next.

Finally – groups. A common myth is that group work is always a method to boost productivity. Not so. I remember when I was teaching in a Sixth Form College, one Faculty Head commissioned a staff review of group work across his department and invited the other department heads to do the same. With nearly 2,500 students we had a good sample size to run the experiment. We staff sat in on each other's lessons, made observations of the classes and spoke before and after the sessions about our lesson design and what we hoped students would learn as a result of the teaching. The findings were that – group work doesn't work that well at all. 'Hang on,' you cry. 'I've been in groups and I got loads out of it.' That's probably true – you got loads out of it, but did the others?

Most group work is badly briefed. Instructions are given out to teams of people where it's assumed the content

ABOVE:
Designing the project delivery. What exercises are going where and why.

LEFT:
A peak moment. Here the problem owner and a facilitator can be seen 'wrestling' with a problem in a scoping session.

is understood. At a distance, group work looks productive and animated; everyone is chatting away in low murmur. But, essentially, it's an instruction adopted by one or two people whilst other people watch what they do. In innovation projects, participants can easily 'lean over a laptop', look busy and not actually add value; the murmur, nodding and agreement could easily be bonding over office politics.

My advice for groups:

- **Split instructions:** Issue specific instructions to each member of the group, so everyone has a task of their own. That way, everyone has to take responsibility for their own actions for the whole group to move forward.

- **Go small:** Five people maximum. Seriously, adults will find any excuse to not join in or say anything. Consider the last event where you were sitting on a round conference table set out for eight, ten or even twelve, and think back to who did all the talking...

- **Allocate a facilitator (with a small 'f'):** This is a person in the group who gives your instructions to others one at a time from a set of your prepared notes

LEFT:
Project participants exploring the merits of one idea over another. Notice the great space they've got to work in.

(or numbered envelopes that people open in turn, for example). Give instructions for this facilitator to keep the group to time and secure output without your direct involvement. These 'little f' facilitators are a great way to manage groups when you send people off for 30 minutes elsewhere around your venue to find a new environment to work in, or out on a consumer safari for an hour or so in the local city to gather information and observations.

- **Give clear instructions:** They should break down a complex activity/topic into small parts that people have to engage with to get from A to B. They can only get to B by applying knowledge (learning) to the situation (A). No more 'And in your tables, talk about what you've just heard and arrive at your table's point of view'. This is not the way.

- **Don't reveal the plan:** Don't tell participants what will happen at the end of the group work when you're briefing it in – they'll jump ahead, skip the 'point' and answer that part of the instruction instead. Get people into groups, then run the activity. Bring the activity to an end and then brief in a group ending. For example, 'Now you've got your answers in your group, you've got three minutes to summarise a concise point of view on this issue as two talking points. One of you will have that written down neatly and be ready to share out loud with everyone here. It's that simple. Go!'

- **Capture output, not discussion:** People tend to discuss a great deal in groups, then leave little time to capture what they've discussed. And when people do capture a discussion, what's written down might not accurately reflect the consensus, perspective or decisions made. It's often best for you to bring all the groups back together 'as one'. Then, hear from each group in turn. This way everyone hears what's been discussed. And at the end of hearing from each group, you write down the agreed output for all to see. This way, you're editing and curating content, and keeping a consistent high standard of project output for all to see and align behind.

7 PACK LIGHT – ESPECIALLY ON INSIGHT

As said earlier in this chapter, if you're facilitating the creative process you can't know the answer on day one. So, you need to 'pack light' and allow plenty of space in your project design for people to discover the 'new', make connections and arrive at ideas. This is especially true at the insight stage where you'll want people to be open-minded. Flooding your project with content is a good way to stifle the design. So, as mentioned, out with the kitchen sink. Packing light is also achieved by:

- Having plenty of breaks and refreshment. A good tip is 'one more break than you think is needed'.

- Referring back to the project brief at the start of each session and allowing for a 10-minute pairs chat to land any creative thinking from overnight.

- Being spontaneous – *phronesis* will help you here.

- Playing games to keep the energy up, and storytelling – always storytelling about the consumer.

- Making plenty of space to think and move.

- Adding a 30-minute 'stepping back moment' in an afternoon for people to pair up and share with each other broader observations about the creative process and key personal learnings from the time they've spent being a project team participant so far.

In summary, it's important to mix up the participant experience by having adults reflecting individually, working in pairs and working in groups. But without clear instruction and fail-safes in design to stop people 'drifting along', any type of work can feel productive but not actually contribute a great deal to the project journey. The point of creative facilitation is to add value to business through inspiring delivery. So, always design for awesome, and you'll deliver better than average and certainly surprise everyone by securing more than they expected.

Interview

Adam Howe

CREATIVE FACILITATOR, EXECUTIVE STRATEGY SESSIONS

Adam Howe lives and works in both the UK and USA, and specialises in advising senior executives on how changes to their organisation's strategy will impact their organisation's design, talent and culture.

You deliver strategy sessions for the senior executives leading some of the world's largest organisations. Give me a sense of what those sessions are like for you to run.
Most of my work is helping execs to build a bridge between how new business models and strategies impact an organisation's culture, design and talent. So, it can be intense. There's a palpable sense of 'we need to get aligned.' There's also an excited vibe at the start, from the execs, about what they'll get, but sometimes also a sceptical vibe about how we'll get there. I think our audiences will naturally be asking what it is that we can do in a few hours or days that ordinarily takes much longer to happen.

What are your observations about how senior executives behave?
I believe the answers are mostly already in their heads. Without overstating the obvious, senior people are clever. Either smart and strategic, and they know they're stuff, or they're clever politically – they know how to manage themselves and the people around them. Our projects are asking them to come up with an answer; they may already have that and it needs refining, improving and aligning, or we can help unlock whatever is blocking it. There's a behaviour of co-operation, but it's easy for them to spout reasons why change won't work, or to list the blockers. We need to watch for that.

What facilitation principles help with seniors, then?
We get out the way. Bad facilitation can be getting in the way with too much storytelling about the usual suspects. Everyone rolls their eyes if you're quoting Facebook, Google and Kodak. It's all been done before. So, we need to frame the issue clearly, agree what a good outcome would be and then aim for it with all of our discussions. Allowing time for these people to really talk it through, too – it's rare they get the opportunity to do that when they're busy running the company.

What have you seen that really gets senior leaders engaged?
It's the stimuli. As I said before, the overused examples are just a mousetrap. All that information is TBU: true, but useless. When we bring an example of how a business has switched its operating model 180 degrees, execs take note. For example, showing a healthcare provider that's sitting on masses of patient data the opportunity to change its business model by following the actions of a global agricultural equipment manufacturer that shifted its business model by doing just that. The answer is already there. Great stories and examples matter. Your stories need to be short, well told, easy to understand and with main points that are easy to remember.

With senior execs – do you sit on the fence and remain impartial or do you share a point of view? What's best and how do you behave/what do you say?
There's the analogy of being on the dancefloor and then the balcony, meaning

being 'in it' and then stepping away to see everyone else. So, first you can be 'in it' with the team as they wrestle with the problem – we've done plenty of projects so I think it's important that as facilitators we share that experience, it's unrelated and potentially a useful stimulus. But then we need to step out and back to see what's going on in the session, and whether we're on track or heading towards a dead end.

What helps you do that?
We always set up our agreements. And with my co-facilitator we agree during the planning process what we think a good outcome for each of our sessions needs to be. Would we be happy with 'x'? Would the client be happy with 'x'? We don't know what that answer is, but we need to create the space for an answer to emerge.

We use a way of having the 'this is how we want to work together' conversation using ROPES (respect, openness, participants, experiment and safety), and we invite our participants to tell us what that standard of behaviour looks like in the session. What will we see people do and hear people say? Execs need this, as so much personal risk and politics exist at the senior level. It's exposing if you're leading a business and feel you don't 'know' the answer when asked. But we can't innovate if everyone thinks that they can't share or can only share the obvious. Our role as the facilitator is to cut through those mental models in a creative way.

What is a final nugget of genius you'd like to share?
It's the time thing. Positive change takes time. There are those who'd argue you can make change happen in a short window – bitesize trainings and small coaching sessions. As part of a series of sessions, yes, change can happen, totally – you can plan and then facilitate a change journey for senior execs and a leadership team. But, you're not going to shift an entire business in the time it takes to watch the *Lion King*.

"I believe the answers are mostly already in their heads."

– ADAM HOWE

The shift

Successful facilitation is when your project participants take total responsibility of the project content.

This is 'the shift' you are aiming for. Your project team are now aware of where they are on the creative journey, what tools are needed at the next stage, how to align their behaviours, choose the right environment and understand what decisions need to be made. It is they who are in control. The management of people's energy, tasks and time has shifted from you (the facilitator) to them (the team).

This takes time and needs to be considered as part of session design.

At the start of any workshop, you'll control almost all the content: what people are discussing, how they are discussing it, for how long and what the outcome will be. For the first few hours of the project you'll be briefing in a series of activities and exercises all engineered to deliver a positive experience for your participants. I'd encourage you to use plenty of short, energetic, activities that get your voice into the room with neat starts and stops.

Establish an environment that is safe, creative and at pace.

For example, a typical GENIUS BOX welcome session takes about an hour – with the proviso that all flip charts will have been completed the night before, and the room set up the previous day – and it looks something like this:

Music is on, facilitators are in their chairs smiling and waiting to receive project participants. There's not a laptop in sight.

We welcome everyone and gather an energy score from everyone in the room.*

We then share a high-level piece about why we're here for context setting. This is supported by one or two flip charts only. We include a brief moment to introduce both ourselves as a business and as the members of the facilitation team. This is not a long business biography (it's boring for others and smells of insecurity).

It's then time to involve everyone in an interactive (cocktail party) game. We never assume everyone knows each other. And if they do, such games are a great way for the team participants to interact with each other differently and for us, as their facilitators to get a sense of everyone's energy and focus.

We land the game to explain that the rest of the project should feel just as easy to follow as our instructions in the game. It will comprise short bursts of focus, with we facilitators looking after instructions, output and timing. We then share the brief for the project (supported by a flip chart and a large visual or prop) and mention that we'll scope that brief out further using specific tools and activities later in the project.

> *
> This could literally be everyone giving a score out of 10 on where their energy levels are at right now, or a drawing of what they're looking forward to doing at the weekend – there's dozens of ways to start the session. What you do will be influenced by the brief, your history with the client, the people who are in the room and the project topic itself. Scores out of 10 is a safe one to start!

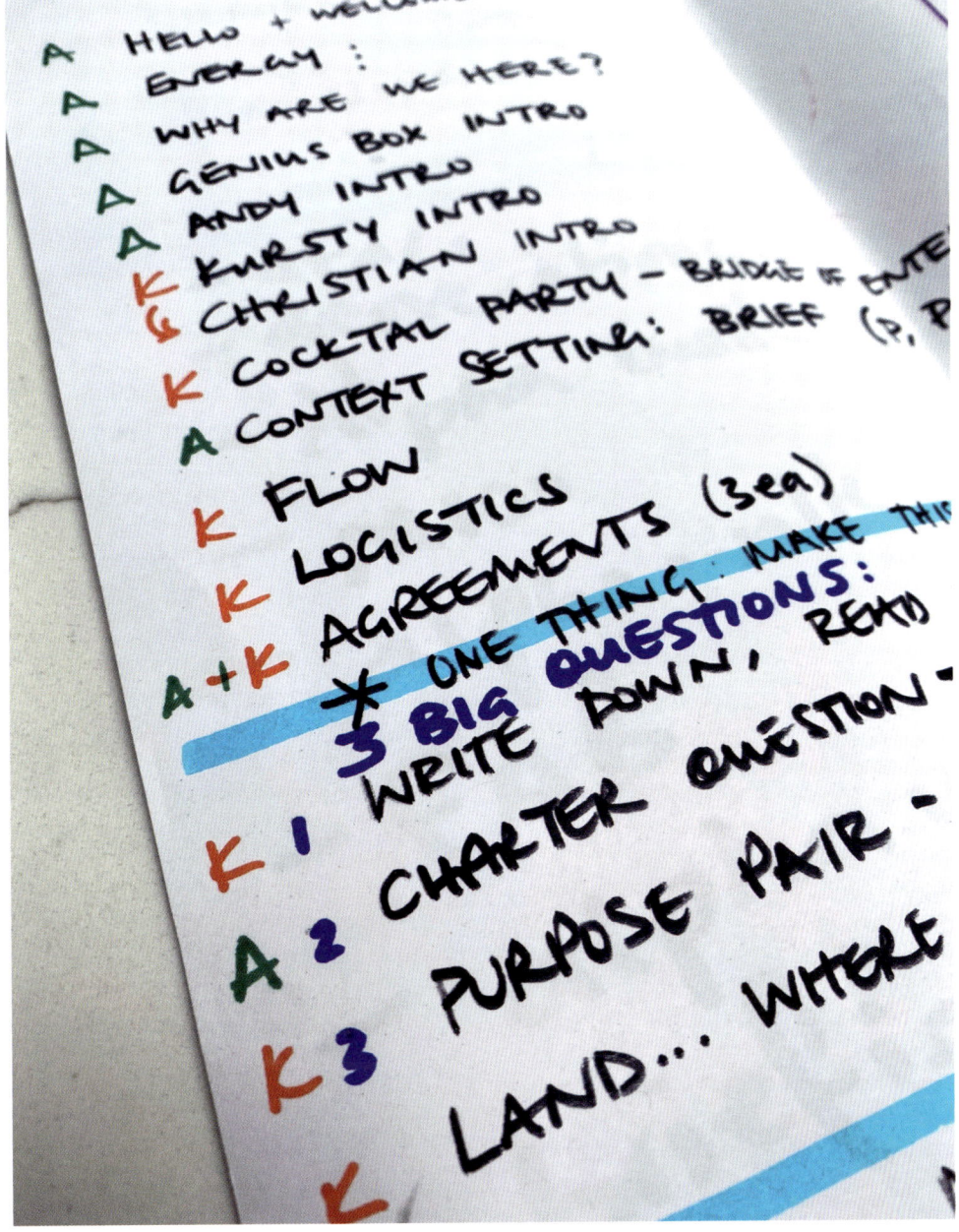

We then reveal a 'flow' or a 'playlist' for the project journey. This is on a series of flip charts, or mapped out on the floor in sequence. We don't use the word 'agenda' as it snaps people back into 'business as usual'. At this time, we often then link to the logistics, timings and health and safety pointers specific to the client and venue.

And finally, we spend a good deal of time setting up the behavioural agreements as a group for getting the best out of each other and the time ahead. These agreements are always referred to at the start of each session. We often say that if the flow or playlist is an engine to a project, then the agreements are the oil that ensures things run smoothly.

It's then time to have a break. We write a time on the flip chart for everyone to arrive back by and set folk off to manage their energy. We then play some music, speak with any participants we feel need a quick check-in and, as a buddy facilitator pair, pin up flip charts and any other visuals or props we've referred to from that set up session.

And now look at that set up again. There is **no project content** – this is not the way. Instead, the set-up is all about building

LEFT:
Have a plan... so you can go off-piste.

the first foundations of the environment in which people can co-create, make new connections and feel safe to explore new challenges to the business status quo.

Too often we see facilitators ask everyone to introduce themselves one at a time and then jump straight into project content only for energy and process to then stall. There's been no time for conditions where a 'shift' can happen. No repeat cycle of activities where trust can be built.

Depending on the context of the project and the number of people in the room, several hours can be dedicated solely to 'setting up' before you even touch the first activity on content. This is the way.

Let's look at the 'the cocktail party' game once more. Invite the group of participants to pair up (randomly), introduce each other to their partner and work through a series of introductory questions*:

> We only do three. Three is a magic number, as studies show that anything more loses power when it comes to adult focus and learning. Three questions are easy to remember and recall. People 'get it' after three rounds of anything – so no need to do any more.

- Where do I have fun outside of work?
- What's something I'm working on right now that I'm proud of?
- What's something I've seen recently that made me smile?
- What's been the highlight of working with my colleagues recently?
- What's my big dream?

...and so on.

You'll notice that all the questions are pretty easy to answer. They require a little thought, but nothing people can't consider and construct an answer to in a matter of moments. Answers can't be right or wrong. The questions can be interpreted in a number of ways; they're almost a guide. And we've noticed that people quickly run off at tangents when they discuss these topics; the questions invite a deeper conversation.

You'll also note that these questions are written in a way so they can only be answered with 'positive' sentiment. They invite happy memories or topics that foster joy and interest. There is nothing hard or challenging here for participants to endure.

All the tools and exercises in this book are designed in the same way; to engineer positive sentiment, joy and confidence. Over time, because of the repeated experience of positive outcomes, the 'shift' will occur. Groups don't magically take control of a project overnight between one phase or another. Your project team participants will develop their confidence at different rates. Some individuals will naturally 'get it' after a few moments, whilst others need more time to see that their efforts made impact. The 'shift' grows slowly over the project journey. But the seeds are sown right on the first meeting and first session.

DON'T TELL ME, SHOW ME
Imagine standing next to a senior leader from your business. You are both observing a group of people from that business, working through a project process. That group are unaware that you're watching them; as if you're a CCTV camera poised in the corner of the room.

When you can see your project team scoping briefs, working in pairs explaining consumer behaviour, sitting in small groups generating ideas and listening to each other, in turn; when they are assessing and selecting ideas, then the shift has happened. This is a critical moment in the narrative of the power of creative facilitation. You can turn to your senior leader and show them how people in their business have the capability to self-organise themselves and a process to tackle live commercial challenges.

If the group are doing this with minimal briefing from you then the shift has happened. That's what you're going for. Teams are now responding to your briefings with the same level of enthusiasm and joy as the earlier introductory games, intros and activities. They've stepped into their project content, but with the same behaviours they had at the start of the project. And, at the same time, those activities will be enjoyable, easy to follow, and yield output that can be shared.

A sign that the shift is happening is the time spent at the start of creative sessions explaining creative activities and briefing in tools is becoming less, and the time spent on activities is more. Similarly, there may be less briefing-in sessions during the day and instead a 'getting going session' at day start and a 'big landing of the day' session at day end; again, strong indications that the shift is occurring.

Remember the shift – but don't hurry to get there by speeding up introductions or cutting out activities. Your facilitated session is likely, for many people, to be a breath of fresh air in an otherwise routine world of work. Projects need a special process filled with specific tools to tackle a range of challenges. And all of that needs facilitating; the shift cannot happen without you.

The Way

Looking back on our journey, I've set out the need for business to up its game in creative capability-building and the case for you to be a brilliant facilitator.

You're reading this book to bring into the world more exciting, energising and creative facilitation. Simply briefing in instruction and keeping to time isn't enough. You'll create value by exciting and energising your project participants; a great facilitator will stop every now and then to develop people (by unpacking the tools you use) in addition to delivering output for the client. Over time the capability of those you work with will strengthen. Your business will flourish. Your people will thrive. And the brand of 'facilitation' can command a deserved premium position. That is our quest.

To start you on your way, I've unpacked in detail what happens in your brain when you're making creative connections. And how, with that knowledge, you can establish creative routines and, over time, develop the habit of constantly doing things in new ways to add value to your personal life and those of others. But knowledge and understanding of what's going on in your head isn't enough on its own. Remember how I described the way Jenny made use of her new knowledge (see pp70–73) in order to approach the facilitation of a project differently – this story provided me with the context to present our GENIUS BOX model. The model is a way of externalising all your thinking before, during and after project facilitation. And by using this model as a reference, you can build your own consistent approach to facilitation that works in harmony with – and amplifies – your own unique style and that of any facilitation buddies you partner with.

I then shared the many tools and instructions we choose from to shepherd project teams through a process so they all arrive at output that gets done. The concepts of a monorail and a radar will help you navigate the journey you're personally experiencing during a project, and help you also empathise with the needs of your project participants.

I've shared tips, tricks, hacks and secrets so your actual facilitation and instruction is clear, impactful and positive. And finally, I've included stories, advice and stimuli from people who I believe are exceptional in the work they do – they are former clients, colleagues and wider members of the GENIUS BOX network; smarter, sharper people are hard to find. Using the insight gathering tools and behaviours in this book, I've looked back on the advice these facilitators have shared with me, and there are three themes I see emerging consistently throughout: safety, style and story.

SAFETY

Change in business is hard. We know why people are wedded to routine. Politics, ego and status all drive our unconscious behaviour. And whilst business *wants* to change, and everyone is signed up to the value of *having* change, rarely will people leap into a project session keen to change their processes or their behaviour.

Creativity demands rule-breaking. Being innovative provokes the status quo. Everyone is on tenterhooks, nervous and expectant for success, but also terrified that a project will expose them and that teams will be labelled with failure. You've got to create a safe environment for people to do new things. You've got to exude confidence that the unknown journey is something you're unphased by. And that you're ready for anything and anyone. The client does not want hear you ask them 'is that okay?' in the break. Project participants who listen to your long CV in the intro are only hearing personal insecurity. And facilitators who are over-polite and constantly seeking permission do not command security in the process. Clients need to know that when the inevitable clash of opinion arises, you're there to take control. They deserve the knowledge that tough decisions will be made without bruising self-esteem. Your team need to know you've got their backs. You've got to engineer every activity to the positive. Safety comes first.

STYLE

The tools and activities in this book will help you to facilitate well, but delivering instruction in a detached and transactional fashion won't add value. As all the tools are human and practical, your personality is an unavoidable component of briefing in instruction and landing session output. Your style and behaviour are the lubricating oil of all these moving parts. Without your particular slant on things, nothing will be differentiating. You absolutely are exposed as a facilitator. So, you have to be you – totally, 100%, genuinely you. If you try to be someone else or emulate the style of others, or worse still, maintain a reassuringly professional distance from the process – it will fail and you will crumble under mental exhaustion.

You've got to pick and own your style. I love the creative process. I enjoy being around other people and I relish the responsibility of looking after them as we solve problems together. It made sense, therefore, to build a business whose proposition and mission is inspiration. I am personally motivated to lead that life and believe there is power in that mission – something attractive to others and a force that can create good within business. My style, I believe, is creative. In order to inspire new thinking, I will need to provoke, surprise, disagree, take a stand, change direction, or bring things to a halt. My style is front-footed. I believe I am a passionate hobbyist who challenges so-called experts – because, surely, there is always another way. And it works – 99% of the time clients are totally delighted. Work is successfully delivered. Awards are won. And repeat work follows. I love that.

But.

Because my style involves pushing boundaries, prodding authority and shaking the tree, what can be a strength can also be strength overdone. And here, where I've taken things too far, I have made mistakes. I have insulted people. I've been rude, cocky and snappy. On good days, I am refreshing and inspiring but on those bad days I've stepped over the fine line between confidence and contumacy. If you're reading this and know me and you recognise those moments, then I am sorry. Truly. Those moments can happen in minutes. And, it only takes a misheard comment or a few poorly thought words to cause offence.

Facilitation that looks easy is hard to do. There's a great deal for me to think about and feel comfortable with before I can relax and be spontaneous. Where one or two elements are missing, that's where I know my style will suffer and I won't be at my best. That's why I prefer to work with a co-facilitator, in a buddy pair, as we can look after each other and calibrate each other's energy. Developing your own style will take time. You need feedback – seek it. Make a note on what themes emerge. But don't turn other people's feedback into direct instruction to become someone you're not.

Your credibility on this journey will be tested from time to time. You'll probably find yourself on a project where it's tough. You'll be in a room and there will be a bit of friction. You'll sense a mismatch between what's expected and what's happening. You'll feel something is up. And, I promise, you'll forget the context and all you've learnt, and totally cock it up. That's fine. You're human. And those people who find that your journey isn't motivating or energising might not warm to you at all. But, remember, it's *your* journey, not theirs. It's up to you to act on what you believe is the best advice. And it's up to you to shape who you are and how you work on the feedback you rate the highest.

The best way to create safety and develop your style is to tell your story.

STORIES

One of the criticisms I cited at the start of the book was that facilitators often believe they should be neutral, and that they need to remain detached and objective. This is not the way.

Tell stories.

And, importantly, be the story.

The GENIUS BOX model helps you to plan your programmes, projects and sessions. In the moment, you'll use the model to switch gear and change the tempo. You'll intuitively know when a group is too big and needs splitting up into pairs. You'll know when to call a break and then land things on a flip chart, or ask for output to be copied up overnight onto the Miro board. And, of course, you'll know when to push back on a thought that's captured falsely as an idea on a sticky note! The one magical element that holds your facilitation together is the story.

Stories have been a consistent theme in this anti-manual. I've told stories about the people in the past I've been inspired by. I've told stories in chapter openings that set the scene. I've used stories to grab your attention before I shared a tool. I've used stories of where people used tools to create success. Stories allow us to share knowledge, theory and information. Stories and anecdotes are vehicles to impart learnings and values. Capturing an insight is, of course, a version of writing a short story:

Sally wants to do this: _____,
but she needs to do that: _____.

An idea is far more easily understood when it's framed in a story. The context of a project is told as a story. And telling stories makes it far easier for people to connect to project sponsors, consumer needs and business opportunities.

When you set up introductions at the start of a project about who you are and what everyone will be doing, you're telling a story. And in the final presentations and celebrations at the end of a project you're telling a story.

Great facilitation is master storytelling. Develop your storytelling style and you'll naturally develop your personal facilitation style. Also bear in mind that people don't remember stories about process, they remember stories about people. Stories paint a picture in the mind. And your project participants will ask themselves 'how would I feel?', 'what would I be thinking?', and 'what would I do?' Stories, therefore, invite your project participants to take ownership and agency of their decisions and project implementation. As someone on the team often remarks: 'if it's going to be, it's down to me.'

Finally, the story you tell yourself of what you do, how you do it and why you do it, will be the ongoing narrative to the work you do. And when you scope a brief, plan a solution and facilitate others to the answers, you'll be adding detail and colour to your own personal facilitation story.

My ask of you is to be that story.

Think about that now – what is your facilitation story?

Are you on a mission to inspire? Do you facilitate to break down creative myths? Will you facilitate delivery only, or will you develop people along the way? Are you going to create a bespoke design each time or can you find a niche that you can scale? Are you going to specialise in technical innovation projects or embrace generic team business briefs? Will you become the 'go to' for strategic workshops, or excel at tactical implementation?

There's a great deal for you to think about.

For many people the world of work is frustrating and complex. It can be dull, tough, and routine. Despite the promise of a highly engaged workforces, value-driven cultures and flexible working conditions, the reality, for many, is the opposite. Your sessions provide a brilliant opportunity for people to leave at the end knowing, understanding and (hopefully) doing something far more rewarding and refreshing than just attending another training day at the end of a commute.

Our world is only going to become more complex, challenging, fragmented and digitised. The glittering allure of a life of leisure, filled with pursuits enriching our personality is a promise from the past yet to be realised. There will always be the need to change and challenge. The tasks of today might be made redundant tomorrow as we continue to implement technology solutions into the way we work, but I believe we will always need to gather people in a room to solve problems, develop ideas and then go make them happen.

You have the potential to create a lasting positive impression with people in those moments. And when challenges are first framed in business, it will be easy for everyone in the room to feel that those problems can't be solved, that work is too hard and that ideas will not be easy.

You'll know that such mindsets hinder creativity.

And you'll say that **this is not the way.**

Importantly, you'll also be able to show them what is.

Now, go lead the way.

Acknowledgements

This book is dedicated to Grandad Scotland (1908–1989), who showed me how to solve problems with my head, and Grandad Worcester (1921–2014), who showed me how to solve problems with my hands.

Enormous thanks to Claire Gell, who took 'what I had written and made it write', Louise Evans for designing the beautiful pages and Becky Miles for project managing me. This book is a dream come true – I was in safe hands, Becky, and learned a great deal from you. Thank you.

Whilst no one can 'own' creative thinking, some tools here will be familiar to those who worked at *?What If! Innovation*. I was a proud *?What If!*-er and it's inevitable its legacy stands the test of time. All of the other tools, names, characters, businesses, events and incidents in the text are the product of my experience, imagination and heavily influenced by the work of countless others – of whom you might be one. I've done my best to point that out as I've gone along, and I mean no harm if I've forgotten to mention you in person. With luck, we'll be leading the way together, so let's talk about it then.

And finally, to Julie. Thank you for the title – 100% your suggestion. I hope you like what came after it.

The author would like to thank the following for their kind permission to reproduce the images in this book:

ALAMY STOCK PHOTO
50 & 103 FlixPix; 161 Carolyn Jenkins; 162 Dave Bagnall Collection; 183 PictureLux/The Hollywood Archive; 187 & 188 (tl) Dave Cameron, (bl) Maximum Film, (tcr) PA Images, (tr) FlixPix, (bcl) colaimages.

SHUTTERSTOCK
© Alex74 151; © Alexander_P 136, 235, 268, 310; © Babich Alexander 236; © Akimd 304; © Nata_Alhontess 127, 288; © Aksol 240, 246; © Adela Belovodjanin 212; © Ava Bitter 79, 84, 196, 229; © Jennifer Chamblee 311; © Dedmityay 198; © Delstudio 197; © Disobeyart 161; © Diviart 137, 238; © Elegant Solution 273; © Everett Collection 81, 107, 176, 331; © Fatig_Studio 288; © Beth French 278; © Frescomovie 279; © Christor Georghiou 221, 236; © Ground Picture 74, 210; © Hacohob 42; © Jiri Hera 187 & 188 (br);
© Kamieshkova 170; © Kari K 161; © Lestyan 143; © Lisjatina 307; © Lynea 78, 228, 246; © Sergii Molchenko 64; © Morevector 10, 202, 218, 281, 282, 285; © Morphart Creation 1, 26, 31, 34, 68, 82, 173, 177, 181, 270; © Navalnyi 260; © Nadiia_Oborska 221; © Channarong Pherngjanda 170; © Maisei Raman 1, 31, 110, 143, 186, 199, 201, 298, 300; © Rawpixel.com 180; © Retroclipart 15, 101; © Sanzhak Marina 83; © Elzbieta Sekowska 59; © Separisa 112; © Charles Taylor 200; © Bodor Tivadar 118; © Irina Trusova 131, 135, 237; © Tupungato 187 & 188 (bcr); © Uncle Leo 152; © Gorbash Varvara 156; © Marian Weyo 161; © Widya Designs 227; © Winwin Artlab 268.

Additional cartoon illustrations: Danny Burgess, 55, 61, 256, 312; Christian Eldridge, 28, 315 (in photo); Will Knight 249 (in photo); Paul Chappell, 46–47, 57, 239; Matt Stone 48, 73, 104–105, 125, 295 (in photo), 302–303.

All other images courtesy of Andy Reid and GENIUS BOX.

First published in 2024 by The Genius Box Ltd in partnership with Whitefox Publishing Ltd

Andy Reid (The Genius Box Ltd) asserts the moral right to be identified as the author of this work. All rights reserved. No part of this publication may be reproduced, stored in a retrieval system or transmitted in any form or by any means, electronic, mechanical, photocopying, recording or otherwise, without prior written permission of the author.

While every effort has been made to trace the owners of copyright material reproduced herein, the author would like to apologise for any omissions and will be pleased to incorporate missing acknowledgements in any future editions.

ISBN 978-1-915635-53-2

Also available as an eBook: 978-1-915635-28-0

Design: Louise Evans
Project Editor: Becky Miles
Copyeditor: Claire Gell
Proofreader: Belinda Gallagher

Printed and bound in the UK by Bell & Bain